Architectures of Colonialism

Kulturelle und technische Werte historischer Bauten
Ed. by Klaus Rheidt and Werner Lorenz

Special Volume

EDITED BY VERA EGBERS, CHRISTA KAMLEITHNER,
ÖZGE SEZER, AND ALEXANDRA SKEDZUHN-SAFIR

Architectures of Colonialism

Constructed Histories, Conflicting Memories

Birkhäuser · Basel

This publication is funded by the German Research Foundation (DFG) in the framework of the Research Training Group 1913 "Cultural and Technological Significance of Historic Buildings," Brandenburg University of Technology Cottbus-Senftenberg; Leibniz Institute for Research on Society and Space, Erkner; Department of Archaeology at Humboldt University of Berlin.

Editors: Vera Egbers, Christa Kamleithner, Özge Sezer, Alexandra Skedzuhn-Safir
Project coordination: Albrecht Wiesener, Sophia Hörmannsdorfer
Copyediting: William Hatherell
Typesetting and proofreading: Sophia Hörmannsdorfer
Cover design: Edgar Endl, Booklab, München
Printing and binding: Beltz Grafische Betriebe GmbH, Bad Langensalza
Cover illustration: "Half Moon" PoW camp in Wünsdorf/Zossen (Germany), photograph from the album "Zossen 1914–17." Photographer: Otto Stiehl (1860–1940). Source: Staatliche Museen zu Berlin, Museum Europäischer Kulturen / Otto Stiehl.

Library of Congress Control Number: 2024934776

Bibliographic information published by the German National Library
The German National Library lists this publication in the Deutsche Nationalbibliografie; detailed bibliographic data is available on the Internet at http://dnb.dnb.de.

ISBN 978-3-0356-2674-2
e-ISBN (PDF) 978-3-0356-2670-4

DOI https://doi.org/10.1515/9783035626704

9 8 7 6 5 4 3 2 1   www.birkhauser.com

Table of Contents

Heritage and Memories

CHRISTA KAMLEITHNER, VERA EGBERS, ÖZGE SEZER, ALEXANDRA SKEDZUHN-SAFIR

Introduction

Over the past decade, decolonial perspectives on built heritage have gained considerable momentum, with the events of 2020 standing out as a turning point. Catalyzed by the Black Lives Matter protests after George Floyd's murder, statues commemorating Confederate generals, colonial rulers, slave owners, and traders were toppled and removed. In the US alone, over a hundred such statues were taken down, with similar actions in Great Britain, Belgium, and South Africa.[1] While activism has been ongoing for years within the Black Lives Matter movement and other interventions to redefine colonial sites and foster de- and postcolonial perspectives both within and outside of academia, the events of 2020 prompted cultural institutions and policy-makers to break their (partial) silence and respond to calls for decolonization in unprecedented ways. The global debate that has since been sparked has brought to the forefront the deep-rooted colonial past ingrained within the built environment and its enduring influence on memorialization and historiography. This discourse urges disciplines engaged with built heritage not only to incorporate such examination into their core focus, but to "carry this expertise into participation and helping to craft new memoryscapes," as Kathleen James-Chakraborty put it at the 2021 European Architectural History Network meeting.[2]

Following the clarion call for decolonization, *Architectures of Colonialism: Constructed Histories, Conflicting Memories* strives to serve as a bridge between historical research and heritage perspectives. This edited volume stems from the International Online Conference of the same title held at Brandenburg University of Technology Cottbus-Senftenberg, Germany, from 16 to 19 June 2021, which brought together international scholars from diverse fields related to the built environment. The book aims to explore historical methodologies and unravel the complexity and contentious nature of built heritage, in both former colonies and metropoles. Through a blend of archaeology, architectural history, and heritage studies, it looks at the entanglement of building histories, histories of use and reuse, perception, and conservation or destruction that make up a place. The case studies in the volume deal with public squares, monuments, residential and functional buildings, urban schemes, and internment camps, through which coloniality operated and was expressed. Some of these architectures have been repurposed as part of the historical process of decolonization, while others are currently undergoing conservation or reconstruction without any awareness of their colonial roots. Still others have vanished over time, yet the power structures established by them persist. Compiling these different cases, the volume asks: Whose heritage are colonial sites? Which possibly silenced memories are attached to them? How are archives and material evidence reassessed to bring forward the stories of marginalized subjects? Creating new memoryscapes requires archival troubling and the search for archives that are not representative of hegemonic narratives in order to find ways that, as Antoinette Jackson has put it, enable "active participation in the construction of other forms, sites, and centers of knowledge that disrupt these silences."[3]

While the volume encompasses case studies from across the globe, some of its chapters shed light on the colonial legacy in Germany and the hesitant and late start to coming to terms with this legacy—which was a major motivation for the conception of this publication. Despite its relatively brief existence, the German colonial empire, marked by extreme violence, wielded significant influence in its colonies, particularly in German East Africa and South-West Africa.[4] Key events in colonial history, notably the so-called Berlin Conference of 1884/85 that formalized and propelled the "Scramble for Africa," were held in the German capital.[5] However, it wasn't until the early 2000s that a plaque commemorating the conference was installed.[6] It took even longer for public funds to support the pilot project "Dekoloniale: Memory Culture in the City," which aims to trace German colonialism in Berlin and foster critical discussions about its continuities. Situated at the venue of the "Berlin Conference," the project's initial activities included creating a guide to colonial sites within the former metropole. This guide not only discusses buildings that were later demolished, but also draws attention to highly visible yet little-known and often-overlooked colonial remnants, such as a frieze that starkly illustrates the brutal colonial mindset. This frieze is an element of the former Deutsche Bank building that was completed in 1908—only shortly after the Herero and Nama genocide. Situated at the entrance to the bank, which financed railway construction in German South-West Africa—a catalyst for war culminating in genocide—, the frieze depicts African warriors bowing and submitting to the "gods of civilization" delivering the railway.[7]

Primarily carried out by Afro-German activists, such memory work draws its strength and visibility from the ongoing movement seeking reparation, as in the case of the descendants of the survivors of the genocide in Namibia, or efforts towards the restitution of looted cultural assets, most prominently the Benin bronzes, some of which have now been repatriated. International scholars have also played a significant role in spotlighting the architectures of German colonialism. Itohan Osayimwese in particular has set new standards in historiography by placing colonial building practices at the center of the history of modern architecture. Likewise, Hollyamber Kennedy's approach, which integrates colonial architectural history and the history of land and property, is pivotal.[8] Such ways of history writing informed by postcolonial theory, complicating the dated binary structure of "center and periphery" and exposing the power imbalances and violence ingrained in constructed spaces, provide a crucial foundation for addressing the legacies of colonialism, as emphasized in this volume. The relevance of such historiographical reflection has grown as the focus on inventories and conservation efforts directed at the architectures of colonialism, most recently the architectures of German colonialism, has increased.[9]

In heritage conservation, the notion of "shared heritage" has developed into a widely used concept when dealing with these architectures. The concept reflects the reality that cultural heritage is often connected to multiple groups. Colonial architecture was and is subject to transcultural dynamics and may have taken on new meaning in the process of postcolonial nation-building. But how can this concept be used in light of the ongoing struggles for redress and the continuing power imbalances between former metropoles and colonies? Local communities may still perceive colonial architecture as a tool and symbol of colonialism. They may also feel disregarded by the European concept of cultural heritage.[10] As the essays collected here make clear, there is a wide range of ways of dealing with the architectures of colonialism. While some of these architectures have indeed become a "shared" heritage, others can be considered nothing but an "uncomfortable heritage" (Leo Schmidt)[11] or a "difficult heritage" (Sharon Macdonald).[12] These conceptual frameworks, initially developed to confront Germany's appalling historical legacies, are applied where the legacies of war and conflict need to be memorialized—this, however, raises contentious questions about how such "heritage is assembled both discursively and materially."[13]

Dealing with cultural heritage and its cultural significance necessitates a continuous process of negotiation and re-evaluation, particularly when dealing with a "shared" heritage amidst unresolved conflicts and substantial power imbalances between the parties involved. In such instances, though, history writing and heritage making can become the starting point for public debate and further political processes. Central to this discourse is the acknowledgment that the question of heritage and its treatment is not a neutral one. The value and meaning of heritage is not inherent in the artifacts and built places but is discursively constructed and changes, based on societal values and debates. The attribution of value to places by heritage experts has therefore been contested, most prominently by Laurajane Smith, who critiques the hegemonic position of experts in assigning values to places without the integration of lay people into this process, ignoring other perspectives on heritage and values divergent from the hegemonic narrative. Only by integrating polyvocality can otherwise marginalized communities participate in the process of identifying values in the built environment. The authority to identify and assign heritage values is thus no longer left to recognized "experts," but is entrusted to a democratic process through participatory procedures.[14] After all, heritage conservation is a political act.

Embracing a decolonizing perspective in particular involves questioning the notion of neutral expertise and reflecting on one's positionality as a scholar, in this way contributing to the inclusion of marginalized knowledge. As Osayimwese points out in her essay, "positionality is part of the conceptual armature of postcolonial theory," whose protagonists, who have experienced exile and otherness, work to reveal the contingency of experience and bias in scholarship—as did the field of postcolonial architectural history that has developed since the 1980s. Current decolonial approaches can draw on this extensive body of scholarship that anticipated many of today's perspectives, as Osayimwese shows. Indeed, it seems that those scholars who have long studied postcolonial architectural history, scholars who are predominantly non-Euro-American immigrant women resident in the US, are rendered invisible because of their positionality, even in a discourse that is very much concerned with positionality. We therefore open the volume with Osayimwese's essay to pay tribute to this substantial work and draw attention to the themes and methods that have emerged from it. These include the global networks and local agencies that were crucial to colonial building, as well as the notion of place and the cultural construction of identities, hybridity, and the question of heritage. Methodologically, archival troubling and the search for new forms of evidence are essential to this work, which has expanded the field of architectural history.

Architectures of Colonialism: Constructed Histories, Conflicting Memories builds upon these efforts, striving to acknowledge actors, memories, and places that are still neglected in architectural history. Integrating archaeology, architectural history, and heritage studies, the volume addresses building processes as well as histories of use, reuse, and appropriation. In this way it expands architectural history to include not only lesser-known buildings, builders, architects, and clients, but also those affected by the architectures of colonialism and those who appropriated them, imparting new stories and memories. Key reference points include studies that deal with the hybrid spaces that emerged in the colonies and the transnational networks through which colonial architecture was developed,[15] underscoring the importance of local building knowledge for colonial architecture, as well as its impact on architecture and urbanism in the metropole.[16] Highlighting the connection between colonialism and modernity, these histories indicate the ambivalence of modernity without reducing modernization to a mere imposition.[17] Particularly, the concept of transculturalism delineates a global history of art and architecture that rejects the idea of culture as a closed entity and eschews the "colonizer–colony binary" in order to avoid repeating the colonial narrative and emphasize the agency of the "colonized."[18] This concept, however, runs the risk of losing sight of undeniable asymmetries. Recent architectural histories instead give precise accounts of colonial violence and refer to the dark legacies of colonialism that still affect people in the former colonies.[19] Decolonial heritage research and practices have turned to oral history, ethnographic fieldwork, and virtual reconstruction, among other methods, to preserve the histories and memories of subaltern groups and individuals.[20] Similarly, critical archaeology seeks to trace the material records of those groups and individuals who typically have not been able to manifest themselves in permanent architecture, to provide forensic evidence or even find a starting point to narratively reconstruct their lives.[21]

Two closely linked parts make up this volume: "Archives and Histories" is about architectural histories that explore new archival sources to show the entanglement of agencies and the experience of the "colonized," the resistance to and appropriation of colonial architectures, and the persistence of colonial settlements and spatial orders. "Heritage and Memories" addresses current cases and issues of colonial built heritage, the historical layering involved, strategies of conservation and local identity, new waves of colonialism leading to demolitions, memory work, and artistic strategies in dealing with colonial monuments, and not least gaps in collective memory.

The first case study by Cornelia Escher employs photographs as testimony to a building process in Cameroon, a German colony, in 1911, of which no other sources are known. Illuminating an archival void, these images, imbued with ethnographic curiosity yet not subject to disciplinary rigidity, unveil elusive perspectives on local construction methods for building in the colonies and the power relations involved. "By capturing bodily presence and material interaction," they show the hierarchical order imposed on Africans in the collective construction of a factory building, and also the white supervisor's dependence on Africans' knowledge.

The next chapter extends into the intricate ways in which colonial architectures intersect with the tapestry of local temporal cultures. Using the concept of "architectural assemblage," Zulfikar Hirji shows how clock towers and printed diaries—operating as interrelated material objects—entered cityscapes and private lives in the East African port cities of Mombasa and

Zanzibar. Part of the British "civilizing mission," these temporal objects were nevertheless adapted to local requirements shaped by Omani imperialism and Swahili polities and communities, as Hirji explores on the basis of the personal archives of Omani governors.

Shraddha Bhatawadekar dissects the image-making mechanisms that elevated Bombay's Victoria Terminus, presently the Chhatrapati Shivaji Maharaj Terminus in Mumbai, to the status of a pivotal edifice within the British Empire. Studying the many actors involved, she questions the assumption that the architecture of the 1880s building was "an outcome of a central and coherent policy" to demonstrate British supremacy. Instead, she shows the local Indian elite's interest in the splendor of the railway station, which was intended to position Bombay in the competition between Indian cities and that still makes the station a symbol of Mumbai even today.

In the following chapter, Elizabeth Rankin and Rolf Michael Schneider discuss a much more controversial piece of architecture: the Voortrekker Monument in Pretoria, which was conceived from 1931 onwards and inaugurated in 1949 to celebrate the Dutch-speaking Voortrekkers who colonized the hinterland of British-ruled South Africa after defeating the Zulu in a bloody battle in 1838. The study analyzes the visual narratives of the frieze inside the monument, examines its design and production process, and shows how artistic and landscape interventions as well as the ANC's reinterpretation of the frieze met the challenge of this symbol of apartheid in the post-apartheid era.

The next chapter turns its gaze to the same geographic expanse. Jens Wiedow undertakes an exploration of the South-West Africa pavilion at the Van Riebeeck Festival in Cape Town in 1952, which, like the Voortrekker Monument, asserted racial superiority. Displaying "developmental progress" against the backdrop of "timeless" and "primitive" Africans, the pavilion recalled patterns of nineteenth- and early twentieth-century expositions. Through the analysis of design, spatial order, and control in and through the pavilion, which mirrored the territorial organization of the country, the case study reveals structures that still shape Namibia today.

In the following chapter, Beatriz Serrazina looks at Diamang's "model city" Dundo, founded in 1919 in northern Angola, presenting transnational corporations as key actors in empire building. This case study navigates the trajectory of Dundo's construction methods and typologies across five decades. It lays bare the layers of racial segregation embedded in the settlement's development, juxtaposed against the backdrop of promises for African workers' "development." Serrazina's exploration exposes a nuanced interplay between the promises of progress and the lived realities of the workforce, leaving a lasting mark on the landscape.

The concluding chapter of this section delves into the intricate landscape of decolonization in Lourenço Marques, now known as Maputo, in the aftermath of the collapse of the Portuguese Empire in the 1970s. Lisandra Franco de Mendonça traces this revolutionary process, which included the removal of colonial monuments and the nationalization of tens of thousands of houses left behind by the departing colonizers. As shown in the case study, the visual redress of public space was accompanied by a musealization and appropriation of colonial heritage by the Mozambique Liberation Front as well as a comprehensive photographic survey, on which the study relies.

Looking back into history, these chapters show the complex entanglement of agencies and the interlocking processes of domination and appropriation that have shaped built space in the post-colonies and that are relevant to the question of cultural heritage today. The second section takes a closer look at current issues of memorialization and heritagization in former colonies and in the centers of former empires.

Jorge Correia unfolds the urban history of Ceuta, now a Spanish enclave in Morocco, known for the recurring dramatic incidents in which refugees and migrants attempt to cross the heavily secured EU borders. The study illuminates the city's violent past, characterized by the process of downsizing. In a destructive move motivated by military considerations, the Portuguese dismantled significant sections of the city, initiating a restructuring of the former Muslim bastion from the fifteenth century onward. The Christian overhaul of Ceuta nearly resulted in the obliteration of its Islamic layers—to whose rediscovery the study aims to contribute.

The chapter by Joaquim Rodrigues dos Santos delves into the contemporary discourse surrounding the conservation of the Basilica of Bom Jesus in Goa—an erstwhile bastion of the Portuguese Empire and currently a thriving tourist destination in India. The case sheds light on the political dimension of conservation and the complexities of transcultural heritage. At its core lies the basilica's de-plastering in the 1950s, which was an intentional effort to underscore the antiquity of the Portuguese heritage in Goa. Paradoxically, this very act now poses a threat to the structural integrity of the building. The consequential red hue of the unplastered brickwork, however, has since become an essential part of Goa's postcolonial identity.

In the next chapter, Ying Zhou presents two cases from Hong Kong and Shanghai—global cities characterized by a demolition-driven urbanism, where colonial buildings are embraced as rare old buildings and symbols of past prosperity. Comparing the histories of the Tai Kwun in Hong Kong and the Rockbund Art Museum in Shanghai, two colonial building complexes that have been developed into arts and culture hubs by international star architects, Zhou discusses the dynamics of heritagization in East Asia: the interplay of state–market alliances, civil society, and heritage policies, and the lack of decolonial perspectives.

The following chapter scrutinizes the appropriation and demise of colonial architectures in the context of contemporary colonialism. Karin Reisinger's study of the Swedish mining town Malmberget, built on Sámi territory, revisits the town's colonial past and looks at the coping mechanisms of present-day inhabitants grappling with the displacement resulting from the progressive extraction of minerals—memory work to which the author has contributed by sharing archival material on the houses' architecture. Employing feminist new materialist approaches, Reisinger also conscientiously reflects on her own positionality, underscoring the importance of reflexivity within the scholarly exploration of such subjects.

Johanna Blokker revisits key events in recent monument toppling and discusses artistic ideas for dealing with colonial statues, such as Banksy's proposal to redesign the Colston statue in Bristol to commemorate the very act of toppling it. She critically assesses the purpose of monuments, heritage conservation, and activism at the intersection of cultural heritage as a social construct and sees the purpose of heritage conservation as a social and political act. Presenting her perspective as a heritage expert, whose profession is to conserve monuments but also to explore the values expressed in monuments, Blokker advocates preserving those objects that are capable of provoking public debate, but eventually removing objects that "do not inspire contestation, but rather engender conflict."

In Germany, such conflicts are not only sparked by historical monuments, as Anna Yeboah highlights in her chapter. The coordinator of the "Dekoloniale" project mentioned above writes about controversial building projects in Berlin and the surrounding area, overt and covert racism, and her own experiences as a Black woman living in Germany. Central to the chapter are the reconstruction of the Potsdam Garrison Church, a symbol of militarism and imperialism, and of the Berlin City Palace, which was crowned by a cross and cupola in 2020—at a time when elsewhere colonial monuments were falling.[22] Under this cupola, which bears an inscription calling for Christian world domination, the Humboldt Forum's non-European collections are now on display.

In a striking way, German collective memory is characterized by colonial amnesia—this is a starting point of the volume and the subject of Reinhard Bernbeck's closing chapter. His essay focuses on the so-called Half Moon camp, a prisoner-of-war camp set up near Berlin in 1915, where not only Muslim prisoners (and others falsely perceived as such) were housed, but which was also a place where the idea of pan-Islamism was spread and prisoners mobilized against the enemies of the German Empire. The first mosque in Germany was built there—the historical photo on the cover shows it surrounded by barracks, both built in timber.[23] Bernbeck recalls the history of the camp and reports on the finds from the archaeological excavations he was involved in, including finds from other historical layers such as those from World War II, when the High Command of the Wehrmacht operated from this site. He further outlines the "material assemblage" that could help reconstruct life in the camp: alongside the archaeological evidence, part of this assemblage includes historical photographs and the voice recordings that were made in the camp, where the prisoners were made objects of ethnographic research. Although heavily "contaminated" by history, no efforts have yet been made to turn the site into a place of historical reappraisal. On the contrary, after 2015, a refugee camp was set up on the site of the former jihadist camp for people who had fled Islamist attacks in Syria or Afghanistan—and the most important evidence of the camp, the voice recordings, were transferred to the Humboldt Forum in the reconstructed imperial Berlin City Palace. Tracing and assembling these various forms of material evidence, Bernbeck reveals German colonial amnesia and at the same time contributes to creating "a new configuration of collective memory."

Acknowledgments

We would like to thank all the participants of the 2021 International Online Conference *Architectures of Colonialism: Constructed Histories, Conflicting Memories,* whose stimulating contributions and discussions laid the foundation for this volume. The conference was organized by the editors of the volume and Albrecht Wiesener, coordinator of the DFG Research Training Group "Cultural and Technological Significance of Historic Buildings" at Brandenburg University of Technology Cottbus-Senftenberg, through which the editorial team met. We extend our appreciation to the group members, whose collaborative efforts played a pivotal role in shaping the conference. Acknowledgments are also due to the peer reviewers, whose insights contributed to the refinement of ideas and bolstered the strength of arguments. It is pertinent to note that all texts underwent a thorough peer-review process, with the exception of the essays authored by Itohan Osayimwese, Johanna Blokker, and Anna Yeboah, as these had been previously published in alternative versions. The conference and this book are dedicated to Prof. Dr. Leo Schmidt, who held the Chair of Architectural Conservation at Brandenburg University of Technology in Cottbus from 1995 to 2020. He coined the term and concept of "uncomfortable heritage" and was a pioneer in the protection of the historical cultural landscape of the former Berlin Wall. Special recognition is extended to the series editors Klaus Rheidt and Werner Lorenz, who made this volume possible, Albrecht Wiesener for his coordination work, Sophia Hörmannsdorfer for typesetting, proofreading, and coordination, and William Hatherell for copy editing. For their support, we would also like to thank Katja Richter, Arielle Thürmel, and Kerstin Protz from Birkhäuser Verlag.

1 A list of removed sculptures and other monuments in 2020 and the year after can be found under https://en.wikipedia.org/wiki/List_of_monuments_and_memorials_removed_during_the_George_Floyd_protests (accessed December 16, 2023).
2 James-Chakraborty 2022, 2.
3 Jackson 2012, 30.
4 Conrad 2012; Osayimwese 2023, 2–4.
5 See Eckert 2013. The 1878 Congress of Berlin on the reorganization of the Balkans can also be considered a colonial event, see Terkessidis 2019.
6 See Rozas-Krause 2020, 67–70.
7 Dekoloniale Team 2022.
8 Osayimwese 2017; Kennedy 2019; Kennedy 2023.
9 See Falser 2023 and the conference *Monuments and Sites de-colonial! Methods and Strategies of Dealing with the Architectural Heritage of the German Colonial Era*, TU Munich in November 2023, organized by ICOMOS Germany and Michael Falser, https://arthist.net/archive/40313.
10 On the concept and criticism of "shared heritage," see Küver 2022 and Vanhee 2016; on heritagization and neo-colonialism, see Coslett 2020.
11 The concept arose from turning the remnants of the Berlin Wall into a memorial landscape—see Feversham and Schmidt 1999; Merrill and Schmidt 2010.
12 Macdonald 2009 examines how the city of Nuremberg dealt with the former Nazi party rally grounds.
13 Macdonald 2009, 4.
14 See Smith 2006; Schofield 2014; Vinken 2021.
15 See Chattopadhyay 2000; Le Roux 2003; Le Roux and Uduku 2004; and the essay by Osayimwese in this volume. Cf. also James-Chakraborty 2014.
16 Avermaete 2010; Crinson 2016; Chang 2016; Osayimwese 2017.
17 Osten, Karakayali, and Avermaete 2010, 12.
18 "Understanding Transculturalism" 2013, 29; on transculturalism and heritage, see Falser and Juneja 2013.
19 See Henni 2017; Kennedy 2023; and "Uncovering the Dark Legacy of Nuclear Colonialism with Samia Henni," https://framerframed.nl/en/dossier/podcast-het-ontdekken-van-de-donkere-erfenis-van-nucleair-kolonialisme-met-samia-henni/ (accessed December 16, 2023).
20 Jackson 2012; Knudsen et al. 2022; Cupers and Kitata 2023.
21 Nitschke and Lorenzon 2020; Pollock 2020; Van Dyke and Bernbeck 2015.
22 For more on cross and cupola, see Jethro 2020 and Oswalt 2023, esp. 122–24.
23 See Bernbeck et al. 2016

Bibliography

Avermaete, Tom. 2010. "Nomadic Experts and Travelling Perspectives: Colonial Modernity and the Epistemological Shift in Modern Architecture Culture." In Tom Avermaete, Serhat Karakayali, and Marion von Osten, eds., *Colonial Modern: Aesthetics of the Past—Rebellions for the Future*, 130–51. London: Black Dog Publishing.

Bernbeck, Reinhard, Torsten Dressler, Martin Gussone, Thomas Kersting, Susan Pollock, and Ulrich Wiegmann. 2016. "Archäologie der Moderne: Ausgrabungen im Gelände der Moschee und des 'Halbmondlagers' von 1915." *Brandenburgische Denkmalpflege* 2, no. 1: 99–113.

Chang, Jiat-Hwee. 2016. *A Genealogy of Tropical Architecture: Colonial Networks, Nature and Technoscience*. London: Routledge.

Chattopadhyay, Swati. 2000. "Blurring Boundaries: The Limits of 'White Town' in Colonial Calcutta." *Journal of the Society of Architectural Historians* 59, no. 2: 154–79.

Conrad, Sebastian. 2012. *German Colonialism: A Short History*. Cambridge: Cambridge University Press.

Coslett, Daniel E., ed. 2020. *Neocolonialism and Built Heritage: Echoes of Empire in Africa, Asia, and Europe*. London: Routledge.

Crinson, Mark, 2016. "Imperial Modernism." In G. A. Bremner, ed., *Architecture and Urbanism in the British Empire*, 198–236. Oxford: Oxford University Press.

Cupers, Kenny, and Makau Kitata. 2023. "Kamiriithu Theatre Virtual Reconstruction." https://africandigitalheritage.org/kamiriithu-theatre-virtual-reconstruction/ (accessed December 16, 2023).

Dekoloniale Team. 2022. "Dekoloniale Erinnerungskultur in der Stadt." In Brücke Museum, Stiftung Deutsches Technikmuseum Berlin, Stiftung Stadtmuseum Berlin, Daniela Bystron, and Anne Fäser, eds., *Das Museum dekolonisieren?*, 137–44. Bielefeld: transcript.

Eckert, Andreas. 2013. "Die Berliner Afrika-Konferenz (1884/85)." In Jürgen Zimmerer, ed., *Kein Platz an der Sonne: Erinnerungsorte der deutschen Kolonialgeschichte*, 137–49. Frankfurt a.M.: Campus.

Falser, Michael, ed. 2023. *Deutsch-koloniale Baukulturen: Eine globale Architekturgeschichte in 100 visuellen Primärquellen*. Passau: Klinger.

Falser, Michael, and Monica Juneja, eds. 2013. *Kulturerbe und Denkmalpflege transkulturell: Grenzgänge zwischen Theorie und Praxis*. Bielefeld: transcript.

Feversham, Polly, and Leo Schmidt. 1999. *Die Berliner Mauer: Denkmalwert und Umgang / The Berlin Wall: Cultural Significance and Conservation Issues*. Berlin: Verlag für Bauwesen.

Henni, Samia. 2017. *Architecture of Counterrevolution: The French Army in Northern Algeria*. Zurich: gta Verlag.

Jackson, Antoinette T. 2012. *Speaking for the Enslaved: Heritage Interpretation at Antebellum Plantation Sites*. Walnut Creek, CA: Left Coast Press.

James-Chakraborty, Kathleen. 2014. "Beyond Postcolonialism: New Directions for the History of Nonwestern Architecture." *Frontiers of Architectural Research* 3, no. 1: 1–9. http://dx.doi.org/10.1016/j.foar.2013.10.001.

James-Chakraborty, Kathleen. 2022. "Black Lives Matter: An Architectural Historian's View from Europe." In *Architectural Histories* 10, no. 1: 1–25. https://doi.org/10.16995/ah.8295.

Jethro, Duane. 2020. "Cross and Cupola: Religious Matters at the Berlin Stadtschloss." https://religiousmatters.nl/cross-and-cupola-religious-matters-at-the-berlin-stadtschloss/ (accessed December 16, 2023).

Kennedy, Hollyamber. 2019. "Infrastructures of 'Legitimate Violence': The Prussian Settlement Commission, Internal Colonization, and the Migrant Remainder." *Grey Room* 76 (Summer): 58–97.

Kennedy, Hollyamber. 2023. "A Spatial Writing of the Earth: The Design of Colonial Territory in South-West Africa." In Itohan Osayimwese, ed., *German Colonialism in Africa and its Legacies: Architecture, Art, Urbanism, and Visual Culture*, 89–119. London: Bloomsbury.

Knudsen, Britta Timm, John Oldfield, Elizabeth Buettner, and Elvan Zabunyan, eds. 2022. *Decolonizing Colonial Heritage: New Agendas, Actors and Practices in and beyond Europe*. London: Routledge.

Küver, Jan. 2022. "The Politics of Shared Heritage: Contested Histories and Participatory Memory Work in the Post-Colonial Urban Landscape." In Marie-Theres Albert, Roland Bernecker, Claire Cave, Anca Claudia Prodan, and Matthias Ripp, eds., *50 Years World Heritage Convention: Shared Responsibility – Conflict & Reconciliation*, 139–150. Cham: Springer.

Le Roux, Hannah. 2003. "The Networks of Tropical Architecture." *Journal of Architecture* 8, no. 3: 337–54.

Le Roux, Hannah, and Ola Uduku. 2004. "The Media and the Modern Movement in Nigeria and the Gold Coast." *Nka: Journal of Contemporary African Art* 19: 46–49.

Macdonald, Sharon. 2009. *Difficult Heritage: Negotiating the Nazi Past in Nuremberg and Beyond*. London: Routledge.

Merrill, Sam, and Leo Schmidt, eds. 2010. *A Reader in Uncomfortable Heritage and Dark Tourism*. Cottbus: Brandenburg University of Technology.

Nitschke, Jessica L., and Marta Lorenzon, eds. 2020. *Postcolonialism, Heritage, and the Build Environment: New Approaches to Architecture in Archaeology*. Cham: Springer.

Osayimwese, Itohan. 2017. *Colonialism and Modern Architecture in Germany*. Pittsburgh: University of Pittsburgh Press.

Osayimwese, Itohan. 2023. "Introduction: Seeing and Building German Colonialism." In Itohan Osayimwese, ed., *German Colonialism in Africa and its Legacies: Architecture, Art, Urbanism, and Visual Culture*, 1–36. London: Bloomsbury.

Osten, Marion von, Serhat Karakayali, and Tom Avermaete. 2010. "Colonial Modern." In Tom Avermaete, Serhat Karakayali, and Marion von Osten, eds., *Colonial Modern: Aesthetics of the Past—Rebellions for the Future*, 130–51. London: Black Dog Publishing.

Oswalt, Philipp. 2023. *Bauen am nationalen Haus: Architektur als Identitätspolitik*. Berlin: Berenberg.

Pollock, Susan. 2020. "Archäologie, Zeugenschaft und Counter-Forensics." In Fritz Jürgens and Ulrich Müller, eds., *Archäologie der Moderne: Standpunkte und Perspektiven*, 271–87. Bonn: Habelt.

Rozas-Krause, Valentina. 2020. "Postcolonial Berlin: Reckoning with Traces of German Colonialism." In Coslett 2020, 65–84.

Schofield, John, ed. 2014. *Who Needs Experts? Counter-Mapping Cultural Heritage*. London: Routledge.

Smith, Laurajane. 2006. *Uses of Heritage*. London: Routledge.

Terkessidis, Mark. 2019. *Wessen Erinnerung zählt? Koloniale Vergangenheit und Rassismus heute*. Hamburg: Hoffmann und Campe.

"Understanding Transculturalism: Monica Juneja and Christian Kravagna in Conversation." 2013. In Model House Research Group, ed., *Transcultural Modernisms*, 22–33. Berlin: Sternberg.

Van Dyke, Ruth M., and Reinhard Bernbeck. 2015. *Subjects and Narratives in Archaeology*. Boulder: University Press of Colorado.

Vanhee, Hein. 2016. "On Shared Heritage and Its (False) Promises." *African Arts* 49, no. 3: 1–7.

Vinken, Gerhard. 2021. "Erbe und Emotionen: Zur überfälligen Re-Politisierung der Denkmalpflege." In Stephanie Herold and Gerhard Vinken, eds., *Denkmal_Emotion: Politisierung—Mobilisierung—Bindung*, 14–23. Holzminden: Mitzkat.

ITOHAN OSAYIMWESE

From Postcolonial to Decolonial Architectural History

A Method

Recent energy around struggles for social justice and their articulation in academic discourse is both inspiring and troubling. The new activity is inspiring because it heralds change in conditions that have long been static. But it is disturbing because it begs the question: *why now?* This energy has found its way into the field of architectural history in the form of a *decolonial turn.*[1] This article aims to articulate a theoretical and methodological framework for this decolonial approach. It does this by reconstructing the evolution of scholarship in architectural history that has probed relationships between power, identity constructs, space-making, and representation. I argue that today's decolonial approach in architectural history builds substantially on the work of non-Euro-American immigrant women scholars in United States institutions in the 1980s. Inspired by their engagement with postcolonial theory, these women pioneered research questions and methods that center global relations, forefront relationships between the present and the past, explicitly engage the political, and seek to transform material human conditions. These themes are precisely what define the work characterized as decolonial in contemporary architectural discourse.

The Decolonial Turn

On looking at the titles of academic conferences and texts published over the past few years, even an outsider to architectural history would notice a change in the tenor, thematics, research questions and methods, and geographical scope covered.[2] The scholars involved share a sense of participating in a sea change in the discipline that mirrors a swell in critical activity in the public sphere. Though it is not always labeled as such from the outset, the term "decolonial" is frequently used during discussion to characterize this work. What does decolonial mean in the context of research and writing on the history of architecture?

    Decolonizing Architecture Art Research (DAAR), a "research and project-based artistic practice" based in Palestine, sees decolonization as a "critical position and conceptual frame" for architecture to participate in social and political struggles "against a present system of inequality and control."[3] Based on this understanding, DAAR pursues both a creative practice of intervening directly in extant colonial buildings and infrastructure, and a historiographical and pedagogical practice concerned with critically examining how architecture has worked under colonialism.[4] Declaring, for example, that Italian "fascist architectural modernism emerged and served as an ideological and technical tool within the larger European colonial project," DAAR posits its approach as a radical departure from previous work.[5]

Another group, *Settler Colonial City Project: Decolonizing Architectural Pasts and Futures*, aims to acknowledge ongoing epistemic and physical violence, and dispossession, and to explore "how the architectural theories and practices of Indigenous people across the globe might impact the writing of architectural stories, the limits, possibilities, and definitions of archives, and even the category of 'architecture' itself."[6] Here, decolonization is concerned with uncovering how colonization continues to disrupt society through the built environment and to distort architectural discourse, and it is implied that this constitutes a new horizon of research.

Likewise, architectural historian Yat Ming Loo suggests that decolonization is concerned with engaging "specific material practices, actual spaces, and concrete politics" in formerly colonized societies, and indicates that this approach transcends previous postcolonial critiques of hierarchies of space, power, and knowledge.[7] Together, these examples highlight some of the characteristic concerns of decolonial approaches to histories of the built environment.

Postcolonial Architectural History

Many of the concerns posited as neologisms in decolonial scholarship have, since the 1980s, been at the center of a body of work that I label "postcolonial architectural history." As I will argue, this scholarship has been relegated to the margins and its interventions have consequently gone either uncredited or unnoticed. Postcolonial architectural history is a subfield that analyzes the built environment primarily through the lens of postcolonial theory. However, as I indicate below, it has all the relevant characteristics of a field, including a set of theoretical and methodological norms, a distinct intellectual history, an accumulated body of specialist knowledge, a set of cultural practices that differentiate it from other fields, and even an institutional manifestation through which it reproduces itself.[8] Though its roots lie in the scholarship and activism of local intellectuals in Europe's colonies in the late colonial period, postcolonial theory itself is often dated to the publication of Edward Said's *Orientalism* in 1978.[9] Said argued that Europe has long engaged in a project of colonial domination by claiming intellectual authority over a place, *the Orient*, which it constructed as the ontological and epistemological other of Europe. Since then, four generations of scholars have studied Europe's historical and ongoing discursive, political, and economic structures of cross-cultural domination. It has been a complex and contested endeavor that has spun off into a larger discipline, postcolonial studies, which is invested in analyzing both the *discursive* practices and the *material* effects of European colonialism "from the sixteenth century up to and including the neo-colonialism of the present day."[10] Notoriously slippery, postcolonialism is used as

> a critique of totalizing forms of Western historicism; a portmanteau term for a retooled notion of class …; the name for a condition of nativist longing in post-independence national groupings; a cultural marker of non-residency for a third-world intellectual cadre; the inevitable underside of a fractured and ambivalent discourse of colonialist power; an oppositional form of "reading practice"; and … the name for a "literary" activity.[11]

To be clear, the *post* in postcolonial studies has never been merely a marker of time. Rather the opposite: *post* is the link between the colonial present and past, or a call to action instigated by the unequal present. Furthermore, postcolonial studies has always been about colonialism's legacies. Indeed, these legacies inspired postcolonial theory in the first instance, as illustrated

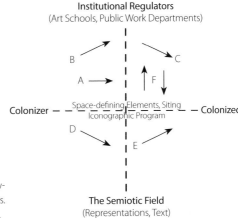

1   Diagram adapted from Stephen Slemon showing how architecture operates in colonial contexts.
Arrows show the direction in which power works.

by the much-debated connection between Said's scholarship and his identity as a Palestinian in exile.[12]

Postcolonial architectural history, then, is at once at home in postcolonial studies and in architectural history. Postcolonial architectural historiography proceeds by conducting a postcolonial reading of its sources. This deconstructive form of reading is based on the original method of postcolonial theory, which highlighted the internal contradictions of colonialism within a literary text, and revealed its ideologies and processes.[13] Unlike this earlier "colonial discourse analysis," however, postcolonial architectural historiography analyzes material objects, space, and the visual field, in addition to language and text. This is its unique contribution to postcolonial studies. Contrary to Arindam Dutta who decries it as merely one of numerous applications of postcolonial theory, postcolonial architectural history offers a unique opportunity to clarify one of the most important conundrums in postcolonial theory: because architecture is simultaneously material(ist) and representational, postcolonial architectural history is able to explain how colonialism functions both through direct forms of domination and via less direct means in the semiotic field (fig. 1).[14] This is also the insight from which much postcolonial architectural history proceeds.

Two Schools of Postcolonial Architectural History

Scholars working in postcolonial architectural history date its beginnings to the publication in the 1970s of the sociologist Janet Abu-Lughod's texts on urbanism in North Africa. Her texts dismantled the orientalist edifice of *the Islamic city*, and sought "to explain the present and to pose a moral problem for the future."[15] Abu-Lughod's work was followed by a series of major publications that reached a crescendo in the 1990s, under the invigorating influence of post-structuralism and deconstruction.

Much of this scholarship has been carried out by women from outside Euro-America who pursued doctoral studies, and developed teaching and research careers, in the United States.

Most of it has emerged from two US institutions: the University of California at Berkeley and Binghamton University. Birthed in 1968, the Berkeley doctoral program set the stage through its unusual commitment to interdisciplinarity. The program's founders believed that other disciplines could offer important insight into their object of study, which they broadened to encompass ordinary buildings and cities. Doctoral students were required to complete courses in other departments such as sociology, cultural geography, and anthropology. Under the leadership of its first full-time member, Norma Evenson, the program gathered a constellation of faculty committed to this ethos and with strong research interests in "nonwestern" topics.[16] These faculty members directed dissertations that turned into monographs in the 1990s. Though diverse in geographic focus, timeframe, and thematic focus, what characterizes this work is a rejection of issues of style in lieu of a focus on space and the social processes that constitute it, including ideology and power, and especially in regions and periods like the Ottoman Empire and South Asia in the late nineteenth century that had not typically been the subjects of architectural historiography in Europe or the United States.[17] The Berkeley school codified its approach with the establishment of the International Association for the Study of Traditional Environments in 1988, and its associated conferences and journal.[18]

The second school of thought developed under Anthony D. King at Binghamton University. King joined the Department of Art History in 1987 but also held a joint appointment in sociology.[19] Soon after arriving at Binghamton from the United Kingdom where he had received his doctoral degree, King visited Berkeley where he taught two graduate-level courses. In recent reminiscences, he notes that this was the beginning of a long-term intellectual exchange.[20] King's first monograph, *Colonial Urban Development: Culture, Social Power and Environment* (1976), set the stage for his subsequent teaching and research through a study of the "colonial third culture" (the product of contact between metropolitan society and the dominant pre-existing local culture) in Delhi, India.[21] Since then, King and his students have theorized the spaces of global cultures, urbanism, and colonialism as part of the world economy, and buildings and cities in relation to identity.[22] Like the Berkeley school, the Binghamton school rejects buildings as primarily aesthetic or technical artifacts, and instead treats them as objects invested with social meaning.[23] Arguably, the Binghamton school is distinguished by its embrace of the global economy as a determinant in the production of built environments. King's approach is codified in the *Architext Series*, which he has co-edited for Routledge since circa 1999.

Scholars of postcolonial architectural history, of course, came from other programs as well.[24] Key scholarship has emerged from the United Kingdom, Australia, Turkey, and Belgium—all countries grappling with legacies of imperialism and colonialism.[25] Given the dearth of doctoral programs in formerly colonized states like India, Indonesia, Nigeria, and South Africa, it is no surprise that representation from these locations has taken on the form I focus on in this essay.[26]

Beyond the structures of doctoral programs and the interests of their faculty, I want to draw attention to the identities of doctoral scholars of postcolonial architectural history. There are at least two reasons to reflect on the female, immigrant, "non-Western," and postcolonial backgrounds of these scholars.[27] First, the fact that they have adopted a common theoretical lens and methodology (described below) justifies searching for other commonalities within the group. Second, scholars from formerly colonized nations have been the standard-bearers of postcolonial studies.[28] This is not a simple question of how subjectivity may shape scholarship. Rather, positionality is part of the conceptual armature of postcolonial theory, where "exile" has been theorized as an experience of otherness from which the "contingency of human experience" can be more fully grasped.[29] As I posit in this article, the positionality of the scholars most closely associated with postcolonial architectural history may have inflected the reception of their work. The problem is generally signaled by under-citation, and it appears in work that is both sympathetic to and critical of postcolonial architectural history.[30] By rendering these women invisible, architectural history is enacting a form of violence akin to the violence that postcolonial and decolonial frameworks both challenge.[31] Consequently, this article centers the work of immigrant and non-European women scholars.

Exemplary Texts

While postcolonial architectural historians have produced a significant number of monographs that illustrate their goals, methods, and insights in excruciating detail, I want to turn my attention to a group of articles that outline the shape of the field.[32] Space does not permit me to summarize all of these publications. In lieu of a comprehensive account, I am offering brief analyses of articles by three authors, Swati Chattopadhyay, Hannah Le Roux, and Ola Uduku, which are only infrequently discussed beyond the subfield.[33]

   In a virtuoso deployment of postcolonial critique within architectural history, Swati Chattopadhyay broke new ground in her 2000 article, "Blurring Boundaries: The Limits of 'White Town' in Colonial Calcutta."[34] The essay brought a postcolonial perspective to one of the discipline's flagship journals, the *Journal of the Society of Architectural Historians*. Building on her 1997 Berkeley doctoral dissertation, Chattopadhyay analyzes the narrative perpetuated by nineteenth-century European observers that the colonial city of Calcutta was divided into black and white zones. Her analyses showed that though English visitors noted that black and white towns existed, they could not agree on where the boundaries of these spaces lay. Conversely, Bengali residents divided the city into a complicated hierarchy of localities. Within this urban landscape, both Indians and the English built for investment. Rooms in these buildings often had no designated functions to accommodate a dynamic rental market that demanded residential properties, warehouses, shops, and other spaces. Further analysis, exemplified in a comparison of Government Hall (Calcutta) to Kedleston Hall (Derbyshire) on which it was modeled, reveals that interior doors lacked locks and there was little separation between service and served spaces. Publications and paintings show that these open plans made it possible for phalanxes of servants to cater to the needs of colonial households (fig. 2). But they also imply severe discomfort with this arrangement, which impinged on bourgeois English notions of domestic privacy and decorum. Racial difference based on skin color was an important aspect of this perceived threat and conventional spatial arrangements were understood as a contributing factor. In theorizing this contradiction, Chattopadhyay draws on postcolonial theories of hybridity and the hypothesis that distinctive "third cultures" were often produced in the "contact zones" of European colonization.[35] She concludes that English observers' distinction between the black and white towns of Calcutta did not align with reality either within individual homes or in urban space. Rather, the "obsessive articulation of delimiting practices" was a rhetorical device that attempted to "fix the signs of difference, in order to resist the effect of the hybrid."[36] It signaled discomfort with the similarities between the so-called black and white towns,

2   Lady Impey with her servants in Calcutta, attributed to Shaykh Zain-al-din, c. 1780.

recognition of the essential hybridity of these spaces, and of Indians' place at the center of colonial life despite colonizers' desires. Chattopadhyay's interpolation of real estate advertisements in newspapers, excerpts from colonial settlers' diaries and travel narratives, building and city plans revealing change over time, and illustrations and paintings of everyday scenes by Indian and European artists, challenged architectural history's reliance on architectural archives containing documents and representations created by architects, and architects' consequent monopoly on defining the terms of architectural history.[37] By analyzing binaries and contradictions, and centering locals as agents in their own histories to challenge an orthodoxy (the dualism of the black/white city) that had not been questioned even in postcolonial circles, Chattopadhyay proves the value of the postcolonial approach. Because of its vacillation between materiality and representation, architecture has the ability to illuminate the workings of empire.

Next, I turn to a body of work published independently and jointly by Hannah Le Roux and Ola Uduku between circa 2003 and 2006.[38] Uduku was one of the first women of African origin to receive a PhD in architecture in the United Kingdom, where she lives and works today, while Le Roux lives and works in South Africa. After meeting at a conference in 1999, the two embarked on a collaboration. The publications that came out of their project thematize a number of topics that were picked up later by other scholars. They focus on the development of "tropical architecture," which was both an educational institution established in 1954 at the Architectural Association in London (at the behest of a Nigerian architecture student, Adedokun Adeyemi searching for a relevant education), and a particular approach to designing for tropical conditions that was institutionalized across the British Empire. Though it was often presented as a rational, technical, ideologically neutral discourse, Le Roux shows that climate discourse and politics were deeply imbricated. In an elegant analysis that utilizes postcolonial and poststructural theories, she considers the built boundary, which tropical architecture obsessively contemplated. According to Le Roux, examples such as Tedder Hall at the University of Ibadan (fig. 3) designed by Maxwell Fry and Jane Drew in 1953–59 in British-occupied Nigeria, illustrate how the triple skin of the boundary (brise soleil, glass windows, and airspace/balcony) structured relations according to an inside/outside binary. At the boundary, architects tried to mitigate the impact of climate on the body, and, through this, the comfort of the expatriate western body became the universal standard for good design.

Boundary-making was racialized since colonizers and colonized did not have the same power to construct space, and it was gendered since the male eye looked out onto a subjugated colonial territory figured as female. The boundary was also a site of the assimilation of local forms like piloti, cantilevered balconies, and brise-soleils, which were denied indigenous authorship and history once they became part of the British discourse of climate responsiveness. Thus, "troubling relations between dominant and subordinated subjects were constructed along with built boundaries."[39] However, Le Roux also shows an ambivalence at the heart of competing colonial desires to modulate colonial space for the European body and to consume the "exotic" world beyond the boundary. This ambivalence creates space for "creative resistance" to the intentions of climatic discourse, as seen at Tedder Hall where users have reclaimed agency by transforming

3   Jane Drew and Maxwell Fry, Tedder Hall, 1953–59, University of Ibadan, Ibadan, Nigeria, detail of the private balconies of a study bedroom wing in 2002, photo by Hannah le Roux.

the thickened space of the boundary into living space.[40] Rather than indefinitely identifying exclusions and illustrating the impossibility of representing the "non-Western" as scholars have charged some postcolonial architectural historiography of doing, Le Roux, through her postcolonial reading, shows that a transformative post-colonial architecture that does not reproduce oppressive power relations is possible.[41] Le Roux's attentiveness to inconsistencies within colonial discourse, and to relations of power and their material and discursive mechanisms and manifestations, are characteristic of postcolonial architectural history.

In her contributions, Uduku argues that tropical architecture was conceptualized, taught, and communicated as a set of universal norms, through entangled global, transnational, trans-imperial knowledge networks centered on London. These networks included long-established colonial agencies like the School of Tropical Medicine and Hygiene; educational institutions like the Architectural Association but also new architecture programs in Ghana and Nigeria; building research stations in Australia, Ghana, India, and South Africa; British architecture firms with branches in Africa, the Caribbean, and South Asia; exiled German architects seeking new pasture for their radical experiments; West African and Caribbean students abroad who formed their own discursive and politically active community; and West African architects practicing at home.[42] This work prefigured a raft of subsequent analyses of the transnational networks of modernism.[43]

Architectural journal articles, technical literature, and photographs were crucial to tropical architecture. However, as Le Roux and Uduku assert, these media distort our understanding of the creation and reception of the phenomenon. Media were almost exclusively produced in England and authored by British subjects embedded in mobile networks that paralleled the original commodity flows of colonialism. Indigenous voices were almost completely absent as were images of use.[44] Consequently, Le Roux and Uduku highlight the complicity of conventional archives in colonialism, and model the importance of identifying counter-sources such as the only professional journal published in West Africa, *The West African Architect and Builder*, or unofficial notes from the 1953 Conference on Tropical Architecture at University College London that record the deep involvement of students from across the colonies in establishing tropical architecture as a course of distinct field.[45]

Modern European Colonialism and Postcolonial Architectural History

These and other foundational articles in postcolonial architectural history reveal shared patterns of thought and analytical strategies, some of which are listed in table 1 below. As the table indicates, these themes and methods resonate beyond the limited scope of modern European colonialism in Africa, Asia, and Australia (typically assumed to be the purview of postcolonial studies). Postcolonial architectural history should therefore be understood as a theoretical orientation and set of methods, rather than a geographically or chronologically defined approach. It exceeds a desire to write the non-Western into history. And it cannot be reduced to a revisionist reworking of modernism via colonialism and orientalism—as it is often mistaken for.[46] Indeed, it can equally well tackle monumentalization and colonial policies for the preservation of a seventeenth-century Sufi monument, and the overlap between the organization of construction labor and penal reform in nineteenth-century Southeast Asia.[47] Methodologically, postcolonial architectural history uses diverse strategies such as discourse analysis, contrapuntal reading, and archival troubling,[48] drawn from poststructuralism, feminist critique, Marxist analysis, and other theoretical frameworks. However, the literature does not support a distinction between a poststructuralist thread of postcolonial architectural history focused on identifying exclusions to prove the impossibility of representing the other, and a humanist approach that posits already existing shared historical values.[49] Rather, these two positions exist simultaneously within individual texts as they do, for instance, in Le Roux's construction of an argument that both reveals how design worked to exclude Nigerians and how Nigerian users overcame this exclusion; and Chattopadhyay's analysis of how narratives insisted on distinguishing the black and white cities of Calcutta in an effort to disregard damning evidence of blurred boundaries.[50] Some scholars are critical of the apparent capaciousness of the field, which seems to encapsulate a wide variety of critical perspectives on the experiences of a range of oppressed subjects as well as nations like Thailand that did not experience formal European colonization.[51] This is a valid concern that has been discussed extensively within the discipline of postcolonial theory itself.[52] Arguably, however, the expansion of the category of the postcolonial is postcolonial theory's greatest success since it lends critical energy and voice to "all types and sites of struggles against hegemonic power," and therefore has the potential for a greater impact on the material human condition.[53] From this vantage point, postcolonial architectural history has a clear path forward—through decolonial critique.

THEMES	THEMES	THEMES	METHODS
Place, space & cultural landscapes	Knowledge-power	Nationalism	Multiscalar formal & spatial analysis
Race	Universal history	The city	Discourse analysis[54]
Cultural construction of identities	The global	Materials & technologies	Archival troubling[55]
Indigeneity	Local agency & resistance	Migration & mobility	Unpacking materiality / representation
Hybridity	Modernities	Networks	(Auto)ethnography[56]
Decolonization & Neocolonialism	Vernacular, tradition, informality	Preservation & heritage	Oral history
Labor	The archive & evidence	Climate & environment	Critical archaeology

Table 1   Characteristic themes and methods in postcolonial architectural history.

Decolonization and Decoloniality

What exactly are decolonialization, decoloniality, and decolonial critique? Like postcolonialism, these terms originate from outside architectural history.[57] In the English- and French-speaking contexts, between the two world wars, colonial policy makers envisioned a gradual transfer of power to "indigenously based, formally sovereign, nation-states," which they called "decolonization."[58] This seemingly technocratic idea was actually a response to widespread anticolonial

THE NATIONAL THEATRE, NAIROBI   NO. 28

4   National Theater, Government Road, 1959, Nairobi, Kenya, photographer unknown.

resistance and national movements that spurred a global shift in values. As we know, events gained unexpected (from European perspectives) momentum, and Europe's nineteenth-century colonial empires in Africa and Asia came to often violent ends between the 1940s and 1960s. However, it soon became clear that political disentanglement was rarely accompanied by economic, social, cultural, and cognitive disengagement.[59] Thus, decolonization is both a constitutional-legal moment and an incomplete process, and both have been preoccupations of postcolonial studies, where scholars have focused on revealing the structural and epistemological dimensions of decolonization's incompleteness and developing practices to dismantle persistent colonial power.[60] Kenyan literary scholar and postcolonial theorist, Ngũgĩ wa Thiong'o, for example, advocates adopting indigenous languages in order to restructure cultural and political life. His open-air community theater rejected both colonial language and architecture, but was violently suppressed by the postcolonial state in the 1970s and 1980s.[61] In place of the monumental, masonry proscenium theater (fig. 4) erected by the British colonial state, where English language productions were held, Kamiriithu Theater consisted of a self-built

> raised semi-circular platform backed by a semi-circular bamboo wall behind which was a small three-roomed house which served as the store and changing room. The stage and the auditorium—fixed long wooden seats arranged like stairs—were almost an extension of each other. It had no roof.[62]

There, the self-funded Kamiriithu group along with local residents scripted and staged Gikuyu-language performances that promoted language learning, taught Kenyan history, provided entertainment, and questioned the nature of contemporary Kenyan society and leadership by a postcolonial elite indebted to colonial political, economic, and cultural systems.[63]

Scholarly approaches to decolonialization have another, concurrent origin story.[64] It emerged from the work of the Peruvian sociologist Aníbal Quijano, which gained traction in the 1990s. "Coloniality," Quijano argued, began with the conquest of Latin America and "the constitution of a new world order, culminating five hundred years later, in a global power covering the whole planet."[65] This power, which was accompanied by an understanding of modernity and rationality as uniquely European phenomena, classified the world according to the mental construct of race, and invented a new structure for controlling labor, resources, and products—global capitalism.[66] Walter Mignolo has expanded on Quijano's definition of decoloniality as the "epistemological decolonization" necessary to "clear way for new intercultural communication … as the basis for another rationality."[67] Mignolo insists that decoloniality is not a conceptual frame for interpreting world events. Rather, it is a practice in which one "extricate(s) oneself from the linkages between rationality/modernity and coloniality."[68] He conceptualizes engagement with these phenomena in spatial terms as dwelling, border thinking, and territorial epistemologies. He also engages with indigenous philosophy and aesthetics, advocating that these be understood as prior to European incursions and be used as the basis for a reconnected past and future.[69]

Postcolonialism and decoloniality are often presented as antagonistic approaches but they are actually closely aligned. In 2020, the journal *Postcolonial Studies* brought these longstanding antagonisms to the fore by staging a dialogue between scholars holding different positions.[70] In his contribution, Ming Dong Gu notes that decolonial scholars have behaved as though "postcolonialism did not exist."[71] Another contributor, Morgan Ndluvu, praises decolonial theory for its "academic humility" and "non-dictatorial" praxis, implying that postcolonial theory is guilty of these sins.[72] Walter Mignolo's contribution contrasts studying the "semiotic dimension of colonisation (of languages, memories and space)" (which I take to mean postcolonialism) with decoloniality as a "praxis of living", while insisting at the same time that decoloniality is only one out of many "options" for confronting the disruptions that coloniality perpetrates.[73] As Sudeshna Guha observes, one strand of current decolonial scholarship has focused on the ethics of curating colonial collections in museums, and, in the process, has "overlooked" the usefulness of understanding "the nationalist politics of decolonization" at the moment of formal independence from European colonialism for "interrogating the cultural imperialisms of the post-colonial states" today.[74] As I will argue, architectural historiography has inherited these tensions.

In fact, though they have distinct disciplinary genealogies and geographical foci, postcolonial and decolonial approaches both challenge insular historical narratives deriving from Europe, and aim to unsettle and reconstitute processes of knowledge production.[75] Two potential distinctions have been tabled. First, decoloniality is said to be more concerned with the afterlife of colonialism and contemporary global inequalities than postcolonialism. Second, postcolonialism is often criticized for a tendency to remain in the theoretical and cultural domains, while decoloniality pays greater attention to material socioeconomic conditions.[76]

However, my summary of the link between personal experience and knowledge production illustrates just one way in which postcolonial theory is grounded in overcoming present inequalities. And a recent exchange in the journal *Postcolonial Studies* reveals that Mignolo's decolonial theory has itself been accused of engaging inadequately with the "material struggle for decolonization" and privileging epistemic work over liberating land and body.[77] What distinguishes postcolonialism and decoloniality may, in fact, be a matter of their degree of political-material engagement (conventionally understood as activism).

Out of the confluence of these and other genealogies, decolonization has gained both academic and popular significance.[78] Eve Tuck and Eugene Wang have memorably protested that instead of focusing exclusively on the "repatriation of indigenous land and life," decolonization has become a metaphor for all social justice initiatives, critical methodologies, and efforts to decenter settler perspectives.[79] Nelson Maldonado-Torres helpfully points out that the current decolonial turn contains equal parts honest discovery and dangerous opportunism.[80] While the decolonization bandwagon raises all sorts of concerns, this essay suggests another, more positive, way of viewing the decolonial turn.

Decolonial Architectural History

The term *decolonial* has been applied most consistently to architectural critique by DAAR. In two recent publications, DAAR argues that existing scholarship on colonial architecture only focuses on the colonial past, and there is therefore a need to investigate the afterlives of colonial architecture in order to do the work of decolonization.[81] Here, we see the misleading insistence that decolonial architectural scholarship represents a new agenda and set of methods. In DAAR's own words, they want to replace the "aesthetic" framework that has been used to analyze colonial architecture with one that "treats architectural space as the product of social, political, and economic transformation."[82] These comments reveal a fundamental misunderstanding of postcolonial architectural scholarship, which takes the interrelation between space and society as a basic premise and often eschews stylistic concerns, and (per its origins in postcolonial studies) is fundamentally a history of the present.[83] Nevertheless, the methods of multi-scalar formal and spatial analysis, discourse analysis, and archival troubling that feature strongly in DAAR's work are characteristic of postcolonial approaches. For example, DAAR replicates the fruitful move that Mia Fuller and several other scholars made years ago of taking built structures and urban ensembles within Italy itself, such as the suburb built for the 1942 *Esposizione Universale di Roma*, as archives of Italian colonialism.[84] However, a distinction exists between decolonial and postcolonial approaches to architectural history in the degree of emphasis placed on the present and on praxis, and in geographical focus. Perhaps, as Hannah Le Roux has recently suggested, postcolonial architectural historiography has not been "anti-colonial" enough.[85]

The scholarly activity that I categorize under the broad rubric of decolonial architectural historiography—because it self-identifies as inaugurating a new, more politically-engaged sensibility in architectural history discourse—has focused on four general areas: the global, race, indigeneity, and gender.[86] There have been several productive recent initiatives to teach and write global architectural histories.[87] Mark Jarzombek explains that "a global history of architecture" is concerned with the "recently emerging geopolitical institutionality of architecture's history," challenging the self-naturalization of the nation-state alongside modernism, and reproducing that which has been suppressed by universalism.[88] Initiatives like Jarzombek's have expanded the discourse in helpful ways. Nevertheless, they have often ignored postcolonial responses to the same questions. Jarzombek misrepresents postcolonial approaches as limited to the period after (European) colonialism, and disingenuously characterizes this work as esoteric and "small in scale."[89] A handful of white male architectural theorists are credited with transforming the discipline in the 1970s and 1980s by parsing the local in relation to the universal, and developing traditional and vernacular architecture as "a type of disciplinary thinking and production."[90] As Swati Chattopadhyay explains, however, postcolonial architectural historiography has long examined the "instantiation of the particular as an effect of the universal," and has conceptualized the global as the possibility of challenging the presumption of the universal.[91] Le Roux and Uduku's transnational actors in the networks of British West African modernism in the 1950s are just one example of this work. Unfortunately, refusing earlier scholarship has consequences. To quote Alice Te Punga Somerville: "Approaches connected to white men, as objects of study or as researchers, are likely to travel along the arteries of our academic worlds in very different ways than, for example, the work of (and about) indigenous peoples."[92]

Recent energy around investigating race in architecture is exciting for the attention it draws to a much-ignored topic, but troubling because it has taken so long to generate broad interest. Race has been the topic of several recent conferences, symposia, and publications.[93] A recent volume, *Race and Modern Architecture: A Critical History from the Enlightenment to the Present*, aims to explore how race—"a concept of human difference that established hierarchies of power and domination between Europe and Europe's 'others'"—has constituted modern architectural discourse from the European Enlightenment to the present.[94] An impressive array of chapters cover topics as diverse as European attitudes towards the Chinese garden and the disparate photographic portraiture of postwar African-American and Euro-American emplaced life. However, the introduction to the volume conflates "modern architecture," "modern architectural history," and the entire discipline of architectural history, whose imbrication with the concept of race is presented as the subject of the book.[95] The authors do not define these much-debated terms from the outset. The text states that "modern architecture entailed spatial practices like classifying, mapping, planning, and building that were integral to the erection of this racialized hegemony," implying that the defining characteristic of modern architecture was/is its racializing bent.[96] If this is the case, then how does this definition relate to other more standard definitions of modern architecture? By contrast, as I have argued in this article, postcolonial architectural history offers a perspective that is useful for analyzing ideologies of exclusion and hegemonic practices that do and do not fit readily into the category of modern architecture.

Like the other scholarship categorized here as decolonial, *Race and Modern Architecture* posits itself as a new turn: "*Race and Modern Architecture* begins the work of exhuming the racial logics embedded in our most canonical histories." Though it acknowledges that postcolonial architectural history has shown that race, modernity, and progress were mutually constructed, the introductory essay goes on to deny their contribution: "If the methodological approaches of critical race theorists and postcolonial scholars already teach us to identify the underlying discourses that structure the gaze of the architect or designer, then the book's chapters identify what tools are still necessary to relate the built environment to these broader cultural processes."[97] It seems to me that a misunderstanding of the goals, methods, and outcomes of postcolonial architectural history is at the root of this aporia. Postcolonial architectural history is misunderstood here as a geographically and temporally bound enterprise concerned with "colonial buildings" and "world exhibitions," and with identifying the "underlying discourses that structure the gaze of the architect or designer."[98]

As I have shown in this article, postcolonial architectural history has a much wider set of theoretical positions, thematic concerns, and methodologies. It has done precisely the kind of work that *Race and Modern Architecture* calls for, by providing "critical hermeneutical methods for uncovering the role of racial thought in familiar objects and narratives."[99] Discourse analysis has been a mainstay of postcolonial efforts to uncover the constitutive role of race, and there is no doubt that "race is there, even when we think it is not" in the postcolonial architectural scholarship summarized in this essay.[100] Furthermore, postcolonial architectural history has paid close attention to the constitution of archives at the nexus of state power and individual subjectivity. It pioneered critical engagement with state (rather than architects') archives and sought alternative archives, and it was instrumental in the elevation of vernacular buildings into objects of study and sources in their own right.[101] However, postcolonial architectural history has not centered race to the exclusion of other constructs, and it can be faulted for not paying adequate attention to the United States, Canada, and South America, though it has addressed the Caribbean.

Recent scholarship on race and the global both lay claim to a heretofore unseen politics of engagement with the present.[102] These claims are even more direct in another wing of decolonial scholarship in architectural history—on settler colonialism and indigeneity. Publications such as "The Settler Colonial Present – On This Land, A Cultural Site," "At the Border of Decolonization," "Indigeneity, Contingency, and Cognitive Shifts," and "Decolonial Ecologies" attest to the importance of these themes in current decolonial scholarship.[103] In "At the Border of Decolonization," Andrew Herscher and Ana María León formulate a new project that seeks to collaboratively produce knowledge about the cities of Turtle Island / Abya Yala / The Americas in relation to settler colonialism, "Indigenous survivance," and decolonial struggles.[104] They assert that "'settler colonialism' has recently emerged as a name for a distinctive form."[105] Furthermore, the architectural theories and practices of Indigenous people, they suggest, have not been adequately examined in light of how these practices might impact the category of architecture itself and the writing of architectural history. In fact, indigeneity, settler colonialism, and the settler colony, are foundational concepts in postcolonial studies. Indeed, postcolonial studies controversially contests the concept of indigeneity as a potentially essentialist trap set by imperialist discourse.[106] For its part, postcolonial architectural history has obsessively examined the status of local/vernacular/traditional/indigenous forms and practices in the built environment.[107] New work like the *Settler Colonial City Project* might profitably engage with the large body of scholarship on architectures of African and indigenous enslavement and genocide in the Caribbean; and on the colonial gaze that emptied local lands of their inhabitants and inserted them into a global network of productive capital, and the problematic architectural and legal regimes that enabled the partitioning and expropriation of indigenous land in the past and in the present in Australia, South Africa, and Namibia.[108]

Unlike the global, race, and indigeneity, gender is one topic that postcolonial architectural historiography has given short shrift, and which decolonial scholarship, under the influence of earlier feminist scholarship, is shining a light on.[109] Torsten Lange and Lucía C. Pérez-Moreno's recent article reflects critically on the explosion of "fourth wave" feminist initiatives insisting on structural transformations in architectural practice and formal architectural education.[110] They identify continuities with earlier "gendered analyses of privacy and domesticity and the 'herstory' mode of writing women into the canon," as well as new directions that analyze women's emotional labor as a form of spatial production, link queer sexuality and gender, and explore collective authorship and non-human forms of embodiment.[111] Their exhortation to write "speculative and performative" histories that intervene in the present and future arguably links their work to the decolonial turn.[112] Another example, the *Feminist Architectural Histories of Migration Project*, engages directly with postcolonial approaches in its emphasis on migrants crossing colonial and postcolonial margins. It too explores design labor without authorship, uses and users who endowed architecture with value, spatial practices of occupation, and "the obscured work of teachers, researchers, and writers."[113] Indeed, my analysis in the current article illustrates the need for a feminist-inspired documentation project targeting the work of non-European women scholars of postcolonial architectural history.

What connects these four bodies of work—on global, race, indigeneity, and gender—is their strongly activist orientation. If indeed an emphasis on material conditions is what distinguishes decolonial from postcolonial frameworks, then architecture's special relationship to materiality/materialism may again offer a bridge. Buildings themselves are material and they play a direct role in shaping socio-economic conditions and inter-human relations, and in creating ideologies. Jyoti Hosagrahar sees a widespread if unspoken acceptance of postcolonial tenets in contemporary practitioners' tendency to see architecture as globally constituted, critique universal design, embrace the local, and pursue social responsibility in design.[114] DAAR's interrogation of the status of Italian colonial-fascist buildings in Asmara, Addis Ababa, and Palermo in the midst of today's neocolonialism and coloniality picks up dangling threads in postcolonial scholarship, while their interventions in Israel's colonial-military infrastructure enact a repossession that resists reproducing colonial relations in a mode similar to the adaptation of the building boundary described by Le Roux.[115] Meanwhile, Anooradha Siddiqi and Kelema Lee Moses relink decolonial efforts to long histories of early anti-colonial activism and contemporary postcolonial scholarship, but propose methodological expansions: Siddiqi invites us to look at the refugee camp as a generator rather than an object of theory and knowledge(s), and Moses suggests that centering contingency in architecture and place-making processes creates openings for multiples ways of knowing such as indigenous design thinking in the United States.[116]

Conclusion

Given the similarities and differences I have summarized between postcolonial and decolonial approaches to architectural history, I would argue that the decolonial turn in architectural history represents an extension of the postcolonial framework across a variety of domains, with a stronger activist bent and an expanded chronological, geographical, and thematic purview.[117] Postcolonialism seems to have finally transformed the canon. However, the transformation remains incomplete if the body of scholarship that has sustained it since the 1980s is rendered invisible.

In an effort to resist the hegemonic logic of academic architectural history and of twenty-first century European and North American social systems, I have chosen to center the scholarship of immigrant, non-European, non-American women scholars of postcolonial architectural history. In academic writing, our historiographical conventions rely on a certain amount of *strawmanning*—new research starts by pointing to flaws in existing scholarship. This in part explains decolonial scholarship's investment in claiming novelty, and accounts for the under-citation of postcolonial architectural history. But strawmanning does not justify the absence of a serious engagement with other work, or the violence wrought by muting the voices of a group that is already under-represented in the discipline. My purpose here is not to discredit decolonial scholarship. On the contrary, I welcome it and the spotlight it shines on inequality and violence of all kinds, and it is my hope that this article will inspire collaboration across the perceived divide between decolonial and postcolonial perspectives in architectural history.

The essay, slightly edited for this volume, was first published in "Rassismus in der Architektur / Racism in Architecture," ed. by Regine Hess, Christian Fuhrmeister, and Monika Platzer, *kritische berichte* 2021, vol. 49, no. 3, 16–38.

1   On "turns" in the humanities and social sciences since the 1960s, see Guldi 2011 and "AHR Forum" 2012.

2   See, for example, Littmann 2021; Loo 2017; *Decolonizing the Spatial History of the Americas*, August 23 – October 15, 2019, The University of Texas at Austin School of Architecture; *Decolonizing Architectural Pasts and Futures*, October 19, 2019, Chicago, IL; Herscher and León 2020a; 2020b. Also see the articles in *Future Anterior*, 2019, vol. 16, no. 2.

3   *Decolonizing Architecture Art Research*, http://www.decolonizing.ps/site/about/ (accessed August 9, 2021); Hilal and Petti 2019, 144; Hilal et al. 2013, 18; Demos 2012.

4   DAAR has published several essays in architectural history venues, and has established a postgraduate program at the Royal Institute of Art in Stockholm that includes courses on the history of colonial architecture. See, for example, Distretti and Petti 2019; "Decolonizing Architecture Advanced Studies", https://www.daas. academy/about/ (accessed March 1, 2023); https://www.artandeducation.net/announcements/320831/ decolonizing-architecture-modernism-and-demodernization (accessed February 10, 2021).

5   Distretti and Petti 2019, 57. In the context of previous scholarship on Italian and other modern European colonial architecture, Distretti and Petti's assertion is a statement of the obvious. Notably, the authors do not cite any existing architectural historical scholarship on Italian fascist colonial architecture. Relevant publications include Giorghis and Gérard 2007, Talamona 1985, Fuller 2007, Denison et al. 2003, Rifkind 2011, Anderson 2015, and McLaren 2006.

6   Herscher et al. [2019].

7   Loo 2017.

8   On what defines a discipline, see Krishnan 2009.

9   Said 1979.

10 Ashcroft et al. 2000, 188.

11 Slemon 1995, 45.

12 For the debate about contemporary postcolonial subjectivity and its relationship to scholarly production as exemplified in the case of Edward Said, see, for example, Armstrong 2003.

13 Ashcroft et al 2000, 192

14 Stephen Cairns calls this the exceptional status of architecture within the broader system of cultural production, and points out that architecture's unique possibilities were already recognized by colonial administrators in eighteenth-century India, who privileged architecture in their machinations precisely because they thought that its materiality/materialism could be used to stabilize notoriously slippery field of signification in colonial discourse. See Cairns 2007. For a critique of postcolonial architectural history as just another application of postcolonial theory, see Dutta 2007, 35.

15 Abu-Lughod 1981, xviii; Abu-Lughod and Hay 1979; Abu-Lughod 1978; Celik 2018. Janet Abu-Lughod's work coincides with the Saidian watershed moment and there are affective ties as well since Said dedicated his *Orientalism* to her and her husband.

16 I use "nonwestern" with immense reservation since one of the major arguments of this essay is that postcolonial architectural historiography is a theoretical framework with a specific methodology rather than a geographical focus.

17 Examples include Celik 1984 and Pieris 2003.

18   James-Chakraborty 2009; 2014.

19   King 2002.

20   King 2016, xvi.

21   Also see King 1974 and King 1973.

22   King's legacy at Binghamton was celebrated in a conference, "Writing the Global City," held in his honor in 2013. The program for the conference offers a preliminary overview of the scope of King's students' work and is available at https://bingdev.binghamton.edu/arthistory/King/KingPROGRAM_FINAL_Letter.pdf (accessed March 1, 2023).

23   James-Chakraborty 2009; 2014.

24   Also see Vikramaditya Prakash's retrospective meditation on the origins of postcolonial approaches to architectural history in Prakash 2019.

25   In Belgium, notable examples include the work of Bruno de Meulder, Johan Lagae, Tom Avermaete, Luce Beeckmans, and others. In the United Kingdom, the work of Ola Uduku, Iain Jackson, Alex Bremner, Lukasz Stanek, among others is notable. Much relevant scholarship from the UK and Central Europe is published in the open access journal *Architecture Beyond Europe*, https://journals.openedition.org/abe/. In Australia, Duanfang Lu, Anoma Pieris, and Peter Scriver are leaders in the field. In South Africa, Hannah le Roux and Huda Tayob have completed important work. Other interlocutors include T. Elvan Altan, Belgin Turan Ozkaya, Kivanc Kilinc, and others. Even a brief survey of these scholars reveals networks of affiliation that confirm the disciplinarity of postcolonial architectural history. Important contributions have also been made by scholars working in cognate disciplines such as anthropology, geography, urban planning, and literary studies. The overview I offer in this article is based exclusively on English- and German-language scholarship as a result of the Anglocentric bias in contemporary academia as well as an artifact of my own scholarly and personal position. For more on language in architectural history scholarship, see "English as the Academic Lingua Franca?", European Architectural History Network, 6th International Meeting, Edinburgh, June 3, 2021: EAHN 2021, 87–88.

26   On the lack of graduate education in architectural history in South Asia and Sub-Saharan Africa, see Hosagrahar 2002; Okoye 2002; Krishna Menon 2000.

27   Kathleen James-Chakraborty points out that postcolonial studies of architectural history have been dominated by scholars from the erstwhile modern European colonies. See James-Chakraborty 2014, 3. Among them, scholars who have explicitly adopted postcolonial perspectives in their work include Zeynep Çelik, Sibel Bozdogan, Gülsüm Baydar Nalbantoğlu, Swati Chattopadhyay, Preeti Chopra, Jyoti Hosagrahar, Anoma Pieris, Ola Uduku, Hannah Le Roux, Madhuri Desai, Mrinalini Rajagopalan, Anooradha Siddiqi, Samia Henni, Mira Rai Waits, Tania Sengupta, and myself, among others. I am not suggesting that only these scholars have explored architectural history using a postcolonial theory framework. Rather, I am highlighting the strange tendency to ignore the contributions made by this core group. Some male, non-European scholars have experienced different types of silencing that this essay does not address. Since nobody is immune to the hegemonic systems, I recognize that the list I focus on in this essay may exclude some scholars who should be included.

28   James-Chakraborty 2014, 3. See also, for example, Armstrong 2003 and Dingwaney Needham 1993.

29   Morgan 2009, iv. The specific group of scholars I am focusing on here have generally not reflected on their identities in their published works. Others like Abidin Kusno have remarked on this topic, see Kusno 2000, ix.

30   See, for example, Jarzombek 2015, 120; Akcan 2014; Cheng et al. 2020, 11; Distretti and Petti 2019, 58.

31   Hilde Heynen notes a similar concern about the suppression of meritorious strands of thought in the historiography of architectural theory, and recognizes postcolonial critique of the problem, Heynen 2020, 299. On the under-citation of scholars of color in general, see Tuck et al. 2015.

32   Several of the articles in this core group were published in the radical architecture journal, *Assemblage: A Critical Journal of Architecture and Design Culture*, which was published between 1986 and 2000. As an experimental publication, *Assemblage* was arguably the only venue where analyses of colonialism, race, gender, class, and sexuality, which, according to Mark Wigley, challenge the "institutionalized and highly protected stories that organize architecture," could be published. Stimulated in part by the neo-conserva-

tive "culture wars" in North America that transformed "identity politics" into an epithet, there was a back-lash against the journal and its brand of architectural theory, and analyses of the politics of subjectivity and the political structures of architecture were forced underground. See Wigley 1995, 88; Burns 2020.

33   A more comprehensive list of articles that establish the historiography of postcolonial analysis in archi-tectural history would include King 1974; Celik 1992; Bozdogan 1988; Ingersoll 1989; Baydar Nalbantoğ-lu 1998; Bozdogan 1999; Baydar Nalbantoğlu 2000; Pyla 1999; Hosagrahar 2012. The list of articles and monographs that are historical rather than historiographical is even more extensive. A helpful bibliogra-phy is included in James-Chakraborty 2014.

34   Chattopadhyay 2000.

35   Chattopadhyay cites Bhabha 1994, 115. Anthony King's discussion of the bungalow-compound complex made a related argument, and both arguments resonate with postcolonial theorist Mary Louise Pratt's concept of the "contact zone." See King 1973 and Pratt 2008 [1992], 8.

36   Chattopadhyay 2000, 176–77.

37   Though familiar today, Chattopadhyay's sources were certainly not orthodoxy for architectural history research in 2000 when this article was published. For example, out of sixteen research articles published in the *Journal of the Society of Architectural Historians* in 2000, Chattopadhyay's was the only piece to use genre paintings as evidence; and only one other article cited real estate advertisements in newspapers. Out of forty-eight articles published between 1999 and 2001, five (including Chattopadhyay's) invoked real estate advertisements, and only Chattopadhyay's analyzed a genre painting.

38   Le Roux 2003; 2004a; 2004b; Uduku 2003; 2006; Le Roux and Uduku 2004.

39   Le Roux 2004b, 440.

40   Le Roux 2004b, 447.

41   Two architectural historians who have engaged with postcolonial theory, Esra Akcan and Sibel Bozdogan, have each expressed this concern. See Akcan 2014, 134 and Bozdogan 1999, 208. Related reservations are expressed, for example, in Berlanda 2017, 71 as well as Southcott and Theodore 2020, 162.

42   See, for example, Uduku 2006, 399, 408–09.

43   Avermaete 2010; Chang 2016; Lee 2015; Stanek 2015.

44   Le Roux and Uduku 2004, 47.

45   Le Roux and Uduku 2004, 49.

46   James-Chakraborty 2014, 3; Akcan 2014, 129.

47   Rajagopalan 2016; Pieris 2011.

48   I take "archival troubling" to mean critiquing institutional archives and institutional time, unearthing hid-den voices or lost patterns, and problematizing the process of unearthing to lay bare the "constitutive incompleteness of the historical archive itself." See Papanikolaou 2017, 47.

49   Esra Akcan makes this distinction in an essay notable as one of few instances in which postcolonial ap-proaches to architectural analysis are thematized in a general publication. See Akcan 2014, 134–35. Also see Bozdogan 1999, 209.

50   Baydar Nalbantoğlu also maintains these two positions simultaneously in her essays, "Toward Postcolonial Openings" (1998) and "Beyond Lack and Excess" (2000).

51   Hosagrahar 2012, 71; Akcan 2014, 133.

52   Chakrabarty 2000, 26; Yaeger 2007.

53   Hosagrahar 2012, 72. For a contrasting view, see Tuck and Wang 2012. For critiques of postcolonial theory, see Chibber 2013.

54   On discourse analysis, see Parry 1987.

55   See Papanikolaou 2017, 47.

56   "Other" as the subject of anthropology; in autoethnography, the ethnographic gaze is framed dialogically, and the ethnographer becomes the "subject-object of observation." See Buzard 2003, 73 and Osayimwese 2014.

57   "Decolonize" has different genealogies in different linguistic and intellectual contexts, including British, French, Soviet, and Latin American. In this article, I focus on the British and Latin American genealogies.

58   Jansen and Osterhammel 2017, 2, 160.

59   Jansen and Osterhammel 2017, 15.

60   See, for example, Ngũgĩ wa Thiong'o 1993 and Ahmad 1992.

61   Ukpokodu 1992.

62   Ngũgĩ wa Thiong'o 1986, 42.

63   Ukpokodu 1992, 31.

64   Here, I am referring to the body of literature known as "decolonial theory."

65   Bhambra 2014, 117.

66   Quijano 2000; Gandarilla Salgado et al. 2021.

67   Mignolo 2020, 615.

68   Mignolo 2020, 615.

69   Mignolo 2020, 615. Also see Mignolo 2011, 113.

70   Prior to 2020, multiple articles were published in *Postcolonial Studies* that attempted to grapple with de-
      colonial theory and its self-understanding as a radical new way of approaching the colonial world order.
      See, for example, Bhambra 2014. For his part, Mignolo has refined his understanding of the relationship
      between postcolonialism and decoloniality over time, and explained it in defense against protestations
      from the postcolonial camp. See Mignolo 2011, xxiii–xxxi, 55. Also see Maldonado-Torres 2020; Mathur
      2020 and Bangstad 2020.

71   Gu 2020, 599.

72   Ndlovu 2020, 579.

73   Mignolo 2020, 613, 615.

74   Guha 2019.

75   Also see Walter Mignolo's comments in *The Darker Side of Western Modernity* (Mignolo 2011, xxvi).

76   Bhambra 2014, 115, 119.

77   Mignolo 2020, 613.

78   For instance, the Decolonize Movement in the United States emerged in 2011 as a splinter group from the
      Occupy Wall Street Movement. See Beeman 2015.

79   Tuck and Wang 2012.

80   Maldonado-Torres 2020.

81   Hilal and Petti 2019, 9; Petti 2019.

82   Petti 2019.

83   For an example of postcolonial architectural scholarship that comments directly on the afterlives of colo-
      nial structures, see Coslett 2020; also see Siddiqi 2017.

84   Fuller 1996; Fuller 2018; Distretti and Petti 2019, 48.

85   Le Roux 2020.

86   It is important to acknowledge that decolonial scholarship in architectural history is strongly informed
      by longstanding developments in a number of disciplines including, in addition to postcolonial studies,
      feminist studies, folklore studies, critical theory, literary studies, critical anthropology, critical geography,
      and others.

87   See, for example, Chine et al. 2010 and the Global Architectural History Teaching Collaborative (of which I
      am a longstanding member), https://www.gahtc.org/ (accessed March 1, 2023).

88   Jarzombek 2015, 112.

89   Jarzombek 2015, 112, 120.

90   Jarzombek 2015, 113.

91   Chattopadhyay 2015, 124–25.

92   Te Punga Somerville 2021, 280. Karen Burns acknowledges this problem for architectural scholarship in
      Burns 2020, 256.

93   Fikeni 2016; *Race, Space, and Architecture*, https://racespacearchitecture.org/index.html (accessed March
      1, 2023); TenHoor and Massey 2015; JSAH Roundtable 2021a; 2021b; *Race, Ethnicity, and Architecture in
      the Nation's Capital*, Thirteenth Biennial Symposium, Latrobe Chapter, Society of Architectural Historians,

February 2021, https://www.latrobechaptersah.org/current-symposium (accessed March 1, 2023); *Architecture and Inequity: New Practices of Care*: London Festival of Architecture Symposium, June 2021, https://www.royalacademy.org.uk/event/lfa-symposium-2021-architecture- and-inequity (accessed March 1, 2023). But also see earlier contributions such as Gürel and Anthony 2006.

94   Cheng et al. 2020, 4.

95   Cheng et al. 2020, 4.

96   Cheng et al. 2020, 4.

97   Cheng et al. 2020, 11, 19. The short list of works in postcolonial architectural history cited by the authors excludes the majority of female, immigrant, and minority scholars who have been at the forefront of this subfield. While the authors use the academic shorthand of gesturing to the vastness of the literature in order to obviate the need for extensive citation, I argue that this practice contributes to a larger pattern of exclusion in the discipline of architectural history. Of the very interesting chapters in the section titled "Race and Colonialism," all three were written by scholars trained in the United States. Two of the contributions are from immigrant, non-white, male-presenting scholars, and two are from established contributors to the subfield of postcolonial architectural history. The disregard for prior scholarship is conspicuous in a chapter from elsewhere in the volume: in Kenny Cupers's chapter, "The Invention of Indigenous Architecture," the author fails to engage with the only three scholars who have conducted critical monograph-length studies of his topic in the last thirty-nine years. See, for example, Osayimwese 2013; 2017; Kennedy 2019a; 2019b; Hollyamber Kennedy, "Against the Migrant Tide: The Prussian Settlement Commission, from Posen to Windhoek," Paper presented at European Architectural History Network, Fourth International Meeting, Dublin, Ireland, June 2–4, 2016; Komeda 2018; 2013.

98   Cheng et al. 2020, 11, 19.

99   Cheng et al. 2020, 11.

100 Cheng et al. 2020, 11.

101 Cf. Cheng et al. 2020, 10.

102 See, for instance, *Race and Modern Architecture*'s caveat that it does not aspire to a more "truthful" history but rather to "provoking architectural historians, students… to become more self-aware." (Cheng et al. 2020, 20).

103 Cordero et al 2020; Herscher and Leon 2020a; Moses 2020a.

104 Herscher and Leon 2020a. I look forward to reading in-depth scholarly treatments in architectural history that explore indigeneity through the lens of decolonial theory. These might include contributions such as Shvarzberg-Carrió 2019 (which is currently embargoed).

105 *Settler Colonial City Project*, https://settlercolonialcityproject.org/Decolonizing-Architectural-Pasts-and-Futures (accessed March 1, 2023).

106 Cf. Good 1976; "Aboriginal/Indigenous Peoples" and "Settler Colony" in Ashcroft et al. 2000, 4, 211; Mudrooroo 1994; Chandler and Reid 2020.

107 While these terms are not equivalent, they are proximate in the way they have been used historically and continue to be used today in architectural thinking (though arguments might be made about their specificity). Examples of postcolonial scholarship on this topic include Micots 2015; Harris and Myers 2007; Hosagrahar 2005; Osayimwese 2014 and forthcoming.

108 Pratt 2008; Pratt 1985; Kennedy forthcoming; 2019; Delle 2014; Nelson 2016; Le Roux 2020.

109 Examples that are arguably grounded in the postcolonial tradition include Pieris 2012; Rajagopalan 2018; some essays in *ABE Journal*, 2019, vol. 16, edited by Anooradha Siddiqi and Rachel Lee. For decolonial feminist architectural history, see Léon et al. 2018; Lange and Pérez-Moreno 2020.

110 Lange and Pérez-Moreno 2020, 1.

111 Lange and Pérez-Moreno 2020, 4.

112 Lange and Pérez-Moreno 2020, 5.

113 Siddiqi and Lee 2019, 4. Also see the recently announced EU-funded project led by Kathleen James-Chakraborty, *Expanding Agency: Women, Race and the Global Dissemination of Modern Architecture*, https://

expanding-agency.com/ (accessed March 1 2023); and *Women in Architecture*, https://www.womenarchitecture.com/ (accessed March 1, 2023).

114 Hosagrahar 2012.

115 For postcolonial analyses of Italian colonial architecture and its afterlives, see, for example, McLaren 2005. On DAAR's interventions in extant colonial buildings, see Hilal et al. 2013, 20; Hilal and Petti 2019, 303; and "Towards an Entity of Decolonization / Verso un Ente di Decolonizzazione," http://www.decolonizing.ps/site/2020/10/towards-an-entity-of-decolonization-verso-un-ente-di-decolonizzazione/ (accessed March 1, 2023).

116 Siddiqi 2020; Moses 2020a; 2020b. Several articles in a 2019 issue of *Future Anterior* devoted to decolonization also interpret it in terms of 1940s–1960s anticolonial nationalism, and center postcolonial theory and its advocates in architectural history (but do not name the group of women discussed in this article). See, for example, Prakash 2019; Griswold 2019.

117 Yat Ming Loo hints at but does not develop a link between postcolonial and decolonial architectural history in Loo 2017.

Bibliography

Abu-Lughod, Janet. 1978. "The Islamic City—Historic Myth, Islamic Essence, and Contemporary Relevance." *International Journal of Middle East Studies* 19, no. 2: 155–76.

Abu-Lughod, Janet. 1981. *Rabat: Urban Apartheid in Morocco*. Princeton: Princeton University Press.

Abu-Lughod, Janet, and Richard Hay. 1979. *Third World Urbanization*. New York: Methuen.

Ahmad, Aijaz. 1992. *In Theory: Classes, Nations, Literatures*. London: Verso.

Akcan, Esra. 2014. "Postcolonial Theories in Architecture." In Elie Haddad and David Rifkind, eds., *A Critical History of Contemporary Architecture 1960–2010*, 119–40. London: Routledge.

"AHR Forum: Historiographic 'Turns' in Critical Perspective." 2012. *American Historical Review* 117, no. 3: 698–813.

Anderson, Sean. 2015. *Modern Architecture and its Representation in Colonial Eritrea: An In-visible Colony, 1890–1941*. Farnham: Ashgate.

Armstrong, Paul. 2003. "Being 'Out of Place': Edward W. Said and the Contradictions of Cultural Differences." *MLQ: Modern Language Quarterly* 64, no. 1: 97–121.

Ashcroft, Bill, Gareth Griffiths, and Helen Tiffin. 2000. *Postcolonial Studies: The Key Concepts*. New York: Routledge.

Avermaete, Tom. 2010. "Nomadic Experts and Travelling Perspectives: Colonial Modernity and the Epistemological Shift in Modern Architecture Culture." In Tom Avermaete, Serhat Karakayali, and Marion von Osten, eds., *Colonial Modern: Aesthetics of the Past – Rebellions for the Future*, 130–51. London: Black Dog Publishing.

Bangstad, Sindre. 2020. "Achille Mbembe's Decolonization." *Africa is a Country*, November 11, 2020, https://africasacountry.com/2020/11/achille-mbembes-decolonization (accessed March 1, 2023).

Baydar Nalbantoğlu, Gülsüm. 1998. "Toward Postcolonial Openings: Rereading Sir Banister Fletcher's *History of Architecture*." *Assemblage* 35: 6–17.

Baydar Nalbantoğlu, Gülsüm. 2000. "Beyond Lack and Excess: Other Architectures / Other Landscapes." *Journal of Architectural Education* 54, no. 1: 20–27.

Beeman, Angie. 2015. "Walk the Walk but Don't Talk the Talk: The Strategic Use of Color-Blind Ideology in an Interracial Social Movement Organization." *Sociological Forum* 30, no. 1: 127–47.

Berlanda, Tomá. 2017. "De-colonising Architectural Education: Thoughts from Cape Town." *Built Heritage* 3: 69–72.

Bhabha, Homi. 1994. *The Location of Culture*. London: Routledge.

Bhambra, Gurminder. 2014. "Postcolonial and Decolonial Dialogues." *Postcolonial Studies* 17, no. 2: 115–21.

Bozdogan, Sibel. 1988. "Journey to the East: Ways of Looking at the Orient and the Question of Representation." *Journal of Architectural Education* 41, no. 4: 38–45.

Bozdogan, Sibel. 1999. "Architectural History in Professional Education: Reflections on Postcolonial Challenges to the Modern Survey." *Journal of Architectural Education* 52, no. 4: 207–15.

Burns, Karen. 2020. "Anthologizing Post-Structuralism: Architecture Écriture, Gender, and Subjectivity." In Sebastiaan Loosen, Rajesh Heynickx, and Hilde Heynen, eds., *The Figure of Knowledge: Conditioning Architectural Theory, 1960s – 1990s*, 255–68. Leuven: Leuven University Press.

Buzard, James. 2003. "On Auto-Ethnographic Authority." *Yale Journal of Criticism* 16, no. 1: 61–91.

Cairns, Stephen. 2007. "The Stones of Orientalism." In Peter Scriver and Vikramaditya Prakash, eds., *Colonial Modernities: Building, Dwelling and Architecture in British India*, 51–65. London: Routledge.

Celik, Zeynep. 1984. "The Impact of Westernization on Istanbul's Urban Form, 1838–1908." Ph.D. Dissertation, University of California, Berkeley.

Celik, Zeynep. 1992. "Le Corbusier, Orientalism, Colonialism." *Assemblage* 17: 58–77.

Celik, Zeynep. 2018. "Reflections on Architectural History Forty Years after Edward Said's Orientalism." *Journal of the Society of Architectural Historians* 77, no. 4: 381–87.

Chakrabarty, Dipesh. 2000. "Subaltern Studies and Postcolonial Historiography." *Nepantla: Views from South* 1, no. 1: 9–32.

Chandler, David, and Julian Reid. 2020. "Becoming Indigenous: the 'Speculative Turn' in Anthropology and the (Re) colonisation of Indigeneity." *Postcolonial Studies* 23, no. 4: 485–504.

Chang, Jiat-Hwee. 2016. *A Genealogy of Tropical Architecture: Colonial Networks, Nature and Technoscience*. London: Routledge.

Chattopadhyay, Swati. 2000. "Blurring Boundaries: The Limits of 'White Town' in Colonial Calcutta." *Journal of the Society of Architectural Historians* 59, no. 2: 154–79.

Chattopadhyay, Swati. 2015. "Seize the Definition." *Grey Room* 61: 123–25.

Cheng, Irene, Charles Davis II, and Mabel Wilson, eds. 2020. *Race and Modern Architecture: A Critical History from the Enlightenment to the Present*. Pittsburgh: University of Pittsburg Press.

Chibber, Vivek. 2013. *Postcolonial Theory and the Specter of Capital*. London: Verso.

Chine, Francis D. K., Mark Jarzombek, and Vikramaditya Prakash. 2010. *A Global History of Architecture*, 2nd ed. Hoboken: Wiley.

Cordero, Jonathan, et al. 2020. "The Settler Colonial Present – On This Land, A Cultural Site." *e-flux Architecture*, October 23, 2020. https://www.e-flux.com/architecture/the-settler-colonial-present/353674/on-this-land-a-cultural-site/ (accessed March 1, 2023).

Coslett, Daniel. 2020. *Neocolonialism and Built Heritage: Echoes of Empire in Africa, Asia, and Europe*. New York: Routledge.

Delle, James. 2014. *The Colonial Caribbean: Landscapes of Power in Jamaica's Plantation System*. New York: Cambridge University Press.

Demos, T. J. 2012. "Decolonizing Architecture/Art Residency." *Artforum* 50, no. 8, https://www.artforum.com/print/reviews/201204/decolonizing-architecture-art-residency-30581 (accessed March 1, 2023).

Denison, Edward, Guang Yu Ren, and Naigzy Gebremedhin. 2003. *Asmara: Africa's Secret Modernist City*. London: Merrell.

Dingwaney Needham, Anuradha. 1993. "Inhabiting the Metropole: C. L. R. James and the Postcolonial Intellectual of the African Diaspora." *Diaspora: A Journal of Transnational Studies* 2, no. 3: 281–303.

Distretti, Emilio, and Alessandro Petti. 2019. "The Afterlife of Fascist Colonial Architecture: A Critical Manifesto." *Future Anterior* 16, no. 2: 46–58.

Dutta, Arindam. 2007. *The Bureaucracy of Beauty: Design in the Age of its Global Reproducibility*. New York: Routledge.

EAHN 6th International Meeting: Conference Proceedings. Edinburgh: The University of Edinburgh. 2021. https://eahn.org/wp-content/uploads/2021/10/EAHN2021-Edinburgh-Proceedings.pdf (accessed March 1, 2023).

Fikeni, Lwandile. 2016. "Apartheid: The Design of Racism in South Africa." *The Funambulist* 5, December 20, 2016. https://thefunambulist.net/magazine/05-design-racism/apartheid-design-racism-south-africa-lwandile-fikeni (accessed March 1, 2023).

Fuller, Mia. 1996. "Wherever You Go, There You Are: Fascist Plans for the Colonial City of Addis Ababa and the Colonizing Suburb of EUR '42." *Journal of Contemporary History* 31, no. 2: 397–418.

Fuller, Mia. 2007. *Moderns Abroad: Architecture, Cities and Italian Imperialism*. London: Routledge.

Fuller, Mia, 2018. "Laying Claim: Italy's Internal and External Colonies." In A. Bagnato, M. Ferrari, and E. Pasqual, eds., *A Moving Border: Alpine Cartographies of Climate Change*, 99–111. New York: Columbia Books on Architecture and the City.

Gandarilla Salgado, José Guadalupe, María Haydeé García-Bravo, and Daniele Benzi. 2021. "Two Decades of Aníbal Quijano's Coloniality of Power, Eurocentrism and Latin America." *Contexto Internacional* 43, no. 1 (Jan/Apr): 199–222, Epub January 15, 2021. https://doi.org/10.1590/s0102-8529.2019430100009.

Giorghis, Fasil, and Denis Gérard. 2007. *The City & its Architectural Heritage: Addis Ababa 1886–1941*. Addis Ababa: Shama Books.

Good, Kenneth. 1976. "Settler Colonialism: Economic Development and Class Formation." *The Journal of Modern African Studies* 14, no. 4: 597–620.

Griswold, Sarah. 2019. "High-Tech Heritage: Planes, Photography, and the Ancient Past in the French Mandate for Syria and Lebanon." *Future Anterior* 16, no. 2: 1–15.

Gu, Ming Dong. 2020. "What is 'Decoloniality'? A Postcolonial Critique." *Postcolonial Studies* 23, no. 4: 596–600.

Gürel, Meltem Ö., and Kathryn H. Anthony. 2006. "The Canon and the Void: Gender, Race, and Architectural History Texts." *Journal of Architectural Education* 59, no. 3: 66–76.

Guha, Sudeshna. 2019. "Decolonizing South Asia through Heritage-and Nation-Building." *Future Anterior* 16, no. 2: 30–45.

Guldi, Jo. 2011. "What is the Spatial Turn?", https://spatial.scholarslab.org/spatial-turn/ (accessed March 1, 2023).

Harris, Richard, and Garth Myers. 2007. "Hybrid Housing: Improvement and Control in Late Colonial Zanzibar." *Journal of the Society of Architectural Historians* 66, no. 4: 476–93.

Herscher, Andrew, and Ana María León. 2020a. "At the Border of Decolonization." *e-flux Architecture*, At the Border, May 6, 2020, https://www.e-flux.com/architecture/at-the-border/325762/at-the-border-of-decolonization/ (accessed March 1, 2023).

Herscher, Andrew, and Ana María León. 2020b. "Editorial." *e-flux Architecture*, The Settler Colonial Present, October 12, 2020, https://www.e-flux.com/architecture/the-settler-colonial-present/353516/editorial/ (accessed March 1, 2023).

Herscher, Andrew, Ana María León, Ayala Levin, and Meredith TenHoor. [2019]. "Indigenous Knowledge and the Decolonization of Architectural Pasts and Futures." http://we-aggregate.org/project/indigenous-knowledge-and-the-decolonization-of-architectural-pasts-and-futures (accessed March 1, 2023).

Heynen, Hilde. 2020. "CODA: A Discipline in the Making." In Sebastiaan Loosen, Rajesh Heynickx, and Hilde Heynen, eds., *The Figure of Knowledge: Conditioning Architectural Theory, 1960s–1990s*, 299–314. Leuven: Leuven University Press.

Hilal, Sandi, and Alessandro Petti. 2019. *Permanent Temporariness*. Stockholm: Art and Theory Publishing.

Hilal, Sandi, Alessandro Petti, and Eyal Weizman. 2013. *Architecture After Revolution: Decolonizing Architecture Art Residency*. Berlin: Sternberg Press.

Hosagrahar, Jyoti. 2002. "South Asia: Looking Back, Moving Ahead-History and Modernization." *Journal of the Society of Architectural Historians* 61, no. 3: 355–69.

Hosagrahar, Jyoti. 2005. *Indigenous Modernities: Negotiating Architecture and Urbanism*. London: Routledge.

Hosagrahar, Jyoti. 2012. "Interrogating difference: Postcolonial Perspectives in Architecture and Urbanism." In Greig C. Crysler, Stephen Cairns, and Hilde Heynen, eds., *The SAGE Handbook of Architectural Theory*, 70–84. London: Sage.

Ingersoll, Richard. 1989. "To the Editor." *Journal of Architectural Education* 42, no. 4: 61.

James-Chakraborty, Kathleen. 2009. "All past buildings will be deemed worthy of study: the Berkeley PhD program and its interdisciplinary orientation." In Waverly B Lowell, Elizabeth Douthitt Byrne, and Betsy Frederick-Rothwell, eds., *Design on the Edge: A Century of Teaching Architecture at the University of California, Berkeley, 1903–2003*, 126–30. Berkeley: College of Environmental Design, Univ. of California.

James-Chakraborty, Kathleen. 2014. "Beyond Postcolonialism: New Directions for the History of Nonwestern Architecture." *Frontiers of Architectural Research* 3, no. 1: 1–9.

Jansen, Jan C., and Jürgen Osterhammel. 2017. *Decolonization: A Short History*. Princeton: Princeton University Press.

Jarzombek, Mark. 2015. "Architecture: The Global Imaginary in an Antiglobal World." *Grey Room* 61: 111–22.

"JSAH Roundtable: Constructing Race and Architecture 1400–1800, Part 1." 2021. *Journal of the Society of Architectural Historians* 80, no. 3: 258–279. https://doi.org/10.1525/jsah.2021.80.3.258.

"JSAH Roundtable: Constructing Race and Architecture 1400–1800, Part 2." 2021b. *Journal of the Society of Architectural Historians* 80, no. 4: 385–415. https://doi.org/10.1525/jsah.2021.80.4.385.

Kennedy, Hollyamber. 2019a. "Modernism's Politics of Land: Settlement Colonialism and Migrant Mobility In the German Empire, from Prussian Poland to German Namibia, 1884–1918." Ph.D. Dissertation, Columbia University.

Kennedy, Hollyamber. 2019b. "Infrastructures of 'Legitimate Violence': The Prussian Settlement Commission, Internal Colonization, and the Migrant Remainder." *Grey Room* 76: 58–97.

Kennedy, Hollyamber. forthcoming. *A Spatial Writing of the Earth: The Borderscapes of Colonial Namibia*.

King, Anthony. 1973. "The Bungalow: The Development and Diffusion of a House-type." *Architectural Association Quarterly* 5, no. 3: 6–26 and no. 4: 4–21.

King, Anthony. 1974. "The Colonial Bungalow-Compound Complex: A Study in the Cultural Use of Space." *Journal of Architectural Research* 3, no. 2: 30–43.

King, Anthony D. 2002. "The Times and Spaces of Modernity (or Who Needs Postmodernism?)" In Mike Featherstone, Scott M Lash, and Roland Robertson, eds., *Global Modernities*, 114–128. London: Sage.

King, Anthony D. 2016. *Writing the Global City: Globalisation, Postcolonialism and the Urban*. New York: Routledge.

Komeda, Ariane. 2013. "Kolonialarchitektur als Gegenstand transkultureller Forschung: Das Beispiel der deutschen Bauten in Namibia." In Michael S. Falser and Monica Juneja, eds., *Kulturerbe und Denkmalpflege transkulturell: Grenzgänge zwischen Theorie und Praxis*, 119–38. Bielefeld: transcript.

Komeda, Ariane. 2018. "Werden, Wandel und Wirkungskraft eines Architekturtransfers in Swakopmund: Deutsche Kolonialarchitektur in Namibia 1884–1914." Ph.D. Dissertation, University of Bern.

Krishna Menon, A.G. 2000. "Educating the Architect." *Seminar (India) Magazine*, no. 494, https://architexturez.net/doc/az-cf-21224 (accessed March 1, 2023).

Krishnan, Armin. 2009. *What are Academic Disciplines? Some observations on the Disciplinarity vs. Interdisciplinarity debate*. ESRC National Centre for Research Methods Working Paper Series 3, https://eprints.ncrm.ac.uk/id/eprint/783 (accessed March 1, 2023).

Kusno, Abidin. 2000. *Behind the Postcolonial: Architecture, Urban Space, and Political Cultures in Indonesia*. New York: Routledge.

Lange, Torsten, and Lucía C. Pérez-Moreno. 2020. "Architectural Historiography and Fourth Wave Feminism." *Architectural Histories* 8, no. 1: art. 26, 1–10, http://doi.org/10.5334/ah.563.

Lee, Rachel. 2015. "Otto Koenigsberger: Transcultural Practice and the Tropical Third Space." *OASE* 95: 60–72.

León, Ana María, Andrea J. Merrett, Armaghan Ziaee, Catalina Mejía Moreno, Charlotte Kent, Elaine Stiles, Emma Cheatle, Jennifer Y. Chuong, Juliana Maxim, Katherine Guinness, Louisa Iarocci, Martina Tanga, Olga Touloumi, Rebecca Choi, S Surface, Saher Sohail, Sarah Parrish, and Tessa Paneth-Pollak. 2018. "To Manifest." *Harvard Design Magazine* 46: 182–89, http://www.harvarddesignmagazine.org/issues/46/to-manifest (accessed March 1, 2023).

Le Roux, Hannah. 2003. "The Networks of Tropical Architecture." *Journal of Architecture* 8, no. 3: 337–54.

Le Roux, Hannah. 2004a. "Modern Architecture in Post-colonial Ghana and Nigeria." *Architectural History* 47: 361–92.

Le Roux, Hannah. 2004b. "Building on the Boundary – Modern Architecture in the Tropics." *Social Identities: Journal for the Study of Race, Nation and Culture* 10, no. 4: 439–53.

Le Roux, Hannah. 2020. "Comfort, Violence, Care: Decolonising Tropical Architecture at Blida, 1956." *ABE Journal* 17, http://journals.openedition.org/abe/8197 (accessed March 1, 2023).

Le Roux, Hannah, and Ola Uduku. 2004. "The Media and the Modern Movement in Nigeria and the Gold Coast." *Nka: Journal of Contemporary African Art* 19: 46–49.

Littmann, William. 2021. "How I Found the Courage to Decolonize my Syllabus." *Platform* (March 1, 2021), https://www.platformspace.net/home/how-i-found-the-courage-to-decolonize-my-syllabus (accessed March 1, 2023)

Loo, Yat Ming. 2017. "Towards a Decolonisation of Architecture." *Journal of Architecture* 22, no. 4: 631–38.

Maldonado-Torres, Nelson. 2020. "A Questionnaire on Decolonization." *October* 174: 73–78.

Mathur, Saloni. 2020. "A Questionnaire on Decolonization." *October* 174: 79–80.

McLaren, Brian. 2005. "The Architecture of Tourism in Italian Libya: the Creation of a Mediterranean Identity." In Mia Fuller and Ruth Ben-Ghiat, eds., *Italian Colonialism*, 167–78. New York: Palgrave Macmillan.

McLaren, Brian. 2006. *Architecture and Tourism in Italian Colonial Libya: An Ambivalent Modernism*. Seattle: University of Washington Press.

Micots, Courtnay. 2015. "Status and Mimicry: African Colonial Period Architecture in Coastal Ghana." *Journal of the Society of Architectural Historians* 74, no. 1: 41–62.

Mignolo, Walter. 2011. *The Darker Side of Western Modernity: Global Futures, Decolonial Options*. Durham: Duke University Press.

Mignolo, Walter. 2020. "On Decoloniality: Second Thoughts." *Postcolonial Studies* 23, no. 4: 612–18.

Morgan, David. 2009. "Critical Distance: The Postcolonial Novel and the Dilemma of Exile." Ph.D. Dissertation, University of Tennessee, https://trace.tennessee.edu/utk_graddiss/624 (accessed March 1, 2023).

Moses, Kelema Lee. 2020a. "Indigeneity, Contingency, and Cognitive Shifts." *Ardeth* 6, 2020, http://journals.openedi-tion.org/ardeth/1171 (accessed March 1, 2023).

Moses, Kelema Lee. 2020b. "Lessons from Hawai'i." *Platform*, October 19, 2020, https://www.platformspace.net/home/lessons-from-hawaii (accessed March 1, 2023).

Mudrooroo. 1994. "White Forms, Aboriginal Content." In Bill Ashcroft, Gareth Griffiths, and Helen Tiffin, eds., *The Post-Colonial Studies Reader*, 228–32. London: Routledge.

Ndlovu, Morgan. 2020. "Well-intentioned but vulnerable to abuse." *Postcolonial Studies* 23, no. 4: 579–83.

Nelson, Louis. 2016. *Architecture and Empire in Jamaica*. New Haven: Yale University Press.

Ngũgĩ wa Thiong'o. 1986. *Decolonizing the Mind*. London: James Currey; Nairobi: Heinemann Kenya; Portsmouth: Heinemann; Harare: Zimbabwe Publishing House.

Ngũgĩ wa Thiong'o. 1993. *Moving the Center: The Struggle for Cultural Freedoms*. Oxford: James Currey; Nairobi: EAEP; Portsmouth: Heinemann.

Okoye, Ikem. 2002. "Architecture, History, and the Debate on Identity in Ethiopia, Ghana, Nigeria, and South Africa." *Journal of the Society of Architectural Historians* 61, no. 3: 381–96.

Osayimwese, Itohan. 2013. "Prolegomenon to an Alternative Genealogy of German Modernism: German Architects' Encounters with World Cultures ca. 1900." *Journal of Architecture* 18, no. 6: 835–74.

Osayimwese, Itohan. 2014. "Architecture with a Mission: Bamum Autoethnography During the Period of German Colonialism." In Nina Berman, Klaus Mühlhahn, and Patrice Nganang, eds., *German Colonialism Revisited: African, Asian, and Oceanic Experiences*, 18–38. Ann Arbor: University of Michigan Press.

Osayimwese, Itohan. 2017. *Colonialism and Modern Architecture in Germany*. Pittsburgh: University of Pittsburgh Press.

Osayimwese, Itohan. forthcoming. *(Re)Translating Hermann Frobenius' Survey of African Architecture*. Leiden.

Papanikolaou, Dimitris. 2017. "Archive Trouble, 2017." In Kateryna Botanova, Christos Chryssopoulos, and Jurriaan Cooiman, eds., *Culturescapes Greece: Archaeology of the Future*, 38–52. Basel: Christoph Merian.

Parry, Benita. 1987. "Problems in Current Theories of Colonial Discourse." *Oxford Literary Review* 9, no. 1: 27–58.

Petti, Alessandro. "The Afterlives of Fascist-Colonial Architecture." In Hilal and Petti 2019, 302–4.

Pieris, Anoma. 2003. "Hidden Hands and Divided Landscapes: Penal Labor and Colonial Citizenship in Singapore and the Straits Settlements, 1825–1873." Diss. University of California, Berkeley.

Pieris, Anoma. 2011. "The 'Other' Side of Labor Reform: Accounts of Incarceration and Resistance in the Straits Settlements Penal System, 1825–1873." *Journal of Social History* 45, no. 2: 453–79.

Pieris, Anoma. 2012. "Between the Home and the World in Violent Conflict." *Gender, Place & Culture* 19, no. 6: 771–89.

Prakash, Vikramaditya. 2019. "Dhārānā: The Agency of Architecture in Decolonization." *Future Anterior* 16, no. 2: 86–120.

Pratt, Mary Louise. 1985. "Scratches on the Face of the Country; or, What Mr. Barrow Saw in the Land of the Bushmen." In Henry Louis Gates, jr., ed., *'Race', Writing, and Difference*, 138–64. Chicago: University of Chicago Press.

Pratt, Mary Louise. 2008 [1992]. *Imperial Eyes: Travel Writing and Transculturation*. New York: Routledge.

Pyla, Panayiota. 1999. "Historicizing Pedagogy: A Critique of Kostof's A History of Architecture." *Journal of Architectural Education* 52, no. 4: 215–25.

Quijano, Aníbal. 2000. "Coloniality of Power, Eurocentrism, and Latin America." *Nepantla* 1, no. 3: 533–80.

Rajagopalan, Mrinalini. 2016. *Building Histories: The Archival and Affective Lives of Five Monuments in Modern Delhi*. Chicago: University of Chicago Press.

Rajagopalan, Mrinalini. 2018. "Cosmopolitan Crossings: The Architecture of Begum Samru." *Journal of the Society of Architectural Historians* 77, no. 2: 168–85.

Rifkind, David. 2011. "Gondar: Architecture and Urbanism for Italy's Fascist Empire." *Journal of the Society of Architectural Historians* 70, no. 4: 492–511.

Said, Edward. 1979 [1978]. *Orientalism*. New York: Pantheon Books.

Shvarzberg-Carrió, Manuel. 2019. "Designing 'Post-Industrial Society': Settler Colonialism and Modern Architecture in Palm Springs, California, 1876–1977." Ph.D. Dissertation, Columbia University.

Siddiqi, Anooradha. 2017. "Architecture Culture, Humanitarian Expertise: From the Tropics to Shelter, 1953–1993." *Journal of the Society of Architectural Historians* 76, no. 3: 367–384.

Siddiqi, Anooradha Iyer. 2020. "The University and the Camp." *Ardeth* 6, 2020, http://journals.openedition. org/ardeth/1179 (accessed March 1, 2023).

Siddiqi, Anooradha Iyer, and Rachel Lee. 2019. "On Margins: Feminist Architectural Histories of Migration." *ABE Journal* 16, 2019, http://journals.openedition.org/abe/7126; https://doi.org/10.4000/abe.7126 (accessed March 1, 2023).

Slemon, Stephen. 1995. "The Scramble for Post-Colonialism." In Bill Ashcroft, Gareth Griffiths, and Helen Tiffin, eds., *The Post-Colonial Studies Reader*, 45–52. New York: Routledge.

Southcott, Tanya, and David Theodore. 2020. "Othering." *Journal of Architectural Education* 74, no. 2: 162–64.

Stanek, Łukasz. 2015. "Architects from Socialist Countries in Ghana (1957–1967): Modern Architecture and Mondialisation." *Journal of the Society of Architectural Historians* 74, no. 4: 416–42.

Talamona, Maria Ida. 1985. "Addis Abeba capitale dell'impero." *Storia contemporanea* 16, no. 5–6: 1093–130.

Te Punga Somerville, Alice (Te Āti Awa, Taranaki). 2021. "OMG Settler Colonial Studies: Response to Lorenzo Veracini: 'Is Settler Colonial Studies Even Useful?'" *Postcolonial Studies* 24, no. 2: 278–282, https://doi.org/10.1080/13688790.2020.1854980.

TenHoor, Meredith, and Jonathan Massey, eds. 2015. *Black Lives Matter*, Aggregate, http://we-aggregate.org/project/black-lives-matter (accessed March 1, 2023).

Tuck, Eve, and Eugene Wang. 2012. "Decolonization is not a metaphor." *Decolonization: Indigeneity, Education & Society* 1, no. 1: 1–40.

Tuck, Eve, K. Wayne Yang, and Rubén Gaztambide-Fernández. 2015. "Citation Practices Challenge." *Critical Ethnic Studies*, http://www.criticalethnicstudiesjournal.org/citation-practices (accessed March 1, 2023).

Uduku, Ola. 2003. "Educational Design and Modernism in West Africa." *Docomomo Journal* 28: 76–82.

Uduku, Ola. 2006. "Modernist Architecture and the 'Tropical' in West Africa." *Habitat International* 30, no. 3: 396–411.

Ukpokodu, I. Peter. 1992. "Plays, Possession, and Rock-and-Roll: Political Theatre in Africa." *The Drama Review* 36, no. 4 (Winter): 28–53.

Wigley, Mark. 1995. "'Story-Time.'" *Assemblage*, no. 27: 80–94.

Yaeger, Patricia. 2007. "Editor's Column: The End of Postcolonial Theory? A Roundtable with Sunil Agnani, Fernando Coronil, Gaurav Desai, Mamadou Diouf, Simon Gikandi, Susie Tharu, and Jennifer Wenzel." *Publications of the Modern Language Association* 122, no. 3: 633–51.

Image Sources

1   Itohan Osayimwese, 2021, adapted from Slemon 1995, 46.
2   Swati 2000, 172.
3   Le Roux 2004b, 449.
4   Age Fotostock.

Archives and Histories

CORNELIA ESCHER

Photographic Approaches to a Colonial Building Site

Ethnography, Architecture, and the Agency of the Artifact

For some time now, architecture researchers seem to have grown a bit weary of discourse analysis and postcolonial studies. The critique stems from different origins. While decolonial critique suggests that postcolonial research has not pursued its critique far enough,[1] others suggest that postcolonial researchers locate their interest too far away from the "actual" material of the discipline, or see the postcolonial critical stance as reducing the richness of historical examples.[2] Yet, the shift from a postcolonial to a decolonial frame of analysis is not only an intensification of critique. Behind these new orientations is also a need to rethink the role of materiality, aesthetic experience, and the positionality of research that postcolonial theory has developed mostly from its structuralist underpinnings.[3]

In colonial architecture history, the so called "material turn," based, mostly, on the growing influence of Actor Network Theory and the theoretical framing of histories of the Anthropocene, has had some effects. On the one hand, studies of colonialism point to landscapes of extraction and material transfers, embedded in the broader timeframes of economy and geology. The colonial phase here appears as a single—yet still important—episode in what is considered the broader change of anthropocenic landscapes.[4] On the other hand, there is a trend towards micro-analysis. The focus here is no longer on the split worlds of discourse and its articulations in material forms, but on the "messy" assemblage that appears in the light of fine-grained analysis. For example, Ariane Komeda has recently described colonial architecture in South Africa as a "medium of exchange and cultural networking."[5] Here, accounts from anthropology, such as Tim Ingold's, seem relevant, as they draw attention to the active qualities of material, and the human engagement with the environment through practices. The new interest is in the actual artifacts with an analysis of how these were experienced in the past. Besides thinking of artifacts as active, this approach brings the field of sensory experience more consciously into research. Photography seems a particularly good tool to access this dimension. Yet, one question remains unresolved with regard to architecture: how can these micro-observations of artifacts and practices, networks and aesthetic experiences be related to an analysis of power?

It is with the background of these questions that I will present my case study based on photographs of a building process in Cameroon taken in 1911, when it was a German colony. In so doing, I rely mainly on a particular photographic series, which is probably the only testimony to this specific event. The series can help to scrutinize the potential of photography for an analysis of architecture and its practices. Here, certain questions regarding the role of the artifact double up: what is at stake is both the agency of the photographic source and the agency of the material setting in the building site. In the following, I will combine different perspectives

1   "Construction of a German Factory, 1911 (probably *Grasland*)"/ VIII A 17816a.

and understand photography and architecture as both aesthetic and discursive, as culturalized forms of expression, which can nevertheless be grasped beyond cultural differences. Thereby, I also build upon postcolonial theories and methodology with a look into practices and the senses.

(De-)Colonial Photography

In order to look into the building process, I selected a series of five photographs from the Ethnological Museum of Berlin (figs. 1–5). The images show successive stages of a building process in Cameroon in the German colonial phase. They have a great level of detail, allowing for the study of the landscape in the background and the fabric of the houses. Moreover, the series has a snapshot quality, which is rare in contemporary photographs from a colonial context.[6] It shows movement and action, instead of frozen postures. These immanent qualities of the series stand in contrast with a certain lack of information on the other hand. To begin with, the name of the photographer and the site photographed on the images are unknown. The series is loosely attributed to the region of the "Grasland" (grassland). This geographical designation has been used since colonial times for a region in the northwestern part of Cameroon, which ethnographers particularly admired for its craftsmanship and its architecture.[7] According to the caption—either added by the museum or by a former owner—the series shows the building process of a German factory, a group of three buildings serving as living quarters, and storage space for a trade post.

Beyond this very rough information, little is known about the context of the origin or distribution of the images. Thus, it seems difficult to set the images' richness and detail of information into a coherent relation with a specific situation. However, the question of how to contextualize a historical photograph seems to be a genuine problem. Here, I would like to refer to Elizabeth Edwards, who has underlined the difficulties of context in using photographs as a historical source. Context, according to Edwards, risks reducing the insights the images themselves could generate. Instead of using the image as a proof for facts or narratives, which are already taken as granted, she suggests addressing photography's relation to historical time as well as its specific potential for historiography. In her analysis, she notably scrutinizes the relation of photographs to the historical event. Moreover, she underlines the photographic capacity to capture atmospheric or phenomenological qualities, which responds to a contemporary interest in the history of experiences.[8]

For the specific case we are looking at, Edwards's analysis of photography and its relation to the historical event is crucial. Edwards argues that the definition of a certain moment as a historical event, which the observer would judge worthy of being written down, is not equally valid for visual material. Here, she sees a specific potential for photography in providing access to moments beyond the colonial perspective. If photography, as Christopher Pinney claims, has blurred the separation between what is intentionally collected as information or unintentionally captured as data,[9] its source qualities might indeed get beyond what seems worthy of being captured in written language. In the case of the photographic series, the "threshold" is not the identification of an administratively relevant event, but a more pictorial question, which is determined from the outset by visual criteria. The author of the photograph thus produces a series from which we can read the process of construction. Besides compositional questions and the desire to depict the different steps of a building process, there is probably also another factor for selecting the moments to be depicted: the spontaneous experience of interest or excitement, which incites the photographer to freeze a specific image. In the series, certain visual high pitches are selected: while the first image offers a pastoral view of the scenery, the other images seem to depict spectacular actions such as lifting up the structure of the roof, collectively raising a wall, or running in order to prevent its falling.

Another aspect, which clearly distinguishes photographic images from other sources, is the spatial situation we are confronted with. Of course, the images are not void of perspective and visual selectiveness, and the photographic lens does not provide a transparent view on a historical reality. Yet, we can extrapolate the configuration of things and humans in the building process. Moreover, there is a photographic process at work in the images that puts all the participants on the same pictorial level.[10] Though the hierarchy of the building process is underlined by the composition of the image (see fig. 1), the images of the series are filled with the sheer presence of humans working on the site, which leads to a very different picture from that given by the written sources, where indigenous workers tend to be neglected or homogenized into a group.

The relation of the series to time and its view onto space have something additional to tell about the situation of the building process and its possible experience. While I assume a specific potential of photography to access history, I do not think that its atmospheric or pictorial mes-

2   "Construction of a German Factory, 1911 (probably *Grasland*)"/ VIII A 17816e.

sages can escape the grip of historical context and discursive power. Therefore, I would claim that the decolonial aspects of the photograph are not so easy to assess for researchers. Our own views are biased in our situated knowledge, taste and previous experience. The message of the photograph originates in relation to a research question and a situated perspective. To put it differently: as in the practice of history writing, which Ariella Azoulay has criticized as a practice of establishing facts that remains largely within a colonial logic,[11] visuals, artifacts, and our more sensual encounters with them, also bear a heritage, which influences our views and perceptions.

Visual and Conceptual Frames of an Ethnography in the Making

Before we go into an analysis of the images themselves, it seems relevant to address the question of the genre to which the image series can potentially be attributed and to set out the frame of interpretation from which this essay analyses the images. The series is credited as showing the building process of a German factory. There is no proof that the image can be ranged among ethnographical photography, neither by an identified author nor by its subject. Yet, I would argue that the photographs we are looking at are also part of a body of ethnographic architecture images in the making. Rather than considering the ethnographic image as something fixed, I will sketch out potential frames of interpretation from ethnography and architecture history, ranging from the colonial period to more contemporary readings.

Generally, for the period under study, we can assume a number of "hobby ethnographers" at work in the region where the photographs were taken. The Cameroon grasslands region was intensively photographed by contemporary travelers, ethnographers, and hobby ethnographers.[12] On a more general level, the use of photography in Cameroon at that time was probably more widespread and may have featured a broader set of contributors than the major body of colonial written sources in Cameroon. We can thus assume a diversification of perspectives and image languages. Still, we might ask if, and how, the image series takes up the pictorial strategies of ethnographic photography as some kind of common denominator. Its implicit rules have been studied notably for people photography. Here, the pictorial strategies were not only established through practice, but also fixed in written sources. They spread beyond ethnographic photography in a narrow sense, as independent photographers hoped to sell their work to museum collections or followed their interest in private popular science.[13]

The ethnographic strategies for architecture photography were probably less codified. In very general terms, ethnographic architecture images often include people, since architecture is framed as "material culture," which means the material output of a specific culture.[14] This "culture" should appear relatively untouched by European influences, so that Europeans would usually not appear in these images. In the visual archives of the ethnologist Leo Frobenius, for example, who travelled to Cameroon in the early twentieth century, we can also discern a certain interest for building processes, since the "fabrication" of material culture helps to understand how specific results are obtained. Particular emphasis is given to the techniques of woven walls. The fabric of the house and the material procedures sustaining it are highlighted. In this context, other serial depictions of building processes carried out by indigenous persons can be found. They are held to show the practices, materials and techniques of building. The photographs of buildings falling apart, which equally occur in the collection, might have a similar background, as they lay bare the constructive principle and the fabric of houses.

There is also another aspect of ethnographic architecture images highlighted notably by architects and architecture research, which seems to have made its way into more contemporary accounts. I here refer to images and texts on non-European architecture, framing it as a "collective building process" and closely associating cultures and built forms. Architecture's fascination with collective building practices goes back at least to Hendrik Petrus Berlage, who highlighted that architecture in Indonesia—then a Dutch colony—delivered an instructive model for building as a collective art (gemeentschapskunst).[15] The idea of collective building in communities held to be intact was then taken up in the postwar period, as a critique of industrialized building processes.[16] Similarly, Wolfgang Lauber, writing in the 1990s on the architecture of palaces and compounds in the Cameroon grasslands, states that there is an "intact community spirit" underlying this "mode of house construction."[17]

Some of the early ethnographic preconditions of viewing might be at work in the use made of the camera while the photographs for the series were taken. Yet, we can only assume the ideological position and potential interest of the photographer. She or he seems rather unconcerned with a "correct" ethnographic framing of a presumably authentic building culture beyond European contacts. Nevertheless, there seems to be a certain familiarity with ethnographic perspectives on architecture—if this can be derived from the image's emphasis on the texture of materials, the building process, and the human practices. The more fluid standpoint

3 "Construction of a German Factory, 1911 (probably *Grasland*)"/ VIII A 17816d.

of the photographer is altered by the later acquisition of the series by an ethnological museum and its integration into its collection,[18] which seems to acknowledge this photograph as an ethnographical document and hereby reinforces possible associations with traditional building techniques.

These ethnographic and architectural image discourses also influence contemporary ways of reading the images in architecture research. My own encounter with the image series, which happened through the museum website, was tainted by a tradition of positive assumptions about collective material practices, and a fascination with texture and craft. The series also responds to my interest in building processes and interactions. The thrilling point is the ambivalent framing of the subject. Though there are reasons to relate it to an ethnographic context, the event it depicts does not fit with colonial ethnography's search for a presumed cultural purity. Precisely because of this ambivalent framing, the series can provide us with material on a practice-related and materially oriented reading of colonialism.

In his famous text "Weaving the world and making culture," Tim Ingold described the practice of weaving a basket as an interactive process in between the material and the producer. The basket does not have a predetermined or conceptual form, but rather evolves out of practice and the properties of the material.[19] If his suggestion is read on a more abstract level as a model for a more ecological relationship of design practices to the world, it seems to emphasize, certainly, not an idea of the presumed purity of culture as heralded by colonial ethnographers. But does his metaphor of weaving also fit the very concrete weaving techniques we see on the construction site in the series of images? Ingold's image promotes a tendency toward harmonious craftsmanship, a certain locality of materials, and a human embeddedness in the immediate environment. His suggestion is a highly valuable methodological proposal to read the interactions of people with a socio-material setting as a dynamic network, with a clear focus on material agencies and processes. However, some of the assumptions and associations contained in the metaphor would, I think, need to be scrutinized and adapted to fit in a colonial context where daily practices are imbued with violence and colonizers strove to press out the environmental riches of the region.

The photographic situation itself problematizes some of the associations the images evoke if they are read in the context of canonical western readings of ethnographical material. Looking at the images, we cannot apply the idea of a harmonious collective of traditional builders, of a society in harmony with its environment, even if some of the visual and aesthetic clues are still at work and might influence interpretations. We are held to ask how questions of power relations, racism, and the extraction of resources enter into the picture as well as into the building process. The questions are thus: Can the photographic series guide us towards a more power-conscious reading of building processes? Can it help us to become warier concerning favorable assumptions about collective building, forged by architects, ethnographers, and researchers alike? How can a perspective on socio-material settings, such as suggested by Ingold, be applied in a society which is disrupted by colonialism, racism, and a struggle for economic power?

Interactions, Agency, and Power on the Building Site

Looking at the images, we can see a relatively complex building process with a differentiated organization. Specific tasks are carried out by individuals or groups of people. In the first image of the series (see fig. 1), the representative of the factory, wearing the typical attire of the colonizers—white clothes and a helmet—, stands against the horizon. A similar position—with an upright, somewhat distanced posture—is occupied by an African wearing a cap, also taking on the role of a supervisor of the building process. In the images, a certain hierarchy and specialization of tasks, with varying degrees of bodily involvement, can be discerned.

In an effort to situate the event within the colonial situation, we could read this as a building process that would normally not raise ethnographic interest, since the presence of European actors is too obvious. Nor is it typical "colonial architecture," since the building is not built for the colonial administration, but belongs to the more informal domain of trade. The site is probably located at a distance from the colonial centers and from the coast, and thus from the transport infrastructure for imported materials.

The abundance of workers in the image can also be read in relation to the economic situation. A system of forced labor existed in the German colonies. Colonized people could be forced to work for public infrastructure by law, but also, more indirectly, through the system of taxation, which forced them to work for the colonizers. Building processes thus relied on an economic system in which cheap labor was made available also to commercial interests. Moreover, the white representative of the factory here probably worked with African intermediaries, who were instructing the working group. For some colonial buildings, groups of workers were acquired

4   "Construction of a German Factory, 1911 (probably *Grasland*)"/ VIII A 17816c.

intentionally from different places as a strategy to maintain power or for their specific skills or education.[20]

Though the construction relies on local material and integrates indigenous knowledge, the organizational scheme seems to be an expression of the colonial system. In this context, the building process is related to an economic system of exploitation which deteriorates the condition of living for the colonized people,[21] though it is impossible to see the long-term and more global effects in the image and track its actual contribution. The sheer abundance of workers is also not an exclusive feature of European colonialism. For example, the involvement of numerous workers in the maintenance of palace architecture in the early nineteenth century in the region of Garoua demonstrated the power of its owners.[22] Thus we are required to focus on the process of building on view in the photograph and ask about the power structures within the interactions that take place in this socio-material setting.

In order to do so, I will for a moment think about descriptions of colonial society and the processes that are possible within them. Older sociological theories have already highlighted the fragmentary nature of colonial societies, since the social existence of its members is incomplete.[23] The outburst of violence directed against the bodies of the colonized was an integral feature of everyday encounters during the despotic but fragmentary regime of German colonialism in Africa.[24] How the racial segmentation of society was reinforced by built structures can be grasped in the color line, which splits colonial residences into a black and a white part. At the very moment of origin of the photograph, the German administration violently reinforced the racial segregation in the city of Douala. But also on the level of architecture, houses were built to clearly separate the domains of African and European private and public lives.

Thus, it seems important to ask how colonial racism enters into practices of building. One strategy to analyze the effects of racism within practices and the sensual domain has been suggested by Sophia Prinz. Building on the work of Frantz Fanon, she argues that racism hampers the perception of the other person's actions as a continuation of one's own bodily and practical intentions.[25] Consequently, the goals in a building process or its successive steps would not be perceived as shared. The collective, and its relation to the material setting, would thus be highly segmented. The experience of the building process itself could then be part of reinforcing racist barriers, as it reinforces this segmentation of experience.

Yet, how we interpret the building process is also dependent on the position we define for artifacts, including buildings and the tools of design. While Prinz builds her theory around sensual perceptions, her view of artifacts could be extended. Instead of underlining the culturalized nature of artifacts and thus their role in maintaining and stabilizing social and cultural traditions, it also seems possible to assign them a more active and processual role. Though partly culturalized, their "affordance" would then extend beyond the culturalized schemes.[26] Moreover, we should mobilize our view in order to see how culturalized or racialized artifacts can also be set in motion and negotiated in the interactions we see.

The photographic series thus guides our view to the conditions under which techniques, knowledge, and building forms were exchanged and negotiated. In fact, some of the features of the house do not fit with what is held to be typical building practices in the grasslands. Though we can assume that the built forms were not static by themselves, the traditional house of the region would consist of large one-room structures with pyramidal roofs, and would be arranged around a central courtyard.[27] An introduction of elements from more European-style architecture, such as the windows cut into the wall facing the courtyard and the partitioning into two separate rooms, seems probable (see figs. 4 and 5). Similarly, the method of drafting and designing the house comes into view, as a process of translation. It materializes in the sticks outlining the floor plan (see fig. 5). Here, the floor plans probably developed by the factory were translated to the building site. If so, they would have to be adapted to the construction technique, which partly determines the shape and the proportions of the house.

The written sources of the colonizers tend to describe artifacts and techniques of building as incompletely mastered by indigenous workers and refer to racist stereotypes. Tools and techniques appear as used against the will of the colonizers and at the origin of conflict and violence.[28] However, the image series can broaden our view of how these tools might work on the site. Do tools and building elements serve to connect the workers, disrupt the hierarchy, translate between cultures? Or are they used to discredit other practices and destroy the climatic behavior of the house? The image series rather suggests the latter, since the windows in the wall would hamper the filtering capacities of the wall against wind and sunlight.

The image series also allows us to look more closely at the interactions of humans with the material setting in the building process and to analyze how the hierarchies mentioned at the beginning of this chapter are actually performed. Here, it seems that bodily involvement in the building process is an important clue in determining hierarchies. The role of the representative

Kamerun

VIII A 17817

Foto:
Erwerb A. Kammeier-Nebel
Markt Hamburg

Aufrichten einer Wand
(wschl. wie 17816)

5 "Raising a wall (probably like 17816)"/ VIII A 17817.

of the factory as a supervisor is fragile, as he is probably not familiar with the technique of build-ing. Nevertheless, he is present in nearly all of the images in order to control the results and to represent power. As he holds a supervising position, he stays at a distance from the actual build-ing process. The African with the cap, who can potentially be identified as a supervisor is also not involved in manual labor. Yet, there is one moment when the building process actively involves the supervising persons (see fig. 5): as one of the wall seems to bend and fall, they start running and moving in order to enter the building process. The photograph here documents a moment in which hierarchies and a status-bound, distinguishing behavior are suddenly challenged by unforeseen events.

Interestingly, the moment when the representative of the factory engages more actively in the building process is not part of the series as I first encountered it on the museum website. It is printed on a different surface, with title and signature more loosely attributed. The liminal status of the photograph can be explained by the compositional disturbance in the image—but also by its power to challenge the hierarchy of the building process itself. The gesture of the merchant as he throws his hands into the air ridicules the superior position that he occupies in the first image of the series and might be read as a factual lack of knowledge on the logic of construction. Even though he is physically involved in the construction process, the distance from the African workers remains relatively large and the movements of the individual actors appear little coordinated.

Conclusion

The photo series contributes to a clearer understanding of power relations in a microanalysis of architecture in a colonial context. Here, photography allows us a special access, not because the domain of the visual is exempt from discursive powers but because of the pictorial logic of portraying a building process. The photographic series can give us insights into specific spatial orders of construction processes by capturing bodily presence and material interaction on the construction site. It shows the potential agency of the construction form, and the turmoil surrounding an unforeseen event that reveals the fragility of the factory representative's position and his fragmentary knowledge of the construction process. Portraying a socio-material setting, the series draws the attention to a recognizable hierarchy of those involved in the building process, but also to a sudden disturbance of this hierarchy. The effects of this disturbance, be they peaceful or destructive, are beyond the frame of the series.

In tracing how the photo series changes when it enters the archive, one can grasp another level of power. This becomes evident in the unclear attribution of the image, which challenges the hierarchies in the building process. Moreover, the ethnological contextualization of the series places it more explicitly into an ethnological context. Looking into ethnographic image discourses, we can trace how later interpretations of the series risk perpetuating categories of colonialism, such as the ethnographically framed indigenous architecture in the grasslands as a supposedly local practice carried out by a peaceful collective.

The actual building process emerges from the image analysis as a more ambiguous undertaking. Though its architecture reunites local features with the probable requests of the factory and is thus a hybrid form, it is embedded in power structures distorting the moment of encounter. The hopeful assumptions about collective practices of building and interactions with materials are not confirmed by the series. Thus, while the image shows a local building process, it can be doubted that its results lead to greater harmony with the surroundings. Nor does the disruption of hierarchy lead to a synchronization of activities. While a hybrid form of building occurs, the practices do not seem to overcome hierarchies and a collective practice or a shared cultural product seems out of view.

An adapted German version of the article will be published in Tobias Becker, Theresa Fankhänel, Dennis Jelonnek, and Sarine Waltenspül, eds. forthcoming 2024. *Der konstruierende Blick: Fotografisches Entwerfen in der Architektur*. Berlin: Schlaufen Verlag. I would like to thank Frederike Lausch, Daniela Ortiz dos Santos, Nina Zahner, Kim Förster, the DFG research group *Lens On*, and the anonymous peer reviewers for their helpful questions, hints, and comments.

1   Osayimwese 2021, 26–29; reprinted in this volume.
2   Moravanszky 2020a, 9.
3   For the broader debate on postcolonial vs. decolonial approaches and the frictions between them, see Colpani et al. 2022; Tembo 2022.
4   See for example the ongoing research on asbestos and cement by Hanna Le Roux, Kim Förster and Monika Motylinska. See also for a proposal to combine varying scales of analysis, Hecht 2018.
5   Komeda 2020, 13.
6   Geary 1986.

7   See for example Lauber 1990. The colonial admiration for this region, its political components, and its enduring impact have been described notably for the Foumban kingdom; see Geary 1990a.

8   Edwards 2016, context: 308–9.

9   With reference to Friedrich Kittler, see Pinney 2010, 165.

10   I here refer to an observation by Pinney, derived from Walter Benjamin, on the idea of the sameness of treatment that photography applies to all the humans it portrays; see Pinney 2010.

11   Azoulay 2019.

12   Geary 1990b.

13   Geary 1990b.

14   See Avermaete 2020, 79. According to Osayimwese, this focus on material culture was coined by Leo Frobenius, see Osayimwese 2013, 14–16.

15   Avermaete 2020, 79.

16   See e.g. Rudofsky 1964. For an analysis, see Moravanszky 2020b.

17   Lauber 1990, 23.

18   On the transfer from the more unstable practice of early tourist ethnographies to "genericization" when ethnographical photographs enter collections, see Hayes 2019, 56–60.

19   Ingold 2000; see also Ingold 2015.

20   Strategic reasons are claimed by the supervisor of constructions of the governments building in 1886 in Douala, Otto Meyer; see Meyer 1911, 38.

21   It would belong to the devastating systems of "Man" that Tsing identifies as the origin of the process of ecological destruction; see Tsing 2016.

22   DeLancey 2016, 43–45.

23   Osterhammel 2009, 98–99.

24   Trotha 1995.

25   Prinz 2018.

26   Escher and Zahner 2021, 12.

27   Lauber 1990.

28   Meyer 1911, 23–37; Seitz 1927, 61–62; 104.

Bibliography

Avermaete, Tom. 2020. "Die beschreibende Tradition: Eine kleine Geschichte der Architekturethnografie." *Arch+* 238 (March): 76–85.

Azoulay, Ariella Aisha. 2019. *Potential History: Unlearning Imperialism*. London: Verso.

Colpani, Gianmaria, Jamila M. H. Mascat, and Katrine Smiet. 2022. "Postcolonial Responses to Decolonial Interventions." *Postcolonial Studies* 25, no. 1: 1–16.

DeLancey, Mark Dike. 2016. *Conquest and Construction: Palace Architecture in Northern Cameroon*. Leiden and Boston: Brill.

Edwards, Elizabeth. 2016. "Der Geschichte ins Antlitz blicken: Fotografie und die Herausforderung der Präsenz." In Herta Wolf, ed., *Zeigen und/ oder Beweisen? Die Fotografie als Kulturtechnik und Medium des Wissens*, 305–326. Berlin and Boston: De Gruyter.

Escher, Cornelia, and Nina Zahner. 2021. "Einleitung: Begegnung mit dem Materiellen in Architekturgeschichte und Soziologie." In Cornelia Escher and Nina Tessa Zahner, eds., *Begegnung mit dem Materiellen: Perspektiven aus Architekturgeschichte und Soziologie*, 9–27. Bielefeld: transcript.

Geary, Christraud M. 1986. "Photographs as Materials for African History: Some Methodological Considerations." *Hist. Afr.* 13: 89–116. https://doi.org/10.2307/3171537.

Geary, Christraud. 1990a. "Photographie als kunsthistorische Quelle." In: Miklos Szalay, ed., *Der Sinn des Schönen: Ästhetik, Geschichte und Soziologie der afrikanischen Kunst*, 113–177. Munich: Trickster.

Geary, Christraud M. 1990b. "Impressions of the African Past: Interpreting Ethnographic Photographs from Cameroon." *Visual Anthropology* 3, no. 2–3: 289–315.

Hayes, Patricia. 2019. "Empty Photographs: Ethnography and the Lacunae in African History." In Gary Minkley and Patricia Hayes, eds., *Ambivalent: Photography and Visibility in African History*, 56–76. Athens: Ohio University Press.

Hecht, Gabrielle. 2018. "Interscalar Vehicles for an African Anthropocene: On Waste, Temporality, and Violence." *Cultural Anthropology* 33, no. 1: 109–141. https://doi.org/10.14506/ca33.1.05.

Ingold, Tim. 2015. "An Ecology of Materials." In Susanne Witzgall and Kerstin Stakemeier, eds., *Power of Material / Politics of Materiality*, 59–65. Chicago: Diaphanes.

Ingold, Tim. 2000. "Making Culture and Weaving the World." In Paul Graves-Brown, ed., *Matter, Materiality and Modern Culture*, 50–71. London and New York: Routledge.

Komeda, Ariane. 2020. *Kontaktarchitektur: Kolonialarchitektur in Namibia zwischen Norm und Übersetzung*. Göttingen: V & R unipress.

Lauber, Wolfgang, ed. 1990. *Paläste und Gehöfte im Grasland von Kamerun: Traditionelle Holzarchitektur eines westafrikanischen Landes*. Stuttgart: Krämer.

Meyer, Otto. 1911. *Unter deutschen Palmen*. Saarbrücken: H. Spieß.

Moravanszky, Akos. 2020a. "Vorwort." In Ariane Komeda, *Kontaktarchitektur: Kolonialarchitektur in Namibia zwischen Norm und Übersetzung*, 7–9. Göttingen: V & R unipress.

Moravanszky, Akos. 2020b. "Architekten als Ethnographen." *Arch+* 238 (March): 46–59.

Osayimwese, Itohan. 2013. "Architecture and the Myth of Authenticity during the German Colonial Period." *Traditional Dwellings and Settlements Review* 24, no. 2: 11–22.

Osayimwese, Itohan. 2021. "From Postcolonial to Decolonial Architectural History. A Method." *kritische berichte* 49, no. 3: 16–38 (reprinted in this volume).

Osterhammel, Jürgen. 2009. *Kolonialismus*, 6th ed. Munich: C.H. Beck.

Pinney, Christopher. 2010. "Camerawork as Technical Practice in Colonial India." In Tony Bennett and Patrick Joyce, eds., *Material Powers: Cultural Studies, History and the Material Turn*, 145–170. London and New York: Routledge.

Prinz, Sophia (2018): "Das Tableau der 'weißen Welt.'" In Susanne Gottuck, Irina Grünheid, Paul Mecheril, and Jan Wolter, eds., *Sehen lernen und verlernen: Perspektiven pädagogischer Professionalisierung*, 45–70. Wiesbaden: Springer VS.

Rudofsky, Bernhard. 1964. *Architecture without Architects: An Introduction to Non-Pedigreed Architecture*. New York: Museum of Modern Art.

Seitz, Theodor. 1927. *Vom Aufstieg und Niederbruch deutscher Kolonialmacht. Vol. 1 Aus dem alten Kamerun*. Karlsruhe: Müller.

Tembo, Josias. 2022. "Do African Postcolonial Theories Need an Epistemic Decolonial Turn?" *Postcolonial Studies* 25, no. 1: 35–53.

Trotha, Trutz von. 1995. "'One for Kaiser'. Beobachtungen zur politischen Soziologie der Prügelstrafe am Beispiel des 'Schutzgebietes Togo.'" In Peter Heine, ed., *Studien zur Geschichte des deutschen Kolonialismus in Afrika: Festschrift zum 60. Geburtstag von Peter Sebald*, 521–551. Pfaffenweiler: Centaurus.

Tsing, Anna. 2016. "Earth Stalked by Man." *The Cambridge Journal of Anthropology* 34, no. 1 (Spring): 2–16.

Images Sources

1–5   Ethnologisches Museum, Staatliche Museen zu Berlin; photographer unknown.

ZULFIKAR HIRJI

Architects of Time

Colonialism, Calendars, and Clocktowers on the East African Coast

In the nineteenth and early twentieth centuries, two forms of temporal materiality associated with British imperialism and colonialism—the printed diary and the clocktower—symbolized British ideas of civilization, industry, discipline, rationality, progress, and modernity, and shaped societal behavior, practices, and outlooks in the imperial metropole and its colonies. Drawing upon archival materials and ethnographic research from colonial coastal East Africa's port cities of Mombasa and Zanzibar, this article starts a conversation about the printed diaries that circulated in these contexts with the clocktowers that were built there. The article proposes the thesis that it was through such an "architectural assemblage" of temporal objects made out of different materials and produced on radically different scales that imperial and colonial powers desirous for land and resources ruptured and restructured local temporal culture and dominated colonized bodies and minds in private and public contexts. The concept of "assemblage" (originally in French, *agencement*), theoretically deployed by philosophers Gilles Deleuze and Félix Guattari, and subsequently used and elaborated upon by scholars in a range of scholarly fields, is here placed in conjunction with "architecture" to refer to different but related objects, knowledges, practices, and affects that brought into being the physical and socio-cultural colonial terrain of coastal East Africa.[1] A particular focus here is on temporal materiality, knowledges, practices, and affects that produced what I am calling *chronometric colonialism*, that part of the colonial terrain made up of an assemblage of objects, including mechanical technologies (i.e., printing presses and clock makers) and an affective culture (i.e., punctuality and laziness), that was made and maintained by the dominant colonial power. But, as with all assemblages, *chronometric colonialism* was a contingent ensemble. Hence, while coastal East Africa's peoples were worked into the flows of colonial temporality and labored within it, they also unmade it through personal and communal acts of resistance and refusal, and by implicitly and explicitly asserting their temporal sovereignty.

Calendars

Imagine yourself suddenly set down amongst stacks of onion-skin paper inscribed with purplish type, piles of books, their spines solid but their pages riddled with worm holes, a stack of personal diaries with handwritten lists and notes in pencil, an assortment of crisply printed invitations, tinted postcards, black and white photographs floating loose or pasted into exercise books and albums, private letters—some written in Swahili and others English, some using embossed letterhead and others attached with metal paper clips to envelopes affixed with colorful postage

1 Photograph of Sheikh Mbarak al-Hinawy at his office desk, Mombasa, late 1940s.

stamps—a bundle of expired passports with neatly clipped corners, packets of telegrams bound with brittle elastic, manuscripts in Arabic script, investiture certificates emblazoned with stamps, signatures, and wax seals, yellowing newspaper clippings, leaflets, notices, files, ephemera, and everything laid out in front of you covered in cough-inducing layers of powdery pyrethrum. This describes my initial encounter in the personal archive of Sheikh Mbarak al-Hinawy (1896–1959).[2]

Sheikh Mbarak's life and career unfolded in the era when coastal East Africa was subject to British, German and Omani imperialism and colonialism.[3] He was born and lived in the port city of Mombasa and became one its most prominent public figures (fig. 1). Today, Mombasa is a city in the nation-state of Kenya, but during Sheikh Mbarak's lifetime it was the administrative capital of the ten-mile strip of coastal East Africa that from 1895 to 1963 was part of the Sultanate of Zanzibar and a British Protectorate. His schooling initially took place in a *madrasa* (Qur'an school) and then a Christian missionary school. During the First World War he enlisted in military service and served as a Private in the 3rd Battalion of the King's African Rifles, a regiment that stayed German advances into the Kenya Colony and Protectorate. After the war he worked in various posts in the local British colonial office. In 1937 he was appointed to the post of Liwali (Governor) for Mombasa by the ninth Sultan of Zanzibar, Sultan Khalifa II bin Harub al-Said (r. 1911–1960). Then, from 1941 until his death in 1959, he served the Sultanate as Liwali for the Coast. Although he self-identified as an Arab of Omani descent, and was an Ibadhi Muslim by faith, as with many other coastal Arabs Sheikh Mbarak's personhood and cultural outlook were historically entangled with the indigenous Swahili communities of coastal East Africa, the majority of whom were Sunni Muslims. A native Swahili-speaker, Sheikh Mbarak was a keen scholar of the Swahili language, literature, customs, and histories, and collected Swahili material culture and manuscripts.[4] Through his independent and collaborative research with local and European scholars, Sheikh Mbarak endeavored to make known the complex heritage of coastal East Africa to a range of publics in East Africa and Europe.

While undertaking research in Sheikh Mbarak's archive, it was the content, form, and materiality of his personal diaries that prompted me to think about the ways in which British coloniality altered Mombasa's nineteenth- and early-twentieth-century temporal culture. The earliest of his diaries dates to 1924 and was produced by Charles Letts & Co., a British family firm that began making diaries in 1812.[5] Its front page (fig. 2) is made of a weighty, textured greyish paper. Printed graphics divide the page into three rectangular blocks. Costing "Two Shillings," the diary was one of the many types of Letts's diaries that the company sold and distributed in Britain and abroad. Its interior pages have "A Week on each Page," with each day of the week given six evenly spaced ruled lines within which the user could write their entries. In addition to calendrical information based on the Gregorian calendar, and the seven-day week beginning with Monday

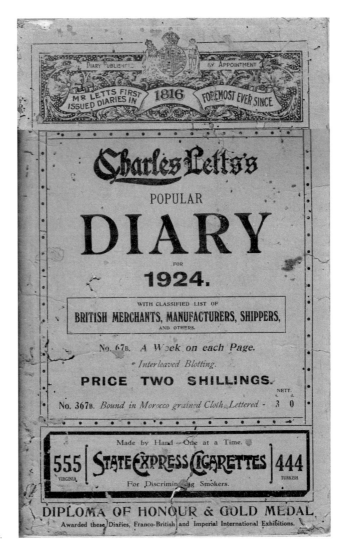

2   Cover of Sheikh
Mbarak's Letts's Diary, 1924.

14 MONDAY [14—352]

All Chiefs & Headmen from every part of the Country arrive. Called in to be shown the Light Cruisers.

15 TUESDAY [15—351]

16 WEDNESDAY [16—350]

1. To visit the Light Cruisers with some 28 Arabs at 10 am.
2. Invited by the Rear-Admiral, Captain & Officers of the Light Cruisers for an "At Home" on board H.M.S. "Delhi" at 9.30 P.M.
3. H.M.S. Dragon arrives.

17 THURSDAY [17—349]

Said M.B.E.b. Said Simsery arrived from Zanzibar.

18 FRIDAY [18—348]

Children Bands stopped by Mr Dickson.

19 SATURDAY [19—347]
S.R. 7.59; S.S. 4.22

E.A. N. Indian Congress 5th Session held opposite Mangoro Offices with Mrs Sarojini Naidu presiding. Mrs S. Naidu arrived today per S.S. Karagola from India.

20 **Sunday** [20—346]
2nd after Epiphany.

Congress sits the whole day.   Bands stopped by Mr

and ending on Sunday, the diary's interior pages also include the Anglican Christian religious holidays and festival days, the times of sunrise and sunset as observed in London, and the number of days in the year in ascending and descending order.

The printed diary form became popular in Britain during the nineteenth century, when time was measured and indexed to gauge societal and personal efficacy, industry, productivity, and worth. Variously linked to the Mechanical Age, the Industrial Revolution and the rise of capitalism, when time became standardized and commodified in order to increase production,[6] the diary was a model of the productive industrial society and a tool for producing this mechanical utopia. More particularly, as argued by Kathryn Carter, through the diurnal practices of scheduling, recording, and writing down both the mundane and intimate aspects of their lives, Britain's diarists from all walks of life produced and instantiated themselves within and according to the diary's temporal logics, and, in so doing, reproduced those logics.[7] Thus, the popularity of Letts's printed diaries and those of other diary-makers in the nineteenth century was symbolic of the desire for people to see themselves as part of a newly ordered world, and the material means by which they could bring this world into being.

In terms of their form, Rebecca Steinitz describes British printed diaries as "texts organized around the concept of organization."[8] And, according to Joe Moran, in Britain diaries remained "conspicuously tactile objects with specific textual and visual conventions."[9] I regard the diurnal form as a producer of *chronometric prose*, an iteratively generated literary genre in which selected traces of life are laid out according to the passing and progression of time graphically demarcated into a culturally determined calendrical system of hours, days, weeks, and months. This was probably as true for people living in Britain as it was for those residing in its colonies. Thus, Sheikh Mbarak's 1924 Letts's diary is replete with British temporal conventions. Like him, through its use, diarists appropriated and reproduced these conventions each time they put pen to paper. Such diaries were an important form of temporal materiality through which European colonial powers were able to regulate and re-inscribe the bodies and minds they colonized.

In the latter half of the nineteenth century, Letts's agents such as Cassell and Co. began distributing its diaries to Britain's colonies in Asia, Africa, Australia, and the Americas.[10] Diary names such as the *Colonial Rough Diary*, the *South African Rough Diary and Almanac*, and the *Indian and Colonial Rough Diary* identified the places they were meant to be used. As such, these geographically identified diaries began to include bespoke content such as the "latitudes and longitudes of colonial ports, cities, and observatories,"[11] and according to contemporary advertisements for these diaries included a "copious directory of foreign, colonial, and country banks, and insurance companies."[12] The diaries also included tables of calendrical information from non-Christian religious traditions and locally relevant astrological tables, such as eclipses and seasons. Apart from the inclusion of this geographically specific content, the basic temporal format of these diaries appears to have remained the same.

Sheikh Mbarak was twenty-eight years old when he wrote in his first Letts's diary (fig. 3). It is difficult to ascertain where he purchased it. It also could have been gifted to him or supplied to him by the colonial office. At this time, he was serving as Arab Assistant to Francis T. Ainsworth Dickson (1881–1935), Britain's Resident Commissioner in Mombasa. As is the case with most of Sheikh Mbarak's diaries, rather than chronicling impressions of events, the diaries contain a clerical-like record of his appointments and events of the day, all handwritten in pencil, using a

3   Inside page of Sheikh Mbarak's Letts's Diary, 1924.

neat, tight, cursive hand. Even details related to his personal life, like his divorces and marriages, are presented in an accountant-like fashion. For example, in his 1927 diary, under "July 30, Saturday," he writes, "Divorced both 2 wives. Handed Sh:400/- to Sheikh Suleman b. Ali El-Mazrui Kathi of Mombasa who paid to Khadija bint Hassan alias Kibibi as her dowry." The diary's internal pages reveal little of his private thoughts or inner life.

Thus, the manner in which Sheikh Mbarak used his diaries, or perhaps, the way they used him—his daily entries written precisely on the rule-lines and within the spaces Letts provided—suggests a type of self-fashioning or self-regulation, discipline, constraint, and the structuring of time expected of a British colonial subject becoming integrated into the colonial administration.[13] His military training and work in the colonial office may account for the precise and reserved style of his diurnal prose. In the latter context, he was likely schooled in the bureaucratic arts of record-keeping as well as the uses and reproduction of the bureaucrat's materials such as files, ledgers, diaries, and letters—the "embodied things" of colonial bureaucracy—or what sociologist Georg Simmel might have regarded as the "objective culture" of British colonialism.[14]

Clocktowers

1896, the year of Sheikh Mbarak's birth, was the same year that the British began constructing the railway line that would run from Mombasa to the eastern shore of Lake Victoria. The British railway enterprise captured the zeitgeist of Britain's industrial age in terms of precision, movement, and speed. As noted by Ravi Ahuja, the railway was also about progress and underwrote Britain's "civilizing mission" in its colonies.[15] Time, timing and schedules were essential parts of the running of the railway, and its architecture reflected this. For example, the railway station at Nairobi, which became the capital of British East Africa in 1905 and the headquarters of the Uganda Railway, had a large clock at the center of its main building. Undoubtedly, like other Mombasa residents, Sheikh Mbarak's outlook was shaped by the railway and the British temporal culture to which it gave rise and which it symbolized.

Whatever the configuration of experiences and sources that shaped Sheikh Mbarak's temporal sensibility, in later life it earned him the reputation of being extremely punctual. During my ethnographic research on his life and career, I was frequently told by family members and former colleagues that, "His office staff knew it was 8 a.m. not by the clock but by the sound of his shoes climbing up the office steps." Recollections of Sheikh Mbarak's embodied temporality are put into further relief by the fact that his office was located near Mombasa's Law Courts building, which housed the city's clocktower.

Completed in 1902, the Law Courts building faced the city's mixed residential and commercial district. The building was located between Mombasa's late-sixteenth-century Portuguese fort and other British Colonial Administration buildings (fig. 4). Its entrance was preceded by a multi-arcaded portico on top of which stood a clocktower that reportedly "chimed every hour."[16] Designed or influenced by the British administrator-architect John Houston Sinclair (1871–1961), the building reflected his peculiar "Saracenic" style: architecture that blended European classical forms with what Sinclair regarded as "Arab" decorative elements appropriate for coastal East Africa's built environment.[17]

4   Picture Postcard, "Main Road of Mombasa", Coutinho & Sons, Photographers, Mombasa, c. 1906.

When Sinclair arrived in coastal East Africa in 1896,[18] Mombasa was the Kenya Colony and Protectorate's main dhow port and steamship harbor as well as the first station of the British-owned Uganda Railway line that ran from the coast to Lake Victoria. As a port city with inhabitants of diverse ethnic backgrounds, faiths, and vocations, Mombasa was the place of residence and work for people who self-identified as Swahili, Bajuni, Somali, Gikuyu, Arab, Omani, Yemeni, Gujarati, Kutchi, among others. Mombasa was also home to different faith groups: Muslims of different doctrinal orientations, Parsees, Jains and Hindus, and Christians of various denominations.

The city's cosmopolitanism engendered a heterogeneous architecture and an associated temporal culture that might be recalled by imagining its soundscape, including the five daily human-voiced Muslim calls to prayer interspersed with the ringing of temple and church bells, and by visualizing its economic circulations such as the tide-led dockings and departures of ships, the dawn arrivals and dusk departures of day laborers, dock workers, trolley-car operators, domestic workers, petty traders, shop keepers, and government employees.

The Law Courts building's chiming clocktower was located in the midst of this temporal flurry (see fig. 4). Its clock face would have been what Sheikh Mbarak and Mombasa's other residents would have seen and heard each day, and when seeking to resolve a dispute, register land, or file any official claim, they would have to enter the colonial edifice that structurally and visually fused the temporal with the socio-legal. Thus, by extension, the Law Courts clocktower not only marked time according to the standard set at Greenwich, which by 1880 had become the official time throughout the British Empire, but was also a synecdoche of British justice, governance, power, and modernity.

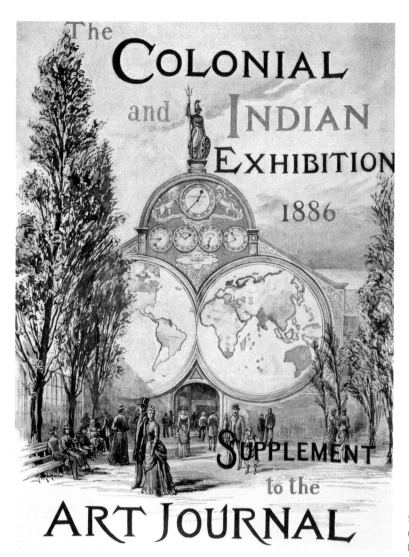

The

COLONIAL

and INDIAN

EXHIBITION

1886

SUPPLEMENT

to the

ART JOURNAL

5   Frontispiece from the *Art Journal* regarding the Colonial and Indian Exhibition of 1886. London, 1886.

Indeed, throughout the nineteenth and twentieth centuries, the clocktower became Britain's most iconic and ubiquitous monument in both its metropole and colonies. According to Trish Ferguson, the clocktower became the "focal point of an increasingly disciplinary industrial world of factories, the mail system and transport schedules, all of which was facilitated by the strict observance of the newly developed concept of public time."[19] In 1859, during the reign of Queen Victoria (1819–1901), London saw the completion of its clocktower, popularly known as "Big Ben." Designed by the architect Charles Barry (1795–1860) in close association with the designer August Pugin (1812–1852), this Gothic Revival clocktower housed the Great Bell and a four-faced clock set to Greenwich Mean Time that was designed by the horologist Edmund Beckett Denison

(1816–1905) in association with the astronomer George Biddle Airy (1801–1892).[20] The clocktower was part of a larger building project that included the rebuilding of the Palace of Westminster that housed the British Parliament. Thus, while the clock itself marked newly standardized imperial time and the temporal turn of the industrial age, the architectural assemblage formed by the clocktower in physical and visual proximity to the halls of legislative power became the paradigmatic iconography of Britain's success at harnessing time in service of its imperial ambition.

The visual expression of how this inordinate determination was inextricably bound up with time is exemplified by a monumental 700-foot painted canvas hung on the wall of a building erected on the grounds of the 1886 Colonial and Indian Exhibition, held in London on the occasion of Queen Victoria's Jubilee, an image of which is reproduced as a frontispiece on the cover of a special supplement of the *Art Journal* published in 1886.[21] The canvas shows two circular hemispheric maps of the world (fig. 5), "each over twenty-one feet," with British territories "coloured in bright red."[22] Above the maps is a decorative arched panel containing five clock faces. The largest of these shows the time at Greenwich, while a row of four smaller clocks shows the corresponding times in the British colonial capitals of Cape Town, Calcutta, Sydney, and Ottawa. Crowning the composition atop a pedestal on the arch's apex stands a triumphant Britannia, a helmeted female warrior figure holding a shield and trident.

Throughout their colonies, the British built many clocktowers, and as was the case in London and Mombasa, these towers were built as standalone structures near central institutions of power or incorporated into prominent colonial-era buildings. In India during the British Raj, for example, clocktowers became ubiquitous, "located at the administrative centre of the township or an important crossroads,"[23] or incorporated into educational buildings like the Mayo College in Ajmer, which was built in the 1870s as a boarding school for Rajasthan's male elite and nobility, and the Rajabai Clock Tower in the University of Bombay, built by the English architect George Gilbert Scott (1811–1878) between 1869 and 1878 in a Gothic Revival style akin to Big Ben. In these and other contexts, the clocktower came to telegraph virtues associated with the West and "Britishness," particularly rationality, industry, exactitude, and punctuality.[24] But conversely, as suggested by Sanjay Srivastava, this imported temporal order fed European stereotypes about the "timeless East" and its "excessive spirituality," as well as the unpunctuality and inherent slothfulness of the native—tropes that were eventually adopted by the colonized as part of their self-imaginary.[25] Thus, once materialized, the clocktower not only reordered the daily rhythms of life, it reshaped the ethos of the colonized other in the image of the colonizer. In sum, as the clocktower and printed diary made their way from the metropole to the colony they became localized and produced, albeit at different scales, *chronometric colonialism*: the temporal domination of local knowledge, ethics, practices, materialities, and aesthetics through direct and indirect acts of erasure, subversion, and replacement.

Returning then to colonial Mombasa, by the 1920s Letts's printed diaries were also localized. Thus, Sheikh Mbarak's 1927 diary was published and printed in Nairobi by *The East African Standard*, an English-language daily newspaper company established in 1902.[26] In form and layout the *Standard*'s diary was similar to that of Letts. Hence, in his *East African Standard* diary Sheikh Mbarak continued to write his entries within the lines as he had done in his Letts's diary. What is curious, however, is that in 1927 he used the diary's "Memorandum of Reference" sections and the back inside cover to chronologically list a range of events with their dates, including

Zanzibar. Bild 7.

Leuchtthurm und Sultanspaläste.

6   Zanzibar's harbor front and Sultan Bargash's clocktower, c. 1890. In "Land und Leute in Deutsch-Ost-Afrika. Erinnerungen aus der ersten Zeit des Aufstandes und der Blokade, in 83 photographischen Original-Aufnahmen / von J. Sturtz; und Schilderungen von J. Wangemann."

the deaths and births of family and community members, religious festivals such as Eid and Ramadhan, and transfers of sums of money. Sheikh Mbarak wrote most of this lengthy list on the rule-lines provided, but he also used a short handwritten line to separate each entry. At the very top right-hand corner of the diary is an entry that reads, "Monday after 1am 25th Jamad El-Awal 1314, 2nd November 1896." The date is Sheikh Mbarak's birth date written in both the standard Islamic (*Hijri*) and Gregorian dates. This and a few other of his similarly handwritten entries suggest, albeit obliquely, that while Sheikh Mbarak used the British pre-printed diary form and its calendrical system and logics, they did not always work for him. As a Muslim and as an Omani Arab with ties to the Sultanate of Zanzibar, the Islamic calendrical system was one that he had grown up with, and it remained an integral part of his *mentalité*. Thus, by inscribing the Hijri date Sheikh Mbarak appears to resist or refuse the diary's logics and write against the colonial grain.

Crowing Clocks

Temporal resistance to European imperialism was not unprecedented in coastal East Africa. One example is the clocktower-cum-lighthouse, built in 1883 in the Sultanate of Zanzibar's capital Zanzibar, by its second Omani ruler, Sultan Barghash bin Said al-Busaid (1837–1888). Oman and its succession of dynastic rulers had centuries-old political, commercial and social ties with the range of coastal East Africa's Swahili polities and communities, and were instrumental in assisting them to oust the Portuguese from their shores in 1729. During the late eighteenth and nineteenth centuries, owing to the imperial and maritime ambitions of Sultan Said bin Sultan al-Busaid (1791–1856), Oman came to dominate coastal East Africa and made Zanzibar its second capital after Muscat. After Sultan Said bin Sultan's death, a succession dispute between his elder sons split the Omani Empire into the Sultanate of Muscat and Oman, and the Sultanate of Zanzibar. Barghash succeeded his brother as the Sultanate of Zanzibar's second ruler.

Barghash was instrumental in modernizing Zanzibar's infrastructure and buildings. The clocktower he erected on the shores of Zanzibar's harbor and his new ceremonial palace, the *Beit al Ajaib* ("House of Wonders"), were the crowning glory amongst his many architectural projects. Both his white-washed, Omani-Arab-style ceremonial palace and the standalone, multi-story clocktower (fig. 6) are said to have been designed by a British marine engineer and inspired by Barghash's visit to London in June 1875, when he was taken on a tour along the Thames embankment.[27] Zanzibar's palace came to be regarded as one of the most modern buildings in East Africa owing to its use of cast iron and electricity and the installation of an elevator, whereas the squarish clocktower itself housed a European-manufactured mechanical four-faced clock and was "crowned by a real electric light."[28]

It is tempting to compare the conglomeration of Barghash's waterfront buildings to London's parliamentary complex insofar as both communicated imperial ambition. And in Zanzibar's case, a palace clocktower, built with the most modern materials produced in Europe and located on the harbor front of one of the Western Indian Ocean's busiest ports, visibly attested to the Sultanate's political and economic dominance in the region, its place amongst the era's leading maritime powers, and Barghash's ambition to firmly establish Zanzibar as the gateway to Africa.[29] However, in so far as the clock in Barghash's tower is known to have been calibrated according to the principles of Islamic time rather than Greenwich time, the building also spoke out about the Sultan's desire for temporal sovereignty. Put differently, like Sheikh Mbarak's diary, Barghash's clock did not work for him, so he changed it.

Some scholars have referred to the temporal system that was used to set Barghash's clock as "Zanzibari time,"[30] but in Barghash's day this system was variously referred to as "*a la turka* (Turkish)", "Ottoman," "Islamic" or "Arabian," or "*ghurubi* (sunset)" time in order to distinguish it from "*a la faranga* (European)" time.[31] The time system divided the day into twenty-four equal hours beginning at sunset and was in keeping with the Islamic daily cycle of prayers, which counted the first prayer at sunset. The system, used since antiquity, also relied on astronomical observations, and thus required European-made twelve-hour mechanical clocks to be reset every day at sunset. Indeed, European visitors to Zanzibar report that the clock setting in Barghash's tower made it both an enigma and a chore. For example, passing through Zanzibar on his return journey from South Africa to England in 1888, the writer John Edward Courtenay Bodley (1853–1925) describes the following scene:

> Moored in the roadstead opposite the town lie a couple of Her Majesty's ships on slave-trade duty, a hundred dhows and a score of steamers flying the Sultan's crimson flag. The whole scene undergoes a striking transformation at six o'clock, which is the sunset hour all the year round in Zanzibar. As the clock strikes twelve, sunset marking the close of the day, a gun is fired in front of the Palace, the band plays the 'Sultan's March,' and from a lofty tower the electric light illuminates the surrounding buildings and a streak of the sea, making Zanzibar, from the harbour at night, with all its squalor hidden in the darkness behind look like a bit of Venice.[32]

Taking a more technical approach, and highlighting the complex calculations needed to convert the time indicated in the clocktower to Greenwich time, in his report, *Meteorological Observation at Zanzibar of Africa, during 1880 to 1881*, Surgeon-Major C.T. Peters (dates unknown) states that:

> As the time is reckoned in Zanzibar from sunset to sunset, according to the Arabian practice, and the hour of sunset is for ordinary purposes considered to correspond with 6 p.m., the clock in the Sultan's Tower, which indicates the sunset time, gave a variation of about 22 minutes during some times of the year, it was necessary to calculate the mean [Greenwich] time. This was done in the following ways: —1. By the mean Greenwich time kindly furnished by the officers of the H.M.S. London and other Royal Navy steamers lying in the harbour; 2. By telegraphic communication from Aden, whence the correct mean Madras time was obtained; 3. By means of a table furnished by the Meteorological Office, Bombay, to reduce the sunset time as indicated by the Sultan's clock into the mean Zanzibar time.[33]

In the nineteenth century, the temporal system Barghash used for his clock was widespread in Muslim contexts, particularly in the Ottoman empire where imperial and local patrons had begun building clocktowers as early as the sixteenth century. For example, Sultan Abdülmecid I (1823–1861) commissioned a clocktower for the imperial courtyard on the banks of the Bosporus, adjacent to the Nusretiye Mosque and Tophane Kiosk in the Beyoğlu district of Istanbul. The four-sided, three-story, fifteen-meter-high structure, known as the "*Tophane Saat*" (Tophane Clock), was designed by the Ottoman-Armenian architect Garabet Amira Balyan (1800–1866) and completed in 1848. Its clock, as was the case with most other Ottoman clocks, was set according to Islamic time.[34] Owing to the constant recalibration requirements of these clocks, a cadre of *muvakkits* (time keepers) was employed and housed near clocktowers in *muvakkithanes* (timekeepers' rooms).[35] As noted by Mehmet Bengü Uluengin, until the latter part of the nineteenth century, Ottoman official public time remained tethered to the rhythms of religious life. Only when the Islamic system started to rub up against the demands of standardization arising in the contexts of military engagements with foreign powers, and coordinating travel by rail and ship, did Ottoman authorities begin adopting Western temporal conventions, albeit with varying degrees of reluctance and with great lamentations by local people.[36]

In Zanzibar, the Islamic temporal conventions used for Barghash's clock also may have been ubiquitous and revered amongst the broader population of clock and watch owners as part of its local temporal culture, which was deeply rooted in Islamic temporal norms and practices, be it calendrically (i.e., using the Lunar Hijri calendar) or chronometrically.[37] The American naval commander William Henry Beehler (1848–1915) records that all of the citizens of Zanzibar set clocks in the same manner as the clock in the tower.[38] According to Jeremey Presthold, during Barghash's reign imported timepieces became fashionable display items in Zanzibar homes. These objects not only indexed personal wealth and cosmopolitan connections, their resetting to "Zanzibar time" exemplified the manner in which Zanzibaris and their Sultan "domesticated global objects."[39] While this interpretative framework provides a useful way to think about Zanzibar's relationship to Western material culture, it does not completely help to explain why Barghash and other Zanzibaris readily embraced European-made mechanical clocks but insisted on setting them to Islamic time. This seeming dichotomy speaks to Leor Halevi's thesis that between the nineteenth and early-twentieth centuries, in the face of encroaching European hegemony, Muslims often readily embraced new things, wherever they were produced, and made them their own in the hopes of retaining their religious and cultural integrity and unity.[40]

The facts on the ground about Zanzibar's temporal culture are made even more complex when it is recalled that in 1879, a few years before he completed his own clocktower, Barghash gifted a clock for the bell tower of Zanzibar's Anglican Cathedral. Built on the former site of the island's largest slave market, Bishop Edward Steere (1828–1882) had overseen much of the church's construction. In his memoir on Steere, R. M. Heanley (1848?–1945) suggests that it was Steere who decided that the clock be set to "Arab" time.[41] However, in her history of the Anglican Mission in Central Africa, the Christian missionary Anne Elizabeth Mary Anderson-Morshead (1845–1928) states that it was Barghash who requested Steere to set the bell-tower clock to "Eastern time," and that this was met with "great satisfaction" from Zanzibar's "natives."[42] Anderson-Morshead also writes that a visitor to Zanzibar commented that,

> … the cathedral clock here keeps Biblical time. … I had landed quite early in the morning, and yet after breakfast I found that by cathedral time it was apparently afternoon. I remarked to the Bishop that his clock had stopped, but he replied, 'No, it is ten o'clock; that is to say the fourth hour of the day,' and so the clock pointed rightly enough to four. This is the way in which natives compute time.[43]

This anecdote suggests that the cathedral clock was not set to "Arab" time but to "Swahili" time. In this coastal East African system, the day starts at sunrise (rather than at sunset in the Islamic system) and is called "*alfajiri*." In Zanzibar, as in other places equatorial East Africa, dawn occurs every day at approximately 6:00 a.m. Daytime hours are counted sequentially from one to twelve beginning at 7:00 a.m. until 6:00 p.m. and are followed by nighttime hours, which are counted sequentially from one to twelve until dawn. Given that the majority of coastal Swahili-speaking communities are Muslims and that the Swahili language has a large number of loanwords from Arabic related to religious ideas, the time-keeping vocabulary also contains such references. Hence, in Swahili, the first hour of the day commences at 7:00 a.m. and is called "*saa moja asubuhi*" [the first hour of the morning]: the terms *saa*, *asubuhi*, and *alfajiri* are all of Arabic origin, the latter referring to the *Fajr*, the dawn prayer, the third of the five daily prayers.

Ironically, a section of a local Swahili story entitled "*Sultani Majnuni*" (Mad Sultan) collected in Zanzibar by Bishop Steere humorously captures Barghash's preoccupation with clocks.[44] In the tale a fictitious sultan visits a local plantation in Zanzibar's countryside during a rainstorm. Upon his arrival, the sultan taunts the plantation owner asking, "You country people, you simpletons, how many clocks do have in your houses?" The plantation owner replies, "Eh! Hweduni, you are making a joke of us; how should we get a clock, we country folk?" The Sultan responds, saying, "You are living with many clocks, not only one, nor two." To which the plantation owner retorts, "I don't even know what such a clock is." The sultan then asks, "Are there no crowing cocks in your plantation? They *are* the country clocks! When you hear the cock crowing you know it's dawn, or early morning; tell me, are these crowing cocks not your clocks?"

If these examples are indicative of Barghash's approach to temporality, then it would seem that the indigenous Swahili time system, be it on the clock in a Christian bell tower or in the farmer's field, operated alongside the official time marked on Barghash's clocktower. Such a rapprochement may have been possible because both were understood as ways of Islamic time-keeping and achieved the Sultan's objective of eschewing Western temporal conventions while embracing and adapting the technology that produced it.

The lifespan of Sultan Barghash's clocktower and his resistance to Western time were short-lived. On 27 August 1897, between 9:02 a.m. and 9:46 a.m., during the "Anglo-Zanzibar War," a proxy war between Britain and Germany as part of Europe's "Scramble for Africa," the British Royal Navy destroyed Zanzibar's clocktower and parts of its neighboring palaces. Thereafter, the Sultanate of Zanzibar, its islands and mainland coastal areas, became a British Protectorate. The post-war reconstruction of the destroyed buildings was overseen by none other than John Houston Sinclair, the British administrator-architect who got his start in Mombasa.[45] Barghash's clock mechanism, which survived the bombing, was reinstalled in a new tower that was incorporated into Zanzibar's ceremonial palace, and the renovated building became the home of the British colonial administration and the headquarters of the newly minted British Protectorate. Presumably, from this moment onwards, the clock in the tower was set to Greenwich Mean Time, synchronized to its counterparts in Mombasa and elsewhere in the British Empire.

Chronometric Colonialism

In coastal East Africa, as elsewhere, diverse temporal objects were critical to Britain's imperial and colonial projects. The mechanically printed diary that circulated in the British colonies was one of the temporal objects through which the colonized came to adopt the chronological logics of nineteenth-century British temporal culture. On a rather different scale, the clocktower, built in the center of colonial capitals, came to govern the chronometry of colonial life. Both these temporal forms, when analytically examined in terms of the knowledges, practices, and affects they employed and engendered as an architectural assemblage, exemplify the temporal means through which coloniality was fashioned and reproduced at personal and societal levels. As such, bringing these distinct objects into conversation with each other as part of a shared and mutually reinforcing temporal architectural assemblage provides a nuanced and critical understanding of how the material, epistemological, and affective enterprise of chronometric colonialism (i.e., the temporal terrain of coloniality) worked and how it contributed toward creating and reinforcing the broader colonial terrain. Moreover, historicizing these temporal objects and tracing their trajectories through the lives of locally situated social actors offers glimpses into the ways that colonial temporalities were resisted, refused, and reimagined.

Finally, I should like to note that it is with great sadness that on December 25, 2020, during the time when I was researching and writing this article, large sections of Zanzibar's Beit al Ajaib and its clocktower collapsed.[46] Ironically, in its demise, the old clocktower reasserted itself into conversations about Zanzibar's pasts, presents, and its futures.

1   Deleuze and Guattari 2004, *passim*; Wise 2014, 91–94.

2   My research in the Hinawy Collection in Muscat (Oman) was conducted over several in-person visits between 2005 and 2010 and in subsequent years using digitized materials. I should like to thank the family of the late Sheikh Mbarak Hinawy for supporting my research and granting me access to their archive.

3   Hirji 2010.

4   See the Swahili Manuscripts in the SOAS Digital Collections (London, UK), https://digital.soas.ac.uk/SWAHILI (accessed January 18, 2022); Hinawy 1950; Hinawy 1964.

5   Letts of London n.d.

6   Mumford 1934, 9–55.

7   Carter 2015.

8   Steinitz 2001, 163.

9   Moran 2015, 144.

10   Steinitz 2011, 66.

11   Steinitz 2001, 165.

12   See, for example, the advertorial, "Diaries," in *The Lancet* from December 22, 1894.

13   See Ruth Watson's case study of the diaries of Akinpelu Obisesan (1889–1963), a railway clerk based in Ibadan, Nigeria for a comparison with another colonial official's diary: Watson 2016.

14   Simmel 1950, 14.

15   Ahuja 2004, 95–96.

16   Nicholls 2016.

17   Longair 2016, 161–62.

18   *Red Book* 1922, 425.

19   Ferguson 2013, 1; see McCrossen 2013, for comparisons with clocktowers installed in industrial contexts in the USA in the nineteenth and early twentieth century.

20   Brindle 2020, 260; McKay 2010, 1–3.

21   Image reproduced and described in Mathur 2007, 53, and Bremner 2016, 144–45.

22   Details of the canvas are included in the *Official Guide to the Colonial and Indian Exhibition*: *Official Guide* 1886, 34.

23   Srivastava 2005, 41–42.

24   Srivastava 2005, 41.

25   Srivastava 2005, 47–49; Metcalf 1989, 78–80; Metcalf 2007, 61.

26   Musandu 2018, 1–2.

27   "The Sultan of Zanzibar" 1875, 575.

28   Smith 1884, 29.

29   Presthold 2018.

30   Presthold 2008, 108.

31   Wishnitzer 2015, 32.

32   Bodley 1889, 405.

33   Peters 1883, 198.

34   Üçsu 2017, 52.

35   Wishnitzer 2015, 25–30; Üçsu 2017, 50. It is not known if the post of time-keeper was instituted in Zanzibar.

36   Uluengin 2010, 17–21.

37   A detailed and critical analysis of Zanzibar's changing temporal culture is provided in Loimeier 2014; see in particular, *Eine Zeitlandschaft*, Chapter 5, 71–85.

38   Beehler 1885, 174

39   Presthold 2008, 107.

40   Helavi 2019.

41   Heanley 1888, 244.

42   Anderson-Morshead 1899, 95.

43   Anderson-Morshead 1899, 95.

44   Steere 1870, 225–6; I have modified Steere's English translation of the Swahili text.

45   Longair 2016, 167; Folkers 2013.

46   Lichtenstein 2020.

Bibliography

Ahuja, Ravi. 2004. "'The Bridge Builders': Some Notes on Railways, Pilgrimage and the British 'Civilizing Mission' in Colonial India." In Harald Fischer-Tiné and Michael Mann, eds., *Colonialism as Civilizing Mission: Cultural Ideology in British India*, 95–116. London: Anthem Press.

Anderson-Morshead, A. E. M. 1899. *The History of the Universities' Mission to Central Africa 1859–1898*. London: Office of the Universities' Mission to Central Africa.

Beehler, William Henry. 1885. *The Cruise of the Brooklyn*. Philadelphia: J. B. Lippincott.

Bianca, Stephano, and Francesco Siravo. 1996. *Zanzibar: A Plan for the Historic Stone Town*. Geneva: Aga Khan Trust for Culture.

Bodley, J. E. C. 1889. "Zanzibar." *Universal Review* III (January to April): 405–17.

Bremner, G. A. 2016. *Architecture and Urbanism in the British Empire*. Oxford: Oxford University Press.

Brindle, Steven. 2020. "The New Palace of Westminster." In Warwick Rodwell and Tim Tatton-Brown, eds., *Westminster II: The Art, Architecture and Archaeology of the Royal Abbey and Palace*, 257–269. London: Routledge.

Carter, Kathryn. 2015. "Accounting for Time in Nineteenth-Century Manuscript Diaries and Photographs." *Life Writing* 12, no. 4: 1–14.

Deleuze, Gilles, and Félix Guattari. 2004. *A Thousand Plateaus. Capitalism and Schizophrenia*. Translated by Brian Massumi. Minneapolis: University of Minnesota Press.

"Diaries." 1894. *The Lancet* 144, no. 3721, originally published as vol. 2, no. 3721 (December 22): 1493. https://doi.org/10.1016/S0140-6736(02)03456-6.

Ferguson, Trish. 2013. "Introduction." In Trish Ferguson, ed., *Victorian Time: Technologies, Standardizations, Catastrophes*, 1–15. London: Palgrave Macmillan.

Folkers, Antoni. 2013. "Early Modern African Architecture: The House of Wonders Revisited." *docomomo* 48, no. 1: 20–29.

Heanley, R. M., Rev. 1888. *A Memoir of Edward Steere*. London: George Bell and Sons.

Helavi, Leor. 2019. *Modern Things on Trial: Islam's Global and Material Reformation in the Age of Rida, 1865–1935*. New York: Columbia University Press.

Hinawy, Mbarak Ali. 1950. *Al-Akida and the Fort Jesus Mombasa*. Nairobi: East African Literature Bureau.

Hinawy, Mbarak Ali. 1964. "Notes and Customs in Mombasa." *Swahili* 34, no. 1: 17–35.

Hirji, Zulfikar. 2010. *Between Empires: Sheikh Mbarak al-Hinawy 1896–1959*. London: Azimuth Editions.

Letts of London n. d. "About Letts of London." https://us.lettsoflondon.com/about (accessed January 14, 2022).

Lichtenstein, Amanda. 2020. "Iconic House of Wonders collapse leaves Zanzibaris wondering about fate of cultural heritage." *Global Voices* (December 28), https://globalvoices.org/2020/12/28/iconic-house-of-wonders-collapse-leaves-zanzibaris-wondering-about-fate-of-cultural-heritage/ (accessed June 25, 2022).

Loimeier, Roman. 2014. *Eine Zeitlandschaft in der Globalisierung: Das islamische Sansibar im 19. und 20. Jahrhundert*. Bielefeld: Transcript.

Longair, Sarah. 2016. "Visions of the Global: The Classical and the Eclectic in Colonial East African Architecture." *Les Cahiers d'Afrique de l'Est / East African Review, Special Issue on Global History, East Africa and The Classical Traditions* 51: 161–78.

Mathur, Saloni. 2007. *India by Design: Colonial History and Cultural Display*. Berkeley: University of California Press.

McCrossen, Alexis. 2013. *Marking Modern Times: A History of Clocks, Watches and Other Timekeepers in American Life*. Chicago and London: University of Chicago Press.

McKay, Chris. 2010. *Big Ben: The Great Clock and the Bells at the Palace of Westminster*. Oxford: Oxford University Press.

Metcalf, Thomas R. 1989. *An Imperial Vision: Indian Architecture and the Britain's Raj*. Berkeley: University of California Press.

Metcalf, Thomas R. 2007. *Imperial Connections: India in the Indian Ocean Arena, 1860–1920*. Berkeley: University of California Press.

Moran, Joe. 2015. "Private Lives, Public Histories: The Diary in the Twentieth-Century Britain." *Journal of British Studies* 54, no.1 (January): 138–62.

Mumford, Lewis. 1934. *Technics and Civilization*. New York: Harcourt Brace Jovanovich.

Musandu, Phoebe Atieno. 2018. *Pressing Interests: The Agenda and Influence of a Colonial East African Newspaper Sector*. Montreal and Kingston: McGill-Queen's University Press.

Nicholls, Christine. 2016. "Mombasa's Law Courts," *Old Africa: Stories from East Africa's Past*, July 22, 2016, https://oldafricamagazine.com/mombasas-law-courts/ (accessed January 14, 2022).

Official Guide to the Colonial and Indian Exhibition. 1886. London: William Clowes and Sons Ltd.

Peters, C.T. 1883. "Meteorological Observation at Zanzibar, East Coast of Africa, during 1880 to 1881." *Quarterly Journal of the [Royal] Meteorological Society* IX: 196–204.

Presthold, Jeremy. 2008. *Domesticating the World: African Consumerism and the Genealogies of Globalization*. Berkeley: University of California Press.

Presthold, Jeremy. 2018. "Zanzibar, the Indian Ocean, and Nineteenth-Century Global Interface." In Burkhard Schnepel and Edward A. Alpers, eds., *Connectivity in Motion: Island Hubs in the Indian Ocean World*, 135–57. London: Palgrave Macmillan.

The Red Book 1922–23: Handbook and Directory for the Kenya Colony and Protectorate, Uganda, Protectorate, Tanganyika Territory, and Zanzibar Sultanate. 1922. Nairobi and Mombasa: East African Standard Ltd.

Simmel, Georg. 1950. "The Metropolis and Mental Life." In *The Sociology of Georg Simmel*. Translated by Kurt Wolff and adapted by D. Weinstein, 409–424. New York: Free Press.

Smith, Alfred. 1884. "From Zanzibar to Nosibe." *Antanarivo Journal and Madagascar Magazine*, VII–Christmas 1883: 29–42.

Srivastava, Sanjay. 2005. *Constructing Post-Colonial India National Character and the Doon School*. New York: Routledge.

Steere, Edward. 1870. *Swahili Stories as Told by the Natives of Zanzibar*. London: Bell & Daldy.

Steinitz, Rebecca. 2001. "Social Spaces for the Self: Organizing Experience in the Nineteenth-Century British Printed Diary." *a/b: Auto/Biography Studies* 16, no. 2: 161–74.

Steinitz, Rebecca. 2011. *Time, Space and Gender in the Nineteenth Century British Diary*. London: Palgrave Macmillan.

"The Sultan of Zanzibar." 1875. *Illustrated London News* 66, June 19, 1875: 575.

Üçsu, Kaan. 2017. "Witnesses of the Time: A Survey of Clock Rooms, Clock Towers and Façade Clocks in Istanbul in the Ottoman Era." *Rúbrica Contemporánea* 142 (December): 43–60.

Uluengin, Mehmet Bengü. 2010. "Secularizing Anatolia Tick by Tick: Clock Towers in the Ottoman Empire and the Turkish Republic." *International Journal of Middle East Studies* 42, no. 1 (February): 17–36.

Watson, Ruth. 2016. "'No One Knows What He is Until He is Told': Audience and Personhood in a Colonial African Diary." *Journal of Imperial and Commonwealth History* 44, no. 5: 815–32.

Wise, J. Macgregor. 2014. "Assemblage." In Charles J. Stival, ed., *Gilles Deleuze: Key Concepts*, 91–102. London and New York: Routledge.

Wishnitzer, Avner. 2015. *Alla Turca Time and Society in the Late Ottoman Empire*. Chicago: University of Chicago Press.

Image Sources

1–4   Courtesy of the al-Hinawy Family Trust, Muscat.

5   https://www.oldeastafricapostcards.com/the-town/ (accessed January 23, 2022).

6   Courtesy of the Victoria and Albert Museum, London.

7   Courtesy of the Herskovits Library of African Studies, Northwestern University Libraries: The Humphrey Winterton Collection of East African Photographs: 1860–1960.

SHRADDHA BHATAWADEKAR

The Image of Railway Architecture in Nineteenth-Century Bombay

Processes and Politics of Representation at Victoria Terminus

The railway station of the nineteenth century represented a complex set of processes and meanings, influenced by a number of developments at the local, national, and international levels. Although the primary purpose of a railway station was to facilitate travel, it came to serve many roles beyond mere transport. As Jeffrey Richards and John M. MacKenzie write, "The railway station more than any other building epitomizes the spirit of the nineteenth century, in its mating of technology and architecture, industry and art, in its conscious appeal to the splendours of the past and its confident striving towards the vistas of the future."[1] This paper looks at these multiple associations and symbolism that the railway station engendered. It particularly probes the role of different actors and events in shaping railway architecture in colonial India. It focuses on a case study of Victoria Terminus[2] (now Chhatrapati Shivaji Maharaj Terminus), a railway station located in Bombay[3] (now Mumbai) to show the interplay of authority in decision-making about its construction.

Victoria Terminus, especially its grand Neo-Gothic administrative headquarters, has come to represent the central building of the British Empire. This paper, however, will demonstrate how image-making through architecture was a heterogeneous process and a product of negotiations involving multiple actors. Using archival research, it investigates how relations between the governing institutions at the national and local levels, the interests of the railway company, and that of professionals like the architect impacted how Victoria Terminus came to be designed and signified. This paper also looks at the role of local Indian elite and media in Bombay in influencing this process. It situates the discussion within the larger architectural and railway discourse of the nineteenth century as well as the global processes of technology transfer and knowledge circulation that characterized this period. It briefly examines the perceptions of this architecture by the local Indian population. This paper further highlights how these early meanings have continued to shape the understanding of heritage at the terminus even today.

Victoria Terminus: Examining Agency and Representation

Built in the late nineteenth century, Victoria Terminus was the principal station and administrative headquarters of the Great Indian Peninsula Railway Company (GIPR). A private company registered in England, GIPR introduced the first railway in India on April 16, 1853, running from Bombay Boree Bunder to Thane. The temporary station at Boree Bunder gave way to a new station in the 1880s along with the adjacent administrative offices, and was named Victoria Terminus in 1887 on the occasion of the Golden Jubilee of Queen Victoria's reign. The administra-

1   An early view of Victoria Terminus, late nineteenth century.

tive building, designed by architect Frederick William Stevens, was an elaborate construction, displaying architectural and sculptural wealth (fig. 1).

The architecture of Victoria Terminus has received scholarly attention and a lot has been written on its architectural importance.[4] While historian Jan Morris saw the building as comparable only to Lutyen's Palace in New Delhi in scale and detail,[5] architectural historian Philip Davies called it "an architectural sensation in perspective and in detail" and "the finest Victorian Gothic building in India."[6] Victoria Terminus was built primarily to house the railway services and offices of the GIPR. Why was it planned on such a grand scale, with a particular emphasis on designing an extravagant administrative building? According to railway historian Ian Kerr,

> The GIPR, like all railways, had to have stations. Places where passengers could quickly and safely, and with some protection from the elements, join or leave trains were required. Terminals had to be larger than less important stations. However, there were no functional imperatives that required VT [Victoria Terminus] to be a massive, ornate, richly decorated building.[7]

Then the question arises, for whom was Victoria Terminus built? What was it meant to represent?[8] In the existing scholarly literature on Victoria Terminus, the building's grandeur is directly correlated with its role in representing British power in India. The creation of monumental architecture in India has been commonly viewed as an outcome of a central and coherent policy on the part of the British Empire to express its political supremacy. Historian Thomas Metcalf writes, "Most central was a concern with political effect. In the public buildings put up by the Raj it was essential to always make visible Britain's imperial position as a ruler, for these structures were charged with the explicit purpose of representing empire itself."[9] In the case of Victoria Terminus as well, British supremacy as a colonial power and the civilizing mission embedded in the discourse on railways and that of architecture seem to be expressed in its sumptuous constructions. Kerr has discussed this aspect in detail:

> … VT was built to represent a set of attitudes, beliefs and relationships: an attitude of British superiority increasingly measured by machines; beliefs in the progressive and civilizing power of railways; relationships anchored in the fact of colonial rule to which compliance was fostered by grand buildings like VT.[10]

While the discussions of the time insisted that the idea of civilization and progress was inherent in bringing the railways to India, and art and architecture were also seen as a medium to educate Indians or to improve their aesthetic tastes, the creation of architecture was much more complex. Davies challenges the myth of imperial unity, highlighting the "climatic, political, economic, racial and regional differences" in the empire that "fostered heterogeneity."[11] Historian Norma Evenson also claims that the British Empire was based on commercial interests and that "the creation of important architecture had been remote from the aims of the British East India Company."[12] She states, "Indifferent to the virtues of imperial image making, the directors grumbled about the cost of even such practical works as fortifications, and they continually fulminated against waste and extravagance in construction."[13] She adds that this attitude remained unchanged even after the British Crown took over the rule of the Indian subcontinent.

It is within this critical frame that this paper deconstructs the image-making involved with Victoria Terminus and its architecture as a product of negotiations at multiple levels. It looks at how the relations between the colonizer and colonized, and between various institutional actors, impacted the creation of architecture and how the interactions between authorities, elite, and laypeople influenced it. These actors and their relations are critically investigated in the socio-political-economic context of the time, in Bombay and in the international context, in order to understand how they determined the form and aesthetics as well as meanings that Victoria Terminus acquired.

Complexity of Railway Construction in India

The railways came to India in the early 1850s, about two decades after they were introduced in England. Seen as important instruments for the British to exert their political and administrative control over India, they were facilitators for the British economy. The railways in India were a controlled affair from the beginning, with a hierarchy in decision-making. Influenced by the governance structures in England, such as the British Parliament and the Court of Directors of the East India Company (later the Secretary of State when the British Crown took over the rule), the Indian Government with its seat in Calcutta had decision-making power related to the railways, even in matters such as determining the railway alignment or the construction of stations. Decisions also went through the provincial governments before reaching the railway company, a rather complex process involving multiple institutional actors, primarily dominated by the British administrators.

The early companies involved in laying the railways in India were private joint stock companies established in England, who managed railways through boards in England and local committees in India. Initially, two companies received their contracts in 1849 for constructing railways in India: GIPR for the Bombay region and East Indian Railway in the region around Calcutta. According to their contracts, the railway companies were to get the land for free or on lease for a period of 99 years.[14] It was decided that the railway, including its buildings, would be taken over by the government after 99 years with certain conditions, but the government also had the right to purchase the railway after 25 or 50 years. The railway companies could, however, give up their lines with prior notice. The railways were organized on a guarantee system: five percent of interest on capital raised was to be given by the East India Company every half-year for a period of 99 years. This system meant that the railway companies were to be paid an assured interest on their investments through public funds in India.

The East India Company was not in favor of extensive outlay of expenditure in India. The Company's dispatch to the Government of India on November 14, 1849, for example, clearly stated that unnecessary and extravagant expenditure on ornamental works should be avoided, especially for stations and railway companies' offices:

> While we should wish that all the works shall be of a useful and substantial kind, it is our special desire that they shall be constructed at the least possible cost, consistent with real utility, and that nothing shall be expended in unnecessary ornaments. We look upon these experiments as of the highest importance, to the future welfare of our Indian Empire, and we are above all things desirous that they shall not in any way be endangered by any useless, or inconsiderate expenditure of any kind whatever.[15]

Railway construction in India was often influenced by developments in England. It dwelled in between various private and government interests in India and England and was negotiated at multiple levels. It is under these circumstances that the first railway was introduced by the GIPR in 1853 from its temporary station at Boree Bunder. The strict control on expenditure and uncertainty about the success of the railways resulted in modest stations being built in the beginning. But as the goods and passenger traffic grew, the need was soon felt by the GIPR to have larger station sheds and administrative offices. This was also facilitated by the changing socio-economic situation in Bombay.

Rise of Bombay as *Urbs Prima in Indis*

Bombay, a humble town of seven islands, gained prominence in the eighteenth and nineteenth centuries after the British took over occupation from the Portuguese. Advantaged because of its natural harbor, Bombay's position as a trade center was strengthened by the opening of the Suez Canal in 1869, which better connected the city to the international trade network. The establishment of railways and mills in the 1850s accelerated the city's progress. The tremendous increase in the cotton trade from Bombay during the period of the American Civil War (1861–1864) and the resultant cash flow led to profound changes in Bombay's architecture and urbanscape.[16] In 1877, the Bombay Municipal Corporation adopted the motto of *Urbs Prima in Indis*—the first city of India. Though objected to by other Presidency towns, such as Calcutta and even locally in Bombay, as seen in contemporary newspapers,[17] Bombay during this period established itself firmly as the principal city of India. *A Report on Bombay Administration* of 1892 added, "Bombay city is more than the capital of the Bombay Presidency; it is also the great manufacturing town and the most important sea-port in India."[18] During this time, the rivalry between cities and different administrations became evident. Newspaper reports show how decisions were taken on several occasions in favor of the national capital Calcutta as opposed to the interests of Bombay. The local Bombay agencies, such as the Bombay Chamber of Commerce, highlighted how "some sinister influence was at work in favour of Calcutta to the detriment of Bombay's interests" in some railway matters.[19] The fight between the cities over the dominant position was reflected in architecture as well. Architectural historian Christopher London states, "Various cities during this period … preferred individual styles of architecture."[20] In Bombay in particular, the creation of grand architecture was the ambition of the Bombay Government to project the image of Bombay as the first city of India.

Neo-Gothic was consciously chosen as a style of architecture for Bombay's restructured Fort area.[21] By the end of the 1870s, grand buildings like the Secretariat, Bombay University, the High Court, and the Telegraph Office were erected by the Public Works Department, all designed in Neo-Gothic style.[22] The choice of Neo-Gothic (and the change from Neo-Classical style) was influenced by the preferences of the city administrators, such as the then Governor Sir Bartle Frere, and also by the ongoing trend in Britain at the time. It helped Bombay claim the status of the "second city of the British Empire" after London,[23] and also "take its place with the finest cities of the East," as the then Governor of Bombay Sir Richard Temple (r. 1877–1880) stated in a speech in 1879.[24]

The creation of an architectural image in Bombay can be jointly attributed to the British and the Indians.[25] Many local Indians, including different communities such as Hindus, Parsis, Muslims, and Jews, were involved in commercial and trade enterprises and earned huge profits. These local elite were quite influential in Bombay. From planning railways in Bombay in the early 1840s[26] to participation in the local committees of the GIPR and civic bodies, such as the Bombay Municipal Corporation, Indians were involved in decision-making in Bombay. They contributed generously to building the city. The public buildings constructed during this time were funded either through Imperial Funds, most of which came as a loan,[27] or through the munificence of members of the local Indian elite, such as Premchand Roychand and Cowasjee Jehangir. Often public subscriptions were called to support various projects. Many Indians worked in the Public Works Department in various capacities. Though often in subordinate positions, they did play an instrumental role in these projects. A few rose to prominent positions, like Raosaheb Sitaram Khanderao Vaidya and Muncherjee Murzban, who went on to design and construct many public buildings in Bombay. As historian Preeti Chopra writes,

> … the joint enterprise resulted in a joint public realm that not only was partially underwritten by Indian philanthropists but was built by native and European expertise. The construction of Bombay was a product of the joint enterprise that called on European architects, engineers, sculptors, artists, and also Indian engineers, artists, craftsmen, and other functionaries to design and construct British Bombay.[28]

This dominant position of Bombay, resulting from its financial and social dynamics and the choice of architecture, continued to characterize the late nineteenth-century development of the city, reaching its climax at Victoria Terminus.

Victoria Terminus: Conscious Choice of Architecture and Sculpture

By the mid-1870s, plans were underway for the construction of a new station and administrative offices for the GIPR at Boree Bunder. While the designs for the station shed were drawn up by GIPR engineers, the directors of the company chose to hire services of Frederick William Stevens for the construction of the administrative offices. The GIPR terminus opened in early 1882, while the construction of the administrative building took ten years to complete. The station, with its four platforms and an iron shed supported by iron columns, was a standard prototype (fig. 2).[29] The design for the administrative building, planned adjacent to the station shed, on the contrary, was very elaborate. The C-shaped building rose to 180 feet in height and was 330 feet in length. It was intricately decorated with a profusion of material, architectural and sculptural forms, and portraits and emblems. Such extravagance in its design can be attributed partly to the ambitions of architect Stevens and prestige of the GIPR.

Stevens, an architect trained in England, came to Bombay in the late 1860s and was employed in the Bombay Public Works Department. His skills were apparent in the Sailors' Home in Bombay that he had completed in 1876.[30] It is clear from the records that the directors of the GIPR were not satisfied with the drawings prepared by the railway company's own engineers. *The Architect* of 1886 notes, "Various plans for the new offices and station were submitted to the directors and the Government from time to time, but none of them were approved of, as they failed to satisfy one of the principal conditions laid down, that they should be suited to the importance of the city, and in consonance with its modern architectural features."[31] The engagement of Stevens for the task resembled an ongoing practice of employing professional architects for designing the railway buildings even in Europe.

2   View of the station shed today; original columns visible.

3　The dome surmounting the administrative building.

Stevens's design of the GIPR offices was influenced by contemporary architecture in Europe, especially the Grand Midland Hotel at St. Pancras and the unexecuted drawings for the Berlin Parliament, both by renowned architect George Gilbert Scott.[32] The choice of architectural elements, such as a west-facing facade and open long verandahs, and the use of sculptural motifs of flora and fauna designed by the Bombay School of Art was commonplace in Bombay's architecture of the time.[33] However, his design became more prominent due to a number of aspects.

The vantage point the site enjoyed was further accentuated by planning a wall along the adjacent station shed similar in design to the administrative building, which helped create a sense of expanse and grandeur for the administrative building itself.

Where Stevens primarily departed from the contemporary counterparts of Victoria Terminus was in the use of an octagonal dome on top of the administrative offices (fig. 3). Circular domes were a typical characteristic of Islamic architecture in India, and examples, such as Gol Gumbaz at Bijapur, existed as testimonies to the architectural achievements of the Islamic dynasties in the sixteenth and seventeenth centuries in western India. Stevens decided to use an octagonal dome, which was a novelty in Bombay at the time. For Stevens, his inspiration for an octagonal dome seems to have come from Scott's unpublished drawings for the Berlin

Parliament, and also Wren's Tom Tower in Oxford, as historian Morris states.[34] The use of domes was associated mostly with royalty in the earlier centuries, but the nineteenth century also saw the adoption of a dome for secular uses to represent the power of democracy, industrialization, and progress.

The dome not only gave an element of novelty to the administrative building, but served to publicize the project more. Even though larger and more complicated domed structures had been built elsewhere before, the octagonal dome designed by Stevens, spanning c. 45 feet, received a large amount of publicity for its scientific and technological achievements in the journals and newspapers of the time.[35] Though not unique in construction, the octagonal dome also came as a pleasant contrast with the steep roofs of the earlier Neo-Gothic buildings in Bombay. This change was highly praised in the media. *The Times of India* reported, "We are glad to say that this elegant piece of architecture, which is constructed on a principle never before introduced in India, of solid masonry supported and strengthened in internal and external ribs of stone, remains as firm as ever."[36] The dome became the crowning feature of the main administrative building and was seen as the climax of the Neo-Gothic and beginning of the Indo-Saracenic phase in the city of Bombay.

The use of elaborate sculpture at Victoria Terminus was directly linked to Stevens's ambitious scheme of creating a monumental structure. Like architecture, the use of sculptures was very

4   Statue of Progress atop the dome.

5　Monogram representing the Great Indian Peninsula Railway Company on the facade of the administrative building.

much debated and discussed during the construction of the earlier buildings in Bombay. The portrait roundels of important personalities and also sculptures representing local communities, local flora and fauna used at Victoria Terminus were common in previous buildings as well. Stevens's choice of statuary for the railway offices also coincided with that used at the time for railway stations worldwide. Representations of progress, civilization, and industry were commonly found on the stations, symbolizing the new-found values of the nineteenth century.[37] The industrial professions were also elevated. Thus, the choice of statuary by Stevens for the offices of the GIPR seems to have been a direct outcome of his encounter with European railway architecture. The sculptural scheme was devised by Stevens to include representations of agriculture, commerce, engineering, trade, and science, symbolizing the railways' integral association with trade and business. The highlight of the sculptural scheme was the statue of progress atop the dome (fig. 4), once again emphasizing the role played by the railways in bringing progress to the city and society. This choice of architecture and sculpture elevated the building's status compared to its counterparts in Bombay.

The administrative building celebrated the achievements of the railways by commemorating in stone eleven men (among them the directors of the GIPR, government officials and the GIPR engineer) instrumental in railway development in India. Two Indians, Sir Jamsetjee Jejeebhoy and Jagannath Shankarsheth, were also commemorated for their important contributions to the development of railways and of the city. But at the same time, the building advertised the GIPR by incorporating the emblems and monograms of the railway company (fig. 5). The construction of Victoria Terminus was influenced by various factors and institutional and individual negotiations as will be shown in the following section.

Processes and Politics of Negotiations

Stevens was an ambitious architect and was interested in making a mark through his designs. He seems to have promoted his designs at the international level. While the terminus was being constructed, illustrations and drawings of the terminus were published in different journals and showcased in various exhibitions. A watercolor drawing by the well-known painter and illustrator Axel Hermann Haig, displayed at the Royal Academy of Arts in London in 1880, also publicized the project.[38] Such was Stevens's association with the project that it came to be known as "Stevens' Pride."[39] The architect took meticulous efforts in designing intricate details and took immense pride in having executed his designs single-handedly, as his letters show.[40]

He also persuaded the GIPR to finish the sculptural scheme he had designed. The directors themselves were not convinced about spending huge sums of money, and the proposal for the sculptural decoration had to wait till 1886 for approval by the Board of Directors. *The Builder* issue of 1886 notes,

> The directors of the G.I.P. Railway Company have accorded their sanction to the execution of the statues which are to be the crowning features of the new terminal buildings at Boree Bunder. This splendid block of buildings has been constructed on such liberal principles in every respect that it would have been a pity to leave out of the design the beautiful figures which Mr. F. W. Stevens, the architect considered would appropriately give completeness to his work.[41]

This building was very much a part of the GIPR's interest in grand modern buildings for its offices. While constructing such large offices was a trend in Europe, it could have also been meant as an advertisement for its achievements and as a symbol of the company's pride in laying the first railway line in Asia. At the time, GIPR was still a private company. In 1874, when the purchase of GIPR came under review after 25 years, as stated in the contract of 1849, the Secretary of State in Britain renounced the rights to purchase GIPR without consulting the Government of India. The defects of the guarantee system were already evident, as the assurance of five percent guarantee with the public money for a private enterprise meant that the money was being misused and lavishly spent by the railway companies. As historian Aruna Awasthi states, "So long as the companies were guaranteed an interest of 5%, they did not observe economy, this led to extravagant and wasteful construction."[42] This resulted in a burden on the Indian taxpayers: "In short the enterprise was called private but the risk was made public."[43] Even though the Government of India objected to the decision by the Secretary of State, it was already apparent that the GIPR would continue for another 25 years in the same manner, with its shareholders getting a guarantee of five percent interest on their investment. It is possible that this extension and the increasing profits and stability prompted the decision of the GIPR to construct the grand offices.

The GIPR seems to have enjoyed an advantageous position in Bombay. There was competition between various railway companies in India before the railways were taken over by the government. Especially in Bombay, GIPR had to fight with Bombay Baroda & Central India Company (BB&CI) for space, alignments, and concessions. GIPR looked particularly influential and was able to sway the decisions of the Bombay Government in its favor on many occasions.

When the administrative offices were being designed, GIPR had to submit its plans to the Government of Bombay as well as the Government of India in Calcutta for approval. The Government of Bombay was pleased with the designs and the efforts of architect Stevens. However, although the Government of India approved these plans, it expressed discontent on a number of occasions about carrying out such a large-scale building, as this was seen as rather a waste of public money. For more than three years, negotiations between the Government of India and GIPR continued via the Consulting Engineer of the Bombay Government to reduce the costs of the building in various ways.

In a letter of April 26, 1878, the Secretary to the Government of India wrote to the Bombay Government,

> … the design of the proposed Terminal buildings for the Great Indian Peninsula Railway in Bombay is somewhat elaborate, and the ornamentation will add to the cost of the building, and therefore to the outlay of what is practically public money. … the character of a design may be made to depend on the artistic arrangement of materials even more than on the work put on them, and that the building in question is perhaps the one extravagance of the Great Indian Peninsula Railway Company in the matter of buildings; … the Railway is a great concern, and the Government of India will not object to the design on the score of needless outlay on ornamentation, but it will trust to the Bombay Government to see that superfluities are kept under.[44]

The Government of India had also suggested delaying construction of the building until the traffic requirements of the city increased to demand such a large construction. It had also recommended that GIPR should share offices with BB&CI, a proposal that GIPR had opposed, saying that the space would not be enough for both companies.[45] The Indian Government, in correspondence of 1881, also recommended that a flat galvanized iron roof be placed over the first floor to finish the building. The Bombay Government persuaded the Government of India against this proposal, suggesting that the GIPR had adequate funds available to complete the building, only after which the construction resumed.[46] Such instances show how the construction process was negotiated at different levels.

Indians were involved in the construction of Victoria Terminus, such as Raosaheb Sitaram Khanderao Vaidya as assistant engineer, M.M. Janardhan as a supervisor, as well as Messrs. Burjorjee and Rustomjee as contractors.[47] About 1.6 million rupees were spent on the construction of the administrative offices. Delays in construction, caused by issues with contractors and other reasons, resulted in the project taking ten years to complete. It is not clear how the local Indians reacted to such an exhaustive spending of public money. There is one instance reported when some Indians, who had requested GIPR to build over-bridges to avoid railway accidents, wrote in a letter of 1881 that GIPR's excuses of poverty were not to be accepted when it was spending lavishly on its administrative offices.[48] Despite these criticisms, generally the situation was amicable in Bombay. As mentioned above, the Indians did play a role in building Bombay and there seems to have been less resistance to the British practices and the British influenced architectural styles in Bombay.

Image-Making through Architecture

There was much academic debate around the architectural style to be used in the colonies. This has been discussed at length by several scholars in their recent writings.[49] Architecture was deemed to have an instructive function and the critics of colonial architecture often stressed the need for an architecture that would suitably represent Western civilization. T. Roger Smith, a staunch supporter of the European style, claimed,

> I hold very strongly, that, as our administration exhibits European justice, order, love of law, energy and honour, so our buildings ought to hold up a high standard of European art. They ought to be European, both as a rallying point for ourselves, and as raising a distinctive mark of our presence, always to be beheld by the natives of the country.[50]

The same idea also seems to have been reflected in the creation of the Bombay School of Art.[51] However, the production of architecture in India required collaborations between Indians and Europeans. Christopher London argues, "The aesthetic solutions required for the successful production of an 'Indian art-form' be it in architecture, painting or interior decoration all required the interaction of Indian minds and traditional practices with British standards of correctness, utility and modernity."[52] New forms of architecture were experimented with, which combined Indian and European forms. As Giles Tillotson writes,

> … the attitudes of many British professionals working in India had changed over time, in their interests in experimenting with the Indian architectural forms and motifs. Supporters of the Indo-Saracenic movement [which combined Indian and European forms] were no less concerned to make an impact on an Indian audience, but rejecting the conqueror's defiant gesture of difference they argued that the time had come to present an image that was more amenable to Indians.[53]

Moreover, even though the Indo-Saracenic architecture has been viewed by some authors as "an instrument by which the British sought to present themselves as Indian rulers, or as they boast of Britain's mastery over India's cultural past," Tillotson claims, "The use of architectural styles from the past had been a standard, indeed universal, approach in European architecture since the renaissance; so that a Briton of the nineteenth or early twentieth century would read the use of past Indian architectural styles as part of that general practice, not as peculiar to colonial India."[54] Victoria Terminus presented this hybridity in architecture, combining national and international trends, using locally established styles and methods, and at the same time experimenting with form and local material.

Local and Media Perceptions

How was this architecture in general and Victoria Terminus in particular perceived by local people? As Chopra has discussed in detail, for laypeople, references to architecture remained local and the use of local flora and fauna and known figures might have created familiarity and affinity with these structures.[55] Moreover, as she adds, these were secular, public institutions and signaled new values to which allegiance was already provided by the local elite.[56] By the time the terminus was constructed, the Neo-Gothic style was well established, so it would not have been a surprise for the locals. As the construction of the building was delayed, it might have caused inconvenience for commuters, resulting in complaints, as in case of delay in the opening of the refreshment rooms at the station.[57] It is quite clear that such a grand building would have become a familiar landmark for local commuters, but have remained a novelty for newcomers, who were struck by its sheer size and magnificence. With Bombay being an important port for many foreign arrivals, Victoria Terminus also became a magnificent entry portal into India for these foreign tourists and dignitaries, also elevating the status of Bombay as an international, modern city.

The image of Victoria Terminus was further promoted by the local and international media. In 1897 *Scientific American* lauded Victoria Terminus as the "grandest railway station in the world" and "the finest modern architectural work in India."[58] In a book *India under the Royal Eyes*, author Battersby eulogized F. W. Stevens for choosing the Gothic design for a tropical climate. He saw VT as "the most striking terminus in the world."[59] The terminus and the architect also received praise from the vernacular media of Bombay. In the competition between cities and city architects for new commissions, Stevens was supported locally as the Bombay man and was applauded for his works. The vernacular newspaper *Rast Goftar* wrote, "We were the first to suggest a decoration for the architect whose genius has adorned Bombay with the noblest of her public palaces – we mean the Victoria Terminus."[60] Such positive reviews and praise helped Stevens to receive further architectural commissions, including the Bombay Municipal Corporation building and offices for the BB&CI, and to stamp his authority in Bombay.

Naturalizing Meanings of Architecture

As the above discussion shows, Victoria Terminus and its architecture cannot be reduced to the scheme of the British Empire as a coherent entity, but it emerges as a product of various processes, conflicts, and intentions, demonstrating hybridity and transculturality. The railway development was controlled by the Government of India to a large extent, though the Government in England, railway boards in England and India, and governments of Presidencies also had a role to play in this process. It was often fraught with conflicts and delays due to a long chain of hierarchies involved in decision-making. The same could be seen during the construction of Victoria Terminus as well. Multiple stakeholders influenced the creation of the terminus. Despite attempts by the Government of India to curtail expenditure by altering the design or use pattern, the grand plans were executed, with persistence from the GIPR and architect F. W. Stevens. The building did fit well with the plans of the Bombay Government and with the architecture already created to project the image of Bombay as the "*Urbs Prima in Indis.*" The support of the local Indian elite for architectural projects in Bombay and positive perceptions by the media and public further helped elevate the image of Victorian Gothic in Bombay. Railway architecture, being a utilitarian infrastructure, signalized progress and the triumph of technology and new values that the railways promoted wherever they went, which did manifest at Victoria Terminus. The place thus incorporated and represented these multiple meanings and negotiations: local, national, and international, as well as individual and institutional, elite and everyday.

Though the building was built for the offices of GIPR, a private railway company at the time, the statue of Queen Victoria on the central facade, and the decision to name the station as Victoria Terminus, linked the building with the imperial aspirations of the British Empire. The building was named as Victoria Terminus in 1887 to commemorate the Golden Jubilee of Queen Empress Victoria. *The Builder* of 1887 mentions, "The statue of H.M. the Queen-Empress, representing the State, the railway being guaranteed by Government, will be placed under the canopy in the central gable of the building."[61] The building was thus seen as an "appropriate compliment to her Majesty, on the fiftieth anniversary of her reign," as *The Builder* wrote earlier.[62] The naming after the Queen set the building in direct association with British imperial power. Over time, Victoria Terminus came to be appreciated as one of the most important buildings of the British Empire,

6   Grand administrative building today.

further elevated through the writings of recent scholars. At the same time, it was internalized and became an integral part of the city fabric and its everyday functioning. It did naturalize the undercurrents and heterogeneity in colonial decision-making.

Continued Legacies

The multilayered associations and identities assumed by Victoria Terminus have been strengthened over the years. Both the station and the administrative building continue to be in use even today (fig. 6). While the terminus has been localized by changing the name to Chhatrapati Shivaji Maharaj Terminus, it still retains its colonial connotations in academic discussions, especially due to contemporary scholarly writings and media and also due to the UNESCO World Heritage Inscription of the terminus in 2004, which have once again highlighted the original construction. Eulogizing the building's architecture and aesthetics in this way has naturalized the colonial heterogeneity. The terminus is integrally linked with the railway discourse and signifies the achievements of the railways, forming an object of pride for Central Railway, the successor of GIPR in the post-independence period.[63] It has received international acclaim as a World Heritage Site and importance at the national level as the birthplace of the Indian Railways, but at the same time, it still remains firmly rooted in the local context, as a symbol of the city of Mumbai. It serves as an advertisement for tourists, but for locals, it has become an assuring presence, symbolizing the hopes and dreams but also the struggles of a life in Mumbai. It is the power of this place to engender multiple images and meanings that has enriched its heritage value and significance.

1   Richards and MacKenzie 1986, 19.

2   The name of Victoria Terminus was changed to Chhatrapati Shivaji Terminus in 1996, and then to Chhatra-pati Shivaji Maharaj Terminus in 2017. However, since this paper discusses the building in the nineteenth century, the old name Victoria Terminus has been used in the title and throughout the text.

3   Bombay was renamed as Mumbai in 1995 and Calcutta was renamed as Kolkata in 2001. However, the old names have been used throughout the text for historical references.

4   The book *A City Icon* (Mehrotra and Dwivedi 2006) gives a detailed account of the construction of Victoria Terminus and subsequent developments, with a particular emphasis on the architecture of the administrative building. The book *Bombay Gothic* (London 2002) also provides details on the architecture of Victoria Terminus along with other Neo-Gothic buildings of the time in Bombay.

5   Morris 2005, 133.

6   Davies 1985, 173.

7   Hurd and Kerr 2012, 100.

8   Stephen Howard has probed the question of why Victoria Terminus came to enjoy a central place in the empire, with a focus on analyzing architectural form and the complexities of colonial architectural production. He shows how the railways invested special meaning into the place (Howard 2012). While the current paper also acknowledges the importance of railways in creating meanings, it differs from previous work in its focus on archival research and in its attempt to outline various stakeholders and their negotiations that shaped the form and image of Victoria Terminus and the resultant hybridity and transculturality.

9   Metcalf 1989, 2.

10   Hurd and Kerr 2012, 100. Ian Kerr has talked in detail about railway representation, particularly how Victoria Terminus has represented different aspects right from its construction until today and also how the terminus has been represented in various media. Hurd and Kerr 2012, 97–135. This paper elaborates on these processes and stakeholder negotiations at the time of the construction of the terminus.

11   Davies 1985, 11.

12   Evenson 1989, 57.

13   Evenson 1989, 57.

14   Awasthi 1994, 55–56.

15   "Despatch by the Court of Directors to the Govt. of India." November 14, 1849, cited in Sharma 1990, 6.

16   "Sir Bartle Frere" 1884.

17   "Editorial Article" 1877; "Editorial Article" 1880.

18   Hunter 1892, 323.

19   Sulivan 1938, 234.

20   London 1994.

21   Bombay Fort, built in the early eighteenth century, was demolished in the 1860s.

22   Gothic architecture of the time in Bombay has been discussed by many historians; see, for instance, Davies 1985; London 2002.

23   Dwivedi and Mehrotra 2001, 175.

24   Douglas 1883, 558.

25   This aspect of the collaborations between Indians and the British in Bombay has been discussed in detail by historian Preeti Chopra (Chopra 2011).

26   The local elite of Bombay, both Indian and British, came together in 1844 to form the "Bombay Great Eastern Railway" to promote the cause of railways in the Bombay region. It was further developed into the "Inland Railway Association" in 1845, which later merged interests with the Great Indian Peninsula Railway Company ("Classified Ad" 1844; "Journal of Commerce" 1845).

27   "From The Times" 1991.

28   Chopra 2011, 30.

29   "Terminal Station" 1875.

30   "Article 4" 1877.

31   "An Indian Railway" 1886.

32   London 2002.

33   For details, see note 51.

34   Morris 2005, 134.

35   "Great Indian" 1887; "An Indian Railway" 1886.

36   "The Victoria Terminus." 1887a.

37   Schröder 2013.

38   London 2002, 86.

39   "The Victoria Terminus" 1887b.

40   "Remuneration" 1877.

41   "Great Indian" 1886.

42   Awasthi 1994, 58. The lines of the GIPR were taken over by the government in 1900 and the railway company continued to manage them until 1925, after which the management was also taken over by the government. Awasthi 1994, 186, 216.

43   Awasthi 1994, 58.

44   "Terminal Buildings" 1878.

45   "Bori Bandar" 1880.

46   "New Terminal Station" 1880.

47   Mehrotra and Dwivedi 2006, 146–53.

48   "Editorial Article" 1881.

49   Chopra 2011; Howard 2012.

50   Cited in Tillotson 1994, 18.

51   The Bombay School of Art was established in 1856 to promote improvements in arts and manufactures in India and local tastes. Indian industrialist Jamsetjee Jejeebhoy provided funds for the school. As art historian Partha Mitter (1994, 4) writes, "After the assumption of government control, the school became a vehicle for disseminating European taste, as part of the grand design of bringing progress to the colonies." The principals and students of the Bombay School of Art were involved in carrying out decorative details and sculptural schemes at many of the buildings constructed in Bombay from the late 1860s.

52   London 1994, preface.

53   Tillotson 1994, 19.

54   Tillotson 1994, 33.

55   Chopra 2011, 58–70.

56   Chopra 2011, 58–70.

57   "The Victoria Terminus" 1891; "Travelling Lubricant" 1889.

58   "The Great Railway" 1897.

59   "India Under" 1906.

60   "The List" 1889.

61   "Great Indian" 1887.

62   "Bombay Railway" 1886.

63   Central Railway is one of the zones of Indian Railways, owned by the Ministry of Railways. Central Railway was formed in 1951 based largely on the original network of the GIPR.

Bibliography

"An Indian Railway Terminus." 1886. *The Architect. A Weekly Illustrated Journal of Art, Civil Engineering and Building* 35: 15–18.

"Article 4—no Title." 1877. *The Times of India,* May 17, 1877: 2.

Awasthi, Aruna. 1994. *History and Development of Railways in India.* New Delhi: Deep & Deep Publications.

"Bombay Railway Terminus Buildings." 1886. *The Builder* 51, no. 2287 (Saturday, December 4): 828.

"Bori Bandar Terminal Station and Offices." 1880. *Abstract of Proceedings of the Govt. of Bombay in the Public Works Department* no. 33–34 (January 5): 8.

Chopra, Preeti. 2011. *Joint Enterprise: Indian Elites and the Making of British Bombay*. Minneapolis and London: University of Minnesota Press.

"Classified Ad 5—no Title." 1844. *The Bombay Times and Journal of Commerce*, July 20, 1844: 462.

Davies, Philip. 1985. *Splendours of the Raj: British Architecture in India, 1660 to 1947*. London: John Murray.

Douglas, James. 1883. *A Book of Bombay*. Bombay: The Bombay Gazette Steam Press.

Dwivedi, Sharada, and Rahul Mehrotra. 2001. *Bombay: The Cities Within*. Bombay: Eminence Designs.

"Editorial Article 1—no Title." 1877. *The Times of India*, November 20, 1877: 2.

"Editorial Article 3—no Title." 1880. *The Times of India*, May 26, 1880: 2.

"Editorial Article 1—no Title." 1881. *The Times of India*, March 12, 1881: 2.

Evenson, Norma. 1989. *The Indian Metropolis: A View Toward the West*. New Haven: Yale University Press.

"From The Times Archives: Edit." 1991. *The Times of India*, July 19, 1991: 10.

"Great Indian Peninsular Railway Terminal Buildings, Bombay." 1886. *The Builder* 51, no. 2281 (Saturday, October 23): 608.

"Great Indian Peninsular Railway Terminus, Bombay." 1887. *The Builder* 53, no. 2319 (Saturday, July 16): 121.

Howard, Stephen Goodwin. 2012. "Chhatrapati Shivaji Terminus." MA Dissertation, University of York. http://etheses.whiterose.ac.uk/3198/2/VT6.pdf.

Hunter, William Wilson. 1892. *Bombay 1885 to 1890: A Study in Indian Administration*. Bombay: B.M. Malabari, Indian Spectator Office.

Hurd, John, and Ian J. Kerr. 2012. *India's Railway History: A Research Handbook*. Leiden: Brill.

"India Under Royal Eyes." 1906. *The Times of India*, July 4, 1906: 6.

"Journal of Commerce." 1845. *The Bombay Times and Journal of Commerce*, April 23, 1845: 273.

London, Christopher W., ed. 1994. *Architecture in Victorian and Edwardian India*. Bombay: Marg Publications.

London, Christopher W. 2002. *Bombay Gothic*. Mumbai: India Book House.

Mehrotra, Rahul, and Sharada Dwivedi. 2006. *A City Icon: Victoria Terminus, Bombay 1887; Now Chhatrapati Shivaji Terminus, Mumbai 1996*. Bombay: Eminence Designs.

Metcalf, Thomas R. 1989. *An Imperial Vision: Indian Architecture and Britain's Raj*. London: faber and faber.

Mitter, Partha. 1994. *Art and Nationalism in Colonial India, 1850–1922: Occidental Orientations*. Cambridge: Cambridge University Press.

Morris, Jan. 2005. *Stones of Empire: The Buildings of the Raj*. 2nd ed. Oxford: Oxford University Press.

"New Terminal Station at Bori Bandar—Proposal to Invite Tenders for the Completion of the Main Building." 1880. *Abstract of Proceedings of the Govt. of Bombay in the Public Works Department* no. 1707 (July 6): 444–45.

"Remuneration to Mr. Stevens for his Design for the new Boree Bunder Terminal Building." 1877. *Abstract of Proceedings of the Govt. of Bombay in the Public Works Department* no. 375 (March 9): 20.

Richards, Jeffrey, and John M. MacKenzie. 1986. *The Railway Station: A Social History*. Oxford: Oxford University Press.

Schröder, Asta Freifrau von. 2013. "Images and Messages in the Embellishment of Metropolitan Railway Stations (1850–1950)." Dr. phil. diss., Technical University Berlin.

Sharma, S. N. 1990. *History of the Great Indian Peninsula Railway: 1870–1900*, p. 1, vol. 2. Bombay: Central Railway.

"Sir Bartle Frere." 1884. *The Times of India*, May 31, 1884: 4.

Sulivan, Raymond J. F. 1938. *One Hundred Years of Bombay: History of the Bombay Chamber of Commerce, 1836–1936*. Bombay: The Times of India Press.

"Terminal Buildings at Boree Bunder." 1878. *Abstract of Proceedings of the Govt. of Bombay in the Public Works Department* no. 966 (May 9): 243–44.

"Terminal station &c., Boree Bunder." 1875. *Abstract of Proceedings of the Govt. of Bombay in the Public Works Department* no. 341 (March 23): 28–29.

"The Great Railway Station at Bombay, India." 1897. *Scientific American* 76, no. 22 (May 29): 344. https://www.jstor.org/stable/10.2307/26121019.

"The List of New Year's Honours." 1889. *The Times of India*, January 9, 1889: 6.

"The Victoria Terminus." 1887a. *The Times of India*, September 14, 1887: 4.

"The Victoria Terminus." 1887b. *The Times of India*, November 5, 1887: 4.

"The Victoria Terminus Refreshment-Rooms." 1891. *The Times of India*, January 8, 1891: 4.

Tillotson, Giles H. R. 1994. "Orientalizing the Raj: Indo-Saracenic Fantasies." In Christopher W. London, ed., *Architecture in Victorian and Edwardian India*, 15–34. Bombay: Marg Publications.

"Travelling Lubricant: To The Editor of The Times of India." 1889. *The Times of India*, May 29, 1889: 4.

Image Sources

1	victoriaterm (columbia.edu), public domain via Wikimedia Commons. https://commons.wikimedia.org/wiki/File:An_albumen_print,_c.1870_of_Victoria_Terminus.jpg

2	Shraddha Bhatawadekar, 2019.

3–5	Shraddha Bhatawadekar, 2014.

6	Shraddha Bhatawadekar, 2017.

ELIZABETH RANKIN AND ROLF MICHAEL SCHNEIDER

Voortrekker Monumentality

Afrikanerdom, Apartheid, Post-Apartheid

Writing this paper prompted us to engage anew with our recent research on the Voortrekker Monument in Pretoria, focusing on the changing views of its monumentality from the outset to the present day.[1] After a brief introduction to the monument, we consider shifts in ideology from the Afrikaners who built it and were to legislate South Africa's extreme form of colonial racism—apartheid—to what might be considered post-colonial counter-responses in the post-apartheid era.

We also ponder how our own responses developed, in terms of approach, analysis, and understanding, after we began our collaboration to reconstruct the monument's history in 2010. And we are particularly conscious of what our research gained from our (initially) divergent viewpoints, dependent more on the circumstances under which we had come to know the Voortrekker Monument than our different academic backgrounds as a German scholar of Greek and Roman art and archaeology ("classical archaeology") and a South African art historian in New Zealand. Rolf Schneider had first visited the monument in 2009 under a post-apartheid government, which allowed him to view its architecture and sculpture beyond the constraints of its Afrikaner Nationalist agenda. Scottish-born Elizabeth Rankin, on the other hand, had grown up in an immigrant family in Johannesburg, and the negative connotations she associated with the monument blocked her from acknowledging its achievements of concept and craftsmanship. Yet from the outset we based our teamwork on mutual trust and constructive criticism, batting ideas back and forward, face-to-face on the rare occasions when we were on the same continent, but chiefly by the constant online interchange that we christened "playing ping pong by email"—a process we happily revisited for this paper. Sharing our different perceptions gave us a wider perspective, alert to further views and particularly concerned to include multiple voices and readings wherever possible to augment our dialog. It was agreed too that our research should encompass visual, verbal, and written narratives alike, and that we should try to look beyond the restrictions of categories such as colonialism, racism, and nationalism, to satisfy our interest in history as an ongoing process of rereading and recontextualizing human stories. Educated within western value systems, thinking patterns, and reception models, we constantly reminded ourselves to try to avoid taking a moral high ground—a challenge that was, however, often difficult to meet. But our different backgrounds provided leverage that encouraged us to think in more depth about these questions and their impact on people and structures.

1 Voortrekker Monument and its ring of wagons, here surrounded by the myriad tents housing participants in the inauguration, December 1949.

The Monument and its Frieze

The Voortrekker Monument (1931–49), elevated on an outcrop outside Pretoria, is generally thought of as a monstrous symbol of South Africa's apartheid regime (fig. 1), and it is hard to comprehend that it was first conceived as an anti-colonial statement, a position unexpectedly acknowledged by Nelson Mandela.[2] Although it ignored the plight of the indigenous peoples of the sub-continent, the monument opposed British colonial rule in the name of burgeoning Afrikaner nationalism. It celebrated the Dutch-speaking Voortrekkers, forebears of Afrikaners, and "colonized people and colonizers themselves."[3] Renouncing British rule in the Cape, they had departed in their covered wagons on the so-called Great Trek beyond colonial control, to open up the hinterland for independent white occupation. In particular, the monument marked the centenary of their crushing victory over the Zulu at Blood River on 16 December 1838, which was a pivotal scene of the marble frieze (see fig. 5). But the republics they set up were taken over by the British, and the aim of the monument was to restore pride in Afrikaner identity after their defeat in the Anglo-Boer War in 1902.

Once the *Sentrale Volksmonumente Kommittee* (SVK; Central Monuments Committee) was set up in 1931 to consider what form the commemoration would take, a decision was reached to erect an architectural memorial, built to house a commemorative cenotaph and a marble frieze with scenes from the Great Trek. The monument was to be surrounded by a ring of wagons, mimicking the laager the Voortrekkers had used for their defense against the Zulu at the Battle of Blood River (see fig. 1). A key consideration for the architect, Gerard Moerdyk, was designing a building that would not draw on styles associated with British imperialism. There would be no classical columned porticoes that had been favored for public buildings in South Africa under British colonial rule. Moerdyk wanted to create a form that was essentially "African," evidently oblivious to the semantic—and socio-political—difference between African and Afrikaner.[4] Moreover, there were formal relationships in its decorative Art Deco details with other contemporary monuments, such as the ANZAC Monument in Sydney. There are older precedents too, notably the 1913 *Völkerschlachtdenkmal* in Leipzig, commemorating the centenary of the Battle of Leipzig. The interest in this monument reflected Afrikaner sympathy with Germany, and their strong resistance to South Africa joining the Allies in World War II under a Jan-Smuts-led government. To emphasize the "great purpose" the Voortrekker Monument "served," Moerdyk did not fight shy of comparing it with much larger structures, not only the *Völkerschlachtdenkmal*, but revered historical examples, such as the pyramids of Egypt, the Great Wall of China, and the Taj Mahal in India.[5]

Moerdyk's initial design makes clear that he had in mind an ancient African tradition: the facade was based on a pylon temple, evoking the grandeur of Pharaonic Egypt.[6] Ultimately, however, a symmetrical monolithic form was conceived, and only the sense of scale and weighty permanence of Egyptian architecture was retained. The monument's block-like mass may have been inspired by environmental aspects of Africa too: it echoed the silhouettes of the flat-topped hills or *koppies* rearing up from the limitless veld of South Africa's interior, while

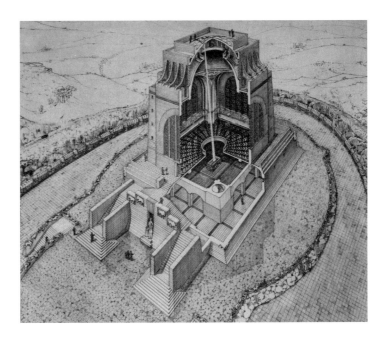

2   Gerard Moerdyk, drawing of cross-section of Voortrekker Monument, 1938.

its stonework was intended to recall the ancient structure of Great Zimbabwe. South African granite formed a *rustica* facing on the enormous construction of concrete and steel, creating a commanding edifice, 62 meters high, with a footing of 40 by 40 meters (see fig. 1).

The monument reveals a spectacular interior (fig. 2). The lower hall houses a symbolic ceno-taph of polished granite,[7] dedicated to the Voortrekkers who died on the Great Trek, visible through a circular opening from the hall above, where one enters. This is the "Hall of Heroes," lit by four huge arched windows with a fretwork of golden glass and surrounded by a marble frieze, 92 meters long and 2.3 meters high, one of the largest in the world. Made of pure white Querce-ta marble, quarried in Italy near Carrara, and mounted at eye level, the frieze tells a heroic story of the Great Trek through a series of twenty-seven scenes with some 200 life-size figures (see figs. 4, 5, 8–11). Finally, the monument is crowned with an imposing dome (see fig. 2), pierced by an oculus that directs the sun's rays each year at noon on the anniversary of the Battle of Blood River onto the seemingly patriotic yet exclusive inscription on the Cenotaph far below—"Ons Vir Jou, Suid Afrika." The inscription declares "We for Thee South Africa," but only in Afrikaans.[8]

Conflicting Ideologies and Responses

The Voortrekker Monument took more than a decade to build and, by the time it was inaugurat-ed on 16 December 1949, the National Party, with its electoral base in the Afrikaner population, had been elected to government. Hence the monument's association is not with the concept of uplifting the Afrikaner underdog, its original intention, but with Afrikanerdom in ascendancy— and inevitably with apartheid, the abhorrent underlying principle of this government's policy from 1948 until the first free elections in 1994. From the time of the monument's completion, the sense of pride it engendered amongst Afrikaners, who visited the shrine and celebrated the heroically presented stories of the Voortrekkers on the marble frieze, was already challenged by the negative attitude of much of the population—both the black majority and English-speaking whites, who were often antagonistic, or at best felt indifferent towards it.

How much stronger would the responses be under the new regime that replaced the Nation-al Party after its long and oppressive rule based on racist principles? To have such an edifice dom-inating the skyline of the approach into Pretoria, which remained one of the capital cities after the election of the African National Congress (ANC) to power, was surely anathema to the "new" South Africa. While the ANC claimed to uphold the principle of tolerance, embracing all cultures, some old monuments associated with apartheid were quietly removed during the early years of its rule—and more vociferously and with ongoing momentum since the #RhodesMustFall cam-paign of 2015, which broadened the definition of colonial oppression to embrace any form of white dominion. Yet the Voortrekker Monument continues to stand, and even to thrive as one of South Africa's top tourist destinations.[9]

It had been fully expected that the monument would somehow disappear under ANC rule after its certain victory in the first free elections in 1994. For a 1992 conference at the University of the Witwatersrand entitled "Myths, Monuments, Museums: New Premises?", artist Penny Siopis designed a program cover that showed the Voortrekker Monument being toppled by a crowd of tiny people pulling on ropes.[10] In contrast to Siopis's left-wing outlook, Louis Eksteen created a work expressing ambivalence about the future of the monument and the Afrikaners it repre-

3   Louis Eksteen, *Quo vadis-triptiek*, 1991, linocut, each 18×15 cm.

sented. His three-part linocut of 1991, *Quo vadis-triptiek* (fig. 3), depicts the monument shaken on its foundations, then lifting off the ground—whether in an implosion or an apotheosis is unclear. But either way, Eksteen's work encapsulated Afrikaner uncertainty about the future. The sheer size and volume of the building, however, rendered removal impossible in practical terms, and there has been no serious suggestion of demolition, although there has been much speculation about what would happen to the monument. One suggestion was that the Afrikaner museum in its basement would be appropriated as a location for commemorating the struggle for freedom and the victory of the ANC. But mannequins in Voortrekker dress with historical accoutrements are still on display.[11]

The survival of the monument is at least in part due to the pre-emptive action of a group of Afrikaners who formed a not-for-profit Section 21 company to take over the site in 1993 before the first democratic elections. Private management re-branded it as the Voortrekker Monument and Nature Reserve, taking advantage of the 341-acre site to offer "apolitical" outdoor activities for game spotters, birdwatchers, picnickers, cyclists, and joggers, and the monument also hosts markets and music concerts.[12] More significantly, under a series of energetic CEOs, management has sought to shift the perception of the monument itself and modify its goals to be more inclusive. Black staff have been engaged as front-of-house guides, and educational programs and exhibitions in the heritage center have shifted away from a purely Voortrekker focus to look at South African history and cultures more broadly, catering for diverse audiences, particularly schoolchildren, both black and white.

Nonetheless, the monument has been a rallying ground for ultra-right-wing groups opposing the move to non-racial democracy in South Africa,[13] and continues to be visited by the faithful as a shrine of nationalist Afrikaner values. This usage reinforces the view of the monument

4   ANC Minister of Arts and Culture, Paul Mashatile, proclaiming the Voortrekker Monument a national heritage site in front of *The Battle of Blood River*, March 16, 2012.

as an icon of apartheid oppression, and its image has provided, and continues to provide, a shorthand symbol for the principles of the old regime. Yet, even when portrayed in a negative or satirical way, images of the monument acknowledge its ongoing power as a symbol.

What was surely required under a new dispensation was a defusing of that potency, or a subverting of its messages. ANC supporters could afford to be magnanimous, and some suggested that the monument stood for what had been overcome to achieve freedom. Tokyo Sexwale, ANC premier of Gauteng province where the monument stands, proposed a new, more complex reading of the edifice when he visited it in 1996. The metal gates to the site are decorated with assegais, the spear-like weapons of the Zulu warriors that the Voortrekkers had conquered

to bring their colonial concept of civilization to the South African interior. At a photo shoot there, Sexwale claimed that the assegais on the gate where he stood represented the armed wing of the ANC, known as *Umkhonto we Sizwe*, which translates as "Spear of the Nation."[14] Referring to South Africa's recent hard-won democracy, he declared that it was the ANC (and hence not the Voortrekkers) that had "opened up the path of civilization." He thus also appropriated the narrative of the historical marble frieze in the Hall of Heroes, which featured many assegais in scenes where Voortrekker firepower overcame the superior numbers of indigenous forces.

A different kind of appropriation came when, lobbied over many years by the staff of the monument, the ANC government finally agreed to proclaim it a national heritage site on March 16, 2012. It seems incongruous that the Minister of Arts and Culture, Paul Mashatile, made the announcement standing in front of the frieze's central scene, *The Battle of Blood River* (fig. 4). But perhaps the ANC minister's unexpected juxtaposition against the iconic Voortrekker victory could be interpreted as acknowledgement that an African government was now in a position to grant status to a monument that embodied white Afrikaner supremacy. However, Mashatile's tone was conciliatory, as he proclaimed that the monument "attained National Heritage status because of its significance in the political history of South Africa and the building's unique architecture," and because "South Africa belonged to all who lived in it"; it would be "a way to heal divisions of the past."[15]

Turning to the frieze, it is easy to understand how its overriding message would have been difficult for Africans to condone, not least in the overall grandeur of its 92 meters of white marble, emulating the classical friezes of antiquity. In portraying selected scenes from the Voortrekkers' journeys, it created a foundation myth for Afrikaner nationalism in monumental visual form. The Voortrekkers are depicted as an upstanding, God-fearing people, their propriety reflected in their upright demeanor and neat dress. The men wear hats and buttoned jackets, even in the heat of battle (figs. 5, 8). The women wear deep-brimmed bonnets and full-length dresses, with

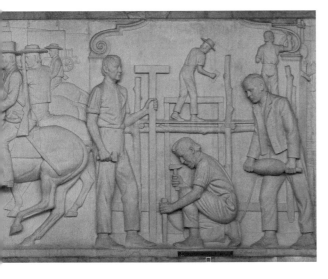

5 *The Vow; The Battle of Blood River; Building the Church of the Vow*, 1949–50. Marble, width respectively 2.28 m; 4.29 m; 2.19 m.

6   Minnette Vári, *Chimera*, 2001. Installation shot of four-channel digital video footage.

high necks and long sleeves, which always appear freshly laundered, even in the most remote wilderness, as in *Women at Saailaer* (see fig. 9). In stark contrast, their African adversaries are expressly presented as semi-naked savages in exotic garb, who act with deceit and ruthless cruelty. When Voortrekker leader Piet Retief attempted to negotiate *The Treaty with Dingane*, a land deal very advantageous to the Boers, Zulu slaughtered his entire company of 70 men and some 130 black retainers (see fig. 8). Soon afterwards they slaughtered 241 Voortrekker women and children and 250 black servants in *Massacre of Women and Children at Bloukrans*. These actions were thought to provide justification for the Voortrekkers retaliating at Blood River, winning against overwhelming odds because of their devastating firepower—although their success is interpreted as God granting victory to the just. To underline this, the flanking scenes depict the Voortrekkers taking *The Vow* to commemorate the day if they are granted victory, and its fulfillment in *Building the Church of the Vow* (fig. 5 left and right). The Voortrekkers are presented as God's chosen people, finding their promised land in emulation of Old Testament chronicles, bringing Christian civilization to what they perceived as an untamed, savage terrain.

More recent historians have written about the Voortrekker story differently, giving credence to an African point of view.[16] Contemporary artists have interrogated the frieze in different ways too. Photographer Abrie Fourie, for example, chose to photograph the tawny marble cladding in a corner of the Hall of Heroes, excluding the frieze altogether as though obliterating its narrative.[17] By contrast, another photographer, Peter Hugo, focused his lens on a section of the relief of Zulu brutally murdering Retief's men, thinking about how his identity as an Afrikaner had been shaped by such images, and questioning how he could explain them to his children.[18] Artist Minnette Vári created a four-channel digital video, entitled *Chimera* (fig. 6), by scraping back the individual frames of the film she had made of the frieze and reconstituting them as animated projections on four suspended screens.[19] Her installation highlights the mythical-historical aspect of the frieze's stories, as her own naked body, masked as a chimera, is inserted into the scenes, provocatively moving amidst the turmoil of the carved bodies frozen in marble. The shifting semblance affords a subtle commentary on the fugitive nature of nationalistic histories and challenges conventional "truths."

The most public of the responses to the Voortrekker Monument is Freedom Park, built by the new ANC government on Salvokop, an outcrop opposite Monument Koppie where the Afrikaner memorial stands (fig. 7).[20] First conceived by Nelson Mandela in 1999, when he spoke of a people's shrine to honor all those who had suffered and died for human rights in South Africa, it was undertaken as a presidential project under Thabo Mbeki from 2000, with a lavish budget. It intends in every way to provide a counter-monument to its neighbor on the other side of the highway entrance into Pretoria. The most obvious difference is the overall appearance. While the Voortrekker Monument is indeed monumental, a dominating intrusion on the skyline and visible from afar, Freedom Park is organic in form and hugs the contours of the land. Instead of an imposing monolithic structure, it consists of a series of inter-linked sites, each named in one of the eleven official languages of South Africa. A sacred site, Isivivane, is centered on a shallow pool emitting plumes of steam, with roughly hewn boulders from the seven provincial areas of

7 Freedom Park, aerial view, 2019.

the country. It was blessed by representatives of the diverse religions of South Africa, and visitors there remove their shoes as a mark of respect. To reach it, they follow a winding pathway down the hillside of Salvokop with an indigenous emphasis: natural stone is stacked to form curving walls and meandering pathways through native planting offset against water features conjuring up ideas of purity and healing. It is in total contrast to the controlled ascent of steep steps leading up to the geometric severity of the overbearing Voortrekker Monument (see fig. 1).

Nor is there a single vaunted narrative in commemorative visual form like that found in the frieze of the Voortrekker Monument's Hall of Heroes. Freedom Park relies on affect, incited by the less parochial symbolism of its architectural forms. There is an account of sorts, however, in the final addition to the Freedom Park complex, completed in 2010—a museum, named //hapo, not an official language in this case, but the language of the indigenous Khoisan peoples, today only a tiny fraction of South Africa's population. The museum narrative presents a history of the sub-continent from prehistoric times to the present day. The key themes are Struggle, Democracy, and Nation Building: the Voortrekkers and the Great Trek are notable by their absence.

The Voortrekker Monument and Freedom Park share a commemorative purpose, although they honor different heroes. At the heart of Freedom Park, Sikhumbuto comprises a contemplative sanctuary with an eternal flame, and a 697-meter Wall of Names, recording some 75,000 people who lost their lives fighting for freedom in South Africa.[21] The agenda is all-encompassing, not only listing those who took part in the recent struggle but accommodating other names going back through history on a series of lower walls, including the World Wars, and even the Anglo-Boer War. There is one omission, however. None of the South African Defence Force (SADF) troops who died on South Africa's borders under apartheid are included.

It is a sign of the ideological rift that remains between the two sites, that the Voortrekker Monument erected its own Wall of Remembrance for SADF soldiers in 2009, signaling that the monument is never likely to be a "neutral" site.[22] In a conciliatory gesture, the Voortekker Monument and Freedom Park were linked by a "Road of Reconciliation," opened in 2011. But such a move cannot reconcile the rival agendas of the two sites, where their predominant dogmas remain oppositional—a colonial commemoration and a post-colonial riposte. Their monumental rivalry, however, entices debates about how colonial statements and post-colonial narratives might help to develop memorials dedicated to a humanity beyond the ideologies of nationalism and racism, color and oppression.

Researching Voortrekker Monumentality and Iconography

Central to our research approach was the analysis of art and architecture, historical places, texts, stories, and biographies and memories of men, women, and children, as well as secondary readings of them all.[23] In doing so, we experienced anew the importance of archives, libraries, and museums, and especially their often unpublished maps, plans, drawings, paintings, sculpture, artwork, photographs, documents, minutes of meetings, letters, newspapers, and magazines. These diverse media also provided invaluable records of people "without history," whose place in history has been too frequently forgotten. Here we benefited greatly from informal and oral accounts, such as those recorded in the James Stuart Archive of Recorded Oral Evidence to the History of the Zulu and Neighbouring Peoples.[24]

8   *The Treaty with Dingane; Murder of Retief and his Men*, 1949. Marble, width respectively 2.14 m; 3.7 m.

Two random examples highlight the kind of surprises we encountered in our research. One is that the Voortrekker Monument was fully conceptualized before the commissioners, the SVK and the architect had clarified what site it would occupy—or even whether it would be erected in an urban or rural context.[25] In the history of such structures, this is exceptional. It points to a remarkable monumental agency that claims contextual independence, paired with (Afrikaner) authority of place and memory. It also speaks of the politics of the time that Pretoria, executive seat of the government, was chosen despite the city's post-dating the Great Trek—a mute acknowledgement of the monument's political potency.

A second example is the puzzling Masonic glass bottle that Piet Retief, leader and appointed governor of the Voortrekkers, is carrying on a strap over his shoulder in *Murder of Retief and his Men* (fig. 8)—an object which has animated scholars to advance far-reaching speculations.[26] We reconstructed the bottle's intriguing biography from its likely production in the Keene-Marlborough-Street Glassworks in New Hampshire in the US in the 1820s to its present home in South Africa, the Voortrekker Complex of the uMsunduzi Museum in Pietermaritzburg. This led us to unfold the close interactions of Christian Voortrekkers and their descendants with Dutch and English Freemasons, amongst them a number of Afrikaner statesmen and Dutch Reformed ministers, who ignored their church's proscription of lodge membership. Yet Retief himself does not seem to have been a Freemason, and we speculate that the bottle must have been a special gift from some of his Grahamstown colleagues who were. That the Masonic bottle finally made its way into the frieze, with the intention of marking Retief's identity with accurate historical detail, is one of the historical paradoxes of its visual narrative.

The SVK, the architect, and the sculptors anticipated achieving the historically impossible, namely that the visual narrative of the frieze would be historically "authentic." The pernickety attention paid to details, evident in myriad SVK documents, suggests that it was believed that accuracy in detail would guarantee veracity for the larger claims of the frieze. A telling example

9 *Women at Saailaer*, 1949. Marble, width 4.01 m.

here is found in a number of handwritten copies of an all-important—but not extant—land treaty, in which the Zulu King Dingane was said to have signed a large swathe of Zulu territory over to the Voortrekker leader Piet Retief in February 1838. This act is depicted in the south frieze scene *The Treaty* as an irrefutable fact, carved in marble forever, its historical reliability reinforced by the careful recording of details such as Dingane's traditional attire (see fig. 8). Yet unpublished evidence from the time around and after the alleged signing led us, ultimately, to argue that this representation is almost certainly incorrect. According to our investigations, at best only a pre-drafted land treaty existed, prepared in advance by Retief but never actually signed by Dingane.[27] Nonetheless, it was claimed that a signed document was found in Retief's satchel, nearly a year after his murder, when his body had been lying exposed to the elements and marauding animals for months. Leading Voortrekkers certified in early 1839 that the texts of the treaty they then began to distribute to the public were true copies of a signed "original," which has been lost to view ever since. It was the Voortrekkers' undoubted intention to legalize their claim to settle in Zulu Natal and establish a republic beyond British control. Such pro-Voortrekker readings of history are typical of the frieze.

In a world where historical narratives are dominated by men, we were intrigued by the rather unusual recurrent presence of women and children in the frieze, the former in sixteen and the latter in ten of its twenty-seven scenes. The women are shown in a variety of social roles. Significantly, they are represented as *volksmoeder* (mother of the Afrikaner *volk*) figures, carrying a baby or protecting their children. These iconic images emphasized that it was the women whose fertility guaranteed the survival of the Voortrekkers. They often remarried rapidly when their husbands died or were killed in conflict, and they produced many offspring, countering very high infant mortality rates. The visual narratives for girls follow the models of their mothers, in training for maternal roles. Women are not only shown as mothers and carrying out domestic tasks, however, but also sharing the dangers of the trek with their husbands: crossing perilous mountains, as in *Descent from the Drakensberg* and *Return from Natal over the Drakensberg*, or undertaking agricultural work, and even fighting against black opponents, as in *Women at Saailaer* (fig. 9). And they play another critical part in the trek. In *Women Spur Men on*, this particular female task is attested by two incidents conflated in this scene, unexpected in view of the patriarchal bent of most Afrikaner communities. The first is that it was the women who compelled the men to remain in Natal and fight back against the Zulu, when the men felt downhearted because of so many Voortrekker deaths. Their subsequent focus, however, was on the British, who were challenging the Voortrekker occupation of Natal, and two concepts of colonialism clashed. In late 1838, the British officer at Port Natal, Major Samuel Charters, reported that the "spirit of dislike to the English sway was remarkably dominant amongst the [Voortrekker] women. If any of the men began to droop or lose courage, they urged them on to fresh exertions, and kept alive the spirit of resistance within them."[28] The women would ultimately play a part in persuading many of their menfolk to abandon Natal, however, and trek back over the mountains to establish a republic in the northern hinterland across the Vaal River, rather than staying in what had become a British colony. It was these women who prompted the complaints of the British commissioner of Zulu Natal, Henry Cloete, that the women would never "yield to British authority" and preferred "to die in freedom as death is dearer to them than the loss of liberty … I consider it a disgrace on their husbands to allow them such a state of freedom."[29] By advocating such liberty, the Voortrekker women were pioneers in a different sense, challenging gender hierarchies, even though their concept of liberation was constrained by their belief in a God-given Afrikaner mission and its racist underpinnings.

Our focus on biographies of people and objects facilitated a more nuanced understanding of the responsibilities of the commissioners and the four sculptors of the Voortrekker Monument frieze. The SVK commissioners wanted to ensure an Afrikaner "purity" for the frieze, so overlooked many competent sculptors to appoint three relatively inexperienced Afrikaners—Frikkie Kruger, Laurika Postma, and Hennie Potgieter—along with a more senior German immigrant sculptor, Peter Kirchhoff. While Kirchhoff was an atheist, the South Africans represented the three Dutch Reformed Churches, central to Afrikaner beliefs and behavior.[30] The SVK and the architect Moerdyk established the topics of the individual scenes, defined the general design, and monitored the implementation of their concept of historical accuracy in the visual narrative. Additionally, the sculptors were required to work together in premises at Harmony Hall in Pretoria,[31] provided by Moerdyk, so that they would produce a *volkswerk* without individuality of styles (fig. 10). Curiously, Moerdyk, who wielded considerable authority in the sculpture studio, recounted that he asked them to "model themselves technically upon two Renaissance sculptors, Donatello and Verrocchio"[32]—advice so ambitious that it was bound to fail.[33] Despite these restrictions, however, the sculptors were given the liberty to divide out the themes among themselves for the initial small-scale maquettes, and to elaborate and change the composition and the iconography, largely without significant interference by the SVK.[34] Surprisingly too, they were able to add extra scenes so that the frieze would be continuous around the entire Hall of Heroes, with additional episodes of conflict and heroic deeds.

10   Interior of Harmony Hall, Pretoria. Sculptors at work on *Departure from the Cape*, 1942.

When our project began, the sculptors were no longer alive to be consulted, but we greatly valued interviews and visits from which we could glean first-hand information. Discussions with the son of one of the sculptors, Werner Kirchhoff, who had lived at the Harmony Hall studio as a schoolboy, helped us to understand the complex process of making the frieze.[35] He had, for example, photographs that showed how the carpenter at Harmony Hall sized up the small maquettes to full scale, making a wooden armature to support the clay that the sculptors worked with to produce the large relief scenes. When the sculptors had finished the relief scenes, they were replicated in some 140 plaster casts (a process in which the original clay reliefs were destroyed) that were then shipped to Italy—a monumental undertaking in its own right. There, in Florence, suitable marble and "first-class Sculptors"[36] were available at the studio of sculptor Romano Romanelli, long known to Moerdyk.[37] Although many of the studio records were lost in the Florence floods of 1966, a single surviving document we found during our visit made us aware of how important this commission had been to local sculptors, providing much-needed employment in the wake of World War II. Some forty of them were commissioned to copy the plaster models into marble, carving the entire frieze in just over a year. Although two of the

South African sculptors were sent to Italy to "guard against any un-Afrikaans elements stealing into the work,"[38] accounts in Potgieter's later memoir, as well as Postma's letters home from Europe, make it clear that there was little for them to do, given the high competence of the Italians (fig. 11).[39] It has rarely been acknowledged, however, that this division of labor made the final marble frieze the work of two parties, the sculptors in South Africa, who developed the models, and the sculptors in Italy, who copied them into Querceta marble. The sculptors of both continents contributed distinctive features to the monumental Afrikaner narrative.[40]

Another novelty for us was the abundant use of non-professional models for the frieze, which also brought more possibilities for interviews, providing further insights into the work of the Pretoria studio. The models seem to have been selected by the sculptors themselves, who endeavored to find sitters with Voortrekker heritage or at least of "good Afrikaner stock." Sculptor Hennie Potgieter later identified and listed the models he could recall.[41] These men, women, and children posed in Voortrekker attire; in some cases, the face would be based on an extant portrait of a historical character or a descendant of that person. For example, the facial features of eleven-year-old Paul Kruger in *The Battle of Vegkop* were based on Louis Jacobs, a great-grandson of the President of the South African Republic (1883–1902), while Peter Kirchhoff's son, Werner, served as Kruger's body model.[42] A press report in December 1949 drew attention to the fact that "Pretoria visitors can recognize a number of their fellow citizens depicted on the walls in the scenes in which their ancestors took part."[43] But for a key Afrikaner figure in the frieze, the Voortrekker governor Piet Retief, Potgieter does not record a model and there was no historical portrait to be found. Surprisingly, Retief's features may have been inspired by the actor who played that part in an early silent movie about the Voortrekkers.[44] The use of living models for most figures, however, linked the monumental frieze to many individuals, biographies and personal histories, which ensured the ongoing topicality of the visual narrative of the Great Trek. The frieze thus has a unique subtext, another layer of narrative that tells, a century after the Battle

11   Romano Romanelli, Gerard Moerdyk, Laurika Postma, Hennie Potgieter, and two Florentine sculptors at work on *Presentation of the Bible to Jacobus Uys* at the Romanelli studio. Full-size replications in plaster of destroyed original clay panels in the background, c. 1948.

of Blood River, of Afrikaners who lived in the city of Pretoria, founded by the Voortrekkers and named after their victorious commander at Blood River, Andries Pretorius. The portraits of the sculptors themselves, together with members of their families and others present at the studio, were used for many anonymous Voortrekkers too, such as those in *Departure from the Cape*, creating yet another micro-narrative, in this case of those who had developed the frieze at the Harmony Hall workshop (see fig. 10).

African models were employed too, but the lack of further information about them is troubling. We know that workshop assistant Piet Malotho, a Sesotho speaker, modelled for the Rolong chief Moroka in *Negotiation*, and that three Zulu models, Ngubeni, Umtetwa, and Ntuli, posed in traditional gear for Zulu in various scenes.[45] Also recorded is a young black woman who agreed to pose for Laurika Postma "in Zulu dress of only a hip covering" to represent the four wives of the Zulu king in *Death of Dingane*, "provided that there was a screen erected around Laurika and her."[46] The models for most of the black people in the frieze remain anonymous, likewise the sitter for king Dingane, the key African figure in the frieze. In contrast to their Afrikaner adversaries, biographies of individual black people were of no interest to Afrikaners—apart from the Zulu kings Dingane and Mpande who feature as individuals in the frieze[47]—which marks another contemptuous form of racism in the visual narrative. Here, the image of African people is generally stigmatized, either by their subservient roles, their aggressive demeanor, or their murdering of white men, women, and children in *Murder of Retief and his Men* (see fig. 6) and *Massacre of Women and Children at Bloukrans*. In *Death of Dingane*, anonymous black people kill the Zulu king, perversely the only scene that shows exclusively Africans. The asymmetry between Afrikaner supremacy and African inferiority in the frieze is profound and is portrayed to be God-given, with repeated elements in the frieze that emphasize the Voortrekkers' (reputed) Christian piety, as in the second scene, *Presentation of the Bible to Jacobus Uys*, as well as *The Vow* and *Building the Church of the Vow*, mentioned earlier (see fig. 5).

Many different actors were involved in the making of the Voortrekker Monument, and numerous uncontrollable circumstances contributed to it too, not least changes of government and the outbreak of World War II. This further complicated the question of how a (or the) reading of the monument and its frieze was established, who had contributed to it, and when. Our question acquired an even sharper edge, as the Board of Control of the Voortrekker Monument published the "authoritative" reading of the structure and the frieze, *The Voortrekker Monument Pretoria: Official Guide*, first printed in 1955 and running through many editions in both Afrikaans and English.[48] This "ur-text" for interpreting the monument was assigned to the architect, Gerard Moerdyk, who contributed three confidently assertive essays, covering both the building and the frieze, mendaciously simplifying difficulties, divergences and disagreements to provide an apparently consensual history. Our analysis of the convoluted processes of transforming memory to marble heightened our awareness of the problems of accounts like these, which favor linear rather than process-related interpretations. Yet only the latter acknowledge that readings are dynamically developed, changed, discarded, and reinvented in response to diverse social, political, and ideological (f)actors.[49] We argue that a supposedly "linear" logic is in many cases formed only in hindsight. Following this line of thought, it is hardly unexpected that the *Official Guide* of the Voortrekker Monument is burdened with all too many historical shortcomings and factual contradictions.

Afterword

When eventually the Voortrekker Monument was inaugurated on 16 December 1949, five of the twenty-seven scenes of the frieze were still missing, among them the iconic *Battle of Blood River* fought in 1838 on that very day, when within a few hours the firepower of some 470 Voortrekkers slaughtered more than 3,000 of an estimated 10,000 Zulu force (see fig. 5).[50] According to the available records, it seems that these conspicuous gaps in the Afrikaner epic of the frieze caused no significant public reaction. How to respond to this "surprising" fact? To us, there is a productive historical shift in the realization that it was the symbolic value of a monument to Afrikanerdom, and the cultural capital it provided, that was of significance to the quarter million people that attended the inauguration,[51] rather than the specifics that had been labored over so intensively. Our explorative journey reinforced many issues encountered in our research, made all the more compelling because we were dealing with a living monument that continues to play a compli-cated part in the arena of a democratic South Africa. It made us doubly aware of the need to approach research from multiple angles, using as wide a variety of sources as possible, and to acknowledge that "historical truth" is a construction—as much for us in our writing, as for those who conceived and carried out the Voortrekker Monument and conceptualized its story. Our project has heightened our affinity with the perspectives of different cultural actors and ideol-ogies, and urged us to rethink our European heritage and the preconceptions it imparts. For us these realizations have been—and will continue to be—both rewarding and challenging, as scholars in the humanities and as social and political beings.

1   The context, concept, process of making, and form of the monument and its frieze (including iconog-raphy and style) are comprehensively discussed in Elizabeth Rankin and Rolf Michael Schneider, *From Memory to Marble: The Historical Frieze of the Voortrekker Monument. Part I: The Frieze* and *Part II: The Scenes* (Berlin: De Gruyter, and Cape Town: African Minds, 2020), hereafter Rankin and Schneider 2020, pt. I and pt. II. We do not reference the individual scenes of the frieze as the section on each can easily be found online in Part II; for clarity, their names are in italics. The two volumes are fully searchable on open ac-cess at https://www.degruyter.com/search?query=keywordValues%3A%28Voortrekker%29&document-TypeFacet=book and https://www.africanminds.co.za/from-memory-to-marble-part-i/. All their images are searchable in the digital database *Spotlight at Stanford* under "Voortrekker Monumentality", https://exhibits.stanford.edu/fmtm.
2   Mandela drew analogies between the resistance of Africans and Afrikaners to British imperialism in a 2002 speech at the Voortrekker Monument, during the unveiling of a statue of a hero of the Anglo-Boer war, saying that "the shared experience of fighting for one's freedom binds us in a manner that is profound" (*The Herald*, March 7, 2002).
3   Giliomee 2003, xiv.
4   *The Voortrekker Monument Pretoria* 1955, 36–37.
5   *The Voortrekker Monument Pretoria* 1955, 37. For the Sydney, Leipzig, and further (inter)national structures considered for the design of the Voortrekker Monument, see Rankin and Schneider 2020, pt. I, 131–37.
6   For Moerdyk's various designs and comparanda, see Rankin and Schneider 2020, pt. I, 80–154.
7   Heymans and Theart-Peddle 2007, 10; *The Voortrekker Monument Pretoria* 1955, 55 identifies it as "Parys granite."
8   Rankin and Schneider 2020, pt. I, 6 fig. 3.

9   There is an unfortunate irony in the fact that, having survived anticipated political closure, the monument has come under extreme financial threat recently because of restrictions preventing its customary high volume of visitors during the Covid-19 pandemic.

10   Rankin and Schneider 2020, pt. I, 410 fig. 328.

11   https://commons.wikimedia.org/wiki/Category:Museum_of_the_Voortrekker_Monument.

12   For the political heritage context, see Parker 2017, 487.

13   Renowned South African photographer David Goldblatt recorded one of these gatherings, *The Voortrekker Monument and a Sunday service of the ultraconservative Afrikaanse Protestantse Kerk (Afrikaans Protestant Church) after a rally of rightwing Afrikaners who threatened war if South Africa became a non-racial democracy, Pretoria, Transvaal, May 27, 1990*; Rankin and Schneider 2020, pt. I, 420 fig. 336.

14   *Sunday Times*, December 15, 1996; Rankin and Schneider 2020, pt. I, 420–21 fig. 337.

15   https://www.sanews.gov.za/south-africa/voortrekker-monument-now-national-heritage-site.   For   the concept of shared cultures, see Parker 2017, 486–89.

16   See, for example, Etherington 2001; Giliomee 2003; Laband 1995; Thompson 1995; Worden 2000; Laband 2021.

17   Rankin and Schneider 2020, pt. I, 459 fig. 378.

18   Rankin and Schneider 2020, pt. I, 458 fig. 377.

19   Rankin and Schneider 2020, pt. I, 455–77; http://minnettevari.co.za/video/chimera-white-edition (accessed July 19, 2023).

20   For Freedom Park, see Oliphant et al. 2014; for a comparison with the Voortrekker Monument, see Rankin 2017; Rankin and Schneider 2020, pt. I, 409–13 figs 330, 331.

21   Rankin and Schneider 2020, pt. I, 412 fig. 331.

22   Rankin and Schneider 2020, pt. I, 430 fig. 343.

23   An unconventional approach that is similar, yet different, is found in Almon 2015.

24   Webb and Wright 1976–2014, published in six volumes. It seemed clear that African oral history was not considered in developing the frieze narrative, although it throws light on many aspects. Laband 2021 exemplifies the historical value of these telling narratives.

25   Rankin and Schneider 2020, pt. I, 60–65.

26   Rankin and Schneider 2020, pt. II, 290–96 figs 13.19–13.22.

27   For discussion and reproductions of the evidence, Rankin and Schneider 2020, pt. II, 203–66.

28   Schoeman 2003, 113.

29   Bird 1965, 259.

30   Rankin and Schneider 2020, pt. I, 177–217.

31   Rankin and Schneider 2020, pt. I, 188–217.

32   *The Voortrekker Monument Pretoria* 1955, 40.

33   Rankin and Schneider 2020, pt. I, 302–4 figs 228, 229.

34   There were minor changes called for on occasion, usually related to the accuracy of detail, particularly in the initial sketches and maquettes during the early stages of design. One major intervention came from the government after the *Rand Daily Mail*, February 15, 1945, claimed that some of the more violent episodes in the frieze, *Murder of Retief and his Men* and *Massacre of Women and Children at Bloukrans*, could stir up racial tension. Rankin and Schneider 2020, pt. I, 252–57.

35   Rankin and Schneider 2020, pt. I, 181 fig. 116, 247–49.

36   So characterized by Romanelli; Rankin and Schneider 2020, pt. I, 265.

37   The Romanelli family still runs the studio: https://www.raffaelloromanelli.com (accessed July 19, 2023).

38   *The Voortrekker Monument Pretoria* 1955, 41.

39   Potgieter 1987; Laurika Postma, Letters from Italy, Postma Folder, University of Pretoria Archive.

40   For the difference in style, Rankin and Schneider 2020, pt. I, 291–351.

41   Potgieter 1987, 11–39.

42   Rankin and Schneider 2020, pt. II, 94–95 fig. 5.13.

43   Rankin and Schneider 2020, pt. I, 221.

44   Rankin and Schneider 2020, pt. I, 224–25 figs. 158, 159.

45   Potgieter 1987, 19, 22–23, 42.

46   Potgieter 1987, 47.

47   *The Treaty with Dingane*; *Mpande Proclaimed King of the Zulu*; *Death of Dingane*.

48   *The Voortrekker Monument Pretoria* 1955—further editions 1957, 1960, 1963, 1966, 1969, 1970.

49   For a wider context, see Foxhall et al. 2020.

50   While Moerdyk insists on the historical accuracy of the scene, Nico Coetzee clarifies that the representa-
      tion, showing the Zulu total subjugation, "has only the vaguest probable historical basis": the message
      is "that thus did the force of order, the white man on his horse, overcome the dark forces of chaos! It is
      propaganda." See Coetzee 1988, 184–85.

51   Rankin and Schneider 2020, pt. I, 401, 403 fig. 321.

Bibliography

Almon, Peta. 2015. *The Design of the Makana Monument in Grahamstown: A Pathway of Memory Inspired by Nature,
    Mediating Public and Sacred Space, as a Regenerative Mechanism of a Forgotten Place*. Grahamstown: Nelson
    Mandela Metropolitan University. http://hdl.handle.net/10948/41283 (accessed May 30, 2023).

Bird, John. 1965. *The Annals of Natal: 1495 to 1845*, vol. II. Cape Town: C. Struik; facsimile repr. of 1888 ed.

Coetzee, Nico. 1988. "Die Voorstelling van die Voortrekkers in die Kuns." In J.S. Bergh, ed., *Herdenkingsjaar 1988:
    Portugese, Hugenote en Voortrekkers*, 177–89. Pretoria: De Jager-Haum.

Etherington, Norman. 2001. *The Great Treks: The Transformation of Southern Africa, 1815–1854*. London: Pearson Ed-
    ucation.

Foxhall, Lin, Hans-Joachim Gehrke, and Nino Luraghi, eds. 2020. *Intentional History: Spinning Time in Ancient Greece*.
    Stuttgart: Franz Steiner.

Giliomee, Hermann. 2003. *The Afrikaners: Biography of a People*. Cape Town: Tafelberg Publishers.

Heymans, Riana, and Salomé Theart-Peddle. 2007. *The Voortrekker Monument: Visitors Guide and Souvenir*. Pretoria:
    Voortrekker Monument and Nature Reserve.

Laband, John. 1995. *Rope of Sand: The Rise and Fall of the Zulu Kingdom*. Johannesburg: Jonathan Ball, 1995.

Laband, John. 2021. *The Zulu Kingdom and the Boer Invasion of 1837–40*. Warwick: Helion & Company.

Oliphant, Andries Walter, Mongane Wally Serote, and Pattabi Ganapathi Raman, eds. 2014. *Freedom Park: A Place of
    Emancipation and Meaning*. Pretoria: Freedom Park.

Parker, Grant. 2017. "Classical Heritage? By Way of an Afterword." In Grant Parker, ed., *South Africa, Greece, Rome:
    Classical Confrontations*, 485–95. Cambridge: Cambridge University Press.

Potgieter, Hennie. 1987. *Voortrekker Monument*. Pretoria: Hennie's Secretarial Services.

Rankin, Elizabeth. 2017. "A Janus-Like Juncture: Reconciling Past and Present at the Voortrekker Monument and
    Freedom Park." In Kim Miller and Brenda Schmahmann, eds., *Public Sculpture in South Africa: Bronze Warriors
    and Plastic Presidents*, 3–28. Bloomington: Indiana University Press.

Rankin, Elizabeth, and Rolf Michael Schneider. 2020. *From Memory to Marble: The Historical Frieze of the Voortrekker
    Monument. Part I: The Frieze* and *Part II: The Scenes*. Berlin: De Gruyter, and Cape Town: African Minds. https://
    www.degruyter.com/search?query=keywordValues%3A%28Voortrekker%29&documentTypeFacet=book;
    https://www.africanminds.co.za/from-memory-to-marble-part-i.

Schoeman, Karel. 2003. *Die Wêreld van Susanna Smit, 1799–1863*. Pretoria: Protea Boek Huis; repr. of 1995 ed.

Thompson, Leonard. 1995. *A History of South Africa*. New Haven: Yale University Press.

The Voortrekker Monument Pretoria: Official Guide. 1955. Pretoria: The Board of Control of the Voortrekker Monu-
    ment.

Webb, Colin de B., and John B. Wright, eds. 1976–2014. *The James Stuart Archive of Recorded Oral Evidence to the
    History of the Zulu and Neighbouring Peoples*, 6 vols. Pietermaritzburg: University of Natal Press, and Durban:
    Killie Campbell Africana Library.

Worden, Nigel. 2000. *The Making of Modern South Africa*. Oxford: Blackwell.

Image Sources

1   Photo courtesy of University of South Africa, Department of Library Services, Pretoria: J.L. van Schaik Publishers, Photograph album 1949, Voortrekker Monument Inauguration.

2   Courtesy of Heritage Foundation Archives at Voortrekker Monument, Pretoria: Photographic Collection, F 39.1.35 k; photo by Alan Yates.

3   Courtesy of the artist; photo © Die Erfenisstigting; Voortrekker Monument 1838–1938, 62.

4   Courtesy of 2012Media24; foto24 Brendan Croft.

5, 8, 9   Courtesy of Voortrekker Monument; photos by Russell Scott.

6   Photo courtesy of the artist.

7   Photo courtesy of Graham Young, retrieved from a downed drone, owner unknown.

10   Photo courtesy of Heritage Foundation Archives at Voortrekker Monument, Pretoria: Photographic Collection, F 39.10.7 k.

11   Photo courtesy of Heritage Foundation Archives at Voortrekker Monument, Pretoria: Photographic Collection, F 39.10.9 k.

JENS WIEDOW

Representing the Mandate
The South-West Africa Pavilion at the Van Riebeeck Festival

Three months of pageantry, parades, and festivities were held in Cape Town between February 1 and April 6, 1952 to celebrate the "achievements" of 300 years of western "civilization" in southern Africa since the arrival of Dutch merchant Jan van Riebeeck in 1652. The Van Riebeeck Festival aimed at displaying the progress of industry in the realization of a modern nation-state, while promoting the aims of nation-building in the Union of South Africa (the Union). Founding narratives surrounding "those who carried the torch of western civilization to this southern corner of Africa" were promoted at the festival under the official slogan "South Africa after 300 years – We Build a Nation".[1]

The mandate territory of South-West Africa (SWA), governed by the Union as a fifth province, presented its exhibit in a pavilion prominently located in the Union section alongside the pavilions for the Cape, Natal, and Free State provinces. This exhibit closely followed the overall themes of the festival, under the motto "We Build a Nation," to show local development in SWA and its contribution to the economic advancement of the Union. This contribution was to be shown in an exhibit displaying "developmental progress" in the territory from pre-history, through the arrival of European civilization posited as the beginning of history, to the establishment of modern industry under Union rule. This pavilion proved to be one of the most popular at the festival, drawing between 7,000 and 10,000 visitors a day. Spectators queued for hours at the entrance of the pavilion (fig. 1), not so much to view the developmental displays, but rather to observe the exhibit of "primitive Bushmen" that had been brought to Cape Town from SWA for the duration of the festival.[2]

This "Native Exhibit" was one of two exhibits at the festival aimed at producing a narrative of primitivism surrounding the indigenous African population to contrast with displays of "European civilisation, modern development and progress," thereby legitimizing settler colonialism in southern Africa. The first exhibit, called the "Bantu" exhibition, for which a special pavilion was built by the Union Native Affairs Department, displayed various African tribes and their social and material "development" under the "guiding hand" of European "civilisation" in a series of spaces showing a developmental "evolution." At the second exhibition, forming part of the South-West Africa pavilion, none of the developmental narratives were played out. Here Africans were framed as being outside of history, incapable of development, and in need of protection from the "deleterious" effects of western civilization.

National exhibitions such as this festival have been important means for countries to strengthen national identities through representations of nationhood to their own residents and the world ever since the Great Exhibition in London of 1851. The national exhibition became

1   Visitors queueing in front of the SWA Pavilion to see the "Bushmen."

a formalized repertoire combining aspects of architecture, didactic display, urban design, and public amusement that were transmitted internationally through an exhibitionary network.[3] Exhibitions provided a stage where industrially manufactured objects, products, and machinery were exhibited to domestic audiences, urban centers could display their modernity, and the nation could celebrate economic, social, and industrial progress. Aiming at producing a homogenous perspective of an orderly world, curated displays in these exhibitions typically followed systems of classification that allocated specific places for everything and everyone. Exhibitions furthermore played an important role in persuading visitors of the necessity for colonial expansion and its civilizing mission by contrasting displays showing exotic "Native Villages" with spectacles of modernity. Displays of colonized peoples were part of the standard repertoire of expositions from the late nineteenth century up to the end of the 1930s, and were intimately related to the aims of colonialism.

The aim of these displays was two-fold. First, they "reaffirmed the colonizing society's racial superiority, manifest in its technical, scientific, and moral development" by constructing binary notions of self /other that were fundamental for the identity production of newly established nation-states.[4] Second, they represented the object of Europe's self-imposed civilizing mission by displaying the colonized as lacking both development and civilization. In this way, the colonial project of bringing enlightenment, development, and progress to the world could be justified and simultaneously communicated to the metropolitan spectators of these exhibitions. As Zeynep Çelik argues, the means of representing these others was to display them in "authentic" settings, dressed in typical costumes and performing typical activities.[5] These representations were informed by ethnographic theories of the nineteenth century that proposed an evolutionary hierarchy along which different people were assigned places according to their stage of development, ranging from the "primitive" to the "civilized." While ethnographic exhibitions were common throughout the world at the turn of the century, by the late 1930s this practice had been largely abandoned due to accusations of racism and emerging critiques of imperialism.[6] In the Union of South Africa, the practice of exporting Africans to international expositions outside of Africa was increasingly viewed with suspicion, primarily due to misplaced fears that they would be "ruined and spoilt" by exposure to "western civilization." However, the practice of hosting ethnographic displays within the Union continued as control over the movement and exposure of Africans could be assured through the mechanisms of segregationist policies commonly known as Apartheid. The role of architecture in the exhibitionary project was to inform visitors with buildings that provided "a quick and realistic impression of the culture and society represented."[7] Pavilions were often designed to emulate national styles, aiming to display national character or even produce hybrid structures that combined stylistic elements from the metropoles with those of the colonies. Within pavilions, hierarchies were established by adopting arrangements where displays of the colonized as timeless primitives were split from those of the colonizers, in order to show industrial and modern progress. This contrast was heightened by differentiating the material palate and construction method of either section, making the difference perceptible to visitors as a tactile experience. Beyond issues pertaining to the differentiation of displays through architecture, the movement and living conditions of the colonized at expositions were carefully controlled through the architecture of their temporary accommodations.

Much has been written about the construction of national displays at national exhibitions through architectural expression, predominantly focusing on those held by European nations between the late nineteenth and early twentieth centuries.[8] Few works, however, deal with exhibitions in southern Africa during the mid-twentieth century when the trend of hosting national exhibitions was experiencing a widespread decline.[9] Those that do discuss these exhibitions focus on the construction of a national history of the Union, without discussing the role that architecture played in these festivals.[10] By focusing on the display of, and control over, Africans exhibited and accommodated at the SWA pavilion, this article aims to uncover the entanglement of architecture and colonialism. In the first section, the colonial relation between the Union and SWA is discussed, highlighting how Africans were administered, and what spaces this colonial administration produced. The second section introduces the SWA pavilion to provide a brief overview of the building and its exhibits, followed by an outline of how the prevailing ethnographic knowledge about Africans in SWA informed the production of architectural space. This is done by examining previously unpublished archival material comprising minutes of the SWA organizing committee meetings and correspondence between its members and actors in the organization of the SWA Pavilion, through which the debates surrounding the pavilion design process and its subsequent development are clarified. This is complemented by examining the architectural drawings of the pavilion that show a development in the design in relation to ongoing debates, primarily surrounding the accommodation of Africans, with an emphasis on which spaces were produced and how these resulted from political and practical considerations.[11]

The SWA Mandate: A Sacred Trust of Civilization

Following the short-lived yet brutal German colonial occupation of SWA, control of the territory was transferred to the Union of South Africa under the League of Nations mandates

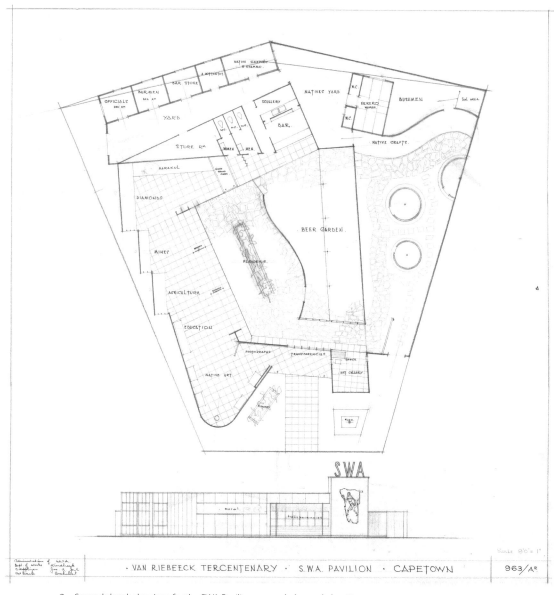

2   Second sketch drawings for the SWA Pavilion, ground plan and elevation.

system.[12] This mandate system provided for stewardship to be granted to "advanced countries" over territories "inhabited by peoples not yet able to stand by themselves under the strenuous conditions of the modern world, there should be applied the principle that the well-being and development of such peoples form a sacred trust of civilisation."[13] Marion Wallace observes that "the [Union] government's objective was to establish a new colonial order, including a smooth-running economy if direct benefit to South Africa. Governance of Africans in the territory was intimately linked to this aim."[14] Thus, the Union imposed a system of governance closely related to its own. The SWA administration was populated by Union civil servants endorsing laws modelled on those in the metropole. Rural land in SWA was allocated for Union settlement programs, while all mineral resources were expropriated for exploitation by Union companies. To effectively develop agricultural production and extract the mineral wealth, the Union imposed a raft of segregation laws and tax regimes, commonly referred to as Apartheid policy, on the African population, thereby bolstering a migrant labor force that had already been established under German rule.[15] African migrant workers travelled to urban centers, mines, and settler farms where they were housed in temporary housing called "compounds," which were often built as rudimentary structures at the least cost to the employer. Movement of Africans in urban compounds was controlled through curfews and restrictive pass laws. Africans were barred from land ownership throughout the territory, and their settlement rights limited to Tribal Areas, Native Reserves and so-called Native Townships. The territory was split between the so-called Police Zone, inhabited by a mix of German, English, and Afrikaner settlers to the south, and African Tribal Areas to the north. This split was articulated by an internal settler and "veterinary" boundary called the Red Line, described by Giorgio Miescher as an "imperial barbarian boundary."[16] This boundary delineated the limits of European settlement and separated areas deemed "civilized" from "darkest" Africa beyond. As a "veterinary" boundary, it furthermore allowed authorities to easily differentiate between what was considered "healthy" as residing south of the line and "diseased" as being present to the north of it, a distinction applied to both animals and people.

After the Second World War, and the replacement of the League of Nations by the United Nations, formal attempts were made by the Union to the UN for official annexation of SWA as a fifth province. To a large extent, this annexation was merely a formal gesture, as the Union had by that stage achieved almost full control over SWA. The UN rejected these annexation attempts, stating that Apartheid legislation and the treatment of Africans under these laws were inconsistent with the terms of the mandate. As with other former mandate territories, the UN preferred the establishment of a trust territory to be administered by a UN trusteeship council in preparation for eventual independence. Central to the Union argument was that the population of SWA remained undeveloped and incapable of running their own affairs.

With this political control being questioned on the international stage, the Van Riebeeck Festival could not have come at a better time for the Union to display its stewardship over the inhabitants of territory at the SWA pavilion. This stewardship was framed both in terms of modern development—albeit for the exclusive benefit of the settler population—and of the necessity of protecting Africans from the dangers of the modern world. These ideas of development and protection strongly influenced the architectural design of the pavilion and the arrangement of its spaces.

The Pavilion and its Exhibits

The SWA pavilion comprised a low-slung horizontal building featuring a vertical tower element at its entrance. Four sections were built to incorporate two exhibition courtyards, an open area for the "Bushmen", and a service yard at the back (fig. 2). Visitors were guided past a representative patch of lawn along a paved walkway to a covered entrance between a staggered exhi-

3   SWA pavilion staff guiding visitors through the evolutionary display in the main exhibition courtyard.

bition wall and the tower, which featured two painted friezes reproducing a famous rock art panel. Passing the main entrance, a central courtyard featured the main exhibition placed under a lean-to roof that wrapped around three sides. A sequence of "evolutionary" displays presented the social, industrial, and economic "development" in the territory, arranged along a diachronic narrative from prehistory to the "highest" forms of industrial production, highlighting the role played by settlers (fig. 3).[17] Spectators were guided past a "traditional" German beer garden representative of a European tradition, doubling back to pass by the tower hosting an art exhibition on the virtues of nature conservation, to enter the second exhibition courtyard through a movable partition gate.[18] This courtyard was placed between the SWA pavilion and the neighboring Natal pavilion and featured the African display that presented two African tribes, the "Bushmen" and "Owambo." Visitors were guided through an open performance space where the "Bushmen" could dance and display their crafts under a shelter built of rough split poles. Behind this "Native" Shelter, the "Owambo" were seen working copper into various artefacts, weaving basket-ware, and crafting timber implements around two traditional rondavels built of natural materials imported from SWA. Reporters wishing to know more about the "Bushmen" could enter an enclosed space at the back of the site, where a white official would mediate questions, and translate replies.[19] Finally, visitors could exit the pavilion adjacent to the tower leading off the African display area.

Two linear accommodation compounds arranged around the service yard were placed behind the main pavilion. Access to these compounds was either via a service passage leading to the central courtyard or from the African Display Area. A service gate connected the service yard to the festival grounds along the eastern elevation. The two accommodation areas provided separated rooms allocated to white officials and four African tribes, each segregated by race and tribe, with buffer spaces consisting of storage rooms placed between spaces allocated to officials and Africans. The entire pavilion, save for the African Exhibit, was built as a modern tim-ber-framed construction covered with smooth asbestos cement sheeting on a low face-brick plinth. Columns surrounding the main courtyard were tubular steel sections and the surface was paved out in pre-cast concrete pavers. In contrast to the main exhibit space, all materials used for the African section were natural and unfinished materials comprising split poles and thatch roof covering. The floor was either surfaced in unfinished slate paving to define the visitors' paths or left uncovered in the areas where Africans were expected to perform their crafts. Most of the structures in the African display were built by the Africans themselves to lend an air of authen-ticity and reduce the overall cost of construction.[20]

Representing and Accommodating Africans

At the festival, African displays were seen as crucial in highlighting the achievements of modern development under settler control against the backdrop of primitive and undeveloped Africans in need of European civilization. This contrast would show the necessity of colonial occupation as well as the self-imposed civilizing mandate of the settler state. At the "Bantu" pavilion, the display of Africans showed their material development under the guiding hand of the Union Native Affairs Department. "Primitive" Africans were shown as becoming "developed" through the influence of "western" education, medicine, and the Christian religion, into a modern work-force. Individual freedom through the introduction of "western law and order" was posited as the highest virtue against the "deprivations" of tribalism.[21]

In contrast to these "developmental" displays, the African exhibit at the SWA pavilion aimed to show a perspective on Apartheid policy as being more concerned with stewardship than "social upliftment." Africans were shown in their "natural surroundings [depicting] a phase in the history of Africa that is fast fading," protected from the dangers of modern civilization by mem-bers of the SWA Native Affairs Department.[22] An article in *Die Suidwester* even proposed a histor-ical link between the "Bushmen" and the landing of Van Riebeeck, when proclaiming that they represented the "closest to [those] Bushmen Van Riebeeck would have encountered."[23] In this display the "Bushmen" were posited as the opposite to everything the modern industrial nation represented, a representation in line with the racialized ideologies informed by the anthropo-logical research of the time.

A Native Affairs Sub-Committee led by P. J. Schoeman and R. F. Morris of the SWA Native Affairs Department (NAD), was established to advise the organizing committee on the selection criteria for "suitable" Africans, as well as their transportation to and accommodation during the festival. As Gordon points out, the NAD had been responsible for the administration of Africans in SWA, based partially on the ethnographic knowledge of the time and on the role of "experts in the field" such as anthropologist-cum-game ranger P. J. Schoeman.[24] Prior to taking up the post as game warden in SWA, Schoeman played a leading role in the study of "Bantukunde" (Bantu Studies) at the University of Stellenbosch Anthropology Department in the 1940s where he strongly argued that Africans "should be isolated in reserves as far as possible so that the western influences could be controlled," fearing that miscegenation would dilute the purity of African, and European, blood.[25] Both Schoeman and Morris were members of the Commission for the Preservation of Bushmen, tasked to investigate the decrease in the "Bushmen" population. Their reported findings attributed this decrease to the presence of "syphilis and other contagious diseases" caused by contact with other cultures.[26] As a remedy, Schoeman proposed the creation of a "Bushmen" reserve in which they "could be controlled and their race preserved."[27] The sub-committee established a clear selection procedure for ten to twelve "Bushmen…of short stature… dressed in their natural clothes" to perform at the festival. All Africans were paid an allowance, provided with free lodging and food, and medically examined before departing for Cape Town. Raw materials for building huts, shelters, and manufacturing crafts were brought along, and the "Bushmen" gathered sufficient natural produce for their subsistence.[28] The sub-committee strongly advised that the Africans be accompanied by white officials at all times. Morris and Schoeman personally selected sixteen "Bushmen" from north-eastern SWA, to be joined by twelve "Owambos", four "Herero" women and three "Hottentot" translators.[29] As the "Owambo" and "Bushmen" were selected from tribal areas north of the Red Line, the fear of contagion was a substantial factor, resulting in the Africans being compounded in segregated accommodations, kept apart from each other and from white officials.[30] The "Bushmen" were medically examined and vaccinated against smallpox at Rundu, then transported ten miles outside Windhoek where they camped for the night before boarding the train the following day.[31] All Africans were seated in a separate train compartment arranged for the trip to Cape Town, and kept under constant medical supervision by Schoeman's wife. This concern for the health of the "Bushmen" continued in Cape Town. Schoeman arranged for another medical examination by Professor J.F. Brock at the University of Cape Town, and requested Brock to arrange for medical students to give the "Bushmen" daily inspections, fearing that their health "might suffer on account of the drastic change in climate."[32]

The staging of African ethnographic displays at the festival was heavily contested. Partly in response to the festival, and certainly in protest against disenfranchisement of Africans through increasingly severe Apartheid legislation, the festival was widely decried by African opposition groups as a festival of hate. These groups banded together to advocate non-collaboration with plans to incorporate Africans in pageants and exhibitions at the festival, resulting in a widespread boycott of the event.[33] Finding local Africans to perform at the "Bantu" pavilion had been impossible for the organizing committee due to this boycott, leaving the organizers no choice but to import Africans from "as far away as Sterkspruit in the Eastern Cape." Initially planned to be accommodated in the African township of Langa, the performers were "made to feel very unwelcome" and had to be relocated to a vacant military camp on the opposite side of the Cape Peninsula.[34] Similar accommodation challenges were faced by the sub-committee to find appropriate housing for Africans and accompanying white officials. Offers to house Africans in the Native Townships were rejected as segregation laws prevented white officials from staying in the locations while, under the same laws, Africans were not allowed to be accommodated outside of the locations unless compounded in segregated accommodation.

Beyond the legal prohibitions, the main concern of the committee was that the Africans from SWA would come under the influence of those who opposed the festival. The Africans were initially to be displayed and accommodated in the "Bantu" pavilion, for which permission from the Union NAD was sought.[35] As the performers at this pavilion were not to be accommodated on the Van Riebeeck Festival grounds, the request was turned down and the suggestion made that the SWA committee find alternative accommodation and host their own display.[36] Recommendations were made by the VRF committee to house "all Natives except the Bushmen… at Langa Native Township," while the Cape Town municipal authorities suggested a "temporary tent site…at Nyanga Native Township."[37] Neither of the proposed solutions suited the SWA committee, who threatened to withhold African participation altogether. Further petitions to the VRF committee to allow accommodation on the pavilion site were initially turned down due to police concerns about having "dangerous barbarians wandering about the fairgrounds," with the Union NAD voicing additional concerns about the bodily odor of the "Bushmen" and their sanitary habits.[38] Bruwer Blignaut, the chairman of the SWA organizing committee, responded to these concerns, in a letter to the Union NAD, claiming that provisions had been made for continual supervision and that the "Native Area" would be surrounded by a "solid high wall" and be locked every night. Additionally, "the Natives and Bushmen would maybe be terrified in such an unfamiliar place, and to assure them, we arranged to have white officials overnight at the pavilion." As the African Exhibition was a key part of the overall narrative of the festival, permission to accommodate Africans was eventually granted, on the condition that they be kept under close supervision and control.[39]

While the design of the SWA pavilion had made provision for an African display area from the beginning, the accommodation of Africans had not been fully resolved until late during the construction of the pavilion, once the question of where Africans would be housed was settled. How different tribes were to be accommodated without subjecting them to inter-tribal contact was another issue that required resolution. These planning problems were resolved by SWA State Architect J. A. Joel, drawing on standardized compound types that were used in public buildings and state housing throughout SWA at the time (fig. 4).

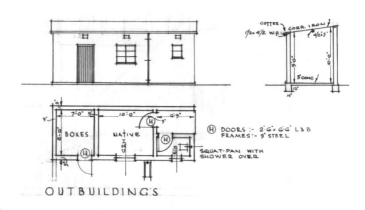

4 Type Compound for African Servants built throughout SWA.

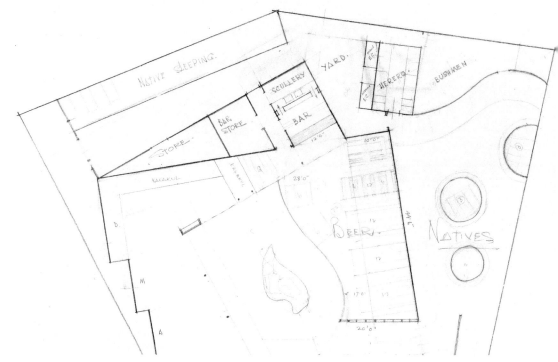

5   First sketch drawings for the SWA Pavilion, detail of the ground plan.

The first draft design proposed by Joel showed three accommodation compounds located behind the main exhibition space. One compound provided sleeping space for "Natives" and another for "Herero" women placed adjacent to the "Bushmen Enclosure," comprising an open space with an enclosed "Soil Area" acting as an ablution space.[40] All spaces were connected by a service yard (fig. 5). By the time of the second sketch design, the African compound had been sub-divided to accommodate European officials who acted as supervisors to the Africans, and dedicated rooms further segregated to reflect the tribal composition of their occupants (see fig. 2).

The construction drawings showed no accommodation compounds, as Joel noted in a letter to Blignaut.[41] Compounds were later added to the construction drawings of November 1951, showing a similar relation between spaces to the second sketch design. Ablutions were changed to differentiate visitors' toilets from those serving Africans. However, a revised drawing of December 1951 showed major changes to the "Bushmen Enclosure." Initially planned to be left wholly uncovered, the space was enclosed to protect them from "the drastic change in climate." All door openings linking the "Enclosure" to the service yard were omitted to prevent contact between the "Bushmen" and members of other African tribes (fig. 6). These changes in the planning indicate that the NAD, specifically Blignaut and Schoeman, had an influence on the planning throughout the design process to align the spatial organization of the pavilion to the prevailing racial ideology of the NAD, strongly influenced by "Bantukunde."

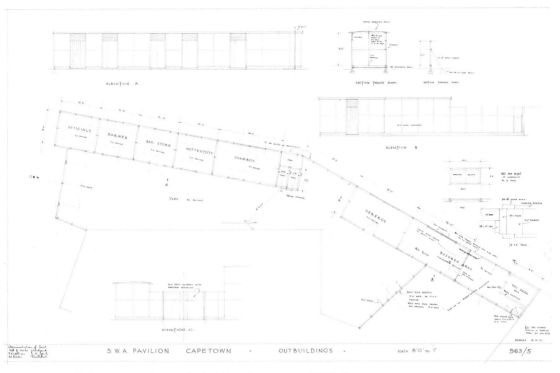

6   Final construction drawings for the African Quarters at the SWA Pavilion.

Conclusion

Beyond providing a didactic display of the territory, its peoples, and industries to the visiting public, the pavilion and its exhibits displayed the practices and policies involved in the colonial development of SWA. Exhibits, comprising both things and people, followed an ordering principle where everything was assigned its "natural" place and arranged in a "scientific" order. The spatial arrangement at the festival closely mirrored the ordering of colonial space in SWA. The split between the exhibition courtyards, one showing modern development brought about by the European settler state, and the other two the supposed a-historical practices of African tribes, emulated the territorial segregation between the tribal areas and the Police Zone. The difference between these spaces was further heightened by contrasting industrial and natural materials used in their construction. By framing Africans as susceptible to foreign influence and in need of stewardship and protection from the "strenuous conditions of the modern world," greater control over African movement was legitimized. This control was exercised at the festival in the two compounds where segregation between people along racial and tribal lines was implemented to prevent "influence and contagion" among those accommodated at the pavilion site and the festival area beyond. Especially the design of the "Bushmen Enclosure" displayed the disposition of the SWA committee towards skewed notions of stewardship. This space provided the bare minimum of facilities, only receiving an enclosed room for sleeping at a late stage in the

125

design process of the Pavilion, to produce a natural setting where they could "sleep under the stars."[42] Spatial segregation of "Bushmen" from the other Africans at the pavilion allowed as little contact as possible, as the entrances to the "Enclosure" and the other compounds were separated and access controlled by NAD staff, to avoid what was perceived as deleterious influence on the supposed "purity and innocence" of the "Bushmen." The extensive health inspections and concerns about the sanitary habits of Africans not only determined the arrangement of space at the festival, but also the logistical arrangements made to transport Africans to Cape Town.

Following the festival, the exhibits were demounted, the pavilion demolished, and the Africans returned to tribal areas north of the Red Line. The exhibition materials were re-used in an exhibition on SWA at South Africa House, London in 1954 to continue representing the colonial narratives of "stewardship and development" to the world.

1   Central Committee 1952, 7.
2   Historical terminology used in the sources is generally retained. When possible the term "African" is used over racializing terms such as "Native", "Bantu", or "Hottentott." Where this substitution detracts from legibility, the original historic terminology is maintained and placed in quotation marks. The same applies for tribal definitions such as "Bushmen," "Owambo," "Herero" etc., which are understood as colonial constructs. The use of binary terms such as "civilized/savage" are used in the historical sources, but it is not the author's intent to reproduce these. All translations from German and Afrikaans are those of the author.
3   Geppert 2010, 6–11.
4   Çelik 1992, 18.
5   Çelik 1992, 18.
6   Corbey 1993.
7   Çelik 1992, introduction.
8   See for example two important works on the Paris Colonial Exposition: Morton 2000 and Çelik 1992.
9   Geppert, Coffey, and Lau 2006 provide a comprehensive overview of literature relating to international expositions; however, the Van Riebeeck Festival is overlooked in this bibliography.
10 For the Van Riebeeck Festival, see Rassool and Witz 1993; Rassool et al. 1996; Witz 2003. For works discussing the Johannesburg Empire Exhibition, see for example Coe 2001 and Robinson 2003.
11 The following holdings in the Namibian National Archive were consulted: Committee Minutes of the Van Riebeeck Festival Organising Committee, the Blignaut Accession, Public Works Department Files, specifically PWD 203. Architectural drawings of the pavilion by state architect J.A. Joel are found in the Namibian Ministry of Public Works and Transport Drawing Archive. Newsprint articles published in the German-language publication *Allgemeine Zeitung*, the Afrikaner *Die Suidwester* and *Die Suidwest Afrikaner* can be found in the Namibian National Library.
12 For the German colonial period, see Wallace 2011, 115–204.
13 League of Nations 1919.
14 Wallace 2011, 244–45.
15 For background to Apartheid policy and its spatial effects, see Christopher 1994.
16 Miescher 2012.
17 Correspondence B. Blignaut to E. Ullmann, February 4, 1952, SWAA fonds, Box 0981, File A/90/21; "Südwest Pavillon" 1952.
18 The beer garden was conceived as a means of showing the contribution to the development in SWA of the German settler community who remained in SWA after the regime change.
19 Witz 2003, 210.
20 The structures in the African Section were marked as being "out of contract" in the plans.
21 NAN A0019 Bruwer Blignaut Accession: Minutes of the Central Organizing Committee, October 29, 1951, 9–10.

22 Witz 2003, 208.

23 "Suidwes se Boesmans" 1952.

24 This ethnographic knowledge was deeply influenced by a book published for the League of Nations called *The Native Tribes of SWA* which used Social-Darwinist theories to characterize African population groups as "primordial and unchanging tribes" and assign the "Bushmen" a place "on the lowest rung of the evolutionary ladder." Wallace 2011, 237.

25 Gordon 2021, 89.

26 An example of this "influence" is observed in a letter by Morris to Blignaut, cautioning about the influence a "Hottentot" translator could have on the "primitive Bushmen" at the fair. He states that this translator had become an alcoholic after being spoilt by the Americans following the Denver Expedition of 1926. Correspondence R.F. Morris to B. Blignaut, February 4, 1952, SWAA fonds, Box 0982, File A/90/21/1.

27 Gordon adds that Schoeman's assessment of the situation ignores the impact of colonialism and exploitation. Gordon 2021, 90–94.

28 Onderkomitee insake Inboorlinge, notule van eerste Versameling, September 25, 1951, SWAA fonds, Box 0982, File A/90/21/1.

29 The selection of Bushmen traveling to Cape Town was framed as Schoeman exercising his "scientific knowledge." See Witz 2003, 209; Rassool et al. 1996, 263.

30 Fears surrounding contagion including a preoccupation with hygiene was widespread amongst colonial settlers, and was one of the root causes of segregation policy in the Union and SWA. See e.g Swanson 1977 or Wallace 2002.

31 "Bushmen pass through" 1952; under the Urban Areas Act, the Bushmen would not have been able to overnight in Windhoek.

32 Correspondence B. Blignaut to Dr. Schoeman, February 18, 1952, SWAA fonds, Box 0982, File A/90/21; Correspondence B. Blignaut to Prof. J.F. Brock, February 11, 1952, SWAA fonds, Box 0982, File A/90/21. The warm Mediterranean climatic conditions at the Cape are indeed different to those of sub-tropical northern Namibia.

33 Witz 2003, 144–79.

34 Witz 2003, 196.

35 Correspondence from Blignaut to Native Affairs Department, September 15, 1951, Bruwer Blignaut fonds.

36 Correspondence from Blignaut to Native Affairs Department, October 8, 1951, SWAA fonds, Box 0981, File A/90/1.

37 Correspondence from Cape Town Divisional Council to SWA Administration Secretary, January 26, 1952, SWAA fonds, Box 0982, File A/90/21/1.

38 Correspondence from Blignaut to VRFC Organiser Cilliers, November 16, 1951, SWAA fonds, Box 0982, File A/90/21/1.

39 Correspondence from VRFC Organiser Cilliers to Blignaut, November 26, 1951, SWAA fonds, Box 0982, File A/90/21/1; Correspondence from Blignaut to Native Commissioner Ovamboland, December 17, 1951, SWAA fonds, Box 0982, File A/90/21/1

40 The terminology used in the drawings requires further explanation: the "Soil Area" is interpreted as an ablution space, "Soil" meaning "Night Soil", an antiquated word for human excreta. An "Enclosure" is a space associated with the keeping of animals. See Black 2010.

41 "…my design is complete leaving the space for Natives as originally arranged. I have not made any drawings of outbuildings as yet. I would rather wait until the matter of Natives is cleared up." Correspondence from Joel to Blignaut, November 12, 1951, PWD fonds, Box 203, File 325.

42 "Suidwes se Paviljoen" 1952.

Bibliography

Black, Duncan, ed. 2010. *Collins English Dictionary*, 10th ed. Glasgow: Harper Collins.

"Bushmen pass through Windhoek on way to Festival." 1952. *Windhoek Observer*, March 5, 1952.

Çelik, Zeynep. 1992. *Displaying the Orient: Architecture of Islam at Nineteenth-Century World's Fairs*. Berkeley, Los Angeles and Oxford: University of California Press.

Central Committee for the Van Riebeeck Festival. 1952. *Official Programme of the Van Riebeeck Festival*. Cape Town: Nasionale Pers Beperk.

Christopher, Anthony J. 1994. *The Atlas of Apartheid*. London: Routledge.

Coe, Cati. 2001. "Histories of Empire, Nation and City: Four Interpretations of the Empire Exhibition, Johannesburg, 1936." *Folklore Forum* 32, no. 1/2: 3–30.

Corbey, Raymond. 1993. "Ethnographic Showcases: 1870–1930." *Cultural Anthropology* 8, no. 3 (August): 338–69.

Geppert, Alexander C. T. 2010. *Fleeting Cities: Imperial Expositions in Fin-de-Siècle Europe*. Basingstoke and New York: Palgrave Macmillan.

Geppert, Alexander C. T., Jean Coffey, and Tammy Lau. 2006. *International Exhibitions, Expositions Universelles and World's Fairs, 1851–2005: A Bibliography*. Berlin: Freie Universität Berlin; Fresno: California State University, https://www.geschkult.fu-berlin.de/e/fmi/astrofuturismus/publikationen/Geppert_-_Expo_bibliography_3ed.pdf (accessed March 13, 2023).

Gordon, Robert J. 2021. *South Africa's Dreams: Ethnologists and Apartheid in Namibia*. New York: Berghahn.

League of Nations. 1919. *Covenant of the League of Nations*. 28 April 1919, available at: https://www.refworld.org/docid/3dd8b9854.html (accessed January 28, 2022).

Miescher, Giorgio. 2012. *Namibia's Red Line: The History of a Veterinary and Settlement Border*, Palgrave Series on Borderlands Studies. New York: Palgrave MacMillan.

Morton, Patricia A. 2000. *Hybrid Modernities: Architecture and Representation at the 1931 Colonial Exposition in Paris*. Cambridge: MIT Press.

Rassool, Ciraj, and Leslie Witz. 1993. "The 1952 Jan van Riebeeck Tercentenary Festival: Constructing and Contesting National History in South Africa." *Journal of African History* 34, no. 3: 447–68.

Rassool, Ciraj, Leslie Witz, and Robert J. Gordon. 1996. "Fashioning the Bushman in Van Riebeeck's Cape Town, 1952 and 1993." In Pippa Skotnes, ed., *Miscast: Negotiating the Presence of the Bushmen*, 257–69. Cape Town: University of Cape Town Press.

Robinson, Jennifer. 2003. "Johannesburg's 1936 Empire Exhibition: Interaction, Segregation and Modernity in a South African City." *Journal of Southern African Studies* 29, no. 3: 759–89.

"Südwest Pavillon am ersten Tag." 1952. *Allgemeine Zeitung*, March 19, 1952.

"Suidwes se Boesmans bitjie skugter in die Kaap." 1952. *Die Suidwester*, March 12, 1952.

"Suidwes se Paviljoen vorder Fluks." 1952. *Die Suidwester*, February 20, 1952.

Swanson, Maynard W. 1977. "The Sanitary Syndrome: Bubonic Plague and Urban Native Policy in the Cape Colony, 1900–1909." *Journal of African History* 18, no. 3: 387–410.

Wallace, Marion. 2002. *Health, Power and Politics in Windhoek, Namibia, 1915–1945*, Basel Namibia Studies Series 7. Basel: P. Schlettwein Publishing.

Wallace, Marion. 2011. *A History of Namibia: from the Beginning to 1990*. Oxford: Oxford University.

Witz, Leslie. 2003. *Apartheid's Festival: Contesting South Africa's National Past*. Bloomington: Indiana University Press.

Image Sources

1   *Die Suidwester*, Windhoek, March 26, 1952.
2   Namibia Ministry of Public Works and Transport Drawing Archive, Dwg. no.: 963/A2.
3   *Allgemeine Zeitung*, Windhoek, April 15, 1952.
4   Namibia Ministry of Public Works and Transport Drawing Archive, detail from Dwg. no.: 725/2.
5   Namibia Ministry of Public Works and Transport Drawing Archive, Dwg. no.: 963/A.
6   Namibia Ministry of Public Works and Transport Drawing Archive, Dwg. no.: 963/5.

BEATRIZ SERRAZINA

Colonial Enterprises and Urban Design

Transnational Knowledge, Local Agency,
and the Diamond Company of Angola (1917–1975)

> From Saurimo to Dundo, 70 km, the journey was made with the ease provided by one of the best roads in the District. The road, curved and flanked by acacia trees, allows for a higher speed than normal. Suddenly, a vague bright that rises between the trees reveals the electric light of the streets and houses. The headlights illuminate a large sign that reads: "Dundo, Diamang." The silent and brightened streets are more like garden alleys. The car stops between a wide carpet of grass, flowered, and a large building with sober lines, colonial style without vulgarity. …
> The Governor did not hide the surprise that this set of things caused him, miles away from the coastline, in a hidden corner of Angola. … Dundo is an oasis in the desert.[1]

Dundo was established in 1919 as the main town of the *Companhia de Diamantes de Angola* (Diamang). After its foundations in the Lunda district, a few kilometers from the north-eastern border of Angola with the Belgian Congo, the Diamang mining company put its best efforts into building a so-called "model" town. Throughout Diamang's lifespan, from the early 1920s to the late 1980s—overlapping with and outlasting the many decades of Portuguese colonial rule in Africa—, Dundo was considered an "oasis in the desert." According to the company's records, this praise was due to the "intelligent, dedicated and enthusiastic work" of Dundo's Urbanisation and Sanitation Team, whose importance in establishing and strengthening Diamang's rule was emphasized.[2] The account cited above of the 1936 visit of António Lopes Mateus, the newly appointed Governor of Angola, clarifies the surprise caused by Diamang's built environment, located in a "corner" of the country. The "plain" houses, the well-kept and "comfortable" gardens, the "hygienic" quarters, and the "well-built" roads all contributed to a much-appreciated setting for the town. Electric light, offered as an "unquestionable sign of civilization," further accentuated the "colonial style" of the buildings.[3]

To celebrate Lopes Mateus's visit, Diamang published a summary of its "origin, development and activity and colonizing action," with charts comparing the material development of the mining region through the growth of towns and roads between 1926 and 1936, and photographs of buildings, gardens, and streets. The document set out the "foundations of a nationalizing action," bringing together old territorial plans, while trying to prove the company's commitment to designing a "perfect" built environment.[4] According to the engineer Quirino da Fonseca, the head of technical operations in Lunda, "major improvements" were then being prepared. "Alongside the industrial work," he underlined, the mining enterprise was eager to sponsor and build a "work of civilization and patriotism … , which can, without the least fear, defy comparison with any enterprise of the most advanced or most prosperous foreign colony."[5]

Fonseca's words were timely and implied key interests. First, Diamang was pursuing a new and different kind of settlement in Lunda, with the goal of claiming a "civilizing" role for the mining venture. Second, the company was committing itself to the renewed Portuguese colonial effort, driven by the nationalistic agenda of the *Estado Novo* (New State) regime. The dictatorial regime in Portugal, lasting from 1933 to 1974, depended not only on colonial extension, as ensured by the promulgation of the Colonial Act in 1930, but also on acts of spatialization, which gave architecture a new goal and role.[6] Along these lines, private companies were seen as crucial agents in empire-building. Diamang, in particular, not only quickly became the major economic and political player in Angola, but was also considered a "stronghold" of the moral, economic, and social values of the Portuguese State.[7] As argued by Mathias Alencastro, Diamang and the New State fostered "one of the most successful public-private partnerships of the entire colonial era," in contrast with the majority of other colonial enterprises. Through the creation of a very profitable "extractive province," Diamang built all the infrastructure for colonization, generated revenue for the Portuguese elite, and strengthened Portugal's position in the international arena.[8]

In fact, the company's early dependence on foreign enterprises to carry out mining works was becoming less heavy, allowing for the construction of a unique, even if always joint, spatial "dialect."[9] From the mid-1930s onwards, some programs that were central to the Portuguese New State's corporative, conservative, and Catholic ideological indoctrination, notably the "*Casa do Pessoal*" (Staff House/Club) and the church, were established in Lunda.[10] Cutting across all other issues, spatial planning was put forward as both pre-condition and consequence of Diamang's rule. Although local conditions could not be ignored—as shown by the accounts of resistance, disease, and climatic difficulties—the company largely followed national and transnational agendas. As a result, stated "concerns" for local populations were always ultimately aimed at the profit and benefit of the company itself.

Considering the interplay between these layers, Benoît Henriet sees company settlements as "peculiar fields of power within the imperial superstructure, where broader tensions are made more visible and challenged."[11] Unpacking such a perspective, this article explores Diamang's built environment as a magnifier of the complex nature of the colonial space(s), merging diverse actors, times, and spaces while diving into the conflicts, contradictions, and dissonant narratives that undermined them. The town of Dundo, in particular, will be used to outline these dynamics. Following Jiat-Hwee Chang and Anthony King's argument that private corporations were among the first imperial actors to enact space-building as a "power-knowledge configuration inextricably linked to asymmetrical colonial power relations,"[12] research on the outposts of these corporations can provide more nuanced pictures of the spatial footprint(s) of twentieth-century colonialism in Africa, engaging with growing calls to diversify archival sources, move away from the canon, "intersect" actors and agendas outside the architectural field, and critically dialogue with concepts of race, labor, and gender.[13]

The following section addresses private companies as key players in the spatialization of colonial empires in Africa. This is followed by a study of Dundo's spatial layout as a "model company town" and then a discussion of the many architectural models adopted and adapted in Lunda, questioning how borderlands, often dismissed due to the absence of aesthetically appealing buildings, may be critical places to uncover other significant facets of architecture built under and over colonialism. The final section focuses on Lunda as a whole to understand the variety of plans across Diamang's space, ranging from struggles to learnings.

Architecture of a Mining Empire

The concession of large "pockets" of land was a fairly common strategy of European powers to support colonialism in Africa at the turn of the twentieth century. After the Berlin Conference of 1884–1885, several private companies were organized as key tools to explore and exploit the colonial ground.[14] Amidst plantations of coffee, cotton, and sugar, mining activities stood out due to their industrialized landscapes, where thousands of African laborers and hundreds of European employees were involved. Operating within fairly bounded areas—carved out as "concessions" and later described as "enclaves"[15]—, mining enterprises achieved significant power in producing and controlling space. A particular group of corporations, from De Beers to Union Minière, Forminière, Bécéka, and Diamang, later known as the "Cape-to-Katanga Miners", "Team," or "Lobby,"[16] paved the way for numerous company towns and workers' villages across Central and Southern Africa.[17] These settlements were often the only manifestation of the colonial apparatus in such remote areas, thus arguably showing up as crucial "scaffolds" in building empires both politically and materially.[18]

The emergence of Diamang was well-timed for Portuguese territorial sovereignty. The organization of the company underpinned the formalization of the so-called "Portuguese Lunda,"[19] coinciding in time and space with the reshuffle of colonial boundaries. Having overcome the European imperial disputes at the turn of twentieth century, colonial Angola was reshaped by a new political framework and gained a generous "slice" that included part of the ancestral Lunda Empire.[20] Despite various plans to occupy Lunda, the region remained under the fragile control of the state authorities until the late 1910s. Overlapping with the ratification of the Treaty of Versailles, and in the face of the so-called "pacification campaigns," Diamang was usefully considered a "buffer" to quell any political ambitions over that part of the territory.[21] Without disappointing these expectations, it became one of the major players in the Portuguese Empire, sometimes called a "state within the state" or the "ninth colony."[22]

Nonetheless, the Lunda border was not a sharp edge. On the contrary, mining companies faced similar economic, technological, and social problems on both sides of the border. Far from the "model" and "perfect" descriptions, the reality on the ground was complex and rough. First, it must be noted that mineral wealth had deep roots and routes in Africa, with local communities having their own uses of land and ownership that had to be negotiated by the colonial power.[23] Later, riots starting in the 1930s and successive labor policies were significant signs of the many struggles that persisted across mining sites.[24] Coercive recruitment led to massive displacements and poor health conditions among workers; the housing conditions offered were often appalling; local families were constrained to a way of life very different from their own; and most work tasks were harsh and poorly paid.[25] Space, from urban planning to village layout and house design, thus became a key asset to sustain company rule and counter such hardships. Over the years, enterprises built an extensive yet exclusive "trans-imperial cloud" of knowledge, which resulted in plenty of shared information, fieldtrips, and intertwined research. As noted by Wendy Roberts, company spaces were "exemplar" evidence of "multiple agents and architectural influences operating on a single project in a region remote from established centres of ideas and practice."[26] Each company built its own particular "architectural dialect,"[27] shedding light on "networked modernities" beyond imperial hierarchies while challenging prevalent colonial dichotomies.[28] Across boundaries and under paternalist guises, managers, doctors, and engineers envisioned and planned mining settlements as "panoptical" spaces, which, while supporting labor productivity, should act as "civilizing" and "modernizing" stations.[29] In particular, "stabilization policies" were enacted as crucial tools to support this informal "mining empire," focusing on house, health, and hygiene as the core aspects of a "social engineering" project.[30]

Converging with Kamissek and Kreienbaum's remarks on the concept of "cloud," this network of connections emerged as a "messy," "fractional," and "diffuse" knowledge reservoir, of creative processes rather than clear-cut transfers, which today ultimately bring not only metropolis and colonies but also different empires and colonies into the same analytical field.[31] Although Diamang had the overall support of the Portuguese state, its remoteness within Angola encouraged long-lasting cross-border connections with Belgian Congo neighbors as well as increased need (and self-government) to experiment with new urban ideas.[32] The following section thus questions how and to what extent the remote and borderland position of mining sites stimulated new urban technologies and architectural repertoires. Was Dundo a real "oasis in the desert"?

Dundo, an "Oasis in the Desert"?

Dundo was founded on a plateau at the intersection of the Luachimo River and the Dundundo tributary, equidistant from the first Diamang mines, in the last months of 1919. The place broadly replicated the physical conditions of Tshikapa, headquarters of Forminière about 150 km to the north. Both towns grew up funneled into river intersections, while making use of the same grid system to functionally organize their space. Dundo was closer to the border than any other Diamang site and therefore guaranteed the best (and much needed) land access to the mining posts in the neighboring colony. After six years of exploratory work, the engineers working in Lunda considered the opening of Dundo as the moment of the "*true* settlement of the company,"[33] illuminating the importance of this particular town in supporting Diamang's venture.

Planned by American engineers with experience in the mines of South Africa,[34] Dundo's center followed the main lines of the "company town" model, later described by John D. Porteous.[35] From its earlier days, the settlement was based on an orthogonal structure, with long tree-lined avenues (fig. 1). Around the town's main square were a club, the Administration House and sports fields. Single-family houses for European employees were lined in spacious blocks with gardens. Workshops and warehouses were placed in the north part of the town, facing a slope down to the river. The hospital for European families, on the other hand, was the farthest possible southwards. By the mid-1930s, 150 white employees lived in Dundo's town center and the site had more than seventy brick buildings.

Just like most company settlements, the city plan mirrored the company's labor hierarchy, reserving the largest and best-placed buildings for the senior staff. By the 1940s, Dundo town center housed an international "European" community of more than 300 people, comprising Portuguese, American, and Belgian experts and families. As part of an industrial machine, both streets and buildings were numbered rather than named. Over time, Dundo became fully equipped with a Native Museum, schools, plant nurseries, a laboratory, and a weather station, picturing the "scientific colonialism" promoted by Diamang. Following the "company town" ethos, the goal was to "qualify and not quantify."[36] Since buildings were frequently demolished to

1   Aerial view of Dundo's streets and bungalows (c. 1970).

make way for new ones, following the finite nature of mining operations, the town did not grow much until the late 1950s. This building synchronicity further emphasized the homogeneity typical of the "company town," namely among the houses for European staff, which showed a great uniformity in typology and materials. The red brick bungalows and well-designed green areas, modelled after both South African and Belgian mining sites,[37] soon became one of Diamang's symbols. Notably, not a single building was planned by an architect.[38] Organizing space in the mining fields was considered under more "practical" and "scientific" standards, turning engineers, doctors, and locally trained drawers, always closely supervised by the management board, into the main planners of the town.

After Lopes Mateus's visit, and confirming Quirino da Fonseca's statement, Dundo underwent a noteworthy spatial renovation. In 1942 the region was reorganized into a "Concession" and a number of teams exclusively dedicated to "urbanization and sanitation" tasks were set up. Three years later, the mining post was suggestively renamed an "urban center." Henceforth, the settlement began to expand southwards, transforming the original polygon into an elongated shape. The "Concession" had plenty of services, including a petrol station, churches, markets, brickyards, vegetable gardens, a swimming pool, a hydroelectric station, the Luachimo River's Touristic Promenade, and an Acclimation Park.

In parallel, both the slope and the river, and later the hospital, were used as physical barriers to separate "Europeans" from African laborers. Different layers of labor and racial segregation

2   Dundo's "indigenous village" to house workers during the "preparation and adaptation period."

were set forward. Around Dundo's central nucleus, more than a dozen "workers' villages" were built for native laborers, and even those had different sizes and shapes according to the origin and role of their inhabitants. Baluba people, for instance, were cherished for their "expertise" in heavy duties, thus being treated with more reverence by the company's administration. Servants from the houses in Dundo, on the other hand, lived closer to the town center, in orderly "neighborhoods." Conversely, laborers newly arrived to work in Diamang's mines, coming from other regions of Angola, were housed and physically evaluated in "acclimation camps," with long rows of adobe houses, located further away (fig. 2). Finally, most local workers, called "volunteers," remained in their wattle and dub huts. All in all, housing was a critical instrument to produce and organize the company space. Lopes Mateus's visit, in particular, coincided with the inauguration of the exclusive Bairro Escola (school neighborhood), built between the workshops and the river, which was regarded as "a hygienic and modern example of the standard of living to which every African can rise through education and work."[39]

According to the company's records, every space in the "Concession area" should obey a "regime of practical sense and beauty," in which concepts of "embellishment," "modelling," and "improvement" *of* and *through* space were key[40] (fig. 3). Notably, the dissemination of the veranda would be considered the main evidence of the transformation of the housing model into a form that was "legible" to Diamang's landscape. Vegetation was also seen as an essential part of this system: on the one hand, it responded to climatic and "moral" challenges faced by European employees, while on the other, this system was a tool for the "civilization" and surveillance of African families. "Model" villages, for instance, were shaped by long rows of trees, orchards, vege-

3   House for the European staff, Dundo, 1945.

table gardens, and even flowers, all of them contributing to a sense of order, while the company demanded that the perimeter around houses be kept completely clean of any vegetation, so that moves inside the villages could be easily spotted.

Unsurprisingly, Dundo was pictured as an "oasis in the desert" by the colonial apparatus—both the state authorities and the national press. The town provoked feelings of strangeness and wonder within the Portuguese imperial scene, so different from the white-washed villages that stood for the Portuguese "national colonization."[41] As previously noticed, both this "oasian" idea and the town's layout were very much in line with the numerous "workingman's paradises" spread around the world to support industrial ventures.[42] Throughout the first half of the twentieth century, the "company town" design had materialized as "one of the most efficient and convenient models of space management, both in practical and political terms."[43] Colonial exploitation sites, in particular, offered the perfect ground to experiment with this model. While both European and African workers were said to benefit from such a "paradisiacal setting," the reality did not comply with these aims. Dundo's history was one of conflict, displacement, dispossession, and destruction since the town's inception.

Broader Circuits: Contact Zones and Transnational Networks

Dundo had its singularities, but it was far from being original. There are many similarities shared between "company towns" built under twentieth-century colonialism(s), from urban planning to the aesthetics of buildings (even if remarkable differences are surely to be acknowledged). The examples of Leverville in the Belgian Congo, studied by Benoît Henriet, the CDC camps in Cameroon, surveyed by Ambe Njoh and Liora Bigon, as well as Robert Home's pioneering work on Natal and Northern Rhodesia workers' housing, are all very close to Dundo and illuminate broad circuits still to be explored, in both their connections and disparities.[44] Beyond this far-reaching background, Diamang's spatial layout would mainly result from the "Miners" circles of knowledge transfer, thus placing emphasis on the particular role of these mining locations in giving shape to the exploitative nature of European colonialism.

Especially from the 1950s onwards, these colonial exploitative borderlands arguably became critical sites to be usefully studied as "architectural contact zones."[45] Corporations were thriving and growing due to substantial post-war demands while international scrutiny became bolder. By the 1950s, "welfare" and "development" flourished as watchwords and were translated into the need for good housing conditions. Transnational meetings, organized by social scientists and institutions that were settling in Africa, such as the Commission for Technical Cooperation in Africa South of the Sahara (CCTA) and the Centre d'étude des problèmes sociaux indigènes (CEPSI), brought mining companies together and made these circuits even stronger.[46] However, the recycling of discourses and ideas dating back to the 1930s, even if sometimes wrapped or named differently, revealed that the reality on the ground did not correspond to the "good" conditions expected and often heralded as "exemplary" among the colonial and business community.

In fact, as the following paragraphs highlight, living conditions in Lunda were far from positive. Although reports were filled with photographs of the already mentioned "model" villages, often presenting a *neutralized* version of Diamang's spaces, these did not correspond to the majority of the workers' settlements. First, the company was never able to house all of its laborers, with many of them remaining in huts built around the pictured settlements. Second, it was not until the early 1960s that the existing adobe houses were in fact almost fully substituted by brick ones. Even in these circumstances, Diamang would report the resistance of local families to being housed in the company's villages. While the colonial authorities celebrated a higher number of "good and big brick and zinc" houses within the "European standard," social scientists acknowledged that the models offered did not correspond to the real expectations of Lunda's communities, who "preferred to live next door, in grass huts they had built themselves, which, according to Western conceptions, arguably did not have all that was necessary for a decent life."[47]

In the face of this challenging reality, Dundo became a major "laboratory" to try out different housing models, therefore adding other layers, challenges, contexts, and goals to be considered within (and further complicate) the impressive "colonial modern" approach.[48] After Orenstein blocks or Kimberley brick houses spread as particular typologies in mining villages—mainly because they were considered "healthier"[49]—, companies experimented with other, more universal, models so that both economic and social demands could be faced. Local issues were never dismissed, from topography and climate to communities' specific demands, pointing to the importance of "editing" skills when it came to the *diffusion* of urban design.[50] A few examples confirm the introduction of new building technologies and methods in Diamang's landscape. The works on the Luachimo hydroelectric station in Dundo, for instance, resulted in the trialing of Wallace Neff's "Airform bubble houses"[51] to quickly house numerous teams of workers. In 1953, twelve houses made out of an air balloon covered with gunite concrete were built in the Bairro Escola, which by then had been renamed Bairro Norte. Unsurprisingly, the camp had been presented as Diamang's first "model neighborhood" to showcase the "best modern buildings" for the so-called "specialized" laborers. After that, two prefabrication systems were tried out to further meet accommodation needs.[52]

It was mainly these models that have endured in the urban imagery of Dundo. While the first adobe houses were lost over time, the new "modern" models, namely the balloon houses and the brick houses with balconies, became symbols of Dundo's urban development. Today, the city remains the main hub of Lunda, despite its infrastructural weaknesses as well as the reproduction of socioeconomic hierarchies in the town plan.[53] Furthermore, some of the above-mentioned typologies were later used in other parts of Angola—such as the balloon houses in the late 1950s along the Benguela Railway line[54]—, suggesting that companies had a role in spreading architectural models throughout the country. Accordingly, Diamang was often asked by the colonial authorities for workers' housing plans that "could be displayed as standards for other enterprises in Angola,"[55] making Lunda a point of arrival, transit, and departure of architectural ideas. Housing built in the Mwinilunga District in Zambia by communities that migrated from Lunda in the 1980s illuminates the resilience of some of these spatial models, particularly through the prevalence of well-kept garden spaces and verandas, and unveils the still unexplored paths that merge colonial and postcolonial periods.[56]

Local Agendas: Conflicting Narratives and (Still) Invisible Expertise

The previous section showed how Diamang presented and advocated its construction activities as innovative and beneficial for African families. By the 1960s, more than 25,000 laborers were employed in the Lunda mining fields. The company's profit was indeed mainly dependent on its ability to engage labor. Learning how to make Lunda's space more manageable—as an example of James Scott's "social gardening"[57]—was Diamang's greatest concern. The growing and fine-tuned "stabilization policies" were a clear symptom of this need. Their supranational scale, while surfing through broad circuits of knowledge, went hand in hand with activity on restricted concessions. It was thus the combination of both scales that resulted in a capillary "infrastructural power,"[58] probably more effective than the state's arterial rule. Yet, even if it is accepted that corporations' control *through* and *over* space was above average,[59] that did not mean that Diamang's authority, just like the colonial government itself, was not "simultaneously strong and weak, with overlapping and ambiguous agendas."[60] In fact, what significantly stems from the company's accounts is precisely a finer view of the conflicts and contradictions on the ground.

Records produced by Diamang's planning and construction services support a mostly benevolent picture. Accounts of the several works in progress, the manufacture and high expenditure of construction materials, and the endless maintenance of buildings evoke a modern, fertile, prosperous landscape. Annual reports, packed with statistics, graphs, and figures, reinforced such a sense of control and achievement, leading Diamang to constantly stress the high number of houses built for the workers as a great "triumph."[61] Labor reports, though, reveal a different, messier scenario. Although accounts of struggles are scant—requiring a careful reading "along and against the archival grain"[62]—, they persist throughout time, pointing to the many histories to be found.

4   Workers' neighborhoods in Caingagi, Lunda,1960.

As expected, housing excelled as an "arena of contestation."[63] The most repeated notes refer to the frequent abandonment of the company's villages. Accounts written in the 1960s, for example, denounced several empty houses around Dundo. By that time, quarters with all the requirements (e.g. durable materials, a yard for each family, kitchen, latrines, running water) were being offered and even a "Diamang's Type House" was proposed (fig. 4). However, workers still preferred to build their own houses in nearby places, where certain rules—particularly the ban on raising animals—were not enforced.[64] In parallel, families would play with the companies' legal demands for housing to easily get a place to live, exposing the ability to use the rules to their advantage. This became particularly true during the "reordering process" of the Lunda district, set up by the Portuguese authorities in the 1960s to fight the liberation movements, when a large number of families moved near mining sites to be sheltered by Diamang.

Diamang's managers would also let their lack of power slip in between the lines. The "Best Village Contest," organised in Lunda since the late 1940s, exposed some of these anxieties. The goal of the contest was to select the settlement built by locals that proved to be most aligned with the company's spatial guidelines, including the application of orthogonal layouts, the construction of verandas, and the use of bricks, doors, and windows. The competition came to an end in the 1960s due to the growing disengagement of the local families, who favored an independent building approach.[65] The company's employees tried to cover the flaw by building a "winning village," but the deliberate assembling of different components—mixing Lunda's painted walls with Diamang's carefully designed windows—was undeniable (fig. 5). In parallel, some old wattle and daub houses still in use had to be neglected because only African workers knew how to master this building technique, showing that it was not only legal regulations to push Diamang towards "definitive", more expensive, adobe houses, but also the critical availability of the local expertise.

5   "Winning village" in Diamang's Best Village Contest, 1962.

The efforts to master Dundo's built environment also engaged many still invisible actors who actively participated in the construction of the settlement and its buildings, namely the non-European designers and builders. Diamang's great autonomy under the Portuguese Empire meant that it had to create and support its own structure. Several departments and teams, as well as brickyards, workshops, and quarries, were organized to plan and carry out construction works. This structure became more specialized over time, evolving from the first general teams in the 1930s to the later Planning Department and the Civil Construction Service in the 1960s. As a result, thousands of men were able to acquire and master new skills, from the production and application of construction materials to the handling of heavy machinery. Dundo's "Concession," for instance, had a team of 1,000 men permanently dedicated to "urbanization issues." In addition, more than 5,000 seasonal contractors and helpers engaged with varied tasks such as bricklaying, transport, road maintenance, and sanitation works[66] (fig. 6). Technical drawings and plans had the signatures of the same African drawers over long periods. Dibué and Domacié, for instance, worked in Diamang's planning services for more than two decades, thus being able to exercise and refine their knowledge in architectural design. Yet, they were never considered "specialized," probably because they remained based in their root communities. Finally, women and children also had a role in Diamang's space, despite records being scarce. Most of them were mainly responsible for cleaning the villages and for less heavy work in bricklaying. Women, in particular, were often key agents in defining the household layouts and materiality, since the company often had to accommodate their agendas and labor requests.

These processes of "specialization" were much celebrated by the colonial apparatus as proof of the alleged "modernization" of Africa. Even if they have to be studied cautiously to avoid the pitfalls of perpetuating untrue linear narratives of "development"[67]—intentionally merging here three very challenging concepts to be dealt with by architectural historiography—, it appears

6   Construction works at Dundo's hospital, 1961.

imperative to acknowledge the extensive and cumulative expertise of Diamang's laborers in building techniques and technologies, which probably influenced later construction works throughout Lunda. Within the rather heterogeneous, erratic, and disputed nature(s) of colonialism, mining locations thus show up simultaneously as pictures of the "repressive developmentalism"[68] as well as places for new skills, offering fertile ground for assessing knowledge that was produced between the silenced layers of the colonial web.

Concluding Remarks

Today, Dundo stands as a thick assembly of layers, connecting different political, social, economic, and technological realities. Recent news show how Diamang's building protocols are still ingrained in Lunda. The company's commitment to its built environment arguably influenced the mining community's relationship with its space. The "exceptional" nature of Lunda continues to be celebrated by today's mining societies, who replicate many of the earlier urban planning lines in the villages they are still responsible for building. For instance, Orenstein red bricks remain acknowledged as the best "solution" for housing while large mining neighborhoods are equipped with green areas and museums.

In particular, Diamang's settlements were designed as part of a larger social engineering project, like an ensemble of shared forms that were (and still are) meant to be exemplary in particular ways. Due to their wide-span chronology and their borderland condition, workers' villages, like those founded in Lunda, challenge the colonial epistemic structure. These places confront us with the need to expand our understanding of architecture and space production beyond nationalist scopes while engaging with local and transnational connections. In addition, since most private companies outlived the end of colonial rule, their housing landscape, as their main tool of control, became a resilient structure. For this reason, we need to focus on these buildings not as inert remains, but as persistent imperial formations that are unfinished histories running in the past continuous, as argued by Ann Laura Stoler.[69] Understanding their role and impact on the spatialization of imperial norms and forms seems paramount to critically engaging with difficult architectural legacies.

The author thanks the two reviewers, as well as the editors of the volume, for the very insightful remarks, which immensely helped to reorganize and improve the article. The author also thanks the Foundation for Science and Technology (FCT) for supporting this work through a PhD grant (SFRH/BD/122658/2016). The article was written as part of the project "*Archwar*. Dominance and Mass-Violence through Housing and Architecture during Colonial Wars. The Portuguese Case (Guinea-Bissau, Angola, Mozambique): Colonial Documentation and Post-Independence Critical Assessment" (PTDC/ART-DAQ/0592/2020 2021–2024).

1   "O Senhor Gov. Geral" 1936.
2   "Diamang's Administration Report, March 1952." ANTT, PT/TT/AOS/D-N/2/10/1.
3   Series of news stories from the newspaper *A Província de Angola*, covering Lopes Mateus' visit to Lunda, July 1936.
4   "Súmula da origem, desenvolvimento e actividade e acção colonizadora da Companhia de Diamantes de Angola, Dundo, June 1936." ANTT, PT/TT/AOS/D-N/2/2/1.
5   "Admirável síntese" 1936.
6   Brites 2017; Brites and Correia 2020.
7   Alencastro 2004; Varanda 2007.
8   Alencastro 2022.
9   Roberts 2014.
10 Rosas 1995.
11 Henriet 2021, 7.
12 Chang and King 2011.
13 Nasr and Volait 2012; James-Chakraborty 2014; Bremner et al. 2016; Itohan Osayimwese, "From Postcolonial to Decolonial Architectural Histories: A Method," keynote lecture at the conference *Architectures of Colonialism: Constructed Histories, Conflicting Memories*, Brandenburg University of Technology Cottbus-Senftenberg, 2021 (see in this volume).
14 Coquéry-Vidrovitch 1972; Honke 2010.
15 Ferguson 2006; Rubbers 2018.
16 Wolfe 1962.
17 Boonen and Lagae 2020; Larmer et al. 2021.
18 Scriver 2007.
19 Carvalho 1895.
20 Vellut 2006.
21 "No distrito da Lunda" 1932.
22 Galvão and Selvagem 1952.
23 Larmer and Laterza 2017.
24 Perrings 1977; Seibert 2015.
25 Dibwe Dia Mwembu 1990; Cleveland 2005.
26 Roberts 2014.
27 Roberts 2014.
28 Lim and Chang 2012; James-Chakraborty 2014.

29   Borges and Torres 2012.

30   Mottoulle 1946; "Social Policy" 1947; Dibwe dia Mwembu 2007; Waldburger 2020.

31   Kamissek and Kreienbaum 2016.

32   Piaton and Bodenstein 2014.

33   Although Diamang was formally established on October 16, 1917 in Lisbon, the agents in Lunda pointed to July 1, 1919 as the official starting date for the company. "Para a história: notas e datas acerca da Diamang, Dundo's Museum Report (1943)." UC/AD.

34   Namely Harold Thomas Dickinson and Lute James Parkinson, both employees of De Beers in South Africa. To learn more about these men see Parkinson 1962, 28; Carstens 2001.

35   Porteous 1970.

36   Morisset and Mace 2019, 8.

37   "Photograph Album of the De Beers Consolidated Mines Ltd. Kimberley, South Africa 1899–1905." John Fuller, Lehigh University Special Collections, SC MS 0230.

38   Nonetheless, Diamang was aware of architectural expertise as a key tool in empire-building, as shown in the hiring of some well-known architects to plan the company's headquarters in Luanda, the capital of Angola, in the late 1940s.

39   "Súmula da origem, desenvolvimento e actividade e acção colonizadora da Companhia de Diamantes de Angola, Dundo, June 1936." ANTT, PT/TT/AOS/D-N/2/2/1.

40   "Report of Diamang's Board of Directors, 1950." ANTT, PT/TT/AOS/D-N/2/5/1.

41   "No distrito da Lunda" 1932.

42   Crawford 1995.

43   Scriver 1999.

44   Henriet 2021; Njoh and Bigon 2020; Home 1997; Home 2000.

45   Avermaete and Nuijsink 2021.

46   Poncelet 2008. Although the role of these institutions remains bound to social and political issues, the study of companies' space points to a significant impact on architectural practices that is still untapped.

47   "Alguns aspectos da cultura quioca. Mensário administrativo, 1962." ANTT, António Soares Carneiro archives, cx. 16, nº3, doc. 1 a 13, PT/TT/ASC/D/0004.

48   Avermaete, Karakayali, and von Osten 2010.

49   Van Nitsen 1933; Dibwe Dia Mwembu 1990; Pesa 2014.

50   Beeckmans 2013.

51   Head 2011. Surprisingly, it seems that the company managers were unaware of the broad impact that Airforms were having on the modernization of the African landscape, especially in Senegal. Some engineers in Lunda even referred to these structures as *casamatas* (bunkers), harking back to earlier military imagery.

52   A 1955 report details the construction of Studal houses around Dundo, pointing to Jean Prouvé's experiments. About this same time, Arcon structures, a British technology disseminated during World War II, arrived in Lunda to quickly house European employees. It was no coincidence that earlier that year Union Minière had built nine examples of these "balloon houses" in Lubumbashi, while prefab systems were being extensively studied across mining sites (Lagae and Boonen 2012). These experiments paralleled *Trajinha* houses, "tropical type", prefabricated bungalows used by both Lunda's engineers and Cahora Bass Dam's teams in Mozambique, a reminder that architectural repertoires travelled diverse circuits, from mining to imperial bonds.

53   Udelsmann Rodrigues and Bryceson 2018.

54   Head 2011.

55   Diamang's head officer in Africa, 1953, "SPAMOI's report: Recruitment (contracts, fees and accommodation), 1953–54." UC/AD.

56   The author thanks Iva Pesa for pointing out this connection. About Mwinilunga, see Pesa 2014.

57   Scott 1998.

58   Mann 1984.

59   For a framework of the multi-dimensions of spatialized power, see Dovey 1999.

60   Myers 2003.

61   "Relatórios por parte dos representantes do Governo." ANTT, PT/TT/CDA/1.

62   Stoler 2009.

63   Barker-Ciganikova et al. 2020.

64   The same question is exposed in an International Labour Organization's report from 1971. "Rapport de Pierre Juvigny, représentant du Dirécteur general du Bureau International du Travail, sur les contacts directs avec le gouvernement du Portugal au sujet de l'application de la convention (no. 105) sur l'abolition du travail force." Geneva, 1971.

65   "SPAMOI's report, 1962." UC/AD.

66   "Relatórios da Concessão do Dundo, 1942–1947." UD/AD.

67   Cooper 1997.

68   Jerónimo 2018.

69   Stoler 2013.

Bibliography

"Admirável síntese da organização e esforço da Companhia de Diamantes de Angola." 1936. *A Província de Angola*, July 14, 1936. ANTT, PT/TT/AOS/D-N/2/2/1.

Alencastro, Mathias. 2004. "Diamond Politics in the Angolan Periphery: Colonial and Postcolonial Lunda (1917–2012)." PhD thesis, University of Oxford.

Alencastro, Mathias. 2022. "Creating Extractive Provinces." *Análise Social* 57: 595–615.

Avermaete, Tom, Serhat Karakayali, and Marion von Osten, eds. 2010. *Colonial Modern: Aesthetics of the Past, Rebellions for the Future*. London: Black Dog.

Avermaete, Tom, and Cathelijne Nuijsink. 2021. "Architectural Contact Zones: Another Way to Write Global Histories of the Post-War Period?" *Architectural Theory Review* 25, no. 3: 350–61.

Barker-Ciganikova, Martina, Kirsten Rüther, Daniela Waldburger, and Carl-Philipp Bodenstein, eds. 2020. *The Politics of Housing in (Post)colonial Africa: Accommodating Workers and Urban Residents*. Berlin: De Gruyter Oldenbourg.

Beeckmans, Luce. 2013. "Editing the African City: Reading Colonial Planning in Africa from a Comparative Perspective." *Planning Perspectives* 28, no. 4: 615–27.

Boonen, Sofie, and Johan Lagae. 2020. "Ruashi, a Pessac in Congo? On the Design, Inhabitation, and Transformation of a 1950s Neighborhood in Lubumbashi, Democratic Republic of the Congo." In Barker-Ciganikova et al. 2020, 66–97.

Borges, Marcelo, and Susana Torres. 2012. *Company Towns: Labor, Space, and Power Relations across Time and Continents*. New York: Palgrave Macmillan.

Bremner, G. A., Johan Lagae, and Mercedes Volait. 2016. "Intersecting Interests: Developments in Networks and Flows of Information and Expertise in Architectural History." *Fabrications* 26, no. 2: 227–45.

Brites, Joana. 2017. "Estado Novo, arquitetura e renascimento nacional." *Risco: Revista de pesquisa em arquitetura e urbanismo* 15, no. 1: 100–113.

Brites, Joana, and Luís Miguel Correia, coords. 2020. *Obras públicas no Estado Novo*. Coimbra: Imprensa da Universidade de Coimbra.

Carstens, Peter. 2001. *In the Company of Diamonds: De Beers, Kleeizee and the Control of a Town*. Ohio University Press.

Carvalho, Henrique de. 1895. "Lunda Portuguesa." *Portugal em África* 2, no. 15: 517–526.

Chang, Jiat-Hwee, and Anthony King. 2011. "Towards a Genealogy of Tropical Architecture: Historical Fragments of Power-Knowledge, Built Environment and Climate in the British Colonial Territories." *Singapore Journal of Tropical Geography* 32: 283–300.

Cleveland, Todd. 2005. *Diamonds in the Rough: Corporate Paternalism and African Professionalism on the Mines of Colonial Angola, 1917–1975*. Athens: Ohio University Press.

Cooper, Frederick. 1997. "Modernizing Bureaucrats, Backward Africans, and the Development Concept." In Frederick Cooper and Randall Packard, eds., *International Development and the Social Sciences*, 64–92. Berkeley: University of California Press.

Coquéry-Vidrovitch, Cathérine. 1972. *Le Congo au temps des grandes compagnies concessionnaires 1898–1930*. Paris: Mouton.

Crawford, Margaret. 1995. *Building the Workingman's Paradise: The Design of American Company Towns*. London: Verso.

Dibwe dia Mwembu, Donatien. 1990. "Industrialisation et santé: la transformation de la morbidité et de la mortalité à l'Union minière du Haut-Katanga, 1910–1970." PhD thesis, Université Laval.

Dibwe dia Mwembu, Donatien. 2007. "Lubumbashi: histoire et mémoire d'une ville industrielle." In Jean-Luc Vellut, ed., *Villes d'Afrique: explorations en histoire urbaines*, 131–144. Paris: L'Harmattan.

Dovey, Kim. 1999. *Framing Places: Mediating Power in Built Form*. London and New York: Routledge.

Ferguson, James. 2006. *Global Shadows: Africa in the Neoliberal World Order*. Durham: Duke University Press.

Galvão, Henrique, and Carlos Selvagem. 1952. *Império ultramarino português: monografia do império*. Lisbon: Empresa Nacional de Publicidade.

Head, Jeffrey. 2011. *No Nails, no Lumber: The Bubble Houses of Wallace Neff*. New York: Princeton Architectural Press.

Henriet, Benoît. 2021. *Colonial Impotence: Virtue and Violence in a Congolese Concession, 1911–1940*. Berlin and Boston: De Gruyter Oldenbourg.

Home, Robert. 1997. "The 'Warehousing' of the Labouring Classes." In *Of Planting and Planning: The Making of British Colonial Cities*. London: E. & F. N. Spon.

Home, Robert. 2000. "From Barrack Compounds to the Single-Family House: Planning Worker Housing in Colonial Natal and Northern Rhodesia." *Planning Perspectives* 15: 327–47.

Honke, Jana. "New Political Topographies: Mining Companies and Indirect Discharge in Southern Katanga (DRC)." *Politique Africaine* 4, no. 120 (2010): 105–27.

James-Chakraborty, Kathleen. 2014. "Beyond Postcolonialism: New Directions for the History of Nonwestern Architecture." *Frontiers of Architectural Research* 3: 1–9.

Jerónimo, Miguel Bandeira. 2018. "Repressive Developmentalism: Idioms, Repertoires, and Trajectories in Late Colonialism." In Martin Thomas and Andrew Thompson, eds., *The Oxford Handbook of the Ends of Empire*, 537–54. Oxford: Oxford University Press.

Kamissek, Christoph, and Jonas Kreienbaum. 2016. "An Imperial Cloud? Conceptualising Interimperial Connections and Transimperial Knowledge." *Journal of Modern European History* 14, no. 2: 164–82.

Lagae, Johan, and Sofie Boonen. 2012. "Des Pierres Qui (Nous) Parlent." In Simon Njami, ed., *Rencontres Picha: Biennale de Lubumbashi*, 19–53. Trézélan: Filigraines.

Larmer, Miles, and Vito Laterza. 2017. "Contested Wealth: Social and Political Mobilisation in Extractive Communities in Africa." *The Extractive Industries and Society* 4, no. 4: 701–6.

Larmer, Miles, Enid Guene, Benoît Henriet, Iva Peša, and Rachel Taylor, eds. 2021. *Across the Copperbelt: Urban & Social Change in Central Africa's Borderland Communities*. Woodbridge, Suffolk: James Currey.

Lim, William, and Jiat-Hwee Chang, eds. 2012. *Non West Modernist Past: On Architecture and Modernities*. Singapore: World Scientific.

Mann, Michael. 1984. "The Autonomous Power of the State: Its Origins, Mechanisms and Results." *European Journal of Sociology* 25, no. 2: 185–213.

Morisset, Lucie, and Jessica Mace. 2019. *Identity on the Land: Company Towns in Canada*. Montreal: Patrimonium.

Mottoulle, Léopold. 1946. *Politique sociale de l'Union minière du Haut Katanga pour sa main-d'oeuvre et ses résultats au cours de vingt années d'application*. Brussels: Institute Royal Colonial Belge.

Myers, Garth Andrew. 2003. *Verandahs of Power: Colonialism and Space in Urban Africa*. Syracuse: Syracuse University Press.

Nasr, Joe, and Mercedes Volait. 2012. "Still on the Margin: Reflections on the Persistence of the Canon in Architectural History." *ABE Journal* 1, https://doi.org/10.4000/abe.304.

Njoh, Ambe, and Liora Bigon. 2020. "Spatio-Physical Power and Social Control Strategies of the Colonial State in Africa: The Case of CDC Workers' Camps in Cameroon." In Barker-Ciganikova et al. 2020, 167–83.

"No distrito da Lunda: Nas Minas de Diamantes." 1932. *Boletim Geral das Colónias* VIII, no. 88: 244–94.

"O Senhor Gov. Geral de visita à Companhia de Diamantes de Angola." 1936. *A Província de Angola*, July 7, 1936.

Parkinson, Lute J. 1962. *Memoirs of African Mining*. Self-published.

Perrings, Charles. 1977. "Consciousness, Conflict and Proletarianization: An Assessment of the 1935 Mineworkers' Strike on the Northern Rhodesian Copperbelt." *Journal of Southern African Studies* 4: 31–51.

Pesa, Iva. 2014. "Moving along the Roadside: A Social History of Mwinilunga District, 1870s–1970s." PhD thesis, Leiden University.

Piaton, Claudine, and Ralph Bodenstein. 2014. "Des entreprises aux lisières des Empires." *ABE Journal* 5, https://doi.org/10.4000/abe.1480.

Poncelet, Marc. 2008. *L'invention des sciences coloniales belges*. Paris: Karthala.

Porteous, John D. 1970. "The Nature of the Company Town." *Transactions of the Institute of British Geographers* 51: 127–42.

Roberts, Wendy. 2014. "Company Transfer: The Architectural Dialect at the Edges of Empire." In Christoph Schnoor, ed., *Proceedings of the Society of Architectural Historians, Australia and New Zealand 31*, 591–600. Auckland, New Zealand: SAHANZ.

Rosas, Fernando. 1995. "Estado Novo, império e ideologia imperial." *Revista de História das Ideias* 17: 19–32.

Rubbers, Benjamin. 2018. "Mining Towns, Enclaves and Spaces: A Genealogy of Worker Camps in the Congolese Copperbelt." *Geoforum* 98: 88–96.

Scott, James. 1998. *Seeing like a State: How Certain Schemes to Improve the Human Condition Have Failed*. New Haven and London: Yale University Press.

Scriver, Peter. 1999. "Company Towns: A Neocolonial Perspective." In *La Città Nouva: Proceedings of the 1999 ACSA International Conference*, 291–95. Washington, DC: ACSA Press.

Scriver, Peter. 2007. "Empire-Building and Thinking in the Public Works Department of British India." In Peter Scriver and Vikramaditya Prakash, eds., *Colonial Modernities: Building, Dwelling and Architecture in British India and Ceylon*, 69–92. London: Routledge.

Seibert, Julia. 2015. "'Wind of Change': Worker's Unrest and the Transformation of Colonial Capital in Katanga – Belgian Kongo." In Babacar Fall, Ineke Phaf-Rheinberger, and Andreas Eckert, eds., *Travail et culture dans un monde globalisé: de l'Afrique à l'Amérique latine = Work and Culture in a Globalized World: From Africa to Latin America*, 253–72. Berlin: Karthala.

"Social Policy of Union Minière du Haut Katanga." 1947. *African Affairs* 46, no. 183 (April): 89–97.

Stoler, Ann Laura. 2009. *Along the Archival Grain: Epistemic Anxieties and Colonial Common Sense*. Princeton: Princeton University Press.

Stoler, Ann Laura. 2013. *Imperial Debris: On Ruins and Ruination*. Durham NC: Duke University Press.

Udelsmann Rodrigues, Cristina, and Deborah Fahy Bryceson. 2018. "Precarity in Angolan Diamond Mining Towns, 1920–2014: Tracing Agency of the State, Mining Companies and Urban Households." *Journal of Modern African Studies* 56, no. 1: 113–41.

Van Nitsen, René. 1933. *L'hygiène des travailleurs noirs dans les camps industriels du Haut-Katanga*. Brussels: IRCB.

Varanda, Jorge, 2007. "A Bem da Nação': Medical Science in a Diamond Company in Twentieth-Century Colonial Angola." PhD thesis, University College London.

Vellut, Jean-Luc. 2006. "Angola-Congo: L'invention de la frontière du Lunda (1889–1893)." *Africana Studia* 9: 159–84.

Waldburger, Daniela. 2020 "House, Home, Health and Hygiene: Social Engineering of Workers in Elisabethville / Lubumbashi (1940s to 1960s) Through the Lens of Language Usage." In Barker-Ciganikova et al. 2020, 141–66.

Wolfe, Alvin. 1962. "The Team Rules Mining in Southern Africa." *Toward Freedom* 11, no 1.

Archival Sources

Torre do Tombo National Archives (ANTT)

António Soares Carneiro archives

Lehigh University Special Collections

University of Coimbra, Diamang's archives (UC/AD)

Image Sources

1   Courtesy of Júlio Pedro, Diamang's photographer.
2   "Report on Indigenous Labor, 1938, given to Dr. Manuel Pereira Figueira, Curador Geral dos Serviçais e Colonos, on his visit to Dundo." UC/AD.
3   ANTT, AOS/COL/UL-8A1 Cx. 713.
4   "Construction Department Annual reports, 1960–63." UC/AD.
5   "SPAMOI's Annual Report, 1962." UC/AD.
6   "Report on Urbanization and Sanitation, 1962." UC/AD.

LISANDRA FRANCO DE MENDONÇA

Boxed Empire

Framing Memories, Architecture, and Urban Space in Maputo
(1974–1976)

Buildings, sites, and landscapes, in their shape and material substance, are precious witnesses to history. They contain answers to questions that we may not have considered but that our children might. As three-dimensional objects, they are more complex than a written source, although less easy to read. And the genius loci—the spirit of the site—is often hard to describe but doubtlessly perceptible to the open minded, and it makes people feel that they share past experiences, as if there were a direct access to history.[1]

Urban built environments are spatial and material archives. ... Most of this dense layering is not immediately legible; it has not been decoded. Rather it is part of a more intuitive, live sense of "urbanity" that generates contemporary individual and collective senses of identity and belonging.[2]

Topographies of Loss and Liberation[3]

On April 25, 1974, the Portuguese Empire came to an end when a military coup in Lisbon deposed the Estado Novo regime,[4] immediately triggering negotiations with liberation movements in "Portuguese Africa" and the end of thirteen years of guerrilla warfare. In Mozambique, the revolutionary turbulence in the metropole was followed by the voiding of the authority of the colonial government and increasing political tension. From this moment on, the idea of an independent government became real for the major part of the population, impacting every ambience and experience in the capital city Lourenço Marques (renamed Maputo in 1976). The signing of the Lusaka Accords (September 7, 1974) triggered a wave of violence that lasted several days, resulting in dozens, perhaps even hundreds (the numbers are uncertain) of victims and arrests. More episodes of violence emerged on October 21 and the flight of Portuguese nationals gained momentum from then on.

Between September 1974 and June 1975, most of the artworks bearing Portuguese iconography in Mozambique, now reinterpreted "as symbols of an [un]authorised version of history"[5] and an impediment to "total liberation," were removed from the public space with the tacit agreement of the Governo de Transição—the transitional government comprising both Portuguese and FRELIMO's[6] lawmakers that had been created in the wake of the Lusaka Accords to manage the transition to independence (set to take place on June 25, 1975). In Lourenço Marques, a considerable part of that repository was deposited in the grounds of the future National Museum of Art (figs. 1–2) and later transferred to a warehouse of the Ministry of Education and Culture. On September 25, 2019, a national holiday in Mozambique commemorating the beginning of the War of Liberation (September 25, 1964), I went to this warehouse located at Av. Forças Populares de Libertação de Moçambique[7] in Maputo to look for statues of colonial origin erected under the Portuguese administration in Lourenço Marques. Many artworks had been

1   The removal of the statue of Mouzinho de Albuquerque, Mouzinho de Albuquerque Square, Lourenço Marques, 1975.

2   Statues in the grounds of the National Museum of Art, Maputo, 1981. In the foreground, on the right, the statue of D. Teodósio Clemente Gouveia; on the left, António Enes; in the center, Gago Coutinho and, just behind it, the equestrian statue of Mouzinho de Albuquerque. In the background, on the left, the "Colony of Mozambique."

lost, a few were going to become part of the new museological program at Maputo Fortress, by then reoriented to the history of colonial occupation and resistance[8]—namely the statue of the former royal commissioner António Enes[9] by Teixeira Lopes, installed in the downtown in 1910, and that of the captain of cavalry and later royal commissioner Mouzinho de Albuquerque by Simões de Almeida (sobrinho), along with two bronze panels depicting heroic deeds of the so-called "pacification" campaigns of the 1890s, both by Leopoldo de Almeida. These latter works were all part of the monumental set installed in Mouzinho de Albuquerque Square (present-day Independence Square) in 1940 (fig. 3), on the forty-fifth anniversary of the so-called "Feat of Chaimite"—the capture of the last Nguni emperor, Gungunhana (c. 1850–1906), by Mouzinho de Albuquerque (1855–1902) in the fortified village of Chaimite. Southern Mozambique's Gaza state had ruled over a substantial part of the territory that now forms Mozambique until its defeat in the context of the military policy of "pacification" of the land led by the Portuguese in the late nineteenth century. The "Feat of Chaimite" was extensively celebrated by the iconography of the early Estado Novo regime as one of the founding moments of Portuguese "civilizing action" in the south of Mozambique, and Mouzinho "appropriated as a precursor of the Estado Novo."[10]

If, on the eve of independence, many of the memorials and much of the overall European urban built environment of the "bifurcated" city[11] of Lourenço Marques were regarded as "un-

desired" or "difficult,"[12] there was, however, a discussion about the conservation of these assets, both in the public realm and within the National Service of Museums and Antiquities (NSMA)[13] and the State Housing Stock Administration (SHSA).[14] The National Service of Museums (later joined by "Antiquities") was established in 1976 and charged with the research, inventory, preservation, and dissemination of the national cultural patrimony. Inventories of (toppled) statues and other artifacts across the country identified several pieces considered consonant with Maputo Fortress's new exhibition program. Several difficulties hindered the development of this project, which ended up never materializing.[15] On another front, the SHSA, which had been created under the umbrella of the Ministry of Public Works to manage the nationalized building stock, organized several workshops to aid the new state tenants in using their houses. Manuals for the maintenance and proper use of these properties were also issued.[16]

In the following years, the public and national discussion would address a considerable spectrum of colonial assets and be formalized, for example, with the process of safeguarding the Island of Mozambique (the first seat of the Portuguese colonial government that lasted from 1507 to 1898) and inscribing it on the UNESCO World Heritage List,[17] and with the drafting of legislation for the protection of the national cultural heritage.[18] It is worth noting that little emphasis was given to the phased visual redress of public space in the Mozambican press.

3   Lourenço Marques *à vol d'oiseau* with the Town Hall building, the Cathedral and Mouzinho de Albuquerque Square with its monument at the center, April 16, 1974.

However, at the beginning of May 1975, the daily newspaper *Notícias* published a survey of
Lourenço Marques residents about the toppling of statues, with around twenty interviews from
people of the most divergent backgrounds and social strata. Practically all the respondents
were unanimous in defending the removal of the statues and their preservation in a museum,
recognizing that "only when the time for historical serenity" arrived, could there be the critical
distance needed to study and evaluate the importance of those "artworks and documents."[19]
The photographic survey of certain public spaces and buildings before, during, and after the
removal of statues, coats of arms, and other heraldic emblems, kept at the Historical Archive
of Mozambique (HAM), attests to contemporary insight into the importance of documenting
this process.[20]

Through long city walks and archival research, I tried to track the pivotal moments in the
events leading to the exodus of colonists in the years around independence (1974–1976) and
migration from suburban areas to the formalized city core (1975–1977), coinciding with major
socio-political transformations in both the former metropole and the colony. I looked at long-
term developments surrounding these events, from the 1950s, when the strong immigration in-

flow from the Portuguese metropole gained momentum, to the signing of the Lusaka Accords, and explored the physical and "urbanity"-related ways in which they impacted the city and its dwellers. My urban excursions stemmed from a premise: that the manner in which colonial ideology has been translated into practice, or the way in which colonial and post-colonial "city-as-idea shaped the city-as-place,"[21] is still very much readable in the built environment.[22] In other words, the urban ambience shows how architecture and urbanism mirrored ideology and how, throughout the protracted War of Liberation (1964–1974), the Transitional Government (1974–1975), and the revolutionary period (1975–mid 1980s) that followed—the latter associated with a civil war (1977–1992) that intersected with southern African and global geopolitics[23]—, the city acted "as 'fields of tensions' for conflicts that related to culture and society," urban and freedom aspirations, and "power and propaganda."[24] Public space within the (formerly European) city—and here one should consider that Africans were subjected to a 9 p.m. curfew up until the beginning of the 1970s and that their access to the city was limited—became the place where one had "the right to exercise one's presence"[25] publicly, but not quite. Among other aspects, the social engineering attempted by Frelimo made use of several instruments of repression, also building "on many pre-existing social currents from the colonial period," following, for instance, an "assimilationist" logic to put the socialist project in place.[26]

Following my wanderings, I traced the history of several buildings and urban spaces by analyzing the building permit processes at the City Council Department of Urban Planning and inventories undertaken by several research teams since the 1990s at the Centre for Studies and Development of Habitat.[27] Some of the buildings I looked at and the overall protected urban ensemble of the downtown area—the city's foundational nucleus—are part of the Municipal Heritage Program and are marked by plaques installed on the walls and sidewalks produced in 2013, with the support of the Spanish Agency for International Development Cooperation. This area is characterized by a mix of modernist high-rise architecture, medium-sized apartment buildings, and a few early twentieth-century two-story houses with cast-iron verandas and columns, along small streets, alleyways, tree-lined avenues, and impressive plazas. At the same time, I conducted semi-structured interviews with a limited group of city dwellers, and looked at historical periodicals, photographic surveys and movies, urban plans and legislation, along with a wide array of literary materials available at the local institutional archives,[28] to find out more about the urban-socio-political transformations that paved the way for and shaped the final stages of colonialism and the initial post-independence period, all interrelated and mirroring a set of events and contested narratives. After independence, relations between Portugal and the new country changed abruptly as they did in the other four post-colonial African Portuguese-speaking countries. The Overseas War and the *retornados*—the more than half a million Portuguese refugees who arrived in Portugal as an outcome of the decolonization processes—"profoundly marked the collective memory of the country's colonial past, to the extent that [these topics] remain taboo," or at least did so until the 1990s, an experience which also "helps explain … 'amnesia' about twentieth-century architecture in Portugal's overseas territories, long after architectural historians had started to rediscover modern architecture in Africa in the late 1980s."[29] This text examines not only the public space and social refashioning in Maputo precipitated by the process of decolonization, but also the cultural complexities of documenting and interpreting post-independence "dissonant" urban heritage.

Visual Redress and the Quest for the Nation

Analysis of the photographic collections of the Photographic Training and Documentation Center (PTDC) and the HAM (both in Maputo) in the context of news stories in local periodicals—relevant editions of Mozambique's weekly national magazine *Tempo* and daily newspaper *Notícias*—, together with recollections from city dwellers, allows us to understand how the removal of the statues, coats of arms, armillary spheres, and crosses (of the Order of Christ) produced by Portuguese colonialism, and later the changing toponomy, provided scope for the immediate re-semanticization of the public space and the visualization of the transfer of power. Beginning at the time of the coup d'état in Portugal, but especially in the weeks that followed the signing of the Lusaka Accords, news articles in the print media described numerous strikes, the halt in the construction industry (leaving hundreds of individuals unemployed and building sites abandoned), major episodes of violence involving hundreds of deaths and detentions in Lourenço Marques (accelerating the flight of colonists), the persecution of so-called "unproductive" citizens or those not aligned with Frelimo's project for a new society, and the progressive dereliction of the city and its services. In the last weeks of the Transitional Government, Samora Machel (1933–1986)—president of Frelimo, soon-to-be President of the country, and until then unknown to a great part of the Mozambican population—addressed numerous rallies throughout Mozambique, adopting an increasingly anticolonial rhetoric that was understood by many settlers as a clear sign of dissatisfaction with their presence in the country. This process was also enabled by the rapid nationalization of some services within weeks or a few months of independence, such as the practice of law, education and health, land surveying services, funeral parlors, and insurance companies, along with land, key industries, and abandoned and rented property.[30] This brought the income-generating businesses and property that belonged, though not exclusively, to Portuguese citizens to a halt, accelerating the substitution of city dwellers, which had been triggered in the months around independence by the exodus of European settlers and mixed-race professionals and entrepreneurs uncertain about their future in an independent Mozambique. The families that decided to leave the new country-to-be started packing their belongings in large wooden crates, which little by little were left on the sidewalks in front of their houses to be dispatched to the Gago Coutinho airport or the port of Lourenço Marques (fig. 4). For months, the sound of hammers nailing crates echoed in the city.

The sudden departure of some 200,000 individuals left behind between 80,000 and 100,000 vacant houses.[31] By late 1974, *Tempo* magazine reports on hundreds of empty houses in Lourenço Marques. Many houses had been empty for months since their owners refused to lower rental prices, thus preventing access to these properties for the vast majority of city dwellers living precariously in the extensive and mostly illegal occupations of the suburbs/*caniço*, which housed about 85% of the capital city's population.[32] By the beginning of 1976 this situation changed radically with the nationalization of vacant houses and rental buildings. This major event unlocked the door to the (European) city for a considerable number of suburban dwellers who only then came into contact with dwellings fully connected to modern utilities, which, on the other hand, and associated with a number of factors, aggravated the deterioration of these houses and buildings, public spaces, and facilities. In this regard, the explanatory brochure with

4 Wooden crate abandoned on the sidewalk on Av. D. Luís, in the downtown area where passers-by have left messages written with white chalk, showing discontent, some of them because of that obstacle on a walkway on such a busy avenue and others "because of its possible meaning"—the reaction of the mass of people that out of disrepute or fear "turned their backs to the construction of the new country."[59] A remark appeared prominently, "*Não leves mais já chega o que roubaste obrigado*" (Don't take more, what you have stolen is enough, thank you), Lourenço Marques, 1974.

the instructions for the correct utilization of the nationalized houses and buildings, a document annexed to the *Lei do Arrendamento* (Tenancies Act) of 1979, is illustrative of the difficulties encountered in the implementation of Frelimo's socio-cultural revolution even though it explains the meaning of the nationalization of urban housing in the context of the "National Liberation Struggle" and the socialist developmental program envisioned for the country.[33]

Adapting Andrew Bellisari's questions when analyzing the request of the Algerian state for the repatriation of French works of art transferred to France on the eve of the Algerian independence, what does it mean for artwork produced by some of the Portuguese metropole's most important sculptors, featuring some of the most celebrated mentors of the Portuguese colonial endeavor, to become the cultural property of a former colony? Or for other types of heritage, designed under colonial rule? Moreover, what is at stake when a former colony deems "it a valuable part of the newly independent state's cultural heritage,"[34] or, on the other hand, condemns it to official scrubbing, subject to *damnatio memoriae*? Such questions challenge our perception of post-independence struggles for identity as primarily concerned with "anticolonial rhetoric of national liberation—with its emphasis on decolonizing the mind as well as the nation"[35]—, which suggests that the valorization and redefinition of national culture would have been in conflict with that of the former colonizer.[36]

5   Building in old downtown area, Rua da Mesquita, Maputo, 2011.

Indeed, Frelimo's initial program focused primarily on contrasting the anticipated achievements of the revolution with the cultural heritage imposed by colonialism. In that regard, the entire state apparatus dedicated to education and culture was reformulated—maintaining, however, "a literacy program that was only in Portuguese (and not in African languages)"[37]—and a campaign to inventory national heritage focused on intangible heritage (for example, the arts and craftsmanship of popular culture), the National Campaign of Cultural Preservation (NCCP), was set in motion between 1978 and 1982.[38] The built heritage produced under Portuguese influence was also surveyed, being generally regarded as recalling "the tenacity and determination of … [the people of Mozambique]" in the face of "humiliation and foreign domination," that is, as "a source of inspiration and instruction for generations to come."[39] On this account, the rich archive (series of photographs documenting building sites, inventories of monuments, urban ensembles, memorials, and archaeological sites meticulously catalogued and illustrated, etc.) put together by the former Commission for Monuments and Historic Relics (active between 1943 and 1975) was dismantled and incorporated into the heritage inventories organized by the NSMA in the aftermath of the NCCP. The NSMA fonds shed light on a number of realities linked to decolonization and its turbulent effects on the social, economic, and administrative landscape in the country. They report, for instance, on the training of new cadres in the absence of qualified teachers, the shortage of trained personnel for the state apparatus, the destruction of memorials by local populations in the aftermath of the Lusaka Accords, and on the consolidation of Frelimo's "master narrative" as the sole bearer of liberation and progress, making use of kaleidoscopic valences of heritage in projecting multiple interpretations, nurturing (somewhat divergent) collective memories that hesitatingly account for, or do not account for, a colonial past. They present "new data" that counter Portuguese narratives around certain memorials. In this regard, historic sites of the Portuguese "pacification" campaigns were then reappropriated under a narrative of resistance and as a means of political legitimation. Chaimite, for instance, no longer represented the location of Gungunhana's defeat and the consequent dismantling of the Gaza Empire, but was rather a physical testimony to the forefathers' resistance against foreign occupation, whose legacy had been fully embodied by Frelimo. As in the previous administration's victor narratives, the recreated deeds of a selected past were now fused with a present that was under construction: "six decades later, with the same ideals that inspired the struggle of Gungunhana, … [the people] took up arms, … submit[ted] the colonial invader into surrender, and expel[led] it from the country."[40]

Using the insightful analysis of Mia Fuller of the relation of present-day Eritreans with their Italian colonial heritage of Asmara, I argue that Maputo's colonial-built environment was, in many ways, also interpreted as representing the "successful national sacrifice, [Mozambicans'] *overcoming* of subjugation, rather than their past colonization."[41] However, unlike in Asmara, the blatant traces of the Portuguese colonial period are not generally regarded by the locals as a value per se, which can be capitalized in various forms. This can easily be gleaned from the Maputo City Structure Plan (*Plano de Estrutura Urbana do Município de Maputo*), partly approved in 2010, which advocates for the densification of the urbanized city center, allowing the undifferentiated demolition and replacement of buildings, with exceptions made only for the old downtown area (fig. 5) and for a small collection of scattered buildings listed as protected or in the process of becoming protected.[42] In reality, although the 1988 law for the protection of cultural heritage provided scope for the designation of the old centers of the main cities, including downtown Maputo, it has not prevented the demolition of buildings in that area.[43]

Celebrating Portugalness in the 1940s and Mozambiqueness in the 1980s

In the backyard of the warehouse, I found three statues: one of the geographer Gago Coutinho, removed from the airport; one of Cardinal of Lourenço Marques D. Teodósio Clemente Gouveia (see fig. 2), which had been erected in the Malhangalene Garden; and the allegory of the "Colony of Mozambique," which stood at the foot of the pedestal of the aforementioned statue of Mouzinho de Albuquerque. This third work caught my attention. Several accounts testified to the destruction of this piece: it represents an austere European female figure, with the coat of arms of the Portuguese Colony of Mozambique on her chest, holding a submissive black child. It now stands in the dunce's corner, staring at the wall: the self-proclaimed great European mother wearied from guiding those she identified as black and backward in the occupied lands overseas. Needless to say, none of the employees I met at the warehouse knew these statues or their provenance. This ignorance regarding Portuguese colonial "iconography (explicit visual or textual referents to [Estado Novo] ideology) and topography, meaning the space and places created by the regime,"[44] is common among the great majority of the inhabitants of Maputo. Several mechanisms produced the ability to "cover" some traces of colonial history in this urban space: the former private and public spaces of the settlers were positively reclaimed by the new power. The street names inscribed onto new power relations consonant with narratives of "self-colonization"[45] socialism and Frelimo's unquestionable rule[46]—all attesting "to new historical and cultural layers on top of a European order that thereby was made less readable, continuing to exist, however, in an altered form."[47]

Over the next few paragraphs, I will explore some background and the basis on which some artwork and urban sites, such as Mozambique Island, the downtown area of Maputo, and Maputo's Independence Square, came to be considered the cultural heritage of the independent state. In doing so, we can better understand how a particular culture of valorization of inherited property emerged during the revolutionary period—as illustrated by the far-reaching legislation for the protection of cultural heritage discussed and approved at this time,[48] and by several projects for the conservation of buildings and urban sites[49] funded by foreign-aid programs. This culture almost faded away from the 1990s on, with the country undergoing important political and economic changes—from a single to a multiparty system, from a state-controlled to a liberal economy, with the denationalization of real estate and the privatization of services, and the end of Civil War in 1992 (which enabled "the development of what many observers dubbed a 'savage' Mozambican capitalism and the rise of a 'neo-colonial' state").[50]

When analyzing the behavior of the Frelimo party-state towards built heritage, one should consider the policies put in place by the previous administration, especially from the 1940s onwards, when a list of Classified Historical Monuments (restricted to colonial heritage) was drawn up and subsequently added to. Built heritage, performing identity, and political legitimacy substantiated by material culture forged collective memory and constituted the "dissonant inheritances" left by colonialism. As already mentioned in the introduction, in 1940—the year in which the Estado Novo celebrated the Foundation of Portugal in 1143 and the Restoration of Portuguese sovereignty in 1640—, the colonial power commemorated the so-called "pacification" campaigns of the 1890s and its heroes with the monument to Mouzinho de Albuquerque and the inauguration of several closely related memorials.[51] The massive Mouzinho de Albuquerque Square, designed in the late 1930s at the top of the city's most important urban axis, the Av. D. Luís (present-day Samora Machel Avenue), towering over the old downtown, with a logo cobbled into the sidewalks stating "Aqui é Portugal" (Here is Portugal), complemented by the Municipal Palace (1947) and the Cathedral (1944), became the site for a considerable number of celebrations and pro-regime rallies. On the same site, a monumental bronze statue depicting the first president of the People's Republic of Mozambique, Samora Machel, produced by North Korean artists and inaugurated on October 19, 2011 (as part of Mozambique's yearlong commemoration of Samora Machel), marked the tribute to the "Father of the nation." Another statue of Samora Machel, installed in 1989, which replaced the stone pillar attesting to the first presidential visit to the colony (President Óscar Carmona, in 1939), stands at the entrance of the Tunduru Garden (former Vasco da Gama Gardens) in Av. Samora Machel. The choice of these places for the tribute to Samora Machel attests not only to the relevance invested by the colonial administration in these places but also to the new frames of the post colony, set, for instance, by numerous celebrations intrinsically linked to the leadership of Samora Machel (fig. 6). In 2004 a resolution of the Municipal Assembly nominated the Town Hall building and the Independence Square for "appropriate use and conservation … for the cultural and historical values that they have and represent in the municipality and for the country."[52]

6 Independence Day, the crowd attends the investiture ceremony for the new president held at the City Hall, Mouzinho de Albuquerque Square, Lourenço Marques, June 25, 1975.

In the wake of independence, many of the material manifestations of colonialism (such as statues, specific iconography, and toponomy) were perceived as a problematic or unwanted heritage and thus silenced, publicly ignored, or removed from the public space. Frelimo too strove to substantiate its envisioned nation's history with a body of material traces, or in other words, "evidence": "'having a heritage'" affirmed its "right to exist in the present and continue into the future."[53] A distinctive repertoire, rooted in the past, populated with (in some cases, appropriated colonial) historical sites, closely followed by highly mediated and controlled practices and rituals, attested to its unquestionable narrative of liberation, its heroes, and its political insight. This was a social and political process borrowed directly from Western concepts of modernity that can now be studied as representative of a particular strand of memory, identity, and legitimacy production at a particular time, reflecting its agendas and perceptions.[54] The fact that, in the wake of independence, Mozambican policymakers sought the protection of artwork, language, and built heritage brought by colonialism illustrates, however, that the reality of Mozambique's cultural refashioning was more nuanced than such assertions would suggest. Many were/are battles over heritage and identity in the post-colony but, as Bellisari argues, "exploring the history of how a former colony came to claim stewardship over … [precise] artwork [and old city centers] emblematic of the former colonizer's culture"[55] unsettles cultural assumptions and "totalizing qualifications often associated with the drama of colonial disentanglement"[56] foremost understood as "the end point."[57] Rather, looking into the turbulent urban history of independence and revolution can present extended insight to begin to investigate dilemmas about contested heritage practices of selection, preservation, public representation, and reception in the post-independence longstanding cityscape and "how the repercussions of colonial divorce reverberate across boundaries"[58] and time.

1   Dolff-Bonekämper 2002, 4.

2   Lee and Misselwitz 2017, 10.

3   This section incorporates material from my article "The Art of Decolonization: Memorials, Buildings and Public Space in Maputo, 1974–1976," in *Heritage 2020: Proceedings of the 7th International Conference on Heritage and Sustainable Development* (see Franco de Mendonça 2020). The research on which it is based was supported by an Alexander von Humboldt Foundation's Postdoctoral Fellowship and a research contract funded by the Fundação para a Ciência e a Tecnologia (FCT), Lisbon (CEECIND/02649/2017). I am also indebted to several scholars at the Eduardo Mondlane University, Maputo, for their insights and for enabling me to use their private archives—especially Júlio Carrilho, Luís Lage, Catarina Torres, and Alda Costa.

4   The Estado Novo (lit. "New State"), a right-leaning corporatist dictatorship, greatly inspired by nationalist and autocratic ideologies and Catholic social doctrine, ruled Portugal from 1933 until 1974. Its policy regarding the Portuguese Empire envisaged the perpetuation of a pluricontinental country constituted by overseas provinces.

5   Schilling 2020, 96.

6   "The Mozambique Liberation Front (FRELIMO) changed its acronym in capital letters to Frelimo in 1977, when the Front became the Marxist-Leninist Vanguard Party." Machava 2021, endnote 1. It had abandoned its self-styled socialist orientation by the late 1980s and has ruled the country since independence in 1975. Because my study deals mostly with the party-state during the post-independence revolutionary period, I will use the name Frelimo for both the Front and the Party.

7   People's Forces for the Liberation of Mozambique (commonly referred to as FPLM).

8   With independence, the Military History Museum, located in the Fortress of Our Lady of the Conception, was permanently closed. Its collection, focused on the Portuguese narrative of the occupation of Mozambique, then became the subject of discussion (see note 15).

9   António Enes (1848–1901), charged with the administrative and legislative organization of Portuguese East Africa, was the mentor of the "pacification" of the lands south of the Save River from 1895 onwards.

10   Verheij 2012, 34. Unless otherwise noted, all translations are my own.

11   The bibliography on the colonial "bifurcated state" (e.g., the institutionalization of double standards for colonized people and citizens), which also translated into a bifurcated city, is extensive; see Mamdani 1996 and Myers 2005.

12   Macdonald 2009.

13   Alda Costa, Director of the Department of Museums, from the National Directorate of Cultural Heritage of the Ministry of Culture from 1986 to 2001, personal communication with the author, Maputo, September 17, 2019.

14   Júlio Carrilho (1946–2021), Minister of Public Works sworn in during the presidency of Samora Machel, personal communication with the author, Maputo, September 18, 2019.

15   The architectural and exhibition projects were outlined by the Historical Archive of Mozambique (HAM). The renovation of the fortress, taking into account the aforementioned curatorial program, took place in the late 1980s with funding from the Norwegian Agency for Development (NORAD), which also funded the restoration of other buildings in the downtown area. "História colonial" 1993.

16   República Popular de Moçambique 1979, 8–10, 45–51.

17   Secretaria de Estado da Cultura and Arkitektskolen i Aarhus 1986.

18   Moçambique 1988, 441–(13)–441–(17). This legislation provides for the legal protection of the tangible and intangible assets of Mozambique's cultural heritage.

19   "Inquérito" 1975.

20   Cf. Collection Arquivo da Câmara Municipal de Lourenço Marques, e. g., Icon. 275–87; 289–90; 297–8; 853.

21   Malone 2015.

22   For instance, in the clear division between the "City of Cement" (the central urban area formally designed and equipped for the settler population during the colonial period) and the *caniço* ("shantytown," lit. "reed," formerly used as construction material in the area), i. e., the formerly unauthorized occupation of the colonial map that lie outside the "city," the location for lower income, African, and *assimilados* (assimilated) groups. Franco de Mendonça 2022, 187 note 2. See also note 11 above.

23   On this argument, see Newitt 2012, 466–67; Cahen 1993, 47; Dinerman 2006, 29–30.

24   Malone 2015.

25   La Cecla 2015, 5.

26   Sumich and Honwana 2007, 8. See also Machava 2021; Dinerman 2006, 11–13, 33.

27   From the Faculty of Architecture and Physical Planning of University Eduardo Mondlane.

28   The HAM, the former Cultural Heritage Archive and current Institute for Sociocultural Research (known by the Portuguese acronymous ARPAC), the Photographic Training and Documentation Center (PTDC), and the National Library of Mozambique, in Maputo.

29   Lagae 2015.

30   Jenkins 2013, 90–91; Newitt 2012, 466–67; Cahen 1993, 51, 54–55; Dinerman 2006, 50.

31   Júlio Carrilho (see note 14), personal communication with the author, Maputo, September 18, 2019.

32   Mendes de Oliveira and Rangel 1974, 42; see also Morton 2019, 42–43. For an overall perception of the socio-economic and demographic distribution in Lourenço Marques from the mid-twentieth century to independence, see Mendes 1985, 92–96, 98, 362–63, 365.

33   República Popular de Moçambique 1979, 8–10, 45–51.

34   Bellisari 2017, 626.

35   Bellisari 2017, 627.

36   Different attitudes towards colonial-built repertoires can be individuated in post-independence contexts (appropriation and reinvention of its meaning being also common): see, for instance, Haile Selassie's regime appropriation of Italian monuments and infrastructural development in Ethiopia in Levin 2016, 453–54.

37   Cahen 1993, 46, see also 50. The Portuguese language was used as the language of instruction and disruption (of ethnic identity), conveyed (by Frelimo) as an instrument of both insurrection and modernization in the context of the liberation struggle and in its aftermath, respectively.

38   Costa 2013, 247–49, 261ff., 276; Hedges 1999, 222–32; Franco de Mendonça 2016, 302ff.

39   Moçambique 1979. This law allowed for each provincial assembly to create an inventory commission of historical places in the province.

40   Excerpt from the speech of Samora Machel held at Chaimite on the occasion of the swearing-in ceremony of several military commanders in 1982. "Marechal Samora" 1982.

41   Fuller 2011.

42   Município de Maputo 2008, 23. Despite being used as a reference by the municipality, this plan was never officially approved by the Council of Ministers under the terms of the Planning Law in force. For an overall perception on the backgrounds, scopes, and characteristics of this plan, see Jenkins 2013, 74–77, 100 ff.

43   This was the case of Casa Coimbra, an emblematic Art Deco building demolished to give way to the 30-story, concrete-and-glass Bank of Mozambique headquarters, inaugurated in 2017, or, very recently, in the same vicinity, the old headquarters of Minerva Central, an historic bookshop established in 1908.

44   Arthurs 2015, 286.

45   Salman Binladen defines the term employed by Hassan Fathy as "in essence, an appropriation of something that has no place in one's own culture and space." Binladen 2018, 6.

46　"One of the basic problems of the history of Frelimo comes not only from the victorious form in which this history has been approached, but above all from the way its knowledge has been presented as unquestionable." Aquino de Bragança and Jacques Depelchin, "Da Idealização da Frelimo à Compreensão da História de Moçambique," *Estudos Moçambicanos* 5/6 (1986), 33, quoted in Machava 2011, 595.

47　Franco de Mendonça 2022, 187.

48　See note 18. Also, the colonial legislation for the protection of historical monuments, relics, and sites was not revoked after independence.

49　E.g., in Mozambique Island and in downtown Maputo. Many projects, however, were held back due to the war. José Capão, Director of the Department of Buildings, from the National Directorate for Cultural Heritage of the Ministry of Culture, and director of the ARPAC (1986/87–1991), personal communication with the author, Maputo, September 17, 2019.

50　Dinerman 2006, 62. According to Jenkins, "as the government negotiated toward peace in the early 1990s after adopting a new market-oriented and multi-democratic constitution, … there was diminishing accountability in central and local government, and growing commoditization of services as well as assets such as land … leading to corruption at all levels." Jenkins 2013, 97. On the impact of the political-economic adjustments put in place, which resulted in escalating state incapacity to pursue urban planning or social policies, see Jenkins 2013, 73–74, 96–98. On the fading interest in heritage discussion from 1990 onward, see Costa and Torcato 1997, 12.

51　"Crónica do Trimestre" 1940, 92–94, 99–101.

52　Município de Maputo 2004.

53　Macdonald 2009, 2.

54　This idea is particularly resonant of writings about the "invention of tradition" and the temporalities of "'heritagisation' as a process." See Hobsbawm and Ranger 1983; Harvey 2001, 320–21, 327.

55　Bellisari 2017, 643.

56　Bellisari 2017, 644.

57　Bellisari 2017, 644–45.

58　Bellisari 2017, 645.

59　"Não leves mais…" 1974, 62.

Bibliography

Arthurs, Joshua. 2015. "'Voleva essere Cesare morì Vespasiano': The Afterlives of Mussolini's Rome." *Civiltà Romana. Rivista pluridisciplinare di studi su Roma antica e le sue intrepretazioni* 1: 283–302.

Bellisari, Andrew. 2017. "The Art of Decolonization: The Battle for Algeria's French Art, 1962–70." *Journal of Contemporary History* 52, no. 3 (July): 625–45, https://doi.org/10.1177/0022009416652715 (accessed February 2, 2022).

Binladen, Salman Salem. 2018. "Foreword by Salman Salem Binladen." In Salman Samar Damluji and Viola Bertini, *Hassan Fathy: Earth & Utopia*, 6–8. London: Laurence King.

Cahen, Michel. 1993. "Check on Socialism in Mozambique: What Check? What Socialism?" *Review of African Political Economy* 57: 46–59.

Costa, Alda. 2013. *Arte em Moçambique: Entre a Construção da Nação e o Mundo sem Fronteiras (1932–2004)*. Lisbon: BABEL.

Costa, Alda, and Maria de Lurdes Torcato. 1997. "Os equívocos e as insuficiências." *MoçAmbiente* 21 (December): 11–13.

"Crónica do Trimestre: Glorificação a Mousinho de Albuquerque." 1940. *Moçambique: Documentário Trimestral* 24: 92–105, http://memoria-africa.ua.pt/Library/ShowImage.aspx?q=/MDT/MDT-N024&p=93 (accessed February 2, 2022).

Dinerman, Alice. 2006. *Revolution, Counter-Revolution and Revisionism in Postcolonial Africa: The Case of Mozambique*. Abingdon: Routledge.

Dolff-Bonekämper, Gabi. 2002. "Sites of Hurtful Memory." *Conservation, The GCI Newsletter* 17, no. 2: 4–10.

Franco de Mendonça, Lisandra. 2016. "Conservação da Arquitetura e do Ambiente Urbano Modernos: A Baixa de Maputo." Tese de dout., Universidade de Coimbra/ Sapienza Università di Roma, http://hdl.handle.net/10316/29573 (accessed February 2, 2022).

Franco de Mendonça, Lisandra. 2020. "The Art of Decolonization: Memorials, Buildings and Public Space in Maputo, 1974–1976." In Rogério Amoêda, Sérgio Lira, and Cristina Pinheiro, eds., *Heritage 2020: Proceedings of the 7th International Conference on Heritage and Sustainable Development*, 751–61. [Coimbra]: Green Lines Institute.

Franco de Mendonça, Lisandra. 2022. "Architecture of (De)Colonization: Heritage, Identity and Amnesia in an African City: Maputo's 'City of Cement'." In Antonella Versaci, Claudia Cennamo, and Natsuko Akagawa, eds., *Conservation of Architectural Heritage (CAH)*, Advances in Science, Technology & Innovation, 185–195. Cham: Springer, https://doi.org/10.1007/978-3-030-95564-9_13 (accessed February 2, 2022).

Fuller, Mia. 2011. "Italy's Colonial Futures: Colonial Inertia and Postcolonial Capital in Asmara." *California Italian Studies* 2, no. 1, https://escholarship.org/uc/item/4mb1z7f8 (accessed February 2, 2022).

Harvey, David C. 2001. "Heritage Pasts and Heritage Presents: Temporality, Meaning and the Scope of Heritage Studies." *International Journal of Heritage Studies* 7, no. 4: 319–38.

Hedges, David. 1999. *História de Moçambique: Moçambique no Auge do Colonialismo, 1930–1961*, 2nd ed., vol. 2. Maputo: UEM.

"História colonial, criação do museu continua um sonho." 1993. *Notícias* [Maputo], October 15, 1993.

Hobsbawm, Eric, and Terence Ranger, eds. 1983. *The Invention of Tradition*. Cambridge: Cambridge University Press.

"Inquérito." 1975. *Notícias* [Lourenço Marques], May 7, 1975: 3.

Jenkins, Paul. 2013. *Urbanization, Urbanism, and Urbanity in an African City: Home Spaces and House Cultures*. New York: Palgrave Macmillan.

La Cecla, Franco. 2015. *Contro l'urbanistica*. Torino: Einaudi.

Lagae, Johan. 2015. "Ana Tostões, ed., *Modern Architecture in Africa: Angola and Mozambique*, Lisbon: ICIST, Técnico, 2013." *ABE Journal* 7: 1–8, https://doi.org/10.4000/abe.2647 (accessed February 2, 2022).

Lee, Rachel, and Philipp Misselwitz. 2017. "Introduction: Things Don't Really Exist Until You Give Them a Name: Unpacking Urban Heritage." In Rachel Lee et al., eds., *Things Don't Really Exist Until You Give Them a Name: Unpacking Urban Heritage*, 8–19. Dar es Salam: Mkuki na Nyota.

Levin, Ayala. 2016. "Haile Selassie's Imperial Modernity: Expatriate Architects and the Shaping of Addis Ababa." *Journal of the Society of Architectural Historians* 75, no. 4: 447–68, https://doi.org/10.1525/jsah.2016.75.4.447 (accessed February 2, 2022).

Macdonald, Sharon. 2009. *Difficult Heritage: Negotiating the Nazi Past in Nuremberg and Beyond*. Abingdon: Routledge.

Machava, Benedito Luís. 2011. "State Discourse on Internal Security and the Politics of Punishment in Post-Independence Mozambique (1975–1983)." *Journal of Southern African Studies* 37, no. 3 (September): 593–609.

Machava, Benedito. 2021. "Re-education Camps and the Messianic Ethos of Mozambique's Socialism." In Françoise Blum et al., eds., *Socialismes en Afrique*, 319–56. Paris: Éditions de la Maison des sciences de l'homme, https://doi.org/10.4000/books.editionsmsh.51435 (accessed January 2, 2023).

Malone, Hannah. 2015. "Revisiting the Fascist City." *Italian Studies* 70, no. 2: 269–74, https://doi.org/10.1179/0075163415Z.000000000100 (accessed February 2, 2022).

Mamdani, Mahmood. 1996. *Citizen and Subject: Contemporary Africa and the Legacy of Late Colonialism*. Princeton: Princeton University Press.

"Marechal Samora Machel em Chaimite." 1982. *Notícias* [Maputo], March 6, 1982.

Mendes, Maria Clara. 1985. *Maputo antes da Independência, Geografia de uma Cidade Colonial*. Lisbon: Instituto de Investigação Científica Tropical.

Mendes de Oliveira and Ricardo Rangel. 1974. "Manter os 'escritos' ou baixar as rendas: Um dilema ilógico." *Tempo* 215, December 15, 1974: 41–47.

Moçambique. 1979. Resolução no. 4, May 3, 1979. *Boletim da República*, I série, no. 50 (May 3).

Moçambique. 1988. Lei no. 10, December 22, 1988. *Boletim [da] República Popular de Moçambique*, I série, no. 51, III suplemento (December 22), 441–(13)–441–(17), https://www.fao.org/faolex/results/details/en/c/LEX-FAOC062319/ (accessed June 12, 2023).

Morton, David. 2019. *Age of Concrete: Housing and the Shape of Aspiration in the Capital of Mozambique*. Athens: Ohio University Press.

Município de Maputo. 2004. Resolução no. 15/AM, August 11, 2004.

Município de Maputo. 2008. *Plano de Estrutura Urbana do Município de Maputo*, vol. 2. Maputo.

Myers, Garth. 2005. *Disposable Cities: Garbage, Governance and Sustainable Development in Urban Africa*. Aldershot: Ashgate.

"Não leves mais…" 1974. *Tempo* 219, December 8, 1974: 62.

Newitt, Malyn. 2012. *História de Moçambique*, 2nd ed. Translated by Lucília Rodrigues and Maria Georgina Segurado. Mem Martins: Europa-América; orig. *A History of Mozambique*. London: C. Hurst, 1995.

República Popular de Moçambique. 1979. *Lei do Arrendamento 4.ª Sessão Assembleia Nacional "Documentos"* 3. Maputo.

Schilling, Britta. 2020. "Afterlives of Colonialism in the Everyday: Street Names and the (Un)making of Imperial Debris." In Berny Sèbe and Mathew G. Stanard, eds., *Decolonising Europe? Popular Responses to the End of Empire*, 95–112. Abingdon: Routledge.

Secretaria de Estado da Cultura, and Arkitektskolen i Aarhus. 1986. *Ilha de Moçambique, Relatório/Report, 1982–85*. Aarhus: Phønix A/S.

Sumich, Jason, and João Honwana. 2007. "Strong Party, Weak State? Frelimo and State Survival Through the Mozambican Civil War: An Analytical Narrative on State-making." *Crisis States Working Papers Series* 2, no. 23 (December): 1–28.

Verheij, Gerbert. 2012. "Monumentalidade e Espaço Público em Lourenço Marques nas Décadas de 1930 e 1940." *On the W@terfront* 20: 11–54, http://www.ub.edu/escult/Water/w-20/onthewaterfront_20.pdf (accessed February 2, 2022).

Image Sources

1,2,4 PTDC, photo by Ricardo Rangel, Collection Ricardo Rangel.

3   HAM, Collection Arquivo da Câmara Municipal de Lourenço Marques, Icon. 4772.

5   Photo by Filipe Branquinho, 2011.

6   HAM, Collection Álbum da Independência.

Heritage and Memories

JORGE CORREIA

Heritage and (Post)Colonial Urban Challenges in the Maghreb

Ceuta and the Moroccan Context

Background and Framework

North-western Africa's history is a palimpsest of powers and regimes where European colonialism has played a significant role in the shaping of cities. An attentive reading of different configurations suggests that tradition has been both a conspicuous and a neglected instrument for post-colonial urban challenges. This text explores the colonial sphere of urbanization in north-western Africa and its legacy, with a particular focus on the city of Ceuta.

At the time of its occupation by the Portuguese in 1415, the Muslim bastion of Ceuta was one of the largest cities on the south side of the Strait of Gibraltar and therefore of great strategic importance. At the same time, the legendary ancient past of the city had turned it into an easily recognizable symbol of power and glory. In fact, several allusions in classical works testify to its greatness and symbolic potency. This aura was very much present in the fifteenth-century imagination, making possession of the city all the more desirable.

The reference to Ceuta in Dante's *La Divina Commedia*[1] is no isolated instance. Across the centuries, the city had been as much a source of inspiration to poets, classical authors,[2] and travellers alike, as an object of greed for neighbors and enemies. Ceuta is located on Mount Acho, traditionally identified as one of the mythical pillars of Hercules, which with its European counterpart, the Rock of Gibraltar, joins two continents and guards over two seas. Later, Arab geographers examined the descriptions and assessments of the site with new rigor and proposed a more accurate version of the city and its history before the Portuguese conquest. Still, if this new vision rejected much of the mythology, the legendary origins of Ceuta remained an important motivation for several conquests.

Once part of the Roman province of Tingitana Mauritania, the city of Ceuta, along with the rest of its neighboring territories, became officially Christianized by the fifth century CE,[3] as did all the territories of late antiquity around the Mediterranean upon the fall of the Western Roman Empire. Christianity was maintained by a strong Byzantine influence in the period immediately following, and only replaced by Islam with the Arab conquest in the late seventh century CE. Subsequent military episodes led to the Arab spread over North Africa, the invasion of the Iberian Peninsula in 711, and the cantonment of Christian forces in the Asturias region from where the *reconquista* would begin.

During the following centuries, Ceuta thrived as a strategic commercial hub and grew to become a *medina* filled with notable public buildings and surrounded by several suburbs. The overall built environment, which had resulted from the Christian-Byzantine and late-antiquity periods, was gradually altered during the centuries of Muslim presence.[4] In the high- and late-Middle Ages, Ceuta reinforced its status as a key player in the political and economic puzzle of the Western Mediterranean. Moreover, the capture of the city by the Portuguese in 1415 can be understood not as an isolated adventure, but rather as the transposition of a religious conflict from Iberia to the Maghreb, underpinned by strategic and symbolic motives.

Such a military move is also to be understood within the context of a long past of social, military, and cultural interactivity between the northern and southern shores of the Strait of Gibraltar. The Portuguese influence in the region lasted from 1415, when King João I (1385–1433) started what would become a series of conquests in the Maghrebi coast, to 1769. For more than three and a half centuries, Portuguese territorial expansion reverberated in isolated enclaves along the Strait and Atlantic coasts, which correspond today to a long seashore stretch in the Kingdom of Morocco, with the exception of the Spanish city of Ceuta. This territorial presence was never seen by the Portuguese crown as a full colony, but neither did it have autonomous jurisdiction. It was rather based on the conquest and occupation of pre-existing Arab and Muslim cities, resulting in a network of possessions directly ruled by the king through local captains and/or governors.[5]

The arrival of a new power, bearing the Christian faith, implied a reconfiguration of the urban fabric. The most frequent military approach was the conquest, which took over pre-existing established cities belonging to Maghrebi historical and political spheres such as Fez and Marrakesh. Occupied cities were, most of the time, too large for Portuguese military resources to maintain in a permanent state of defensive readiness. So, the Portuguese adopted a pragmatic attitude to the rule of these cities, oriented towards sustainability in a hostile environment. Therefore, urban appropriations shrank cities, erased suburbs, and promoted the opening of new streets and squares, closer to a built environment that could be identified as Portuguese. Significant reductions in the city's perimeter and surface were carried out in a procedure known as *atalho* (downsizing). In some cases, opportunities to experiment with more elaborate systems have left an urban heritage that is still present today, simultaneously echoing early-modern bastioned military systems, grid-planning urban spaces, and the scars of cultural clashes as far as the built environment is concerned.

With the exceptions of Ceuta and the Spanish conquest of Melilla further east in the Mediterranean, all strongholds were lost to the royal Moroccan dynasties in the following centuries. Later, during the first half of the 1900s, Spain and France divided the kingdom into protectorates, respectively in the north and the central south, leaving an urban footprint that still resonates today, more than half a century after Moroccan independence in the mid-twentieth century. Once again, conflicting urban patterns starred in a complex political scenario.

Portuguese Ceuta: Dimensions and Military Impact

Ceuta represents a peculiar case study. It offers a different model from the colonial and political history that interrupted the Arab and Muslim continuum of traditional cities in the Maghreb—conducted by the Portuguese in coastal townships in the fifteenth and sixteenth centuries, and by the Spanish and the French in the twentieth century. The still-Spanish enclave of Ceuta, for centuries an important Muslim commercial stronghold, has remained in European hands ever since it was conquered by the Portuguese in 1415.

This colonial history is responsible for some of the most important features of the city, still readable today. The arrival of the new Portuguese lordship and the Christian creed led to a re-evaluation of, and a reduction in, the built urban space. The key issues were around the foundation of a new Christian image where the cathedral would not only replace the former main mosque, but also new fortifications would mask Islamic defensive systems.

Medieval Muslim Ceuta was formed by an urban nucleus, called a *medina*, in the narrowest part of the peninsula and by several suburbs to the east and west, which recent archaeological excavations and coeval descriptions by Arab geographers have helped to locate.[6] This was definitely too large a territory for the Portuguese to defend after the conquest. A shortening of the perimeter reduced the whole area to 14 %, confined to the former *medina* area.[7] This downsizing technique—*atalho*—was an extreme decision about the urban space, selecting a specific perimeter and surface, and deleting the rest.

The necessity to concentrate the defense of the city in the isthmus area enabled a demographic concentration in that zone. Integrated under the Portuguese crown, Ceuta found itself secluded and with a hostile hinterland, having lost some of the favorable conditions that had turned it into a mercantile emporium in the Middle Ages. Now, with only a meager European population, its limits retreated to the narrowest strip of the peninsula, which was more easily defensible as it had a shorter land frontline. In the first phase, soon after the conquest in 1415, the Portuguese downsized the city which immediately excluded the suburbs to the east and west, blocking the peninsula and reducing the urban area.[8] For the east, the urgency of the downsizing was not so great, since an attack would require a less-probable enemy water landing at the edge of the peninsula that surrounds Mount Acho. The eastern outskirts were progressively razed and transformed into farmland to supply the city's reduced population. The devastation of the houses eliminated potential shelters for the enemy, preventing possible ambushes. In this sector, the downsizing and its implications dragged on throughout the fifteenth century. As can be seen in the engraving by Georg Braun,[9] at the beginning of the following century, the destruction of built structures on the hills between the Portuguese city and the tip of the peninsula was still visible, while the contour walls also showed the marks of Portuguese penetration, later described by Valentim Fernandes between 1505 and 1507 (fig. 1).[10] By the time of the reign of King Manuel I (1495–1521), almost a century of Portuguese presence in this Maghrebi city had elapsed and with it a slow but consistent process of landscape metamorphosis.

Military architecture did not undergo major changes when the Portuguese took over. The continuous carrying out of maintenance works was a constant in a battleground like Ceuta. From the beginning of the sixteenth century, however, records of repairs in the city's fortifications increased. It was a clear sign of the weakness, and even the obsolescence, into which the defensive perimeter of the former *medina*, used by the Portuguese for almost a century, had fallen. There was an urgent need to renovate military structures in all Portuguese positions, at a time when, besides Ceuta, the Portuguese crown ruled Ksar Seghir, Tangier, and Asilah, all located in the Strait of Gibraltar region, and was further expanding beyond the kingdom of Fez, on the southern coasts of Morocco and Sus. With renovation purposes in mind, master Francisco Danzilho travelled from Portugal in 1511.[11] What is known of his works was measured by master Boytac and Bastião Luiz over a number of days starting on June 28, 1514.[12] In Ceuta, the intervention on the eastern side of the fortifications definitively concluded the process begun almost a century earlier.

1   A 1572 engraving depicting a view of Ceuta in the beginning of the sixteenth century under Portuguese rule.

Francisco Danzilho's renovation works, with additions by Boytac, constituted the main constructive and reforming impulse since the conquest of the city. However, despite having marked Ceuta's morphological landscape at the beginning of the sixteenth century, they already reflected a mismatch with the importance of the site, fuelling the enemy's greed that was increasingly avid for the recovery of lost territories. In 1541, governor D. Afonso de Noronha wrote to King João III (1521–1557) calling attention to the bad condition of most of the city's walls and gates, particularly in view of the movements of the Turks.[13] Faced with the permanent threat of the Ottoman fleet near the Strait of Gibraltar, the monarch sent a team to Ceuta made up of Italian engineer Benedetto da Ravenna and architect Miguel de Arruda. Finding the city in very poor condition and incapable of defending itself, Ravenna drew up a plan that Arruda would take to the king for consideration and approval.[14]

The Italian engineer formulated a project that is reflected in a sketch (lost) and notes[15]—a fundamental tool for the analysis of the modernization of fortifications that took place after 1541. The general design focused on strengthening the fortified structures around the city's perimeter, that is, the Portuguese downsized rectangle, with emphasis on the mainland front where two new bastions were proposed. The fortification works, completed in 1548/49, provided for flooding the moat for use as a maritime channel (fig. 2).[16] The north and south angles of this new fortress line showed the same defensive unit: the early-modern bastion. Straight, interrupted by canon embrasures and accessible by an upper *chemin de ronde*, a walled curtain stretched between two opposing orillons that enabled one of the main principles of flanking, the crossing of fire and mutual defense.[17]

By the mid-sixteenth century, the city of Ceuta projected a strong and impregnable image onto its narrow front of contact with enemy territory. Indeed, given the fragility of the land border between the isthmus and the rest of the continent, which actually meant the frontier between the new Christian stronghold and the belligerent hinterland, military architecture has always played a fundamental role in Ceuta. Summing up, after an initial immediate appropriation of the Islamic defenses, this sector saw major transformations during the sixteenth century when a new bastioned fortification was built over the former segment, originally built by the Umayyad Caliphate of Cordoba. Thus, and besides the obvious survival quest, a complete obliteration of the Muslim past helped convey a European image of a city belonging exclusively to the Portuguese in the Maghreb.

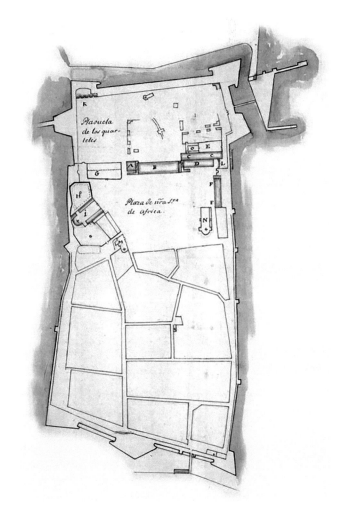

2   An early-eighteen century plan of
Ceuta, already under Spanish rule.
B   Old Portuguese Castle
i   Former Portuguese Cathedral
N   Church of Our Lady of Africa

A European Quest: Urban Development in Ceuta

Besides the profound downsizing, reconfiguration, and military delimitation, intervention in the new walled city suggests another significant heritage impact on the urban history of Ceuta. Updating and employing a novel rhetorical language were key factors, at a time when urban concepts and practices were being progressively contaminated by early-modern ideals. Important actions were seen in the opening of a new square and new street, clearly intended to unblock the dense inherited fabric.

When conquering the city, the Portuguese uncritically adapted many existing urban elements. Nevertheless, a more exteriorized city, reflecting the social practices of towns and cities in metropolitan Portugal, was required. Therefore, the opening of a large square became an urgent matter. Faced with less demographic pressure, the ideal location proved to be in front of the old castle, thus unblocking and opening up the north facade of the former mosque, now turned into a church. As depicted in Braun's engraving (see fig. 1), the city's square or *terreiro* (yard), called Aira in the fifteenth century, was assumed to be the most important public space, organizing internal routes and enabling access to the most notable buildings.

Later on, during the 1500s, the early-modern renovations of the city's military architecture offered the urban agglomeration a peaceful period of development and stabilization, as a result of the impregnability of its new defensive system. The available area of the Portuguese city was approximately 8.5 hectares during the second half of the sixteenth century and the first half of the seventeenth century.[18] In general terms, the interior of the fortified rectangle of the city had two sectors equivalent in area, both roughly square and arranged side by side. The eastern half displayed a densely populated grid of about eleven blocks of houses, shops, and gardens, while the western half housed practically all public facilities, whether religious, military, or civil, around the public *terreiro*.

The street layout process emerged as a natural continuation of the operation initiated by the downsizing operation. Less demand for free territory, due to a scarcer population density, contributed to a regularization of streets that gradually accommodated more and more orthogonality. The newly named Rua Direita (main straight street) remains the only major thoroughfare of the urban space, parallel to the north and south coasts. This organization resulted from a balance between the network of streets inherited from the Islamic fabric and a desire to rationalize the public space, particularly through its laneways, clearly distinguishing public and private spaces, as can be seen from donation letters.[19] Streets tended towards a regular grid, favoring junctions at 90-degree angles in T-shaped crossroads. Jerónimo de Mascarenhas counted, in 1648, 450 dwellings and about 1,900 people of communion—that is, all Catholics regardless of age—in this prime residential sector.[20]

Portuguese Ceuta in the second half of the sixteenth century and the first decades of the following century, until it passed into Spanish hands in 1640, was characterized by the military architecture and urbanism explained above. Afterwards, during Madrid's rule, the image of the city would be deeply marked by the long years of siege by Sultan Moulay Ismail (r. 1672–1727), starting in 1694 and continuing until his death.[21] The rectangle of the former Portuguese city remained stable, despite the destruction perpetrated by the Alawite bombings. Nevertheless, there were important changes in the urban morphology, both east and westwards. Towards

Mount Acho, the path that started at Almina gate was defined as a street, flanked by new constructions for a population that was fleeing the threat of projectiles launched from the mainland. It came to constitute the main axis of the mesh of the new *ensanche*, today visible in Paseo del Revellin, Calle Camoens, and Calle Real. To the west, the separation from the mainland was accentuated with the erection of successive bastioned frontlines between the moat and the outer camp of the besieging Arabs. During the second half of the siege, in the first decades of the eighteenth century, the Spaniards redesigned the land front, multiplying the bastions, ravelins, gorges, and hornworks, in order to keep enemy fire as far as possible from the limits of the inhabited core. Coeval cartography exhaustively illustrates the stages of such works, a Vauban-style military architecture that secluded the island/peninsula even more.[22]

In summary, the colonial city was characterized by the Portuguese legacy in the center (confined to the former Arab *medina* limits), the expansion towards Almina, and the defensive curtains of the land front. Late-medieval and early-modern decisions still resonate in the city center's current urban stratigraphy, further developed by Spain since 1640. After Moulay Ismail's siege and new shifts in power, mainly in the twentieth century, Spanish Ceuta has recovered much of its medieval area and has been extended towards the mainland, beyond its continental walls, in a process that reoccupies the ancient Islamic domains. Curiously, a majority of Moroccan immigrants now live in these new neighborhoods.[23]

Christian Reimagining of Ceuta

Until recent times, Spain had a deliberate policy that claimed Ceuta as an eternal Christian site since late-Roman domination brought Byzantine influences to the region. Hence, more than seven centuries of Islamic rule were to be subordinated to the legitimation of European control that the Portuguese conquest of 1415 had supposedly fairly reclaimed for the Papacy from the hands of the "infidel" occupant. So, what happened inside the former Portuguese quadrilateral surface was to become another crucial moment of heritage clash, particularly fostered by twentieth-century policies. The historical claim over this disputed territory has led to an active obliteration of the Muslim legacy in order to favor the signs of European presence and, most drastically, to modernize historical Ceuta with the opening of Gran Via and its conspicuous contemporary design of public space. Although the intention is based on a tabula rasa method, the permanence of the Islamic general layout persisted, and to this day still signals significant axes and limits of the city, even if masked by later constructions.

The religious built heritage shows another way of reimagining Ceuta as a Christian stronghold. In a chronologically parallel process, a sign of such transformation lies in the former Portuguese cathedral, to which the original medieval mosque was converted. The oldest data for the mosque assigns a wrong orientation to its *qibla*, in 937, before a major reconstruction by the Almoravid Sultan Youssuf Ibn Tachfin in the eleventh century.[24] The building was then extended almost to the sea, under the orders of mayor Ibn Isa.[25] Al Bekri describes the mosque as having five naves, the central one being the highest, and a courtyard,[26] while Al Ansari counts twenty-two naves, surely counting both transverse and longitudinal naves.[27]

Consecrated to Our Lady of the Assumption upon the Portuguese conquest in 1415, the cathedral maintained its layout in five naves, whose tension was now longitudinal, favoring a ba-

3   Ceuta: View over the city with the cathedral in the foreground.

silical section of the structure, since the central nave was higher.[28] As noted above, the opening of a central main square (*terreiro*) in front of the cathedral allowed the most important entrance to face north, giving a sense of symmetry to the new Christian elevation. The minaret was transformed into a bell tower in the first phase, but given its antiquity, it would have been degraded in 1422[29] but kept at the back of the church, as Braun's engraving seems to suggest in the early sixteenth century (see fig. 1). Inside, one would have found a hypostyle hall with some 180 columns, as counted by Lanckman of Valkenstein.[30]

Until the end of the seventeenth century, that is, covering the entire period of Portuguese occupation, the cathedral was always housed in the former mosque building, adapted to the functions of a Christian church.[31] In 1570, the diocese of Ceuta merged with that of Tangier,[32] but this did not introduce any morphological change in the cathedral. Given the ruinous state of the church since the beginning of the seventeenth century, works took place from 1685, under the direction of Juan de Ochoa.[33] The previous structure was demolished and a new one built on the same site; the new cathedral was consecrated in 1726. It would eventually undergo a second important renovation in the twentieth century, between 1944 and 1955,[34] which defines its current aspect. Indeed, its ruined state determined reconstruction efforts by the Spanish authorities,[35] which led to a significant twist with the introduction of a novel neo-Baroque style (fig. 3). A dome and twin towers helped to give a new grand look to the building, now the most visible structure in Ceuta, as an unquestionable Christian landmark in Africa. Little by little, the image of the city witnessed transformations according to European desires to erase the pre-colonial layer.

Another religious building played a fundamental role in this colonial enterprise. The history of the Portuguese city of Ceuta by the 1400s was not only about physical appropriations of pre-existing buildings from the Muslim medieval past. There was also new construction. Perhaps the most paradigmatic new building project of this period was the erection of the church of Our Lady of Africa, which still exists today, the church of the first parish in Africa. There is no certainty as to the precise date of the church's construction; however, it already existed in 1437, when it was visited by princes Henrique and Fernando on their way to the assault on Tangier.[36]

Braun placed this church where it still stands today, depicting it in two low volumes without a tower (see fig. 1)—the larger nave(s) at the front and the apse at the back, smaller and oriented to the east. This common typology of two adjacent rectangles, which is rooted in the more rural Portuguese tradition, is clearly assumed to be a new creation in Ceuta, ruling out the possibility of the church's being a repurposing of the Notaries' mosque, which would have been located somewhere else.[37]

Occupying the northeast corner of the main public square, the church's appearance must have been quite different from today's, since it would have remained a small chapel for quite some time, as described later in the seventeenth century.[38] At the beginning of this century, this church, chapel, or hermitage was still the surviving structure of the fifteenth century, except for a high choir added later. Some decorative care was applied by 1677, when it housed the Cathedral of Ceuta, already Spanish, due to the ruined state of the original cathedral building. This was also its image in 1695, still lacking the transepts that later would reshape it as a Latin cross. Successive interventions contributed to the building that can be admired today in Ceuta, of which the intervention of 1721 to 1726[39] stands out, symmetrizing the church in a three-nave plan. Like the neighboring neo-Baroque cathedral, it is the heavily renovated and augmented church of Our Lady of Africa that reached the twentieth century and still embellishes the main square.

French and Spanish Colonial Periods in Morocco

As mentioned earlier, together with Melilla, Ceuta is the exception to the European colonial rule in North Africa, having remained under the Spanish crown until the twentieth century. However, the protectorate period in Morocco (1912–1956) introduced another period of interruption in the Arab *longue durée*, which was manifested in the built environment. This was a period when Ceuta was not isolated, but rather integrated into a wider colonial domain.

Acting as de facto colonial powers during the first half of the twentieth century, France and Spain's policy in African cities was never to touch the historical centers—*medinas*—but rather to build new European and "Western" quarters on adjacent grounds. These additions to pre-existing cities, called *villes nouvelles* for the French and *ensanches* for the Spanish, were established in the vicinity of the *medina*'s walls (fig. 4). *Ensanches* usually followed a grid-pattern disposition of streets, clearly influenced by Cerdà's plan for Barcelona during the previous century, with an Andalusian art deco flavor expressed in the language of the facades[40] (fig. 5). Indeed, the choice of such a style can be associated with a colonial expansion of southern Spain into north-African territories, reclaiming them from autochthonous rights. For the French, urban choices relied on similar geometric patterns, more often using the ring system or the *étoile* crossroads for the street layout to accommodate the necessary infrastructure for buildings inspired by the Beaux-Arts or Modern movements to arise along its sides.[41]

4   A mid-twentieth century plan of Asilah, Morocco, showing the former *medina* south of the *ensanche*.

5   Tétouan, Morocco: Street view of the Spanish *ensanche*.

The urban policies of both colonial powers were based on divisions that marked a clear and prejudiced clash between sectors, favoring the settlement of European residents and others over the native population. In the novel "Western" neighborhoods—despite the liberty that many modern architects felt in territories outside Europe—models of mass housing were imported from the old continent and uncritically erected on North African soil, serving the visual identity needs of an expatriate population. Colonialism neglected deeper research on traditional ways of living and building, thus leaving no fertile terrain for post-colonial urban renewals and expansions that instead have been copying Western prototypes of mass housing to shelter the fast growing Moroccan population.

In fact, the French and Spanish colonial period did not pursue a path of understanding tradition. Traditional Islamic cities such as Marrakesh or Fez have gathered orientalized gazes and perspectives, picking up from misconceptions and stereotypes that had evolved during the second half of the nineteenth century and were perpetuated by colonialism.[42] Only quite recently has scholarship shed light on the urban organization and composition of such urban tissues,[43] most of them confined to old quarters or historical centers of thriving contemporary cities. On the one hand, colonial policy ended up having an important and non-deliberate side effect by freezing the traditional built environment of the pre-existing *medina*'s quarters. On the other hand, it prevented preservationist efforts from fighting increasing insalubrity problems. Its response to these problems lacked attention to social needs still indexed to Islam and only perceived progress as an acritical import of Western models, a kind of approach that was continued after independence (fig. 6).

6   Fes, Morocco: New housing blocks next to the old medina El Bali.

The Islamic urban tradition, on the contrary, is more closely related to social aspects of daily life than to geometrical questions of regularity. Built for pedestrian movement, cities show a grade from public to private, from *halal*—what is allowed or profane—to *haram*—what is forbidden or sacred.[44] These cultural dimensions work as filters at different levels of the urban structure or the building composition. The courtyard represents the private spaces of a house, its domestic *haram*, and it is the basic spatial unit in the traditional Islamic city. Thus, everyday social practices, expressed in codes of privacy and neighborhood relationships and structured around courtyard houses, accessed by a hierarchy of thoroughfare streets leading to dead-end lanes, have been replaced by heavily pierced block facades. These units reverberate the colonial paradigm, forcing many inhabitants in Morocco to keep windows shut, to introduce opaque barriers in balconies or shared stair landings,[45] and often to find refuge in walled top terraces when available.

Urbicide Versus Apartheid (Post)Colonial Strategies

In Spanish and French areas of colonial influence in the first half of the twentieth century, a clear system of apartheid was put into practice. Not only did it divide cities into sectors, but it also associated the autochthonous population with vernacular ways of building and urbanizing. The colonizer, to whom modernity was claimed as an exclusive attribute, manifested its technological superiority by controlling the physical world. The colonized was seen as less talented technologically, and thus inferior and irrelevant to the architectural and urban design process. A post-colonial analysis reveals contexts of segregation and the resilience of Spanish and French colonialism in the production of residential spaces, noticeably contrary to traditional standards still valid in North Africa.

This attitude of accentuating the "us" and the "other" also has echoes in poorer or clandestine neighborhoods of Ceuta. However, the panorama one could witness across Protectorate areas differs from Ceuta, due to its exceptional character as a lone enclave on the southern shore of the Strait of Gibraltar for over six centuries. Here indeed an intentional legitimation of Iberian heritage favoring a neo-Baroque skyline for the city, rather than assuming continuity with Islamic layers, shows how policies of Europeanization have challenged conceptions of identity in a disputed border territory. In spite of the subsequent wide expansion beyond walls and more recent urban reconfigurations, the original nucleus keeps traces of its historical stratigraphy. Despite Europeanization and westernization efforts in the last century, late-medieval and early-modern decisions still resonate in the city center's contemporary urban morphology, such as the location of the main religious landmark, the main square, and the structural axes of the central area.

One can speak of deliberate "urbicide"[46] strategies in Ceuta that, in the *longue durée*, have progressively destroyed Arab-Islamic landmarks or urban footprints. Sometimes these strategies were more diffused in time, such as the initial Portuguese occupation process between early-fifteenth and early-sixteenth centuries. At other times they took the form of blunter attitudes towards the built heritage of the city that introduced a novel and rhetorical Western look in the 1900s, the obliteration and replacement of buildings suggesting firm objectives of a political statement through architecture and urbanism.[47]

The impact of an institutional policy of heritage manipulation has masked a past in this city that has only recently been rediscovered. But recent changes in Ceuta's political approach towards heritage point to a rediscovery of the Muslim past through important archaeological excavations[48] and structural rehabilitations that found in the city's urban palimpsest a touristic opportunity for Western visitors in search of safe exotic havens amidst the political and military turmoil of Northern Africa and the Middle East. Paradoxically, such a novel and almost orientalist "postcard" view of the city is offered merely a few miles away from one of the most heavily secured borders of Europe, with walls, electric fences, and ditches along the eight kilometers that separate the enclave from Morocco.[49] Cyclic episodes of trespassing by Maghreb and sub-Saharan (im)migrants, followed by police counteroffensives and scenes of death and despair, are unfortunately part of the picture as well. Thus, Ceuta's political positions and the local psyche stand on a fragile and narrow line that not only divides Europe and Africa, but also reflects an atavistic colonial standoff. In fact, the western wall and bastions with which the Portuguese separated Ceuta from the hinterland in the sixteenth century, turning it into a fortified island, are very much overshadowed by other lines of fortifications constructed by the Spaniards in the 1700s, pushing a few miles further into the outer territory, and now the administrative frontier between two countries.

Today, with fewer than 90,000 inhabitants, the city nevertheless wishes to reclaim its historical gateway status as the threshold between the Mediterranean and the Atlantic. Having accepted its specific position as a European city in the Maghreb with a multi-ethnic composition,[50] the recovery of its medieval and late-medieval past allows Ceuta to reconnect to the growing

Moroccan population and sell itself as a crossing point of cultures rather than emphasizing the dominance of the Iberian-Christian part. All chronologies and styles, monuments and tissues are now a resource for the current marketing aspirations of the city, while the dilemma of being situated between Europe and Africa remains.

1   Alighieri 2006, canto 26, 35–37.

2   Circulating among several classical authors, the story was told in great detail in Pomponius Mela's *De Chorographia* (Mela 1998, book 1, 5, 27); it is better described in Pliny's *Naturalis Historia* (Pliny 1969, book V, 2).

3   Gozalbes 1981, 160–61.

4   Aspects of the city's medieval image will be further developed in the next section.

5   On Portuguese conquests and presence in North Africa, see Dias Farinha 1990 as well as Oliveira and Serrão 1998.

6   On these matters, cf. three different translations of Al Ansari's description (Al Ansari 1947, 10–52; 1962, 398–442; 1982–83, 113–162) and studies by Gozalbes Cravioto (Gozalbes Cravioto 1988; 1993).

7   Correia 2008.

8   Posac Mon 1967, 22. In letters from 1443, the Aljazira valley was already identified as "outside" the city; see: *Carta de doação de umas casas a Rodrigo Afonso de Azevedo, escudeiro do Infante D. Pedro, que ali residia desde a conquista da cidade*, Sintra – July 12, 1443 (Chancelaria de D. Afonso V, liv. 24, fl. 85), in Azevedo 1915–1934, 246.

9   Braun et al. 1572.

10   Azevedo 1915–1934, 20.

11   Sousa Viterbo 1988, I, 272–274.

12   *Livro das medidas de Arzila, Alcácer, Ceuta e Tânger, feitas por mestre Boytac e Bastião Luiz em 1514* (IAN-TT - Núcleo Antigo, nº 769, fls. 41–47v).

13   *Carta de D. Afonso de Noronha a D. João III*, Ceuta – March 13, 1541 (IAN-TT, Corpo Cronológico, parte I, maço 69, doc. 64), in Ricard 1948, 318–320.

14   *Carta de D. Afonso de Noronha a D. João III*, Ceuta – June 7, 1541 (IAN-TT, Corpo Cronológico, parte I, maço 69, doc. 125), in Ricard 1948, 433–439.

15   *Castello da cidade de Cepta*, in *As Gavetas da Torre do Tombo* 1960–1977, vol. V, 1965, 79–81.

16   *Carta de Maria de Eça a D. João III*, Ceuta – February 14, 1548 (IAN-TT, Corpo Cronológico, parte I, maço 80, doc. 33) in Ricard 1948, 261–62; *Carta de D. Afonso de Noronha a D. João III*, Seinal – May 30, 1549 (IAN-TT, Corpo Cronológico, parte I, maço 82, doc. 106), in Ricard 1948, 328–30.

17   Moreira 1989, 149.

18   The construction of the bastioned fortification perimeter meant a small reduction in the actual availability of the intra-wall space compared to the medieval Muslim *medina* area.

19   *Carta de confirmação de umas casas em Ceuta a Garcia de Céspedes*, Lisboa – July 6, 1454 (Chancelaria de D. Afonso V, liv. 10, fl. 57), in Azevedo 1915–1934, 213; *Carta de doação de umas casas a Rodrigo Afonso de Azevedo, escudeiro do Infante D. Pedro, que ali residia desde a conquista da cidade*, Sintra – July 12, 1443 (Chancelaria de D. Afonso V, liv. 24, fl. 85), in Azevedo 1915–1934, 246.

20   Mascarenhas 1995, 16.

21   Gomez Barceló 1995, 387.

22   For a comprehensive selection of Ceuta's cartography, see Bautista Vilar 2002.

23   Statistics show a growing Moroccan population in Ceuta within the last fifteen years. For detailed and comparative graphics, consult: http://ine.es.

24   Ferhat 1986, 7; Gozalbes Cravioto 1995, 86–87.

25   Ferhat 1993, 360.

26   Al Bekri, 1918, 204.

27   Al Ansari 1962, 414.

28   Al Ansari 1962, 414.

29   Al Ansari 1982–83, 130.

30   For a tentative reconstruction, see Gozalbes Cravioto 1995, 93.

31   Perez del Campo 1988, 42–43. In 1648, Mascarenhas attests to the same in his description and history of the city of Ceuta, see Mascarenhas 1995, 17.

32   Lopez 1941, 202.

33   Perez del Campo 1988, 44.

34   Perez del Campo 1988, 46.

35   Brásio 1973, 68.

36   Brásio 1973, 74.

37   Gozalbes Cravioto 1995, 106.

38   Ros y Calaf 1977, 177.

39   Brásio 1973, 77.

40   On Tétouan's *ensanche*, the capital of the Spanish Protectorate in Morocco, see Akalay Nasser 2012. For other colonial interventions in the Maghreb region, see Nunes Silva 2016.

41   The case of Casablanca is paradigmatic of such an urban approach; see Cohen and Eleb 1998.

42   On these aspects, see Beaulieu and Roberts 2002; Oulebbsir and Volait 2009.

43   Amidst a vast bibliography on the subject produced since the 1970s, see in particular Hakim 1986.

44   Petruccioli 1990, 39.

45   This could be understood as a clear reference to the practice of *driba*, an appropriation of outside space as explained by Hakim 1986, 27.

46   The term was first coined by writer Michael Moorcock in 1963 and has ever since been used in contexts of urban destruction and organised violence against urban environments, notably by war, such as Bosnia or the Israeli–Palestinian conflicts. See Coward 2009.

47   Read Perez del Campo 1988 to follow the stages of transformation of the cathedral in detail over time.

48   Some examples were published by archaeologists Fernando Villada Paredes and José Manuel Hita Ruiz: Villada Paredes and Hita Ruiz 2015a; 2015b; 2016.

49   On this particular border and the political entanglements associated with it, see Figueiredo 2011.

50   In 2011, the Fundación Ceuta Crisol de Culturas 2015 was created with the purpose of preparing the commemorative activities for the sixth centenary of the Portuguese landing. Despite evoking such a date as the entrance of Ceuta in modernity, its objectives often refer to the "encounter of cultures" or "interculturality" of the city; "cultures," in plural, is in its very denomination. See *Ceuta2015* 2012.

Bibliography

Akalay Nasser, Mustafa. 2012. *El Tetuán español: Síntesis de su historia urbana y arquitectónica (1860–1956)*. Granada: Universidad de Granada.

Al Ansari. 1947. "Descrição de Ceuta muçulmana no século XV." *Revista da Faculdade de Letras* XIII, 2ª série, no. 1: 10–52.

Al Ansari. 1962. "Una descripción de Ceuta musulmana en el siglo XV." *Al-Andalus* XXVII: 398–442.

Al Ansari. 1982–83. "La physionomie monumentale de Ceuta: un hommage nostalgique a la ville par en de ses fils, Muhammad B. Al-Qasim Al Ansari." *Hespéris-Tamuda* XX–XXI.

Al Bekri, Abu Obeid. 1918. *Description de l'Afrique Septentrionale*. Alger: Typographie Adolphe Jourdan.

Alighieri, Dante. 2006. *The Divine Comedy I: Inferno*. Translated by Robin Kirkpatrick. London: Penguin Books.

As Gavetas da Torre do Tombo. 1960–1977. 12 vols. Lisbon: Centro de Estudos Ultramarinos da Junta de Investigações Científicas do Ultramar.

de Azevedo, Pedro, dir. 1915–1934. *Documentos das Chancelarias Reais, anteriores a 1531, relativos a Marrocos*, 2 vols. Lisbon: Academia das Sciências.

Bautista Vilar, Juan. 2002. *Limites, fortificaciones y evolución urbana de Ceuta (siglos XV-XX) en su cartografía histórica y fuentes inéditas*. Ceuta: Ciudad Autónoma de Ceuta / Consejería de Educación y Cultura.

Beaulieu, Jill, and Mary Roberts, eds. 2002. *Orientalism's Interlocutors: Painting, Architecture, Photography*. Durham, N.C.: Duke University Press.

Brásio, António. 1973. "A primitiva catedral de Ceuta." In *História e Missiologia. Inéditos e Esparsos*, 56–83. Luanda: Instituto de Investigação Científica de Angola.

Braun, Georg, Franz Hogenberg, and Simon Novellanus. 1572. *Civitates Orbis Terrarum*, 6 vols. Cologne: Philippus Galleus.

Ceuta2015. Fundación Crisol de Culturas. 2012. Ceuta: Ciudad Autónoma de Ceuta.

Cohen, Jean-Louis, and Monique Eleb. 1998. *Casablanca: Mythes et figures d'une aventure urbaine*. Paris: Éditions Hazan.

Correia, Jorge. 2008. *Implantation de la ville portugaise en Afrique du Nord: de la prise de Ceuta au milieu du XVIe siècle*, 2 vols. Porto: FAUP publicações.

Coward, Martin. 2009. *Urbicide: The Politics of Urban Destruction*. London: Routledge.

Dias Farinha, António. 1990. *Portugal e Marrocos no séc. XV*, 3 vols. Lisbon: FLUL.

Ferhat, Halima. 1986. "Un nouveau document sur la grande mosquée de Sabta au Moyen Age." *Hespéris-Tamuda* XXIV: 5–16.

Ferhat, Halima. 1993. *Le Maghreb aux XIIe et XIIIe siècles: les siècles de la Foi*. Casablanca: Wallada.

Figueiredo, Patrick. 2011. "Muros do Mediterrâneo: Notas sobre a construção de barreiras nas fronteiras de Ceuta e Melilla." *Cadernos de Estudos Africanos* 22: 153–75.

Gomez Barceló, José Luis. 1995. "Evolución de calles y barrios, en el istmo de Ceuta, coetánea al cerco de 1694–1727. Esbozo de un nomenclator para su studio." In Eduardo Ripoll Perelló and Manuel F. Ladero Quesada, eds., *Actas del II Congreso Internacional "El Estrecho de Gibraltar"*, vol. IV, 387–404. Madrid: Universidad Nacional de Educación a distancia.

Gozalbes, Enrique. 1981. "El culto indígena a los reys en Mauritania Tingitana: Surgimiento y pervivencia." In *Paganismo y cristianismo en el occidente del Imperio Romano. Memoria de Historia Antigua*, vol. 5, 153–164. Oviedo: Universidad de Oviedo / Instituto de Historia Antigua.

Gozalbes Cravioto, Carlos. 1988. "La estrutura urbana de la Ceuta medieval." In Eduardo Ripoll Perelló, ed., *Actas del Congreso Internacional "El estrecho de Gibraltar"*, vol. II, 345–50. Madrid: Universidad Nacional de Educación a distancia.

Gozalbes Cravioto, Carlos. 1993. "La topografia urbana de Ceuta, en La cronica de Tomada de Gomes Eanes de Zurara." In Alberto Herratzi, *Ceuta Hispano-Portuguesa*, 189–206. Ceuta: Instituto de Estudíos Ceutíes.

Gozalbes Cravioto, Carlos. 1995. *El urbanismo religioso y cultural de Ceuta en la Edad Media*. Ceuta: Instituto de Estudios Ceutíes.

Guevara, Adolfo L. 1940. *Arcila durante la ocupación Portuguesa (1471–1549)*. Tanger: Publicaciones del Instituto General Franco para la Investigación Hispano-Arabe.

Hakim, Besim S. 1986. *Arabic-Islamic Cities: Building and Planning Principles*. London: KPI.

Lopez, Atanásio. 1941. *Obispos en la África Septentrional desde el Siglo XIII*. Tanger: Instituto General Franco para la Investigación Hispano-Arabe.

Mascarenhas, Jerónimo de. 1995. *História de la ciudad de Ceuta (1648)*. Ceuta: Instituto de Estudios Ceutíes / Málaga: Editorial Algazara.

Mela, Pomponius. 1998. *Pomponius Mela's Description of the World*. Translated by F. E. Romer. Ann Arbor: University of Michigan Press.

Moreira, Rafael, dir. 1989. *História das Fortificações Portuguesas no Mundo*. Lisbon: Alfa.

Nunes Silva, Carlos, ed. 2016. *Urban Planning in North Africa*. London: Ashgate.

Oliveira, A.H., and Serrão, Joel, cords. 1998. *Nova História da Expansão Portuguesa. A Expansão Quatrocentista*, vol. II. Lisbon: Editorial Estampa.

Oulebbsir, Nabila, and Mercedes Volait, coords. 2009. *L'Orientalisme architectural, entre imaginaires et savoirs*. Paris: Picard.

Perez del Campo, Lorenzo. 1988. "Etapas en la construcción de la catedral de Ceuta." In Eduardo Ripoll Perelló, ed., *Actas del Congreso Internacional "El estrecho de Gibraltar"*, vol. IV, 41–50. Madrid: Universidad Nacional de Educación a distancia.

Petruccioli, Attilio. 1990. *Dar al-Islam*. Brussels: Pierre Mardaga,

Pliny. 1969. *Natural History*. Translated by H. Rackham. Cambridge, MA: Harvard University Press.

Posac Mon, Carlos. 1967. *La última década Lusitana en Ceuta*. Ceuta: Publicaciones del Instituto Nacional de Enseñanza Media.

Ricard, Robert, dir. 1948. *Les Sources Inédites de l'Histoire du Maroc*, Première Série – Dynastie Sa'dienne. Archives et Bibliothèques de Portugal, Tome III (Janvier 1535 – Décembre 1541). Paris: Paul Geuthner.

Ros y Calaf, Salvador. 1977. *História Eclesiástica y Civil de la celebre ciudad de Ceuta (1912)*. Ceuta: Ciudad Autónoma de Ceuta.

de Sousa Viterbo, Francisco. 1988. *Dicionário Histórico e Documental dos Arquitectos, Engenheiros e Construtores Portugueses*, 3 vols. Lisbon: Imprensa Nacional / Casa da Moeda.

Villada Paredes, Fernando, and José Manuel Hita Ruiz. 2015. "Huerta Rufino." In André Teixeira et al., coords., *Lisboa 1415 Ceuta – historia de dos ciudades / história de duas cidades*, 57–59. Ceuta: Ciudad Autónoma de Ceuta / Câmara Municipal de Lisboa.

Villada Paredes, Fernando, and José Manuel Hita Ruiz. 2015. "El baño árabe de la Plaza de la Paz (Ceuta)." In André Teixeira et al., coords., *Lisboa 1415 Ceuta – historia de dos ciudades / história de duas cidades*, 126–128. Ceuta: Ciudad Autónoma de Ceuta / Câmara Municipal de Lisboa.

Villada Paredes, Fernando, and José Manuel Hita Ruiz. 2016. "Una mezquita de barrio de la Ceuta mariní." In André Teixeira, coord., *Entre les deux rives du Détroit de Gibraltar: Archéologie de frontières aux 14–16e siècles / En las dos orillas del Estrecho de Gibraltar: Arqueología de fronteras en los siglos XIV-XVI*, 275–321. Lisbon: CHAM-FCSH/UNL-UAç.

Image Sources

1   Septa, in Braun et al. 1572, vol. I, fol. 57r.
2   Plano del recinto de Zeuta, 1718. Archivo General de Simancas – MPD. LXIII-73.
3   Jorge Correia, 2011.
4   Torres Quevedo S. A. (T. Q. S. A.) Telecomunicaciones, Plano de Arcila (n. d.).
5   Jorge Correia, 2016.
6   Jorge Correia, 2019.

JOAQUIM RODRIGUES DOS SANTOS

(Re)Contextualizing *Goencho Saib*'s Basilica

The Basilica of Bom Jesus in Goa as a Paradigm of Contested Transcultural Heritage

When one imagines Goa (India), two images immediately come to mind: paradisiacal beaches with white sand framed by clear seawater, blue sky, and green palm trees; and the impressive reddish-brown Basilica of Bom Jesus. The Goan beaches are marvelous, like so many other beaches around the world, but the Basilica of Bom Jesus, undoubtedly the Goan *ex libris*, is truly unique.

The basilica is a major symbol of Goa: it houses the tomb of Saint Francis Xavier, the "Apostle of the East"—also known locally as *Goencho Saib*, "Lord of Goa," in the Konkani language—and gives a glimpse of the "Golden Goa" and "Rome of the East," the former capital of the Portuguese Eastern Seaborne Empire that was then one of the most cosmopolitan cities in the world. Built by the Jesuits at the turn of the seventeenth century, the Basilica of Bom Jesus received the saint's remains soon after his death and subsequently became a major site for Catholic worship in Asia.

In the first half of the 1950s, facing the independence of the Indian Union and its claims over Portuguese India, the Portuguese dictatorial regime, as part of its intention to use heritage as an ideological propaganda instrument, restored[1] the Basilica of Bom Jesus, causing a radical change in its image and simultaneously provoking problems with its conservation. After the integration of Goa into India, the basilica became a paradigm of contested transcultural heritage, incorporating multiple challenges: this Goan architectural masterpiece, with Portuguese and Indian influences, is the subject of a robust debate among those who consider it a colonial symbol, those who reclaim it as a Goan symbol, heritage lovers who demand effective measures to preserve it, those whose subsistence relies on (hazardous) touristic commodification, and Goan Catholics who merely wish for their church to be free of ideological meanings.

This essay intends to analyze the Basilica of Bom Jesus in Goa as a paradigm of contested transcultural heritage, briefly mentioning its historical background and architectural characteristics, considering its religious and ideological meanings and their impacts on actions to preserve the basilica's heritage, and especially focusing on the contemporary debate about the preservation of this monument, referring to the main questions and people involved (in which I am also included).

A Jesuit Building and a Pilgrimage Site

But before we analyze the heritage context around the basilica, it is fundamental to know its background. The history, art, and architecture of the Basilica of Bom Jesus have been studied by several researchers, such as Viriato Brás de Albuquerque, Francisco Gomes Catão, Mário Chicó,

Carlos de Azevedo, José Pereira, Pedro Dias, António Nunes Pereira, Paulo Varela Gomes, and Cristina Osswald.[2] It is widely known that Saint Francis Xavier and his two companions were the first Jesuits to reach Asia in 1542. In the following decades, several buildings were constructed: the College of Saint Paul of the Arches, the College of Saint Roch, the Seminary of the Holy Faith, the Novitiate of Our Lady of Immaculate Conception (all in the city of Goa) and a few other small churches and chapels spread along Tiswadi Island.

The construction of the Professed House of Bom Jesus began at the end of 1585 (or the beginning of 1586) within the city of Goa, according to a plan by the Jesuit provincial Alessandro Valignano (1539–1606) with the likely collaboration of Domingos Fernandes (fl. 1578–1597), architect of the Society of Jesus in Goa, and Júlio Simão (fl. 1596–1625), master engineer of Portuguese India.[3] In 1593 the building would have been near completion, and the construction of the basilica, attached to the Professed House, commenced the following year; construction of the main facade began only in 1597 (figs. 1 and 2).

Pedro Dias identified Domingos Fernandes as the probable author of the basilica's plan (a single-nave basilica plan),[4] while António Nunes Pereira proposed that due to the figurative complexity of the basilica's facade, it might have been the creation of Júlio Simão.[5] The facade is divided horizontally into three stories by friezes and vertically into three bays by pilasters; a gable with a Flemish bas-relief cartouche top ends the facade. Italian influences can be seen on the ground floor (portals with Serlian motifs), French influences on the first floor (rectangular windows with French Serlian moldings), Flemish influences on the third floor (oculus with carved cartouche frames), and Indian influences at the top (side *chakra*-type adornments instead of side volutes at the gable). With the exception of the four pilasters in plastered and whitewashed laterite stone that divide the facade into three bays, the whole facade is in granite stone; the rest of the basilica is in plastered and whitewashed laterite stone.

1   Church of Bom Jesus (c. 1855–62).

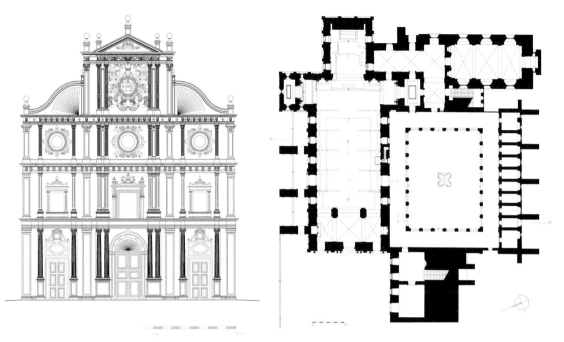

2   Elevation and ground plan of the Basilica of Bom Jesus in Goa (2000).

Another feature of the basilica draws attention: the monumentality of its facade. Portuguese early-modern churches generally had two stories with a pediment or analogous top, but the Basilica of Bom Jesus marked the emergence of a new type of facade, replicated later in the churches of Our Lady of Grace, Saint Anne of Talaulim, and the Cross of Miracles—all in Goa or in its immediate surroundings. This extra level of the basilica's facade, together with its profuse ornamentation, might have been influenced by Indian aesthetics, where there is no monumentality without multiplicity—that is, the more component forms a building has, the more monumental and beautiful it is, regardless of its proportions.[6] Whereas Hindu temples (especially Dravidian ones) have many squat levels due to a more flexible system of proportion, Western aesthetics are attached to the rigid classical proportion system. Therefore, instead of having a facade with many squat levels, the Basilica of Bom Jesus has a three-level facade (an extra story compared to the usual Portuguese facades) yet maintains the Western proportion system, thus creating a higher facade that could compete with local temples.[7]

The basilica's facade became perhaps the most paradigmatic case of Goan architecture, and one of the two Goan types of church facade that are unique in the world (the other is the much later cupoliform church type, such as the Church of Saint Stephen on Juá Island). According to Paulo Varela Gomes, the Basilica of Bom Jesus might have triggered the development of a local taste merging European and Indian influences to create a very distinctive kind of transcultural heritage: it "could have been the building that allowed Indian artisans to domesticate European architectural and ornamental vocabulary, to make it their own."[8]

The unfinished basilica was consecrated by Fr. Aleixo de Meneses (1559–1617), Archbishop of Goa, in 1605. The basilica was finally completed in 1624 and then received the remains of Saint Francis Xavier. The construction of a new vaulted sacristy began in 1652, and in 1659 two chapels were added to the basilica on each side of the false transept: a chapel housing the saint's tomb and a chapel containing the Blessed Sacrament.

Then in 1683, an event occurred that gave more prominence to the basilica: facing the imminent invasion of Goa by the Maratha forces of Sambhaji Bhosale (1681–1689), the Portuguese viceroy Francisco de Távora (1646–1710), Count of Alvor, came to the basilica, opened Saint Francis Xavier's coffin and offered his vice-regal baton, his royal credentials, and a letter pleading for the saint to protect Goa. As Sambhaji had to retreat suddenly to resist a Mughal invasion, this incident was considered a miraculous intercession from the saint. Later, in commemoration of this event, Portuguese viceroys and governors became invested in the basilica.[9]

After two centuries of significant missionary activity across Asia and East Africa, the Society of Jesus, with its center in Goa, was suddenly banned from all Portuguese territories in 1759 by the Marquis of Pombal, Sebastião José de Carvalho e Melo (1699–1782), Portuguese chief minister at the time. The Jesuit complex was assigned to the Congregation of the Mission of Saint Vincent de Paul (known as Vincentians or Lazarians), until this order was also banned in 1790; thereupon, the basilica and Professed House came under an administrator nominated by the Goan Archbishop.[10]

A section of the Royal Archaeological Museum of Portuguese India dedicated to religious art was installed in the Professed House from 1900 to 1935;[11] related to this development, the roof of the Professed House was replaced by one with a slight inclination, substituting Mangalore tiles for the existing country tiles. The importance of the basilica as an essential Catholic pilgrimage site in Asia grew enormously with the initiation of periodical public expositions of the remains of Saint Francis Xavier (also known as Xaverian celebrations), which attracted pilgrims from across the East. During Portuguese rule, these celebrations occurred in 1782, 1859, 1878, 1890, 1900, 1910, 1922, 1931, 1942, 1952, and 1961.[12] The importance of the building grew further with its classification as a Portuguese National Monument in 1932[13] and after Pope Pius XII (1876–1958) elevated the church to a minor basilica in 1946, thus recognizing its vital role in the evangelization of the East.

The Basilica as a Colonial Symbol

The independence of the Indian Union in 1947 and its claims over Portuguese India caused an enormous disturbance within the Portuguese nationalist and imperialist dictatorial regime. Unable to defeat the Indian Union in an armed conflict, the Portuguese regime diplomatically sought support from other countries by justifying the cultural, historical, and religious closeness of Goa, Daman, and Diu to Portugal rather than to India.[14] As had happened in Portugal, Goan monuments and historical celebrations were used by the dictatorship as powerful instruments of ideological propaganda. The Basilica of Bom Jesus, a major symbol of Goa and the pilgrimage place of the Apostle of the East, was chosen for restoration in the context of the celebration of the fourth centenary of Saint Francis Xavier's death in 1952.

Baltazar Castro, a famous Portuguese architect, led the mission to restore the national monuments of Portuguese India from 1951 to 1953. Castro had been the visible face of the regime's program for the restoration of monuments in Portugal in the 1930s and 1940s. His legacy was marked by a huge number of interventions in monuments, many of them through extensive actions that were facing criticism by the end of the 1940s.[15]

In 1952 Castro ordered the removal of the limestone plaster from the basilica's exterior, leaving the laterite stone exposed after receiving a chemical treatment. Castro had used this kind of feature in numerous "reintegrations" (as the vast heritage works in Portugal, tending to recover the alleged pristine shape of monuments, were referred to by the Portuguese dictatorial regime). Medieval buildings became privileged targets for nationalist reintegrations because they were considered witnesses of the nation's birth—Portuguese roots were supposedly traced to the Middle Ages. Moreover, many medieval buildings survived into the nineteenth century with no plaster, an image appreciated by Romanticism—even if most of the old buildings had originally been plastered. Consequently, images of buildings with a stone wall face became associated with antiquity and, increasingly, with monumentality due to the large Portuguese castles, palaces, and monasteries with this characteristic of a lack of plaster.[16]

It is unsurprising, then, that Castro would opt to deplaster the basilica. By leaving the laterite exposed, Castro was providing the Basilica of Bom Jesus a kind of medievalized image, enhancing its ancientness and monumentality by correlating it with the revered Portuguese medieval cathedrals and monasteries. Moreover, by boosting its agedness, highlighting the monument was even more ancient than the famous Taj Mahal, the dictatorship's propaganda was justifying historically and culturally the maintenance of Portuguese India. These intentions were complemented by the massive pilgrimage of Catholics from all over the East to Goa for the Xaverian celebration of 1952 (fig. 3).

This situation was exploited by the Portuguese regime to display Goa, Daman, and Diu as an overseas province belonging to a multicontinental country with historical, cultural, linguistic,

3   Public exposition of the remains of Saint Francis Xavier (1952).

4   The Basilica of Bom Jesus in 2018.

and religious affinities, following Gilberto Freyre's (1900–1987) Lusotropicalist premises. Goans were encouraged to absorb Portuguese-influenced characteristics to manifest their differences from the people of the Indian Union. This strengthening of the role of the Basilica of Bom Jesus as a symbol of the territory was, therefore, disseminating a subliminal message: Goa was Catholic with a westernized culture and, thus, closer to Portugal than to the Indian Union.[17]

Up to 1952, there had been little contestation over the Basilica of Bom Jesus, but from this date on, this would become a constant in the basilica's history. The basilica's drastic change in image from whitewashed lime plaster to reddish-brown laterite began to attract criticism from a segment of Goan cultural elites—even in newspapers, despite the regime's censorship.

These criticisms were triggered by the collapse of the Arch of the Viceroys at the beginning of August 1953. This monument had also been restored by Baltazar Castro, who had removed its plaster. A couple of weeks after the restoration was completed, the arch collapsed under heavy rainfall during a storm. This event was a blow to the dictatorship's propaganda efforts, and soon it drew criticism in Goan newspapers, blaming Castro for the disaster.[18] The exposure of laterite to the monsoon's effects weakened it, leading to its collapse.

The criticism was then extended to what had been done to the Basilica of Bom Jesus: the recreation of an idealized image for the basilica that had never existed before, prioritizing its aesthetic value over its historical value and conservation. Besides the know-how Castro acquired in Portugal, his restoration criteria might have been influenced by a misconception that Goan churches had not originally been plastered; however, local technicians were aware that lime plaster was always used to protect laterite stone, especially against rainwater—in fact, due to the vulnerability of the laterite stone of the basilica walls, three arch buttresses had already been built in 1862 to support the basilica's north facade.

In 1957, only five years after the basilica's deplastering, the Government-General of Portuguese India sent a telegram to Lisbon urgently requesting Baltazar Castro to replaster the basilica, since the laterite was disaggregating; however, this request was denied by engineer Eugénio Sanches da Gama (1892–1964), who demanded the maintenance of the deplastered facade for aesthetic reasons, according to the regime's speech.[19] Newspapers branded this change to the basilica's image an atrocious disfigurement that was the product of a deformation of taste.[20] Such criticisms of Castro's actions became criticisms against the dictatorial regime, and the basilica itself consequently came to be regarded as an imperialist symbol by many who were struggling against the colonial regime. Additionally, the immense pilgrimage of 1952 created some constraints as not only pilgrims but also tourists began visiting the basilica in increasing numbers. The year 1952 was indeed a disruptive key moment in the history of the basilica.

Another problem emerged for the Basilica of Bom Jesus in 1959, relating to preparations for other major celebrations used by the Portuguese regime for ideological purposes in the following year: the fourth centenary of Prince Henry the Navigator's death and the 450th anniversary of the Conquest of Goa by Afonso de Albuquerque. By order of the Portuguese Governor-General Manuel Vassalo e Silva (1899–1985), a musealization plan for Old Goa was proposed by a committee led by José António Ismael Gracias Jr. (1903–1993); two years later, the restorer Luís Benavente (1902–1993) was sent to Goa to coordinate work on the monuments.[21]

Benavente immediately noticed the disaggregation of the basilica's laterite stone, and by November 1961, he had produced a report calling the basilica's deplastering, which he claimed had occurred without satisfying a single justifiable criterion, a huge error. Consequently, he ordered the replastering of the basilica as soon as possible to correct this error—not only to recover the monument's initial character but, above all, to preserve the durability of the building.[22] However, there was no time to implement Benavente's directive. In December 1961, a mere month after his report was released, the Indian army entered Portuguese India in Operation Vijay and ended 450 years of Portuguese domination.

Jurisdictional and Identity Idiosyncrasies at the Basilica

This former Jesuit basilica in Goa remains a paradigmatic case of contested transcultural heritage, incorporating multiple challenges (fig. 4). For four and a half centuries, during the Portuguese administration, this heritage was created and conserved by following Western premises moderated by local influences: little by little, along with its increasing religious importance, the basilica also began acquiring an ideological meaning linked to Portuguese colonialism, which grew exponentially during the nationalist dictatorship at the end of Portuguese rule. The incorporation of Goa into India brought some idiosyncrasies concerning the preservation of the Basilica of Bom Jesus, not only by intensifying problems originated by the aforementioned intervention of 1952 but also by creating new ones.[23]

With Goa's integration into India, the basilica and all other listed monuments of former Portuguese India came under the jurisdiction of the Archaeological Survey of India (ASI), the Indian state institution responsible for cultural heritage, including national monuments. During the Portuguese era, although the basilica was listed as a national monument, it continued to belong to the Catholic Church: maintenance and repair work could be done by the Catholic

Church itself, albeit with authorization from the Portuguese administration and usually with its financial support—a remnant partially inherent to the commitments of Portuguese Overseas Patronage.[24]

Under the ASI's surveillance, the Catholic Church is also allowed to use the Basilica of Bom Jesus for religious purposes, but all interventions are restricted to ASI technicians or are under the ASI's scrutiny. Classified monuments of Goa, Daman, and Diu are, in fact, *sui generis* cases among India's national monuments. In India, religious monuments with liturgical usage require the consent of their owners to be listed as national monuments, and only after securing positive consent can they be placed under the ASI's management.[25] Therefore, only very few cases of "living" religious monuments are under the ASI's management. However, after the integration of Goa, Daman, and Diu into India, a mere formal transition placed all monuments listed by the Portuguese—including religious monuments still in use, such as the Basilica of Bom Jesus—under the ASI's jurisdiction.

This jurisdictional idiosyncrasy of the Catholic monuments of Goa, Daman, and Diu started causing friction between the Archdiocese of Goa and Daman and the ASI. As the most important Catholic religious buildings in Goa are listed as national monuments, and are thus under the responsibility of the ASI, the Catholic Church's authority over these buildings is substantially conditioned—unlike the places of worship of other religions that are still in use and therefore are not classified as national monuments. Indeed, while Hindu, Muslim, Jain, and other religions' places of worship can freely undergo maintenance, extension, remodeling, and other modifications according to the owners' wishes, Catholics cannot do the same with the major churches of Goa, Daman, and Diu. This jurisdictional situation has left Catholics from the Archdiocese of Goa and Daman feeling somewhat discriminated against, leading to conflict with the ASI. Tense relations have been nurtured by situations pushing the limits on both sides.[26]

The Basilica of Bom Jesus is at the center of these disputes: along with the See Cathedral, it is one of the most important churches of Goa, used daily for religious celebrations and as a place of pilgrimage—perhaps the main place of Catholic worship in the East due to the presence of Saint Francis Xavier's tomb. Despite this importance, however, the ASI's rules rigidly curtail the Archdiocese of Goa and Daman's authority over the basilica.

The postcolonial significance of the basilica has also been a target of ideological clashes, often provoked by misunderstandings. The last decade has seen the rise of Hindu nationalist feelings throughout India, which have been reflected, to varying degrees, in government policies. Goa was not immune to this ideological wave, with serious effects on Catholic heritage and especially major monuments, such as the Basilica of Bom Jesus.

Just as the Portuguese regime ideologically explored the basilica as a colonial symbol, those who opposed the colonial regime—especially non-Catholic freedom fighters—did the same. In the postcolonial period, the basilica's image as a colonial symbol persisted within many strata of the Indian society, including in Goa. By extension, many people in India, especially in the last decade, have associated Catholics with these ideological meanings as colonial remnants, with the progressive radicalization of many segments of Indian society. Among the contemporary Catholic community, it is commonplace to hear lamentations from those who increasingly feel that they are part of a contested minority after decades of being merely Indian citizens, like everyone else, irrespective of their religion.

Older people among the Catholic elites still have a nostalgic affection for the Portuguese period and continue to speak in Portuguese, thus exacerbating the anti-Catholicism of the right-wing Hindu nationalist ideology. For those who wish to erase the Portuguese layer from India, the eradication of the Basilica of Bom Jesus would certainly be desirable. Moreover, many Catholics might consider the ASI's refusal or delay in performing repairs to the basilica as signaling its intention to hasten the decay of the monument, leading to its eventual collapse.[27]

An (Alleged) Goan Architectural Feature: The Laterite Stone Wall Face

The strained relations between the ASI and the Archdiocese of Goa and Daman have exacerbated the main threat to the Basilica of Bom Jesus today—namely, the lack of plaster on its facades. Visible signs of deterioration of the basilica's laterite stone have increased the polemic about replastering since at least the 1990s (fig. 5). Water infiltration from monsoon rain unleashed the disaggregation process of the laterite stone, and the ASI intended to take measures to tackle the problem. Paradoxically, however, the ASI was halted by protests from Goan Catholics, supported by a substantial portion of the Catholic clergy.

In fact, until a couple of years ago, a considerable number of Goans believed that the basilica in its current form, without plaster, had always existed. This "illusion of immanence" was a consequence of the fact that most people had only known the contemporary basilica's structure; only a few elders remember when the basilica was plastered and whitewashed, and these individuals are disappearing rapidly.

5 Detail of the condition of the laterite stone (left) compared with the granite stone (right) (2018).

As a matter of fact, the simple, sober, and robust image of the deplastered basilica became part of the construction of the postcolonial Goan identity.[28] The exposed laterite used in buildings came to be considered a Goan architectural characteristic. It is easy to find churches with lateral facades without plaster, such as the Church of the Holy Spirit at Margao or the Church of Our Lady of Mercy at Colva. However, there is persistent doubt about whether the facades of these other churches were always in laterite or if they were deplastered at some point in the past—and if so, one needs to know if it happened before or after the deplastering of the Basilica of Bom Jesus in order to assess possible influences on the removal of plaster from these churches.

It is also curious to observe the Chapel of Saint Sebastian at Arpora, with its side facade painted in red, as it was deplastered—perhaps due to the influence of the Basilica of Bom Jesus or perhaps motivated by an intention to concede a Goan architectural image. For instance, the new facade of the Chapel of Santa Cruz in Calangute is made of laterite,[29] and a new chapel built in Baga, located between Calangute and Arpora, is completely devoid of plaster, something unusual in Catholic religious architecture in Goa. Similarly, a few newly built houses have adopted the characteristics of a traditional Goan Catholic house but without plaster. In fact, the use of laterite wall face in Goan architecture seems to be a postcolonial input—but not necessarily with a decolonial meaning.

In the 1960s, right after Goa's integration into India, architects Bruno Souza (b. 1925) and Sarto Almeida (1924–2020) decided to establish their own offices in Goa; Souza was born in Goa, while Almeida was the son of Goan emigrants to Tanzania. Soon after, Souza and Almeida's architecture increased their visibility and associated them with the new architectural identity of a recently assimilated territory of India. The laterite stone-wall face was a feature of some of Souza and Almeida's buildings.[30]

Like other famous Indian architects of their generation, Souza and Almeida absorbed influences either from Le Corbusier (1887–1965) or Louis Kahn (1901–1974), who worked in India respectively in the 1950s and 1960s. Le Corbusier and Kahn used raw materials (concrete, bricks, stone) in their buildings in Chandigarh and Ahmedabad, showcasing bare building materials and structural elements—the "honest use of materials" was by then defended in modernist and brutalist architecture.

Yet the most influential architect undoubtedly would have been the British-born architect Lawrence "Laurie" Baker (1917–2007), who designed a long list of buildings across India. Unlike modernist architects, Baker's architecture was based on regional building practices and the use of local materials, adopting methods from Indian vernacular architecture combined with modern technologies and creative designs; the focus was on creating low-cost, efficient buildings. Baker's multi-volume buildings with curvilinear shapes and raw materials were indeed a source of inspiration for many Indian architects beginning their careers in the post-independence period.

In this way, Souza and Almeida marked the postcolonial architectural panorama of Goa, made of old-fashioned or kitsch buildings. They were joined by Charles Correa (1930–2015), another Goan-descendant architect who designed some buildings in Goa. His Kala Academy, located in Panjim, became a landmark of contemporary Goan architecture, where laterite wall face is abundantly used. In fact, these three architects received and blended modernist influences, together with Baker's ideas and vernacular influences, to create a local architecture.[31]

This use of laterite wall face as a characteristic of Goan architecture affected the preservation of Goan built heritage. For instance, the Reis Magos Fort was restored in the 2010s according to the plan of Gerard da Cunha (b. 1955), a Goan-descendant architect who had worked with Laurie Baker before establishing himself in Goa. Cunha removed the remaining plaster on the fort walls, assuming that Portuguese forts in Goa had not been plastered.[32] However, this was a tremendous misunderstanding, since all Portuguese forts had indeed been plastered. His opinion might have been influenced by Baker's works and the assumptions of Souza, Almeida, and Correa, but the deplastered Basilica of Bom Jesus might have also had some influence on his assumption regarding the use of laterite wall face in Goan architecture.

At the same time, the "rediscovery" of ancient pre-Portuguese monuments in Goa, especially from the Kadamba Empire period, might have contributed to the debate on Goan architecture. Some pre-Portuguese temples were listed as national monuments by the Indian government in 1982:[33] Structures such as the Manguesh Temple at Cortalim, the Saptakoteshwar Temple at Khandepar, the Mahadev Temple at Tambdi Surla, and the Jain Basti Temple at Bandora, all abandoned, presented a laterite stone face. However, the lack of plaster does not necessarily mean that these structures were deplastered. The plaster might have been lost over the years, with the abandonment of worshippers; in fact, plaster samples were found in some of these monuments. This feature could have contributed to the assignment of whitewashed limestone plaster as a characteristic introduced by the colonial presence; therefore, using exposed laterite in buildings might mean a return to Goan architecture's initial physiognomy.

The Contemporary Debate on the Basilica's Preservation

The Basilica of Bom Jesus was confirmed as an Indian national monument in 1982, during the reformulation of the listed monuments of Goa, Daman, and Diu.[34] In 1986 the basilica, together with other churches and convents of Goa, was also listed as a UNESCO World Heritage Site. In the proposal, a specific criterion was dedicated to the basilica: beyond its fine artistic quality, the presence of the tomb of Saint Francis Xavier was considered a symbol of an event of universal significance for the influence of the Catholic religion in Asia.[35] In addition, in 2009, the basilica was ranked as one of the "Seven Wonders of Portuguese Origin in the World" through a popular vote.[36]

Nevertheless, the damage to the Basilica of Bom Jesus observed by Luís Benavente in 1961 continued to increase, and by the new millennium, disaggregation was clearly visible in the exposed laterite stone of the facades. Conscious of the basilica's vulnerability, archaeologist Nizamuddin Taher, by then in charge of the ASI Goa Circle, began raising awareness with the aim of preventing further damage to the basilica. However, Taher's intention was met with vehement opposition by the Catholic Church and Catholic believers: on the one hand, the opposition was caused by tense relations between the ASI and the Archdiocese of Goa and Daman; on the other hand, Catholic believers who had never known a plastered and whitewashed version of the basilica, and thus believed it had never been plastered, had difficulty accepting change to the basilica's image.

In response, Taher proposed the use of a new technique that he had developed, the "laterite pack," used to restore the Dhamnar caves in Bhopal and parts of the ruins of the Augustine convent in Old Goa. The laterite pack is a composite mortar, made of lime mortar, laterite lumps, and powdered broken bricks, used to fill cavities of deteriorated laterite surfaces, mimicking both the texture and color. Although not a solution to effectively preserve the exposed laterite, at least this technique could temporarily stall the stone's disaggregation. Eventually, Taher considered his technique a first step in the slow process of changing the mindset within the Goan community, leading to the replastering of the basilica.[37]

The laterite pack was, however, merely a palliative, temporary, and located solution, since the real conservation problem continued to exist. Furthermore, when applied, the laterite pack was revealed to be a kind of pinkish patchwork standing out from the original reddish-brown laterite, thus affecting the global image of the monument—not to mention the lack of studies on the long-term effects of the laterite pack on laterite stone. The consolidation of a heterogeneous stone like laterite, which has large pores, is not feasible, and if not plastered with a sacrificial layer, such as plaster, it continues to erode; moreover, the wetness caused by rainfall leads to the bio-colonization of the stone, accelerating its degradation.[38] These issues ultimately bolstered the opposition to the use of the laterite pack technique, including among heritage lovers.

The mid-2010s marked a turning point in the contemporary debate about the preservation of the Basilica of Bom Jesus. In 2016, Taher's intentions were still being criticized, and a few supporters of the basilica's replastering were publically rebuked, including by Catholic priests.[39] However, little by little, the awareness-raising about the importance of safeguarding Goa's cultural heritage began to yield results, not only among opinion-makers and cultural elites but also among the Goan public.

There have been a few reasons for this change in perspective. One was the arrival in Goa of some Portuguese researchers with new perspectives free from local conditioning and in possession of knowledge from documental sources in Portuguese archives. Investigations by art historians and architects, such as Pedro Dias, António Nunes Pereira, Paulo Varela Gomes, Cristina Osswald, and me, allowed us a deeper knowledge of the history and artistic characteristics of the basilica.

The role of Paulo Varela Gomes also requires a special mention. By studying the basilica within the context of Goan Catholic religious architecture, Gomes developed the idea of the uniqueness of Goan architecture in many of its features, refusing the use of the expression "Indo-Portuguese." As mentioned before, by stating that the Basilica of Bom Jesus might have initiated a kind of architecture unique to Goa—a Goan architecture—Gomes's assertions surely contributed to instilling feelings of pride among Goans, who started to recognize the exceptional nature of their heritage.

Also meriting special attention are my efforts to explain the restoration process performed by Baltazar Castro in 1952 and Luís Benavente's intention to replaster the basilica at the end of the colonial period, based on official documental sources found in Portuguese archives. In fact, as Benavente had done half a century earlier, I argued that replastering the basilica would both increase its durability and recover its historical and artistic authenticity.

Goan scholars and heritage lovers also became more involved in safeguarding the basilica: Edgar Ribeiro, Vishvesh Kandolkar, and Fernando Velho, among others. While Ribeiro has been defending for a long time the implementation of a heritage protection zone in Old Goa, Kandolkar analyzed the basilica as part of the construction of the postcolonial Goan identity in his PhD thesis. All of these actors have engaged in awareness-raising actions (e.g., newspaper articles, seminars, meetings) with local priests and communities, the Archdiocese of Goa and Daman, political decision-makers, and even ASI technicians. In fact, while scientific articles and other papers by Portuguese and Goan scholars provide scientific support for the preservation of the basilica, these awareness-raising efforts are gradually bearing fruit by educating people, explaining the problem, resolving their doubts, showing documental evidence, and supporting their concerns.

Recent worries increased the Goan community's interest in the preservation of the basilica. Protests against the construction of new buildings, and especially a flyover inside the protected zone of the Basilica of Bom Jesus, have gained momentum.[40] However, energetic protests against the rainwater damage, which were lodged during some lengthy maintenance work performed by the ASI on the roof of the Professed House, presented an opportunity to unite the Archdiocese of Goa and Daman, Catholic believers, and heritage lovers around the same preservation aim.[41]

In fact, this rainwater damage became a warning about a major future concern: the impact of climate change on the basilica, which must be mitigated.[42] It is not only rainwater problems that are now affected by climate change, increasing the disaggregation of the laterite and fomenting the invasion of infesting herbs and other microorganisms; vibrations caused by heavy traffic from the nearby highway affect the basilica's structural integrity, and air pollution, also related to the highway, causes severe harm to the basilica, since carbon monoxide reacts with water, forming acids that attack the laterite stone. Besides the highway, deforestation in and around Old Goa, caused by unplanned urban expansion, is contributing to the drainage of increasingly heavy rainwater directly to the low terrain where the historic center of Goa is located, causing massive flooding of the unprepared drainage system of the site.[43] The basilica, which is situated lower than the surrounding ground, undoubtedly suffers from substantial problems of capillarity infiltration.

Epilogue

For the first time, the replastering of the basilica is being discussed as a feasible option.[44] It has been a long time since Baltazar Castro removed the plaster of the basilica in 1952, but now some of the stakeholders in Goa seem to be heading toward a common position on the basilica's preservation. Several experts in conservation from India and abroad have been called upon to take part in the debate and have given their input in a clear and pedagogical way. Local priests, such as Fr. Patrício Fernandes, with the support of the Archdiocese of Goa and Daman, are raising awareness in their communities; heritage lovers and scholars persist in their efforts to safeguard this unique heritage; and even the general public has started to progressively accept the idea of replastering the basilica.

However, the problem now seems to be of a different nature: since at least the nineteenth century, the Basilica of Bom Jesus has been a pilgrimage site that is especially crowded during the Xaverian celebrations, but its classification as a World Heritage Site, together with the state jurisdiction of the ASI, turned it into a buzzing touristic hotspot. The intense pressure of cultural and religious tourism placed on the basilica has several consequences, such as greater degradation owing to massive use and, consequently, higher maintenance costs.

Tourism is a major source of revenue but is also twisting the local reality.[45] The commodification and touristification of monuments in Old Goa are generating economic gains, visible in souvenir shops, eating places, and new houses that are multiplying, without any planning, across Old Goa's lands with potential archaeological remains, but this tourism is not offering significant benefits to the preservation of these monuments. There is a lack of sustainable touristic management (fig. 6).

Indeed, the most peculiar fact is that, right now, it seems that tourists, even unintentionally, are themselves an obstacle to the preservation of the basilica—especially those coming from other parts of India. The "red basilica," as the Basilica of Bom Jesus is often called, is a sought-after *ex libris* of Goa, different from all the other old, whitewashed Catholic churches in India, making it unique. In fact, this epithet conjures images of several Indian monuments where red is the prominent color (red fort, red palace, red temple, etc.) and one of their charming aspects. For instance, the main gate of the city wall of Diu, another former Portuguese territory, was painted in red after its integration into India and now resembles a red fort. In fact, one may wonder if the deplastering of the basilica might have been adopted somehow as part of an "Indianization" process, based on premises related to the debate on Goan architecture with a laterite wall face.

6 Touristic advertisement about Goa with an illustration of the Basilica of Bom Jesu, 1966.

To conclude, the Basilica of Bom Jesus is today a contested transcultural heritage site seen as a Goan peculiarity by Indians, as a colonial remnant by right-wing Hindu nationalists, a Lusitanian cultural legacy by Portuguese (and Westerners), and as a symbol of Goan identity by Goans, especially Catholic believers. However, its preservation is far from assured, while the contestations continue and time continues to pass without any concrete measures taken to protect this legacy of humankind.

This essay was developed within a contract funded by the FCT – Foundation for Science and Technology, under the Decree Law nº 57/2016 and the Law nº 57/2017.

1   The terms "restoration" and "restorer" used in this essay must be understood in the same way as they were perceived in the mid-twentieth century by the Portuguese dictatorial regime, when heritage was used as an instrument of ideological propaganda.

2   See, for instance: Osswald 2013; Gomes 2011; Pereira 2005; Dias 1999.

3   Pedro Dias also mentions the Jesuit master builders Luís Castanho and Francisco Domingues, as well as Giovanni de Manolis, as being in charge of the woodwork and Diego Ferrán as responsible for the quarries in Bassein, from where the granitic stone of the facades was brought. Cf. Dias 1999, 290–91.

4   Dias 1999, 288.

5   Pereira 2005, 228–29.

6   On Indian aesthetics, see for instance Dehejia 2014; Hussain and Wilkinson 2006; Sudhi 1997.

7   Santos 2009.

8   Gomes 2011, 68–70.

9   Saldanha 1990, vol. 1, 174–75.

10   Kloguen 1831, 79.

11   Melo 1952, 240–47.

12   On the Xaverian celebrations, see Kandolkar 2021a; Gupta 2014; Vicente 2002.

13   "Ordinance no. 1.360," *Boletim Official do Governo Geral do Estado da Índia* 27 (April 1, 1932), 405; "Decree no. 532," *Boletim Official do Governo Geral do Estado da Índia* 15 (February 19, 1932), 205.

14   On the end of the Portuguese colonial regime in India, see Lopes 2017; Stocker 2011; Bègue 2007; Couto 2006.

15   Santos 2015.

16   On the "reintegration" of monuments in Portugal during the dictatorship, see Tomé 2002 and Neto 2002.

17   On the Lusotropicalism, see Santos 2020; Souza 2001; Freyre 1961; Freyre 1952.

18   "Recordando o Passado" 1953. See also Neves 1953.

19   "[Official Report]" (typescript), Lisbon: Historical Overseas Archive, 'Former Overseas Ministry' Fund, 'Estado da Índia' Collection, file no. 632024, 1957.

20   Ry 1959.

21   On the musealization plan for Old Goa, see Santos 2016.

22   Benavente 1961.

23   Santos 2017.

24   Kandolkar 2020.

25   "Act no. XXIV of 1958: The Ancient Monuments and Archaeological Sites and Remains Act 1958," *The Gazette of India* 221, Part II (August 29, 1958), 155–69.

26   Santos 2017, 243–54.

27   This statement can be easily observed in talks with the local Catholic community and by reading newspaper articles—some of them mentioned in this essay.

28   On the construction of the postcolonial Goan identity see Kandolkar 2020b; Kandolkar 2015.

29   Silveira 2020.

30   Velho 2020.
31   Kanekar 2019.
32   Cunha 2017.
33   "Notification 9–4–79–WET," *Official Gazette – Government of Goa, Daman and Diu*, Series 1, no. 22 (August 26, 1982), 183–84.
34   Ibid.
35   https://whc.unesco.org/en/list/234 (accessed in June 2021).
36   https://projetos.7maravilhas.pt/portfolio-items/7-maravilhas-de-origem-portuguesa-no-mundo-old (accessed in June 2021).
37   Taher 2020. See also Taher 2017.
38   Rodrigues and Santos 2021. See also, among others, Das 2008 and Kasthurba et al. 2006.
39   "Plastering Basilica" 2016.
40   "Amid Pressure" 2020.
41   Fernandes 2020; "ASI Has Neglected" 2020; Joseph 2020; "Rector Slams ASI" 2020; Gama 2020; "Take immediate steps" 2020.
42   Kandolkar 2021b.
43   Fernandes 2021b.
44   Fernandes 2021a; Souza 2021; Monteiro 2021.
45   On tourism in Goa see Kandolkar 2020c; Kandolkar 2016; Trishur 2013.

Bibliography

"Amid Pressure, Goa Drops Move to Urbanise Heritage Church Complex." 2020. *National Herald*, December 2, 2020.
"ASI Has Neglected Conservation of the Basilica at Old Goa." 2020. *Herald*, April 24, 2020.
Bègue, Sandrine. 2007. *La Fin de Goa et de l'Estado da Índia: Décolonisation et Guerre Froide dans le Sous-Continent Indien (1945–1962)*. Lisbon: Ministério dos Negócios Estrangeiros.
Benavente, Luís. 1961. "[Official Report]" (typescript). Lisbon: National Archive of the Torre do Tombo, 'Luís Benavente' Fund, 'Estado da Índia' Collection, box no. 79 'Índia (Diversos)', file no. 548, document 10 "Acerca dos Paramentos Exteriores da Basilica do Bom Jesus em Velha Goa".
Couto, Francisco Cabral. 2006. *O Fim do Estado Português da Índia – 1961*. Lisbon: Tribuna da História.
Cunha, Gerard da. 2017. "Reis Magos Fort, Goa." In Kulbhushan Jain, ed., *Conserving Architecture*, 306–17. Ahmedabad: Aadi Centre.
Das, Sutapa. 2008. "Decay Diagnosis of Goan Laterite Stone Monuments." Paper presented at the *11DBMC International Conference on Durability of Building Materials and Components* (Istanbul, May 11–14, 2008), https://www.irbnet.de/daten/iconda/CIB13224.pdf (accessed in June 2021).
Dehejia, Vidya. 2014. *Indian Art*. London: Phaidon Press Limited.
Dias, Pedro. 1999. "A Construção da Casa Professa da Companhia de Jesus em Goa." In Mário Barroca, ed., *Carlos Alberto Ferreira de Almeida: In Memoriam*, vol. 1, 287–97. Oporto: Faculdade de Letras da Universidade do Porto.
Fernandes, Paul. 2020. "A Plaster of Poise for the Basilica." *Gomantak Times*, May 17, 2020.
Fernandes, Paul. 2021a. "Goans Accustomed to Seeing Laterite Walls of Basilica, but it Needs Restoration." *Times of India*, March 27, 2021.
Fernandes, Paul. 2021b. "Heritage Lovers Raise Flooding Alert, Call for Expediting Basilica Work on Priority." *Times of India*, May 6, 2021.
Freyre, Gilberto. 1952. *Um Brasileiro em Terras Portuguesas: Introdução a uma Possível Luso-Tropicologia*. Lisbon: Edição 'Livros do Brasil'.
Freyre, Gilberto. 1961. *Portuguese Integration in the Tropics*. Lisbon: Tipografia Silvas.
Gama, Danuska da. 2020. "Urgent Efforts Needed to Ensure Basilica Is Protected for Future Generations." *The Navhind Times*, April 23, 2020.
Gomes, Paulo Varela. 2011. *Whitewash, Red Stone: A History of Church Architecture in Goa*. New Delhi: Yoda Press.

Gupta, Pamila. 2014. *The Relic State: St. Francis Xavier and the Politics of Ritual in Portuguese India*. Manchester: Manchester University Press.

Hussain, Mazhar, and Robert Wilkinson, eds. 2006. *The Pursuit of Comparative Aesthetics: An Interface Between the East and West*. London: Routledge.

Joseph, Verghese V. 2020. "Shoddy Restoration Work at Goa's Basilica of Bom Jesus Causes Deep Anguish." *Indian Catholic Matters*, April 23, 2020.

Kandolkar, Vishvesh. 2015. "Local Identity, Global Architecture." *The Goan Everyday*, July 19, 2015.

Kandolkar, Vishvesh. 2016. "Tourism's Unsustainable Consumption of Goa." In Emanuela Delfino, Carlo Vezzoli, eds., *Sustainable Energy for All by Design: Proceedings of the LeNSes Conference*, 365–72. Milan: Edizioni POLI.DESIGN.

Kandolkar, Vishvesh. 2020a. "Restoring Basilica of Bom Jesus, and the Role of Archaeological Survey of India." *Economic & Political Weekly* 55, no. 36 (September 5, 2020), https://www.epw.in/engage/article/restoring-basilica-bom-jesus-and-archaeological-survey-india (accessed in October 2021).

Kandolkar, Vishvesh. 2020b. "Architecture and the Structure of Goan Identity in the 'Postcolonial' Period." PhD thesis, Manipal Academy of Higher Education.

Kandolkar, Vishvesh. 2020c. "Consuming Goa Portuguesa: Vacationing in a Postcolonial Colony." *Journal of Human Values* 26, no. 3: 266–76.

Kandolkar, Vishvesh. 2021a. "Itinerant Saint: The Architecture of Golden Goa and the 1952 Exposition of St. Francis Xavier's Relics." *The Journal of Hindu Studies* 14, no. 2: 149–70.

Kandolkar, Vishvesh. 2021b. "Rain in the Basilica: Protecting Goa's Bom Jesus from the Ravages of Climate Change." *eTropic: Electronic Journal of Studies in the Tropics* 20.2: 95–113.

Kanekar, Amita. 2019. "Charles Correa in and out of Goa." *Namasté: The ITC Hotels Magazine*: 48–57.

Kasthurba, A. K., Manu Santhanam, and M. S. Mathews. 2006. "Weathering Forms and Properties of Laterite Building Stones Used in Historic Monuments of Western India." In Paulo B. Lourenço et al., eds., *Structural Analysis of Historical Constructions*, vol. 2, 1317–22. New Delhi: Macmillan India.

Kloguen, Denis Cottineau de. 1831. *An Historical Sketch of Goa, the Metropolis of the Portuguese Settlements in India*. Madras: Gazette Press.

Lopes, Filipa Sousa. 2017. "As Vozes da Oposição ao Estado Novo e a Questão de Goa (1950–1961)". PhD thesis, University of Oporto.

Melo, José Afonso de. 1952. "A Basílica do Bom Jesus." *Boletim Eclesiástico da Arquidiocese de Goa* 5–6: 240–47.

Monteiro, Lisa. 2021. "Basilica can collapse 'at any moment', must be plastered soon." *Times of India*, January 25, 2021.

Neto, Maria João. 2002. *Memória, Propaganda e Poder: O Restauro dos Monumentos Nacionais (1929–1960)*. Oporto: FAUP Publicações.

Neves, Mário. 1953. "A Queda do Arco dos Vice-Reis Constituirá um Aviso a Considerar nas Obras da Velha Goa?" *Diário da Noite* 10576, August 13, 1953: 1, 4.

Osswald, Cristina. 2013. *Written in Stone: Jesuit Buildings in Goa and Their Artistic and Architectural Features*. Saligao: Goa 1556.

Pereira, António Nunes. 2005. *A Arquitectura Religiosa Cristã de Velha Goa*. Lisbon: Fundação Oriente.

"Plastering Basilica; Church Says Oh God, Please Don't." 2016. *The Goan Everyday*, February 10, 2016.

"Recordando o Passado." 1953. *O Heraldo* 13094, August 4, 1953: 1.

"Rector Slams ASI over Gross Neglect of Basilica." 2020. *The Goan Everyday*, April 23, 2020.

Rodrigues, José Delgado, and Joaquim Rodrigues dos Santos. 2021. "A Historical Blunder: Exposing the Laterite of the Basilica of Bom Jesus." *Herald*, August 15, 2021.

Ry, Ludovico Toeplitz de Grand. 1959. "Salvaguardar a Tradição." *Heraldo* 14727, February 25, 1959: 1.

Saldanha, Manuel José Gabriel de. 1990. *História de Goa (Politica a Arqueológica)*. Madras: Asian Educational Services.

Santos, Joaquim Rodrigues dos. 2009. "As Portas da Jerusalém Celeste: Proposta de Síntese Formal para as Fachadas de Duas Torres na Arquitectura Religiosa Portuguesa entre os Séculos XVI e XVIII." *Artis* 7–8: 273–74.

Santos, Joaquim Rodrigues dos. 2015. "On the Trail of Baltazar Castro, a Portuguese Restorer in India." In Vladan Djokić, Ana Nikezić, and Ana Raković, eds., *EAHN 2015 Belgrade: Entangled Histories, Multiple Geographies*, 244–53. Belgrade: Arhitektonski Fakultet Univerziteta u Beogradu.

Santos, Joaquim Rodrigues dos. 2016. "'Reinstalling the Old City of Goa as an Eternal Light of the Portuguese Spirituality': The Plan for the Reintegration of Old Goa at the End of the Colonial Period." *Architectural Histories* 4, no. 1, art. 9: 1–21, http://doi.org/10.5334/ah.58.

Santos, Joaquim Rodrigues dos. 2017. "Cultural Idiosyncrasies and Preservation Challenges in the Indo-Portuguese Catholic Religious Architecture of Goa (India)." In Joaquim Rodrigues dos Santos, ed., *Preserving Transcultural Heritage: Your Way or My Way?*, 243–54. Casal de Cambra: Caleidoscópio.

Santos, Joaquim Rodrigues dos. 2020. "'A Western Light in Eastern Lands': The Study Missions to the Estado da Índia and the Development of an Indo-Lusotropicalist Rhetoric." In Marta Pacheco Pinto and Catarina Apolinário de Almeida, eds., *Portuguese Orientalism*, 108–40. Eastbourne: Sussex Academic Press.

Silveira, Lester. 2020. "Renovated out of Existence: The Sorry State of Architectural Conservation in Goa." *Herald*, May 31, 2020.

Souza, Gerard de. 2021. "Goa's Basilica of Bom Jesus Could Lose Iconic Red Look to Conserve the Structure." *Hindustan Times*, April 2, 2021.

Souza, Teotónio de. 2001. *Gilberto Freyre na Índia e o "Luso-tropicalismo Transnacional."* Lisbon: Centro Português de Estudos do Sudeste Asiático.

Stocker, Maria Manuel. 2011. *Xeque-Mate a Goa: O Princípio do Fim do Império Português*. Alfragide: Texto Editores.

Sudhi, Padma. 1997. *Aesthetic Theories of India*. New Delhi: Intellectual Publishing House.

Taher, Nizamuddin. 2017. "Preserving the Exfoliated Weathered Fabric of Basilica of Bom Jesus, Old Goa." In Joaquim Rodrigues dos Santos, ed., *Preserving Transcultural Heritage: Your Way or My Way?*, 303–11. Casal de Cambra: Caleidoscópio.

Taher, Nizamuddin. 2020. "Preserving a World Heritage Monument," *Herald*, May 10, 2020.

"'Take immediate steps to repair basilica urgently', rector writes to ASI." *The Times of India*, April 23, 2020.

Tomé, Miguel. 2002. *Património e Restauro em Portugal (1920–1995)*. Oporto: FAUP Publicações.

Trishur, Raghuraman. 2013. *Refiguring Goa: From Trading Post to Tourism Destination*. Saligao: Goa 1556.

Velho, Fernando. 2020. "The Long Shadow of Goa's Dying Basilica." *Herald*, December 13, 2020.

Vicente, Filipe Lowndes. 2002. "A Exposição do Corpo Sagrado de S. Francisco Xavier e as Exposições Industriais e Agrícolas em Goa." *Oriente* 4: 55–66.

Archival Sources

"Act no. XXIV of 1958: The Ancient Monuments and Archaeological Sites and Remains Act 1958." *The Gazette of India* 221, Part II, August 29, 1958, 155–69.

"Decree no. 532," *Boletim Official do Governo Geral do Estado da Índia* 15, February 19, 1932, 205.

"Notification 9–4–79–WET," *Official Gazette: Government of Goa, Daman and Diu*, Series 1, no. 22, August 26, 1982, 183–84.

"Ordinance no. 1.360," *Boletim Official do Governo Geral do Estado da Índia* 27, April 1, 1932, 405.

"[Official Report]" (typescript), Lisbon: Historical Overseas Archive, 'Former Overseas Ministry' Fund, 'Estado da Índia' Collection, file no. 632024, 1957.

Image Sources

1   Photo by William Johnson and William Henderson; Southern Methodist University – Digital Collections.
2   Survey and drawings by António Nunes Pereira.
3   Photo by James Burke; LIFE Archives.
4, 5 Photo by the author.
6   *Goa Today*, October, 1966; Krishnadas Shama State Central Library.

YING ZHOU

Confounding Decolonizing Etiquettes

Cases from Hong Kong and Shanghai

The spate of reckoning with colonial legacies, sometimes involving toppling sculptures and architectural monuments, seems to have taken a global turn. Developing political economies in the Global East, however, have largely ignored these modes of interrogation, confounding the prevalence of decolonizing etiquettes circulating around the world. Here, colonial legacies are not spurned. Rather, their architectural manifestations have been popularly regarded as a source of progress and prosperity, and they have been part of the enthusiasm for heritage conservation in the region since the 2000s.

Part of an ongoing research examining art spaces in Shanghai and Hong Kong, this essay analyzes two cases celebrated for the conservation and reuse of colonial-era built structures. In Hong Kong, the former Central Police Station compound was gazetted as a historic monument and then converted into an arts and heritage hub known, since its opening in 2018, as Tai Kwun. In Shanghai, the block surrounding the former Royal Asiatic Society building, which was converted into the Rockbund Art Museum and opened in time for the 2010 World Expo, has been redeveloped and conserved as a historical district. The physical conservation of the two sets of buildings seems to confirm an uncritical embrace, both popular and institutional, of the material legacies from the colonial era and a disengagement from the nuances of historical trajectories. By examining their original uses, transformations over time, and reuse, this piece unpacks how these two colonial-era structures have been embraced and appropriated as part of the contemporary development of the two cities.

The inceptions of Shanghai and Hong Kong as cities in the mid-nineteenth century under the same colonial contracts, their post-1949 divergence as political economies, and then a slow convergence since China's reform and opening in the 1980s, make them remarkable comparative cases[1] for the contemporary "heritagization" that has become prevalent in the two cities since the mid-2000s. As urban geographer David C. Harvey asserts, "heritagization," the development of heritage as a process, is not only "a selective portrayal contingent on present-day requirements," but also fundamentally tied to "the production of identity, power, and authority."[2]

In Shanghai, the material manifestations of colonial-era global linkages were appropriated to jump-start accelerated economic liberalization in the 1990s after nearly four decades of a planned economy. Historic buildings have come to symbolize both Shanghai's past prosperity, and through their reuse, the city's economic revival.[3] In Hong Kong, where the end of colonialism in 1997 did not result in independence, selected old buildings are valued not only for their rarity in a prevalently demolition-driven urbanism. These buildings have also come to be embraced as representing a local identity that many see as being eroded, including, amongst other things, the rule of law.[4] The specificities, in the drivers, actors, and pathways, of the heritagization processes highlight the uniqueness of the "One Country Two Systems" framework that is itself undergoing transition.

In both cases, heritagization is simultaneous with a seeming disregard for the colonial past. In contrast to the economically developed and politically liberal contexts of the West, where heritage recognition and implementation, including established norms for conservation, grew out of the rapid urbanization of a nineteenth-century modernity,[5] heritagization itself is nascent in the economically developing but politically differing social contracts of the non-West. Historical buildings and their reuse have begun, since the 2000s, to play into the aspirations of the rapidly rising cities of the Global East.[6] Heritagization here satisfies the growing demand sophistication of local market tastes, while fulfilling aspirations to reach the standards of the developed world. In these contexts, where buildings that are not demolished for being outdated, nor their plot-ratios maximized for economic value, remain atypical and exceptional, inhibiting the first progress towards saving old buildings by calling out the colonial-era wrongs represented by them would be to undermine the global aspirations at the heart of heritagization in these cities. The seeming oversight of the colonial past embodied by the old buildings nevertheless warrants further unpacking. Examining the historic developments of these two cases elucidates the processes of selecting and recognizing buildings as historic and having heritage value in these developing economies. The cases also contextualize the role heritagization plays for economic transition, which is fundamental to understanding the lack of criticality towards colonial legacies in these contexts.

From the Royal Asiatic Society Building to the Rockbund Art Museum

Imperialism, resource extraction, industrialization, and nation-building are all interconnected parts of a global modernity. For nineteenth-century China, growing demand for tea led to deficit of silver for the West and the consequent cultivation of the opium trade by the West to pry open the vast but closed Chinese market. The Opium War was fought and Qing imperial China defeated. With the signing of the Treaty of Nanking in 1842, strategically selected coastal locales as treaty ports became the new hubs of globalization's opportunities.

In Shanghai, conceded areas, "Concessions," became places where extraterritorial global trade rapidly grew. While the beginnings of the Concessions were by no means glamorous affairs, the soldiers and the merchants were also accompanied by a group of people interested both in civilizing the "natives," as locals were regarded, and by the rich cultures of such indigenous peoples. The Royal Asiatic Society (RAS) was founded in London, when King George IV granted a Sanskrit scholar, Sir Henry Colebrooke, the Royal Charter in 1824, "for the investigation of subjects connected with and for the encouragement of science, literature and the arts in relation to Asia."[7] In October 1857, in the library housed in the Masonic Hall, an American Protestant missionary and highly regarded Chinese linguist, Elijah Coleman Bridgman, was elected the first president of a society—founded by eighteen high-minded British and American men, of whom six were missionaries—that would be granted affiliation with the RAS the following year.[8] The Northern China branch of the RAS was thus established in Shanghai in 1858 as a gathering place for like-minded expatriate thinkers curious about the "civilization" of the region, against the backdrop of the West's rapid economic expansion. In the early 1860s, the RAS fell into decline with the death of Bridgman. With the help of US Consul General, it was soon revived in 1864, launching the publication of a journal,[9] and setting up a library and a museum.[10]

The RAS was also soon granted a site for its first building. A plot, in a new block at the bend where Suzhou Creek flows into the Huangpu River and behind the British Consul's building, was leased to the RAS. Designed by architect Thomas William Kingsmill, the RAS building opened in 1871, with a reading room, a library of books on the Orient, and a lecture hall on the ground floor.[11] Three years later, the newspaper *Shun Pao* reported that its upper floor was opened as a museum with a zoological and geological collection. In 1886, the road in front was renamed Museum Road, showing the rising status of the RAS and its cultural function.

With the rapid growth of Shanghai, the RAS became an important intellectual hub in the city, though its use was restricted to its non-Chinese members. By the 1920s, the RAS reading room received more than 3,000 users every year. It was clear that the RAS was outgrowing its premises, and its wooden structure vulnerable to termite infestations. In 1927 fundraising began for a new building, and in 1930 the British Consul, showing his support, donated the plot to the RAS, which it had previous leased.[12] The late 1920s and early 1930s was also the time when many of the buildings in the same block, which remain today, were erected. The Young Women's Christian Association and the Baptist Publication and Christian Literature Society buildings, alongside the Capitol Theater and the Yuanminyuan Apartments, complemented the trade houses and bank buildings growing along the Bund, forming a cultural block in proximity to the British Consul.

Construction of the new RAS building was completed in October 1932. At the opening of the building in February 1932, the chair of the International Concession's Municipal Council, A.D. Bell, officiated, and the Republic of China's Minister of Education, Cai Yuanpei, gave remarks,[13] showing the importance of the RAS as a cultural organization to the new republic. By this time, the RAS membership had also been extended to include the Chinese.

The new six-story building was designed by Palmer and Turner (P&T) architects, who were already known in the now commercially vibrant metropolis for their Hong Kong Shanghai Bank building and Sassoon tower along the Bund (fig. 1). Built of reinforced concrete structure, the composition and ornamental motifs of the building's façade are designed to express its mission as a modern repository of knowledge of the arts and sciences of the region as well its locality. The façade is symmetrical, with two octagonal windows at the base citing the traditional Chinese form. Above the gray stone base, the body of the building is red brick, suggesting its Western extractions.[14] A horizontal plate on the façade between the second and third floors is engraved with the Chinese name of RAS: the characters chosen are in antique seal script,[15] the type of which would be found in its collections. Both the horizontal nameplate and the parapet are carved with the cloud pattern, a classical motif that would have been found on the carved bronzes or jade relics in the RAS's collection.

Soon after the new building's opening, the second Sino-Japanese War that began in 1937 would make the building a destination for an increasing number of donations as many expats departed in response to the political turbulence.[16] In 1943 Museum Road was renamed Huqiu Road, a first attempt at decolonization.[17] Two years later, the building that had been requisitioned by the Japanese Army had been returned to RAS use, but soon, the last edition of the *Journal of the Northern China Branch of the RAS* would be published. In 1949, with the founding

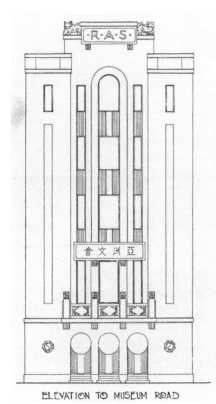

ELEVATION TO MUSEUM ROAD

1   Elevation drawing (left) and photograph (right) of the Royal Asiatic Society building in the 1930s.

of the People's Republic of China (PRC), which the Chinese Communist Party (CCP) dubbed the "Liberation" for their emancipation of the country from imperialist dominance, the RAS closed. In the following years, as nearly all foreigners departed the new China, the RAS collection was dispersed, with the geological and zoological artifacts sent to the Natural History Museum, and the books and documents to the charge of the Shanghai Library.[18] The building itself has variously served as storage for the Shanghai Library and as the offices of the Natural History Museum between 1949 and the 1990s.

From an extraterritorial "special economic zone" and a city known for its consumption, central planning after 1949's Liberation turned Shanghai into a city of production. The architectural symbolism of an area like the Bund that manifested Western imperialism and capitalism became the scourge for the new nation that prided itself on socialism and self-sufficiency.[19] The Western- and hybrid-styled buildings that had represented free-dealing market economics, cosmopolitanism, or China's subjugation to foreign powers, depending on one's perspective, were despised. The Cultural Revolution starting in 1966 further pushed for the obliteration of the old. It would be another thirty years until China would embark on economic transition starting in the 1980s, which the government called "Reform and Opening." Opening again to the outside world, a slow but growing recognition of buildings in places such as the Bund began to take on popular support and eventually state backing.[20]

At the end of 1986, the municipality convinced the central government to include modern-era Shanghai in its second batch of National Historical Cultural Cities,[21] which the municipality advocated for as the birthplace of the CCP. In the first batch, only traditional Chinese cities such as Xi'an and Beijing were selected and none of the colonial-era cities. It was thus on the basis of the official acknowledgement that the foundation of the PRC was itself a product of global modernity, that the historical importance of stylistically Western-looking modern-era buildings to China could be affirmed. In 1989, the Shanghai municipality would name the first batch of buildings as Outstanding Modern-era Architecture for protection against future demolition.[22] In 1999 the former RAS building was one of 162 protected buildings included in the third batch of the city's list, now renamed Outstanding Historical Architecture.[23]

The same year, the former Nissin building at Number 5 reopened, branded as M on the Bund. In 2001 the adjacent Union building by P & T at Number 3 reopened, branded as Three on the Bund, after careful restoration by the American architect Michael Graves. The commercial success of these restorations after decades of neglect, as well as the growing number of expats and returnees beginning to settle in Shanghai in the mid-2000s who appreciated such developments, would not go unnoticed.

The growing heritage movement was not only a reaction to the demolition-based urban development fundamental to the restructuring of the city to accommodate accelerated economic liberalization, for which Shanghai was anointed the Head of the Dragon in the aftermath of the Tian'anmen Square Incident in 1989.[24] Nostalgia literature and television period pieces, by both local authors and the overseas Chinese diaspora, glamorizing the 1930s Republican-era city dubbed as "the Paris of the East," also fed a new and growing popular recognition of old buildings, which were rapidly disappearing. The prosperity, decadence, and cosmopolitanism associated with Shanghai's pre-war era were contrasted with the socialist period of enforced austerity, poverty, and international isolation. In the marketization and re-globalization that began under Reform and Opening, the modern-era architectures and what they represented were harked to for the city's revival.[25] It would soon become obvious that the buildings were not merely symbols. With the 2000 opening of an area branded *Xintiandi*, literally "New Heaven and Earth," a successful commercial development converting historic housing into a new shopping block,[26] the patina of age and the grace of history became economically valuable. By the mid-2000s, both the government and private sectors became interested in "old buildings," a term used locally for buildings built before 1949.[27]

At the end of 2001, China joined the World Trade Organization. In the Tenth Five-Year Plan released in this year, the area at the mouth of the Huangpu River became branded in Chinese as *Waitanyuan*, literally the "originary source of the Bund," a name that gives credence to the development site's historicity. In 2006 the name was approved by the Office for Management of Place Names in Shanghai. In 2002 the district's developer organized a call for "International Concepts for Waitanyuan Area Urban Design."[28] The international investors of the Rockefeller Group, eyeing the growth market, signed on for the development of Lot 174, encompassing the blocks around and including the former RAS building in 2004 (fig. 2). In 2005 the Chinese developer Sinolink joined in the new company established to develop the lot, named the Shanghai Bund de Rockefeller Group Master Development Co. Ltd.

In the mid-2000s, teams from Tongji University's architecture faculty undertook the mapping, surveying, and historical research of the area now branded the "Rockbund." The name is a catchy shortening of the two prominent parts of the development company's long name, that of the Rockefeller and the Bund. Researching and documenting historical buildings made up many of the dissertations undertaken in this premier school of architecture in Shanghai. In 2006 the developers engaged David Chipperfield Architects for the renovation of the old buildings.

The architects and researchers found the buildings in a sad condition. Like most areas in the city, the accumulation of demographic demand since Liberation, coupled with neglect, had transformed many of the grandest buildings into informal squalor. Though the RAS building was somewhat shielded because it had been managed by the Shanghai Library, its top floors were turned into residences, and multiple partitions and additions were built. In the 1990s, when marketization accelerated and local state-owned enterprises were compelled to corporatize, the spaces of the RAS building were even rented to a financial enterprise.[29] David Chipperfield Architects, who were already known for their work in the restoration of the Neues Museum in Berlin's Museum Island, undertook a careful restoration and addition to the former RAS building (fig. 3). While the eastern addition accommodates contemporary infrastructure needs, a new façade to what was formerly the back of the building responds to the creation of a new plaza in the masterplan.

After the World Expo in May, the new Rockbund Art Museum (RAM) was the first in the area to open in October 2010, the branding vehicle and centerpiece of the entire Rockbund development. For a block that had been known for its cultural functions in pre-Liberation times, and has since become a socially impoverished area, the insertion of an art museum was part of the real estate strategy to raise the profile of the area (see fig. 2). The inaugural exhibition by artist Cai Guoqiang, followed by the solo shows by Zeng Fanzhi and Zhang Huan, all well-known representatives of Chinese contemporary art in the 2000s, set the tone for the new RAM by developing inquiries into the historic building as well as contemporary developments. Zeng's show, for example, referred to the former function of the upper floor as a natural history museum and installed an abstraction of a mammoth figure as the centerpiece of the double-height space. Zhang Huan's large sculpture of Confucius, located in the former auditorium level of the RAS, similarly commented on the institution's collection of Chinese historical artifacts. The rapid rise of Chinese contemporary art and the museum boom would quickly reverberate in the city in the aftermath of the Expo. Across from the RAM and outside of the Rockbund development, the Amber Building, built in 1937, was also restored and opened in 2018, housing the international galleries Perrotin and Lisson.

From the Central Police Station Compound to Tai Kwun

If the revival of the old buildings in Shanghai, in what is branded as the Rockbund area, represents the re-embrace of global capital flows and cosmopolitanism, the reuse of the former Central Police Station in Hong Kong, a poster child for laissez-faire governance and global flows, evokes a different kind of nostalgia (fig. 4).

After the British occupation of Hong Kong in 1841, the settlement known for its drug smuggling, piracy, and robberies grew rapidly.[30] The extraterritoriality of the colony outside Chinese

2   Plan of the contemporary neighborhood around the Rockbund development, outlined in black, with the former Royal Asiatic Society building, now Rockbund, in solid black (left); the Rockbund Art Museum (right).

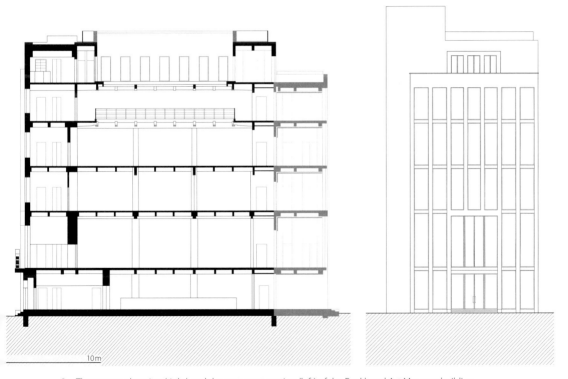

3   The eastern elevation (right) and the east–west section (left) of the Rockbund Art Museum building indicating Chipperfield Architects' interventions (in gray).

jurisdiction attracted legal offenders. One of the first buildings of the colony's establishment, thus, was built for the first Chief Magistrate, William Caine, in 1841, who was charged with the police and the prison. The steep site, about 300 feet above sea level and protected by rocky ravines on the sides, was chosen for its defensibility from local incursion. After the police force was established in 1844, the first buildings, shoddily constructed, were converted into a prison, while a magistracy was constructed as part of a program of works, in 1845, on the eastern end of the site.

The growth of prisoners accompanying rapid urbanization compelled the expansion of the penitentiary buildings. Soon a decision was made to move the police force to the site of the prison. In the 1860s Indian officers were recruited to Hong Kong, and in the 1870s reforms expanded the force to include Chinese police officers. For the 125 European officers, 171 Sikhs, and the 315 Chinese, the building enforced racial segregation, reflecting the colonial order of the time. Urbanistically, the arrangement was made so that the prison was marked off by the magistracy and the police barracks.[31]

Starting in 1897, the radial layout of the prison was demolished, and its building materials were recycled for new cells in a new hall. During the following decade, a new central magistracy was built atop the demolished former one. With walls made of Canton red brick, and pillars finished in a molded cement concrete, the building manifested the orders of colonial rule. The year before, the northern plot, Inland Lot 3, was also obtained for a Headquarters Block for the police force, designed with a three-story public façade to the north and a two-story façade with long verandas facing onto the inner Parade Ground. While the road-facing façade was built in red brick and rendered in cement plaster, the other elevations were finished in Formosa facing bricks. A granite staircase connected the levels with the mosques, billiard halls, interrogation rooms, and other facilities. Part of the compound was destroyed during the Second World War, and restorations took place afterwards, with new technological upgrades.

Responding to the large influx of refugees, the police headquarters also moved to new premises, and the compound in the district of Central became the Island Headquarters and eventually the Central Police Station, colloquially referred to as the CPS. The Victoria Prisons

4   The block around the former Royal Asiatic Society building, now Rockbund development (left), and the former Central Police Station compound, now Taikwun (right).

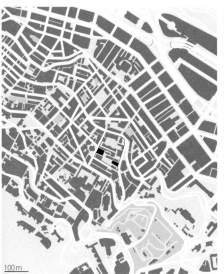

5   Plan of the contemporary neighborhood around Tai Kwun, outlined in black, with the newly added volume in solid black (left); the upper courtyard with Tai Kwun Contemporary building (right).

site also eventually stopped serving as a convict prison and became a detention center for refugees,[32] most notably after the Vietnam War. As China's Reform and Opening, starting in the 1980s, further propelled Hong Kong from being an Asian Tiger of industrial exports to one that served as a conduit for international financial flows into and out of the PRC, the visible rise of the skyline of Hong Kong's Central district manifested this shifting role of the city, which accompanied China's re-globalization. In 1984 the British-Chinese Joint Declaration was signed for the Handover of Hong Kong from British to Chinese sovereignty in 1997. The first Chinese police commissioner would be appointed in 1989.

Following the 1993 opening of the Mid-Levels Escalator, bringing pedestrians up and down the steep slopes of Central and epitomizing the rapid growth of the area (fig. 5), and the impending decommissioning and development on the table, the site of the CPS compound was declared a monument in 1995. The first years after the Handover saw the conscious branding of Hong Kong as "Asia's World City." The first Chief Executive of the Special Administrative Region (SAR) began to push forward an eighteen-billion HKD tourism plan, which included a sixty-million HKD pilot for the area around the CPS.[33] In business-oriented Hong Kong, the newly established Tourism Commission was charged with the compound's future.[34]

Despite economic contractions in Hong Kong resulting from the SARS Pandemic at the end of 2002 lasting into 2003, the idea of a restoration project for tourism was set. The government saw private sector involvement as fundamental to the economic feasibility of the development.[35] In April 2003, the Tourism Commission and its parent Economic Development and Labour Bureau (EDLB) proposed the conversion of the CPS compound into a "heritage tourism attraction,"[36] and opened the tender to the private sector.[37]

One of the proposals suggested converting the site into an arts complex, funded by donation, and run by a non-profit foundation or trust. This proposal was turned down, but it seeded a direction for the site's reuse. The burgeoning rhetoric of the "creative class" was also being touted by urban bureaucrats internationally in the mid-2000s.

At the same time, protests against the demolitions of the Star Ferry and Queen's Piers, as well as the profit-driven single-developer West Kowloon development, were magnifying voices alarmed by what was increasingly seen as an erasure of local cultural identity.[38] Colonial-era buildings, under threat from the government's infrastructure-focused developmentalism, thus became symbols for this unique local identity that distinguished Hong Kong from the PRC's mainland. With this growing civic consciousness, local concern groups and professional associations questioned the commercialization of historic sites such as the CPS. They took their complaints about the way in which the Tourism Commission and EDLB planned for the future of the CPS to the government's Home Affairs Bureau,[39] until then not actively involved with the CPS development.

At the end of 2004, the Legislative Council's Panel on Home Affairs put forward the motion to "put on hold the tendering procedure for the tourism project at the Central Police Station."[40] The Hong Kong Jockey Club, a semi-public philanthropic organization led by local elites, in the meanwhile commissioned the Swiss architecture firm of Herzog & de Meuron (HdM) for a conceptual proposal for the site. From London's Tate Modern to the Unterlinden Museum in Colmar, HdM's works have put adaptive reuse on the international cultural map with their creations of high-quality museum spaces in historical buildings. Nevertheless, their proposal for latticed towers, the details of which were made public in October 2007, garnered critical feedback from both the professional associations and concern groups. The towers, inspired by bamboo scaffolding and intended to lift a series of programs above the office buildings surrounding the site, especially irked the concern groups, who saw keeping the old buildings as they were as the only legitimate form of preservation.[41] Public consultations, which ended in April 2008, made clear that the towers, however transparent they could tectonically be achieved, were not acceptable.[42]

In 2008 the Hong Kong and Shenzhen Bi-City Biennale of Architecture, held for the first time in Hong Kong on the grounds of the former CPS, opened the premises to the broader public. Entitled "Refabricating City," the potential of the centrally located site was further highlighted. With two large open-air courtyards surrounded by low-rise buildings, the CPS offered a rare uncongested space in the center of the high-density city. The same year, amendments to the Outline Zoning Plan (OZP) emphasized the importance of the compatibility of the new developments with the historic site.[43] The tower scheme rejected by the public gave way to a second scheme of a floating bar that hovered above the existing buildings.[44] The third and realized scheme, shared in 2010, reduced the volumes of the new additions to conform to a stringent OZP, which also requested preservation of much of the existing historic compound. The scheme preserved the area as a rare low-rise urban oasis surrounded by high-rises.

The shifts in the CPS development, moreover, seemed to change the SAR's approach to heritage in general. In May 2007, a Subcommittee on Heritage Conservation was established, and in July, a new Development Bureau was established to take over the responsibility for heritage policy that had been under the Home Affairs Bureau.[45] The fact that heritage, often seen as

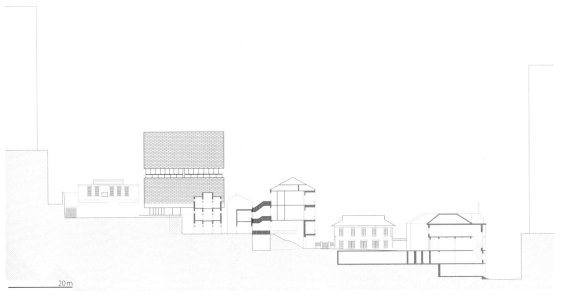

6   A north–south section of the Tai Kwun compound looking west, showing the newly added volume, in black, of Tai Kwun Contemporary.

antithetical to development, is under the oversight of a government body named for development, reveals the conceptualization of historic buildings in an urban context of rapid renewal. The Chief Executive's annual Policy Address on October 10, 2007 formally announced heritage as important to the SAR.[46] Heritage conservation became, belatedly in Hong Kong, a new buzzword, and a more autonomous concept no longer primarily tied to tourism and economic development.

The selection for the commercial operation of the heritage site also went through several rounds, with the Jockey Club deciding finally to establish The Jockey Club CPS Limited to oversee this new Centre for Heritage and Arts, rebranded as Tai Kwun, literally meaning "large station" in Cantonese. In 2018 the compound would open to the public after nearly two decades of conceptualization and a decade of design, conservation, and construction. Two new HdM-designed polished cultural vessels hover above the masonry base of the historic granite walls (fig. 6), totaling around one-fifth of the total floor area. Demolition of a one-story building used as offices and a building for laundry had made these new structures possible. The introduction of a necessary selective demolition and the implementation of new structures also became an unprecedented innovation in the treatment of historical buildings deemed heritage in Hong Kong. The new volume on the eastern edge of the complex houses a performance venue accommodating 200 seats, and a second volume for the new contemporary visual art institution, Tai Kwun Contemporary, stands on the western edge (see fig. 5). Modeled on the German *Kunsthalle*, Tai Kwun Contemporary has since become representative of the development of an arts scene in Hong Kong, long considered a cultural desert.

Contemporary Heritagizations

The development of these two cases shows how they are products of their specific contexts (fig. 7). The former RAS building had been a pinnacle of the kinds of orientalist learned societies that had been as important a part of the imperialist endeavor as commercial or military conquests. The building's architectural ornamentation, as well as its spatial hierarchy, was designed to communicate its role as a repository of artifacts and a gathering place for this colonial project. RAS's expulsion after Liberation, the dispersal of its collections, and the dilapidation of the building show the disdain for material history under a planned economy, where vestiges were tolerated only because there had been no alternative. It had not been a deliberate decolonization as much as a kind of forgetting without intention. The rental of the building's spaces by the local state to a financial firm in the 1990s underlines this apathy, especially in the first decade of rapid economic transition. Whereas the use of the former RAS building underwent turbulent changes, the CPS compound experienced an institutional continuity from the beginnings of the colony. It expanded from the first buildings for control and orderliness to a central node in the heart of the city, though anachronistic in form and density by the 1980s when Hong Kong's economic rise made its surrounding context one of the most intense urban forms in the world. The decommissioning of the compound in the 2000s came only with the moving of its functions to a more modernized facility, and the symbolic significance of its materiality rendered only in

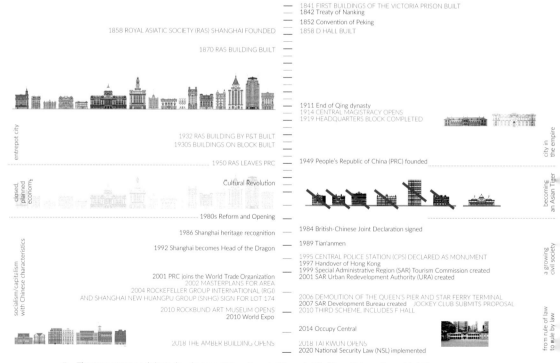

7   The two cases and their development timelines in Shanghai (left) and Hong Kong (right).

commercial terms. It was civil society groups, in the face of growing disenchantment with the SAR government, who amplified popular affection for the iconographic meaning of the compound, representing a pre-Handover Hong Kong.

Even though the cities diverged in their political economies and development trajectories, their contemporary heritagizations converge in certain ways. That selected historical buildings are no longer simply torn down for higher density and for more profitable new developments shows a broader shift in regard, both popular and institutional, for the concept of cultural heritage, especially since the mid-2000s in East Asia. This is especially notable in Hong Kong, where the pressures of market economics and the protection of private property rights have resulted in few old buildings being left. In Shanghai, it was the circumstances of poverty that preserved almost all of the physical fabric of the city until the 1980s. It was only in response to the large-scale demolition-based urban development in the 1990s that the remaining areas became protected in the mid-2000s. In both cases, the public nature of their ownership has facilitated their valuation as heritage and eventual conservation. The role civil society played in the active conservation efforts in Hong Kong, however, is markedly different from that in Shanghai.[47] The clamors of the non-governmental organizations changed the way the former CPS building was to be re-developed, and also led to the institution of a new government bureau dedicated to cultural heritage. Even though public sentiments against demolition also influenced the implementation of heritage policies in Shanghai in the 1990s, it was, however, the commercial potential of the area of the former RAS building that shaped the state-market alliance in the development of the historic district in time for the Expo.

That both the former RAS building and the CPS have been repurposed for new cultural functions also reveals the global aspirations for the creative class since the mid-2000s,[48] and how heritagization is an integral part of culture-led urban developments. For both projects, prominent international "starchitects" were engaged to deliver new architectural icons. They reflect a pattern of commercial success, reusing selected types of historical buildings, and capitalizing on their stylistic cachet to new market tastes, as well as the insertion of the apex industry of aesthetic goods as a new function for old buildings. Bypassing the more prickly questions of keeping these colonial-era legacies of the RAS and the CPS helps to focus on the heritagizations and their successes as markers for adopted developed-world tropes.

It becomes even clearer which symbolic values are prioritized, when Tai Kwun and the Rockbund Art Museum are contrasted to other buildings that could have been selected as cultural heritage, yet do not elicit similar popular sentiment (fig. 8). In Hong Kong, the demolition of the 1970s General Post Office (GPO), a colonial product as much as the CPS, but evoking much less nostalgia from local concern groups, shows that it is less the crutches of colonialism that have been popularly embraced, than that of the historicist style of architecture itself. Even though the contemporary version of the GPO is a public building that rose with the growing status of Hong Kong as one of the Asian Tigers, its modernist architectural language of white walls, brise-soleils, and band windows could not appeal to the popular sentiment the way CPS / Tai Kwun's red brick and classical orders are able to. Without this iconography of historicism, neither its civic function nor the adaptability of its gridded open plan—more suited for contemporary art functions than older buildings—could prevent its already-decided fate of being redeveloped. Similarly, in Shanghai, the 1980s Friendship Store, the site on which the Peninsula Hotel is built, has also been demolished. Perhaps because many other much older buildings were demolished already,

8   The demolished Friendship Store (upper left) and the to-be-demolished General Post Office (upper right), contrasted to the conserved former Royal Asiatic Society building, now Rockbund Art Museum (lower left) and Block 1 of the former Central Police Station, now Tai Kwun (lower right).

its demise raised no eyebrows, and its function as the sole conduit for foreign capital in the early 1980s garnered little sentimental value. In both Shanghai and Hong Kong, the selections of the visibly classicist rather than modernist buildings show a nascent popular understanding of what is heritage.

The pathways and spatial production mechanisms of the rapidly developing cities of the Global East have compelled what seems to be an embrace of the material symbols of their colonial pasts, without the kind of confrontational reckoning with their meanings that seemed to have gripped the world in the 2020s. If heritage is "a contemporary product shaped from history,"[49] and a practice that "clarifies pasts so as to infuse them with present purposes,"[50] then the contemporary circumstances of Shanghai and Hong Kong also explain the seeming disregard for colonial legacies. From these accounts of two cases from two cities, other specific pathways between development and social contracts as legacies of a global modernity, and from diverse geographies, deserve further unpacking.

The funding support of the HK RGC General Research Fund 17604122 is gratefully acknowledged.

1   Robinson 2004.

2   Harvey 2001.

3   See, for example, Ren 2008.

4   See, for example, Ku 2010.

5   See, for example, Choay 2001.

6   For a discussion of the global aspirations of developing world cities, see, for example, Bunnell 2015.

7   In 1838 the RAS Bombay branch was established, the RAS Ceylon in 1845. Following the Opium War, the RAS Hong Kong branch was established in 1847. Branches in Japan, Malaya, and Korea would be established in the late 1800s.

8   Otness 1988.

9   In 1858, the *Journal of the Northern China Branch of the RAS* began its publications and would continue until the closure of the branch in 1949.

10   Royal Asiatic Society n.d.

11   With the donation of the London Missionary Society's Alexander Wylie's 718 volumes in 1871, the RAS library soon had around 1,300 titles. Danielson 2004.

12   Otness 1988.

13   Wang 2007.

14   Whereas the red brick was decreed for use in the French Concessions, the gray brick was forbidden because it suggested Chineseness. The symbolism of the materiality would carry through from the Concession era predilections to the contemporary era of heritagization, since the 2010s.

15   The use of seal script, which is a calligraphic type that evolved from the scripts carved on bronzes during the first millennium BCE, is another instance where the research function of RAS, as part of which its artifact collection would have included bronzes with similar scripts, is shown through its architecture.

16   In 1939, donations of 3,000 Western-language books and 1,000 Chinese-language books from the International Institute of China expanded the RAS library to 12,677 volumes. Otness 1988.

17   In December 1941, after the Japanese had attacked Pearl Harbor and launched the US's entry into World War II, the Japanese occupation of the International and French concessions in Shanghai became official. In 1943 the Japanese-controlled government overseen by Wang Jingwei took over the management of the Concessions and renamed 240 roads, including the Museum Road. Tang 1989; Peng 2007.

18   In 1955, the Shanghai Library took over the RAS's library collection, which was counted as having 94,000 volumes. In 1957 the Shanghai Library took over the collection of the Maritime Customs Museum and the Zikawei Bibliotheca Major, which had been known in Chinese as the Xujiahui Library or Catholic Church Library. Danielson 2004.

19   Talks of demolishing such a visible manifestation of national shame were only halted by the reality of not having enough funds to rebuild and thus having to reuse the spaces.

20   A tourist map of Shanghai from the early 1980s would have shown places like the traditional Yu garden at the center of the former Chinese walled city and the zoos and the parks, but no mention of the buildings along the Bund or those modern-era buildings in the former Concessions would have been made. Henriot 2010.

21   State Council 1986.

22   Shanghai Municipal Government 1989, § 62.

23   The listing in 1999 of the third batch of Outstanding Historical Architecture also included the Lyceum Building on 185 Yuanmingyuan Road. In the second listing from February 15, 1994, the former YWCA Headquarters building, the former China Baptist Publication, the former Christian Literature Society building, and the former Ampire & Co. building, all in the same block as the RAS building, were also listed. See Shanghai Municipal Government 1994, § 8; Shanghai Municipal Government [1999], § 57.

24   The central government's decision to continue economic liberalization without a political liberalization was a crucial decision that made itself clear in the events at Tian'anmen Square in 1989. In the aftermath, the international embargo halted the inflow of needed investments that were fundamental to economic

liberalization. The successful control of mass protests in Shanghai led to the rise of its municipal leadership to central government positions. Under this realignment of powers in the state hierarchy, Shanghai, which had been suppressed since Liberation in 1949, was anointed the Head of the Dragon to lead the acceleration of economic liberation. For elaboration, see Zhou 2019.

25   Zhou 2017a.

26   *Xintiandi* is often considered a seminal development for China, in which the commercially successful renovation and reuse of old buildings for new commercial functions paved the way for a popular recognition of historic architecture as well as market promotion for such practices.

27   For an unpacking of this term "old houses," see Zhou 2017a.

28   Dai 2003; Lou 2009.

29   Photos from the time showed the banner of the company Qingdao Securities Company on the front of the building. Zhang 2007.

30   Carroll 2007.

31   Crisswell and Watson 1982.

32   Sinclair 1994.

33   LegCo 2000, 1999–2000.

34   The Tourism Commission was formed in May 1999 under the Economic Services Bureau, which became the Economic Development and Labour Bureau (EDLB) in 2002, and since 2007 the Commerce and Economic Development Bureau (CEDB).

35   Price Waterhouse Coopers Consultants, for 1.27 million HKD, was tasked to formulate a heritage and tourism concept for a development at the Central Police Station, Victoria Prison, and the Former Central Magistracy. LegCo 2003b.

36   Within this framework, the document stipulated that "mandatory preservation requirements would be kept to the minimum… leaving as much flexibility as possible to the future Project proponent" and there would be "flexibility to preserve the facades only for some of the buildings." HKSAR 2003.

37   LegCo 2003a.

38   Ku 2012; Zhou and Choi 2019.

39   Central Police Station 2004; Action Group 2004a; Action Group 2004b.

40   LegCo 2004.

41   Law 2008.

42   The Hong Kong Institute of Architects (2008) publicized a letter to the Jockey Club, questioning the tower scheme as the structures "do not appear to be compatible with the local urban context in terms of bulk, scale and expression."

43   The Outline Zoning Plan of 2008 specified that "the applicant of application for planning permission should demonstrate with a comprehensive scheme for the whole site that, among other things, the nature and scale of the proposed use/development would be compatible with the historical setting of the Compound in terms of height and design as well as the general planning intention for the site." LegCo 2008.

44   Mack and Herzog & de Meuron 2010, 94–101.

45   The newly established Development Bureau took over the responsibility of planning and lands administration from the Housing, Planning and Lands Bureau, public works from the Environment, Transport and Works Bureau, and heritage policy from HAB.

46   Tsang 2007.

47   Not explicitly stated in this piece, it presumes an a priori knowledge of the dominance of the state in China. Though cases with bottom-up initiatives do exist, notably in residential areas in Shanghai, the ownership and function of the buildings in the Rockbund preclude this approach. For such cases, see, for example, Zhou 2017b.

48   See, for example, Kong 2007.

49   Tunbridge and Ashworth 1995, 20.

50   Lowenthal 1998, xv.

Bibliography

Action Group on Protection of the Central Police Station Historical Compound. 2004a. "CB(2)155/04-05(06) Submission from Action Group for the Protection of Central Police Station Historical Compound on 'Review of built heritage conservation policy'." Hong Kong, November 4, 2004.

Action Group on Protection of the Central Police Station Historical Compound. 2004b. "CB(2)180/04-05(01) Submission from Conservancy Association on 'Review of Built Heritage Conservation Policy'." Hong Kong, November 4, 2004.

Bunnell, Tim. 2015. "Antecedent Cities and Inter-Referencing Effects: Learning from and Extending Beyond Critiques of Neoliberalisation." *Urban Studies* 52, no. 11 (August 1): 1983–2000.

Carroll, John M. 2007. *A Concise History of Hong Kong,* Critical Issues in History. Lanham, MD: Rowman & Littlefield.

Central Police Station Heritage Task Force. 2004. "CB(2)155/04-05(05) Submission from Central Police Station Heritage Task Force on 'Review of built heritage conservation policy'." Hong Kong, November 4, 2004.

Choay, Françoise. 2001. *The Invention of the Historic Monument.* Translated by Lauren M. O'Connell. New York: Cambridge University Press.

Crisswell, Colin N., and Mike Watson. 1982. *The Royal Hong Kong Police, 1841–1945.* Hong Kong: MacMillan.

Dai, Gaoming. 2003. "Rockbund Project Starts," in *Huangpu District Yearbook 2003*, 203. Shanghai: Shanghai Century Publishing Group.

Danielson, Eric N. 2004. "Shanghai's Lost Libraries Rediscovered." *Journal of the Royal Asiatic Society Hong Kong Branch* 44: 83–90.

Harvey, David C. 2001. "Heritage Pasts and Heritage Presents: Temporality, Meaning and the Scope of Heritage Studies." *International Journal of Heritage Studies* 7, no. 4 (January 1): 319–38.

Henriot, Christian. 2010. "The Shanghai Bund in Myth and History: An Essay through Textual and Visual Sources." *Journal of Modern Chinese History* 4, no. 1: 1–27.

HKSAR Economic Development and Labour Bureau. 2003. "CB(1)1495/02-03(01) Central Police Station, Victoria Prison and the Former Central Magistracy: A Heritage and Tourism Concept." Hong Kong, April 24, 2003.

Hong Kong Institute of Architects. 2008. "HKIA Views on Conservation and Revitalization for the Former Central Police Station Compound." March 18, 2008.

Kong, Lily. 2007. "Cultural Icons and Urban Development in Asia: Economic Imperative, National Identity, and Global City Status." *Political Geography* 26, no. 4 (May): 383–404.

Ku, Agnes Shuk-mei. 2010. "Making Heritage in Hong Kong: A Case Study of the Central Police Station Compound." *The China Quarterly*, no. 202: 381–99.

Ku, Agnes Shuk-mei. 2012. "Remaking Places and Fashioning an Opposition Discourse: Struggle over the Star Ferry Pier and the Queen's Pier in Hong Kong." *Environment and Planning D: Society & Space* 30, no. 1: 5–22.

Law, Violet. 2008. "Herzog & de Meuron Face Opposition in Hong Kong." *Architectural Record*, February 6, 2008.

LegCo. 2000. "PWSC(1999–2000)86 Tourist District Enhancement: Pilot scheme in Central and Western District." In "Minutes of meeting of the Public Works Subcommittee," Hong Kong, January 26, 2000, 1999–2000.

LegCo. 2003a. "Development of the Central Police Station, Victoria Prison and the former Central Magistracy compound into a tourism-themed development and the reprovisioning arrangement for existing users at the compound." In "CB(1)2084/02-03 Minutes of joint meeting of the Panel on Economic Services and Panel on Security," Hong Kong, April 28, 2003, 4–10.

LegCo. 2003b. "Consultancy Studies Commissioned by Government on Formulation and Assessment of Policies." In "Official Record of Proceedings," Hong Kong, April 30, 2003, 5697.

LegCo. 2004. "CB(2)343/04-05 Minutes of meeting of the Panel on Home Affairs." Hong Kong, November 9, 2004.

LegCo. 2008. "No. S/H3/22 Sai Ying Pun & Sheung Wan Outline Zoning Plan (OZP)." Hong Kong.

Lou, Chenghao. 2009. "Past and Present of 'Waitanyuan'." *Shanghai Memory*, February 20, 2009.

Lowenthal, David. 1998. *The Heritage Crusade and the Spoils of History*. New York: Cambridge University Press.

Mack, Gerhard, and Herzog & de Meuron. 2010. *Herzog & de Meuron: das Gesamtwerk (1997–2001)*, vol. 4. Basel: Birkhäuser.

Otness, Harold M. 1988. "'The One Bright Spot in Shanghai': A History of the Library of the North China Branch of the Royal Asiatic Society." *Journal of the Hong Kong Branch of the Royal Asiatic Society* 28: 185–97.

Peng, Guoyue. 2007. "Naming of the Roads in Shanghai: Basic Research for Naming in Social Linguistic Theory." *Bulletin of the Institute for Humanities Research*, 33–43.

Ren, Xuefei. 2008. "Forward to the Past: Historical Preservation in Globalizing Shanghai." *City & Community* 7, no. 1 (March 1): 23–43.

Robinson, Jennifer. 2004. "In the Tracks of Comparative Urbanism: Difference, Urban Modernity and the Primitive." *Urban Geography* 25, no. 8 (December 1): 709–23.

Royal Asiatic Society. n.d. "About RAS." https://ras-china.org/About%20RAS (accessed April 13, 2021).

Shanghai Municipal Government. 1989. "Notice of the Submission for Outstanding Modern Era Architecture to Be Included in the Municipal Roster [First Batch]".

Shanghai Municipal Government. 1994. "Second Batch of Outstanding Historical Architecture."

Shanghai Municipal Government. [1999]. "Third Batch of Outstanding Historical Architecture."

Sinclair, Kevin. 1994. *Royal Hong Kong Police 1844–1994*. Hong Kong: Police Public Relations Branch Royal Hong Kong Police Force.

State Council. 1986. "State Council Approves and Transmits to the Department of Urban and Rural Development and Environment Protection and Department for Culture Regarding the Announcement of the Second List of Renowned National Historic Cultural Cities". People's Republic of China.

Tang, Zhijun. 1989. *Annals of Modern-Era Shanghai*. Shanghai: Shanghai Lexicographical Publishing House.

Tsang, Donald. 2007. "Policy Address 2007–2008: 'A New Direction For Hong Kong.'" October 10, 2007.

Tunbridge, John E., and Gregory Ashworth. 1995. *Dissonant Heritage*. Chichester, NY: John Wiley & Sons.

Wang, Fang. 2007. "Study of the Area around the Former British Embassy on the Bund and the Evolution of the Architecture (1843–1937)." PhD Thesis, Shanghai, Tongji University.

Zhang, Ming, ed. 2007. *Shanghai's Waitanyuan Historical Architecture (Phase 1)*. Shanghai: Far East Press.

Zhou, Ying. 2017a. "The Cultural Street." In *Urban Loopholes: Creative Alliances of Spatial Productions in Shanghai's City Center*, 143–229. Basel: Birkhäuser.

Zhou, Ying. 2017b. "The Midtown of China." In *Urban Loopholes: Creative Alliances of Spatial Productions in Shanghai's City Center*, 230–334. Basel: Birkhäuser.

Zhou, Ying. 2019. "Lujiazui Shanghai: Urban Paragon for a Post-Socialist China." In Kees Christiaanse, Anna Gasco, and Naomi Hanakata, eds., *The Grand Projet: Towards Adaptable and Liveable Urban Megaprojects*, 105–48. Rotterdam: nai010.

Zhou, Ying, and Desmond Choi. 2019. "West Kowloon, Hong Kong: A Transport-Oriented Development with Culture." In Kees Christiaanse, Anna Gasco, and Naomi Hanakata, eds., *The Grand Projet: Towards Adaptable and Liveable Urban Megaprojects*, 149–98. Rotterdam: nai010.

Image Sources

1   From the magazine *Architecture Monthly*, April 1933.
2   Map drawn by the author and Zoe King Man Cheung; photo by the author, 2019.
3   Section and elevation drawn by the author and Jane Mengyao Li.
4, 7, 8 Drawn by the author.
5   Map drawn by the author and Zoe King Man Cheung; photo by the author, 2021.
6   Drawn by the author and George Jin-yu Guu.

KARIN REISINGER

Doing Material Positionality while Listening to the Prolonged Coloniality of a Mining Town on Indigenous Ground

As part of the project *Lifelike Appendix to the Archive* (figs. 1 and 2), I added fragments of local on-tologies to archival material held by ArkDes Stockholm while I was a scholarship holder there (2018–19).[1] Specifically, I appended photos to the original drawings by the architect Folke Hederus, which allow viewers, particularly researchers, to get an impression of what is currently happening to the hopeful architectural projections of the 1950s for the mining town Malmberget, Sweden. This critical appendix shows the current destruction of the town and is accessible, together with the original drawings from the 1950s, at the ArkDes Collections. These collections store Swedish ar-chitectural drawings in the archives of the capital city of Sweden, Stockholm, more than 1,000 km away from the current destruction of Malmberget, a result of expanding the extraction of iron ore in the town. Stockholm has also been the place where many of the plans for mining in the faraway town of Malmberget were drawn up. Malmberget in the arctic region was built around mining pits to exploit iron ore, a material used all over the world, particularly by architects. Today, the town is disappearing in a slow and unstoppable process to make way for further mining.

The colonization of northern Sweden is frequently narrated in male, heroic histories along with specific infrastructures and architectures.[2] The perspective of the Indigenous Sámi is often left out, although Sábme[3] has already been inhabited by the Sámi for a very long time. It has been subject to repeated acts of colonization,[4] controlling and limiting the Sámi's access to their environments, and on many occasions requiring the Sámi to adapt and change nomadic prac-tices due to settler colonialism, as Elsa Laula explained in 1904,[5] or even to be displaced.[6] The extensive infrastructure of mining is even today in conflict with reindeer herding.[7] The situation is conflictual, and in the face of the complex continuities of hopes (for minerals and jobs) and losses (of homes), simplified binary understandings of architecture neither grasp the complexity at work, nor provide an understanding of the prolonged colonialities enacted by and readable in architectures. Therefore this text investigates the complex roles of architectures within the process of a colonialism linked to extraction of resources (iron ore) that we architects need for building. Architectures have been part of the colonization, and colonial architectures have of course also become home to the Indigenous population. In today's situation, people in Malm-berget are losing their homes as a result of the advancement of resource extraction, the north of Sweden being one of the most mineral-rich zones in Europe, supplying the "centers" with minerals to build and communicate, with far-reaching but distinct impacts on various agencies.

Which and whose architectures and practices do we reproduce in discourse, canons, and archives? In the search for an inclusive and non-binary understanding of the architectures and spatial practices[8] of a disappearing mining community, I follow, as a non-Indigenous researcher,

1 | 2 *Lifelike Appendix to the Archive No. 1* (2018), collages by Karin Reisinger, based on drawings by Folke Hederus (1957–1958).

those who have come before me, who have re-considered and re-narrated histories and struggled for visibilities for silenced voices. Many Indigenous researchers and their allies have contributed to unfolding the coloniality in Sámi territory on the Swedish side, which is also connected to gender binaries. My aim is to look at this together with the disappearing architectures of the extractive mining environment, informed by my own exercise of listening to local practitioners and researchers in numerous conversations, shared activities and reading, as well as reacting to the comments of the generous peer-reviewer of this paper, May-Britt Öhman, an Indigenous and feminist researcher on the History of Technology. These practices of listening and learning, and thinking about how architectural research can respond to local knowledges, result in a creative critique of dominant practices of building and knowing based on extractivism. All of this describes an ongoing process and aims to offer some small steps to contribute to decolonizing architecture, a profession involved in the extraction of minerals in many ways.

Expanding Extraction

Malmberget's underground mine for the exploitation of iron ore is one of the mines owned by LKAB, the Luossavaara Kiirunavaara AB, the Swedish mining company 100% owned by the state. LKAB is the largest iron ore producer in Europe with 15.5 million tons of crude ore mined each year in Malmberget alone—equivalent to approximately the volume of a seven-floor building per day.[9]

Malmberget is located in Sweden, but it is also a town in Sábme, the land of the Sámi. Malmberget's Lule Sámi name is *Málmmavárre*.[10] Conflicts between reindeer herding and mining are inevitable as both activities require significant amplitudes of land, and mining needs infrastructure that crosses reindeer herding paths. The discussion of the colonization of the area is still ongoing. In 1920 Karin Stenberg, pioneer in activism for Sámi rights and associations, wrote about Swedish colonial politics and included international comparisons.[11] More than 100 years later, Åsa Össbo, a researcher at the Várdduo Center for Sámi Research, described the current process of intensifying the exploitation of resources from Norrland as "Tillbaka till den koloniala framtiden" ("Back to the Colonial Future").[12] Kristina Sehlin MacNeil, her colleague, unfolds the re-

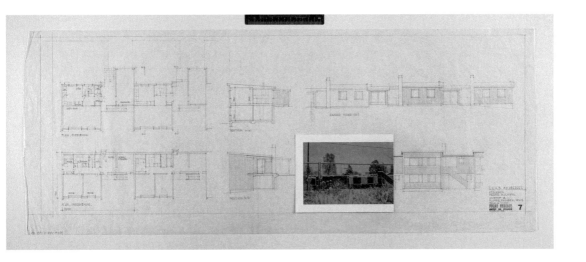

lationship between extractivism and colonialism through the Sámi's "connection to the Country," which is in conflict with "colonialism, capitalism and neoliberalism, where extractivism is the ruling force."[13] Or, put differently, the close connection to the country, which has manifold aspects concerning language, communication, knowledge, spirituality, and practicalities, is affected by direct violence against nature or the land itself, thereby affecting the people who live in close connection to the land,[14] whereas settler colonialism treats people as movable.[15]

Understanding Swedish colonialism is crucial for understanding the ongoing losses in Malmberget. A frequent official Swedish position is that Sábme is not subject to colonialism, preferring the terms "integration" or "colonization" to describe the "cultivation" of Sábme, thereby avoiding an engagement with colonialism and its atrocities.[16] As Gunlög Fur puts it, explaining the specificity of Swedish colonialism: "Describing Swedish expansion as inner colonization makes it possible to view Sámi country as an inherently Swedish territory" and negates the contextualization of colonialism. Such discursive actions have "enabled Scandinavia to emerge in the modern period as untainted by colonialism and thus in a position to claim trustworthiness as mediators and as champions of subaltern and minority rights."[17]

Indigenous researchers and allies have elaborated on such theoretically and practically consequential notions of colonialism and feminisms.[18] Astrid Andersen, Kirsten Hvenegård-Lassen, and Ina Knobblock as well as Madina Tlostanova, Suruchi Thapar-Björkert, and again Ina Knobblock propose a basis for discussing the relationships of colonialism and feminism:

> Like other Indigenous peoples around the globe, the Sámi and the Inuit have been subjected to very direct processes of colonization and exploitation over the course of history, in the form of the theft of land and natural resources, as well as policies of assimilation and separation based on racialized discourses.[19]

> … at the centre [of colonial processes] lies the historical and on-going dispossession of Sami people of their land in the name of (settler) nation-building and industrial development.[20]

In the Swedish side of Sábme, where mining started in the seventeenth century, Kristina Sehlin MacNeil explains in *Extractive Violence on Indigenous Country* that Sámi were sometimes forced to transport the minerals across the snowy fields with their reindeer.[21] Many fled because this was not compatible with their ways of life, and the consequences were often punishment and physical abuse. Given the strong interest in the minerals of northern Sweden—Sweden hoped to compensate for what other countries gained through overseas colonization—the rights of the Sámi have constantly been weakened since the seventeenth century. A number of regulations and duties ensured that they were forced to keep their traditions—as interpreted through the colonizer's eyes: the Lapp-shall-be-Lapp ideology (*lapp skall vara lapp*)[22] was based on preserving stereotyped nomadic lifestyles[23] based on reindeer herding to keep the Sámi away from lands for which the colonizers had other purposes in mind, in line with the Swedish industrialization,[24] or rather "industrial colonialism."[25] The segregation policies were consciously enforced by the mining industries,[26] although the Sámi have also been part of the colonizing structures.[27] Malmberget was a core area for the colonization due to the national interest in the iron found there, based on settler colonialism, centrally administered by the Swedish Crown, which promoted the settlements in the north. Malmberget's ore was reported to the Crown in the early eighteenth century, and further specified by groups of experts. That extraction of the ore was continuously and in many complex ways in conflict with Sámi ways of life, laying the foundation for Sweden not ratifying the Indigenous and Tribal Peoples Convention (ILO).[28] All these reasons, better described by the researchers cited, contribute to putting the relationships of Sàbme/Sweden/Malmberget on the map of sites to be discussed through the lens of architectures' contribution to colonialism.

Architecture, Gender, and Coloniality

Lennart Lundmark reports on the struggles of the Sámi to be allowed to build, possess, and live in houses instead of, or in addition to, the *lavvu* (or Swedish *kåta*, traditional huts or tents). Even in the twentieth century the housing question was determined by the "Lapp-shall-be-Lapp" ideology.[29]

Architecture and planning have been complicit with the actualization of colonialism and thus in very practical terms with mining. To mine the iron ore, a local workforce was needed and therefore had to be housed. In Malmberget the first workers' wooden "shacks," affectionately called *kåkstaden*, had been built very near to the open pits. The harsh climate, with winter temperatures down to −40°C and lower, made long trips to work impossible. Therefore the first shacks clustered around the pits, above all around "Captain's Pit," the central pit, today more than 250 meters deep, splitting the community in two parts. These "shacks" housed the settlers from the south, who came from many regions, attracted by the minerals. The housing situation was cramped around 1900, shortly after the train line strongly intensified the mining activities.[30] The last replicas of *kåkstaden* shall be moved to another place.

Malmberget was already of interest to well-known Swedish architects in the 1940s and earlier. Commissioned by LKAB, Hakon Ahlberg, the renowned Swedish architect and first president of the Swedish Architects' Association, planned the town's *Allhelgokyrkan* (All Saints Church) with lots of careful details and a freestanding clock tower covered with wooden shingles. The church had to be disassembled and re-built in another place due to the expansion of the mine.[31] The rebuilding was planned for the next couple of years, but demolition has been under consideration since early 2022.[32] Ahlberg also planned the *församlingshem* (parish home) of the mining society. The local cemetery is built around a chapel by Olof Lundgren. Eskil Sundahl, a well-known Swedish architect planned the shop, *Kooperativa*,[33] and his son Sune Sundahl, Sweden's most

3   *Tjännstemannavillor* (managers' villas) in Malmberget, arch. Folke Hederus, photo by Sune Sundahl, 1957.

influential architectural photographer, preserved the new buildings and hopeful futures of the young town in his photos.

In the 1950s LKAB commissioned Folke Hederus, at that time a lesser known architect with an office in Stockholm, to experiment with housing typologies in Malmberget and Kiruna and to develop high-quality homes for the workers[34] who had often moved to their new workplace from the south. He designed from *ungkarlsbostäder* (housing for young men) to *tjänstemanna-villor* (managers' villas, fig. 3)—names that announce that these typologies were built for male workers. Furthermore, class distinctions in the building styles are reflected in names and designs. In the approximately fifteen managers' villas[35] in elevated places of the town, the design of stair-ways and chimneys received special attention in these family buildings with many rooms. The housing for young men, on the other hand, were row houses with small apartments. Hederus designed many row houses with multi-variant ground floors with thoughtful and careful design for the workers. The only drawing of a woman in the rich material of ArkDes Collections shows a woman pushing a pram along a row of *kedjehuserna* (row houses, literally "chain houses," see fig. 1).[36] Today in Malmberget, all of the buildings I have mentioned here, from villas to row hous-es, have been demolished. Only some selected buildings have been transported to sites nearby.

"Colonialism also came with ideas regarding sexuality, gender and gender identities such as nuclear family systems, two-binary gender systems and how work was supposed to be divided according to ideas of gender," Emma Rasmusson summarizes in her innovative master's thesis,

4 Malmberget Östra (Eastern Malmberget) with around 75 % of the houses already demolished, 2021.

which moves beyond colonial practices within the planning frameworks of mining to suggest ways towards alternatives.[37] She traces a continuity of colonialism, racism, and discrimination up to current circumstances through planning and its frameworks. A researcher into Indigenous feminism and knowledge production, Rauna Kuoakkanen, confirms that colonialism in the Nordic countries is not past but ongoing:

> Although there are critical differences between the Nordic countries and settler colonial states, the Nordic states are very much built upon exploiting the Sámi and dispossessing them of their traditional territories. Also, as in settler colonial states, a lot of the wealth in the Nordic countries comes from the Sámi territory. Colonialism is an existing structure in society, not a past event.[38]

For this awareness of prolongation and continuity,[39] I want to borrow from South American decolonial thinkers and feminist decolonial researchers the term "coloniality": Madina Tlostanova, Suruchi Thapar-Björkert, and Ina Knobblock explain that "coloniality is a full dependence of the models of thinking, making, and interpreting the world on the norms, created and imposed by/ in Western modernity."[40] These authors build on the seminal work of Maria Lugones for whom coloniality is "not just a classification of people in terms of the coloniality of power and gender, but also a process of active reduction of people," of dehumanization. The denial and "robbing them of validity and co-evalness" is coloniality.[41]

> As the coloniality infiltrates every aspect of living through the circulation of power at the levels of the body, labor, law, imposition of tribute and the introduction of property and land dispossession, its logic and efficacy are met by different concrete people whose bodies, selves in relation, and relations to the spirit world do not follow the logic of capital.[42]

Coloniality is exerted on bodies and genders, and it comes with hierarchical distinctions based on dichotomies, such as the distinction between human and non-human, or men and women.[43] It "is a pattern of power that emerges from an invisible part of history."[44] Considering such complex relationships in the Nordic countries, I suggest that the colonial gender aspect is also readable in the design of architectures in addition to planning, as Rasmussen has already elaborated. Architectures designed by architects from the south were not only built to support the extraction of mineral resources, but also built for specific gender roles and family structures. This becomes visible in sketches, plans, and photos. Furthermore, I want to suggest that a further extension of coloniality becomes visible in the disappearance of homes and architectures in Malmberget. Today, every( )body, regardless of ethnicity, class, and race, is affected by this loss since the entire town is about to be demolished (fig. 4, see figs. 1 and 2).

To study the Sámi's experiences of vast environmental changes, Össbo draws on the environmental philosopher Glenn Albrecht's concept "*solastalgia*, which sheds light on environmentally induced anxiety and distress" and explains how dislocations and drastic changes in the environment also lead to losses of knowledge.[45]

> Trauma, sorrow and distress as effects of this extractive violence can be borne over generations, especially for people who are connected to the landscape and certain traditions, which is often the case in Indigenous cultures and societies.[46]

As Glenn Albrecht elaborates, non-Indigenous people also experience such losses deeply, as colonialism comes in waves. He identifies a "second wave of colonization, ironically impacting on the descendants of the original colonists" which leads to "complete dispossession for some and solastalgia for those left behind."[47]

Facing the loss, a diverse group of local women came together in the *Handarbetscafé* (embroidery café) of Gällivare-Malmberget, founded by Karina Jarrett, to embroider the environmental changes.[48] They embroidered the architectures of Malmberget that got lost during the process called urban transformation, *stadsomvandling* (fig. 5). It has been my privilege to be in constant

5   Malmnedles / Handarbetscafé Gällivare-Malmberget at the exhibition *Fences Insects Embroideries (material communities)*, Geological Survey of Austria, Vienna, September 17–30, 2022, curated by Karin Reisinger, part of Wienwoche festival. With works from Margit Antilla, Berit Backe, Carina Engelmark, Karina Jarrett, and Eeva Linder.

6   Karina Jarrett, embroidery, *Av järn är du kommen* (Of Iron You have Come), 2019.

exchange with the group since 2018, when we embroidered together for the first time. I shared with the group archival material that has influenced small details of their embroideries, as shown in *Av järn är du kommen* (Of Iron You have Come) by Karina Jarrett (fig. 6). This direct influence was surprising to me. The relationship of architecture from the 1950s and its current dismantling (hope and loss) was embroidered, and the image of the house drawn in Stockholm for Malmberget made it finally back "home" in an unexpected way. However, when Karina Jarrett explained her work to the audience in Vienna at the exhibition *Fences Insects Embroideries (material communities)*,[49] she offered her own local narratives about these architectures and their gender attributions, wisely explaining the experimental architectures planned by Folke Hederus as "female architectures." Her narratives opposed familiar biases of architecture and gender and therefore destabilized them. While the group of local women is interested in the preservation and creative re-narration of the lost homes, Stockholm's archive houses the images of the experimental drawings and images of architectures drawn in the center. The narratives can and do differ, but what holds them together?

Doing Material Positionality

Today, the number of buildings in Malmberget is shrinking rapidly (see fig. 4) in line with the extraction of iron ore, above all in the center of the town. The only high-rise building has been demolished piece by piece because its construction did not allow for blasting. Malmberget has been dismantled in large parts whereas, due to the Covid 19 pandemic, my travels to Sweden have become difficult and rarer than in the previous years. I am not Sámi, I am not even Swedish. After my first contact with Malmberget in 2016 and numerous stays in the community thereafter, I wrote this text in Vienna in 2022 where my daily practices rely on minerals exploited from several regions inhabited by Indigenous people all over the world. This paper was written on a laptop which functions due to minerals, and the presentation at the conference *Architectures of Colonialism* was streamed with the help of the same material. My actions depend on resources from Indigenous lands. This is one of the inextricable connections that makes it necessary to understand and think with places like Malmberget, especially from an architectural perspective. So, how are we architects *and* researchers involved in it? How can we give an account of ourselves?[50] Wendy E. Rowe explains in the *SAGE Encyclopedia of Action Research* a basis for working with local knowledge holders:

> Positionality refers to the stance or positioning of the researcher in relation to the social and political context of the study – the community, the organization or the participant group. The position adopted by a researcher affects every phase of the research process, from the way the question or problem is initially constructed, designed and conducted to how others are invited to participate, the ways in which knowledge is constructed and acted on and, finally, the ways in which outcomes are disseminated and published.[51]

In a workshop on research ethics with the Várdduo Center for Sámi Research at the end of 2020 Kristina Sehlin MacNeil gave me the opportunity to discuss how I could do research in Sábme without epistemic extractivism of Indigenous knowledge cosmologies, and without infringing local knowledge strategies and survival practices but rather supporting them instead. One of these suggestions was to deepen my work on a material positionality.[52] Feminist new materialisms and critical materialisms are helpful when looking for conceptual models based on interdependency and interconnectedness, for staying with the tensions, and at the same time insisting on anti-binary work. Sarah E. Truman describes material-based research with the help of an example:

> Consider a phone constructed from metal, frequently mined at the expense of violent racialized human labor and Indigenous sovereign rights over land. In considering the 'value' of a phone, feminist new materialist research might ask questions about the ways that humans and metal and phone and land and capitalism and economy and militarism, and so on, are already imbricated in each other.[53]

In the context of material connections that means asking uncomfortable questions to ourselves and staying with the discomfort. "Who are you?" asks researcher May-Britt Öhman in a book chapter with the multilingual title "Gut la dån? Vem är du? Kukas sie olet? – Who are you?" She commences with a material relationship: "The Iron ore mine, the forest industry and the hydropower sector in the northern Sámi territories … have for a long time been essential to the provision of the unsustainable way of life that most of us – perhaps even you – lead today."[54]

In particular, the production of iron ore is important for building urban centers all over the world. LKAB advertises the productivity of their Swedish mines with claims of six Eiffel towers potentially being built every day. They also visually refer to mega-cities that rely on the exploitation of iron ore being transformed into building materials: "A world without steel is unthinkable."[55] The virtual production of architecture (renderings and drawings) likewise has a material basis. Renderings being calculated rely on minerals to be produced. We can also look at the rooms we are in, and determine which building parts depend on the extraction of iron ore. We can even look at our desks and see how dependent and entangled we are in the extraction of iron ore in a material way: the paper clip, the binders, the stapler, the tea egg, the spoon, …[56]

With this, everybody is immersed in a complex connection between center and periphery, where usually the center is taking from the peripheries, repeating a colonial connection. As researchers we are always at risk of repeating these connections. To speak, formulate, and make productive in a self-critical way, how we researchers and architects are involved in hegemonic relationships based on colonialism in the form of extractivism, for me started from a material account of myself as architect and researcher while listening to local researchers and practitioners,[57] to those who have lost their homes and survived, or to those locals who are just about to lose their homes and are currently dealing with the pain and the loss.

The handling of architectural information can support local struggles of mourning. In 2018 I organized a participatory lecture in Gällivare, sharing architectural information stored in the architectural archive and contained on about 200 slides of the presentation in the local context of exactly these architectures, allowing it to make new sense through local knowledge. "I don't know if this sauna still exists," I reported to the audience while showing plans by Hakon Ahlberg. "Oh, this is my sauna!" somebody replied from the audience… The encounter created a sort of dialogue, although difficult due to the large interest in the event, for different forms of knowledge coming together through the architectures which are becoming lost.

Indigenous researchers have emphasized that there is knowledge extractivism as much as there is material exploitation of the land.[58] Indigenous peoples have been objectified for research. Research has become a productive component of colonization and colonialism with strategies of classification, representation, and evaluation according to Western standards.[59] Although resistant, Sámi subjectivities are shaped by colonial knowledge production, which manifests in scientific racism, explains Katarina Pirak Sikku. They question dichotomies of culture/nature and civilized/non-civlized[60] and even gender binaries.[61] Andersen, Hvenegård-Lassen, and Knobblock also witness numerous binaries in research:

> The current uptake of the exotic—as was the case with colonial conceptions of the primitive and the distinction between good and bad savages—is both racialized and gendered and criss-crossed with (other) binaries such as nature versus culture.[62]

A further dichotomy is the one of center and periphery. While material is taken from the peripheries to centers and the centers therefore materially exist of peripheries, architectural knowledge about the extractive and extracted peripheries is stored in the archives of Sweden's capital: the ArkDes Collections have collected the historic future visions, drawings, and photos of newly built miners' homes and public buildings in Malmberget. The people of Malmberget, who are currently losing their homes, have no access to the archive, which is more than 1,000 km away.

The archive shows the visions, the great plans of the architects. Commissioned by LKAB, they could experiment with architectural advancements, but often implemented gender stereotypes. In 2021 the center of the town was deconstructed and finally everybody is losing their home. In December 2018 I was looking for the terraced houses by Folke Hederus, and to my surprise just came upon their destruction. I added the photos so they became a continuation of the architect's original drawings from 1957 and 1958, and donated them to the archive for international researchers to have access to the information that these architectures are being, or have been, dismantled in the course of extraction (see figs. 1 and 2), critically questioning the centralized practices of gathering and keeping knowledge. I added some of the details that are not shown in the archive: the destruction of past projections of the future.

A Conclusion Which is Just the Beginning

When I revised this chapter, news spread throughout Europe about an enormous find of rare earth minerals in Kiruna, just 125 km away from Malmberget. Under political pressure from 2022 onwards, the history of the *framtidsland* (land of the future)[63] looks about to be repeated once more in a time of "new extractivsm" and "new industrialism."[64] The need for mineral resources accelerates building activities to house further mining workforce. The continuity of building and losses is guaranteed because mineral resources are limited.

Throughout history, material flows have changed intensities and directions. Colonialism, entangled with extractivism, has led to the changes in local ways of life. It has also led to specific architectures in the course of extraction that are linked to structures of dominant gender requirements. However, a situation of prolonged coloniality and extended extraction now makes also the architectures, which have become home to so many, unlivable because the ground has been destabilized. Within these inextricable complexities of the Anthropocene, I tried to argue for methods of collage as supportive tools (see figs. 1 and 2) because they allow for thinking about ambivalent situations together, such as architectural projections in the center and actual destructions in the peripheries, and for approaching uncomfortable connections and continuities. They open up new questions, especially within a discussion of Swedish colonialism that is neither concluded nor widely acknowledged, nor established in the academic curricula of architecture. Many of the local researchers quoted in this contribution have thought about histories and gender in the imbrications of extractivism and colonialism, which provide an entry point into discussing architectural histories, showing the complexity of colonization, and understanding it as part of our daily (architectural) lives and practices.

Doing material positionality gave me first of all a possibility to answer the local question, "Why are you here?," but also serves as a way of foregrounding interconnectedness and building a first step towards reciprocities and self-critique of the hegemonic knowledge production, as Kuokkanen demanded in *Reshaping the University: Responsibility, Indigenous Epistemes, and the Logic of the Gift*.

In that regard and complexity, how can we deal with architectures that have been supporting colonialism and capitalist extraction, and are at the same time precious homes to many? Losing the familiar environment is a slow and painful process, and creative techniques for urgent heritage and local preservation, like the embroideries of the women of the embroidery café, are practices of dealing with the loss. Epistemic and archival decolonization, on the other hand, based on awareness of involvements in colonialisms and extractivisms, is a collective task of ongoing dialogue. Bringing critical narratives so far considered peripheral into the central archives of architecture is a first step to revive architectural projections of the past with its current extractive and colonial effects. Starting with the old feminist practice of giving an account of ourselves as researchers and architects, at least in a material way as a first step, has turned out to be a good point of departure to open up discussions.

I am very much indebted to May-Britt Öhman's peer review of the paper. Listening to her comments was an intense learning process, mostly about how much avoiding saviorism has to do with language, details, references, tenses, or even single letters. Her engagement with my paper allows me, as the non-Sámi and non-Swedish person that I am, to take small steps in resisting binaries that the process of colonization has left in many forms and formats, practices and buildings. Also, I want to thank Vera Egbers for her encouraging support and patience for the development of these difficult and complex questions, and Christa Kamleithner for the close reading of the text.

This research was funded by the Austrian Science Fund (FWF), project no. T1157-G. For the purpose of open access, the author has applied a CC BY public copyright license to any author accepted manuscript version arising from this submission. *The Lifelike Appendix to the Archive* (figs. 1 and 2) is from the time of my fellowship at ArkDes Stockholm in 2018–19.

1   The Swedish Centre for Architecture and Design in Stockholm.

2   This can be seen in numerous publications that concentrate especially on industrial development and on creating an infrastructure to transport the extracted minerals.

3   The region inhabited by the Sámi people, stretching over Norway, Sweden, Finland, and Russia. Sábme is the local expression used in the area of Malmberget.

4   See Öhman 2021a, 433.

5   Laula 1904.

6   The exhibition *Sielu biedganeapmi / Själens splittrande* (*The Broken Heart*) deals with the forced migration of the Sámi, Museum Ájtte, Jokkmokk, opened February 2, 2023. https://i-on.museum/sweden/ (accessed January 18, 2023). It is part of the research project *Identity on the Line*.

7   Öhman 2021a, 433.

8   Jane Rendell (2000, 101) describes such an interdisciplinary notion of space as space as it is found, "used, occupied and transformed through everyday practices."

9   This comparison is foregrounded by LKAB. Data from and calculations based on https://www.lkab.com/en/about-lkab/from-mine-to-port/mining/ (accessed February 22, 2022).

10   Malmberget also has a Meänkieli name: *Malmivaara*. See also Knobblock 2021.

11   Stenberg 1920, esp. 69–70. Also, these researchers have written about the colonization of Sábme: Össbo and Lantto 2011; Lundmark 2008; Öhman 2010.

12   Össbo 2022a.

13   Sehlin MacNeil 2017, 6.

14   Kristina Sehlin MacNeil and Niila Inga explain precisely in Sehlin MacNeil and Inga 2019, esp. 44. In *Extractive Violence on Indigenous Country*, Sehlin MacNeil also points to the distinction between "utilitarian logic" (extractivism) and the "partnership logic" according to which Indigenous people live; see Sehlin MacNeil 2017, 6. See Stammler and Ivanova 2016.

15   Össbo 2022a, 22.

16   See Sehlin MacNeil 2017, 4.

17   Fur 2013, 26. See also Sehlin MacNeil 2017, 5.

18   As mentioned above, the work of the researchers Elsa Laula, Karin Stenberg, and May-Britt Öhman, and many more, needs to be acknowledged here.

19   Andersen et al. 2015, 241.

20   Tlostanova et al. 2019, 292.

21   See also Stenberg 1920, 33.

22   See Lundmark 2008. See also Laula 1904.

23   Stenberg 1920, 52. See also Laula 1904; Öhman 2021a.

24   Sehlin MacNeil 2017, 8.

25   Åsa Össbo explains "industrial colonialism" based on large-scale transformations due to hydropower in Össbo 2014. See also Össbo 2022b. In the later publication Össbo summarizes how the concept *colonialism* has been recently used in historiography and research on the "relations between the Swedish state and the Indigenous Sámi people" (Össbo 2022b, 1/14).

26   Sehlin MacNeil describes for example the politics of Hjalmar Lundbohm, LKAB's first manager in Kiruna: see Sehlin MacNeil 2017, 9; Persson 2018.

27   For example, the role of Johan Graan, described in Arell 1977; Stenberg 1904, 70.

28   The local researcher Alice Ahnqvist published a comprehensive two-part work on the Sámi history of the area: *Våra förfäder levde här: Samerna – En historisk betraktelse från forntid t.o.m. är 1899* (*Our Ancestors Lived Here: The Sámi – A Historical Observation from Ancient Times to 1899*, self-published 2021), especially 216 and 220–223. The Indigenous and Tribal Peoples Convention (ILO 169) is binding to the signing nations and secures the rights of the Indigenous peoples. Twenty-four nations have signed the treaty so far, but not Sweden.

29   Lundmark 2008, 217–236.

30   The women's role at that time was described in Reinfors 1989.

31   The Collections of ArkDes in Stockholm have available the plans of the original building (1942–1944) as well as the plans for the reconstruction after the first relocation from the early 1970s, including a new parish home and a house for the staff.

32   Ahl 2022.

33   Drawings from Olof Lundgren (1925) and Eskil Sundahl (1930) at ArkDes Collections.

34   Folke Hederus's son, Per Hederus, published *Folke Hederus arkitekt*, see Hederus 2021, esp. 30–48. Many of the buildings have been documented by the architectural photographer Sune Sundahl (see fig. 3).

35   According to a 1953 position plan by Folke Hederus, Collections ArkDes, Stockholm.

36   See also Reisinger 2018. The plans of the row houses have been used for the *Lifelike Appendix to the Archive*, figs. 1 and 2.

37   Rasmusson 2017, 19. Rasmusson points to the "indigenous feminists and/or indigenous queer thinkers" Ina Knobblock, Rauna Kuokkanen, and Qwo-Li Driskill et al. 2011. See also Berman and Lindquist 2014. Ina Knobblock shows how settler colonialism is related to gender in Knobblock 2022.

38   Knobblock and Kuokkanen 2015, 279.

39   Linda Tuhiwai Smith (2012) has argued that the colonial condition is not over for the Indigenous people. See also Ledman 2021, 30–31.

40   Tlostanova, Thapar-Björkert, and Knobblock 2019, 290.

41   Lugones 2010, 746 and 749.

42   Lugones 2010, 754.

43   Lugones 2010.

44   De Lissovoy and Fregoso Bailón 2019, 83. The authors draw on Aníbal Quijano Obregón's work.

45   Össbo 2021, here esp. 18.

46   Össbo 2021, 29.

47   Albrecht 2005, 57–58. Albrecht describes "a wave of aggressive colonialization by large scale, extractive and power-generating industries owned by State, national and multinational corporation" which "dispossessed the Indigenous people of the Valley [Upper Hunter Region, Australia] and for them post-colonial shock waves continue to the present day expressed, in part, as both nostalgia and solastalgia."

48   Jarrett and Reisinger 2021. See also Reisinger and Jarrett 2021.

49 The exhibition *Fences Insects Embroideries (material communities)* at the Geological Survey of Austria, September 17–30, 2022, was curated by Karin Reisinger as part of the Wienwoche festival, https://wien-woche-archiv.com/de/1147/fences,_insects,_embroideries_(material_communities) (accessed November 7, 2023). The workshop "On Dealing with Loss" by Karina Jarrett and Eeva Linder took place in the exhibition on September 17, 2022. For another event of speaking together see Pernilla Fagerlönn, Karina Jarrett, Jelena Micić, and Karin Reisinger, "Curatorial Threads – Connecting Situated Knowledges in the Face of Extraction," panel at the *Transformations Symposium* (Swedish Research Council symposium on artistic research), November 17, 2022, Luleå.

50 See also Rendell 2016. Rendell builds on Butler 2005.

51 Rowe 2014, 627. Itohan Osayimwese also used the concept of "positionality" for her keynote lecture "From Postcolonial to Decolonial Architectural Histories: A Method" at the conference *Architectures of Colonialism: Constructed Histories, Conflicting Memories* at Brandenburg University of Technology Cottbus-Senftenberg on June 16, 2021 (see in this volume).

52 See also my paper "Struggles at the 'Peripheries': Situated Knowledge Production and Feminist Visions for Post-extractive Environments," further elaborating the claim of interdependency and co-production of knowledge (Reisinger 2022).

53 Truman 2019, 9.

54 Öhman 2021b, 238.

55 Johansson Jänkänpää 2014.

56 Lilja and Reisinger 2022. The publication contains the collage of a "mineral desk" which I use for workshops and lectures.

57 These dialogues with the people onsite are constant negotiations, Antoinette Jackson reported in her keynote lecture "Plantation Spaces and Memory – Heritage Interpretation, Memorialization, and Tensions of Public Use at Antebellum Plantation Sites, USA" at the conference *Architectures of Colonialism: Constructed Histories, Conflicting Memories* at Brandenburg University of Technology Cottbus-Senftenberg on June 17, 2021.

58 See for example Kuokkanen 2008a. See also Kuokkanen 2008b; Karin Stenberg 1920.

59 See for example Linda Tuhiwai Smith's seminal work, *Decolonizing Methodologies* (Smith 2012).

60 Katarina Pirak Sikku, "Nammaláphán," exhibition folder (Umeå: Bildmuseet 2014). Summarized in Tlostanova et al. 2019, 293.

61 See for example in Tlostanova et al. 2019 and Lugones 2010.

62 Andersen et al. 2015, 241.

63 Össbo 2022a. According to Össbo (p. 1), the third wave of *framtidslandprojektion* (projection of the land of future) is taking place.

64 Sörlin 2023.

Bibliography

Ahl, Dina. 2022. "Kyrkan i Malmberget kan rivas: 'Vi tar hellre bort byggnader än personal'." *P4 Norrbotten*, January 5, 2022. https://sverigesradio.se/artikel/allhelgonakyrkans-framtid-osaker-utredning-om-eventuell-rivning-pa-gar (accessed February 16, 2022).

Ahnqvist, Alice. 2021. *Våra förfäder levde här: Samerna – En historisk betraktelse från forntid t.o.m. är 1899.* [Malmberget]: self-published.

Albrecht, Glenn. 2005. "'Solastalgia:' A New Concept in Health and Identity." *PAN Philosophy, Activism, Nature* 3: 44–59.

Arell, Nils. 1977. *Rennomadismen i Torne lappmark: Markanvändning under kolonisationsepoken i fr.a. Enontekis socken.* Umeå: Umeå University.

Andersen, Astrid, Kirsten Hvenegård-Lassen and Ina Knobblock. 2015. "Feminism in Postcolonial Nordic Spaces." *NORA – Nordic Journal of Feminist and Gender Research* 23, no. 4: 239–245. https://doi.org/10.1080/08038740.2015.1104596.

Berman, Elfrida, and Sara Lindquist, eds. 2014. *Queering Sápmi: Indigenous Stories Beyond the Norm.* Umeå: Qub Förlag.

Butler, Judith. 2005. *Giving an Account of Oneself*. New York: Fordham University Press.

De Lissovoy, Noah, and Raúl Olmo Fregoso Bailón. 2019. "Coloniality: Key Dimensions and Critical Implications." In Derek R. Ford, ed., *Keywords in Radical Philosophy and Education*, 83–97. Leiden and Boston: Brill.

Driskill, Qwo-Li, Chris Finley, Brian Joseph Gilley, and Scott Lauria Morgensen, eds. 2011. *Queer Indigenous Studies: Critical Interventions in Theory, Politics, and Literature*. Tucson: University of Arizona Press.

Fur, Gunlög. 2013. "Colonialism and Swedish History: Unthinkable Connections?" In Magdalena Naum and Jonas M. Nordin, eds., *Scandinavian Colonialism and the Rise of Modernity: Small Agents in a Global Arena*, 17–36. New York: Springer.

Hederus, Per. 2021. *Folke Hederus arkitekt*. Stockholm: self-published.

Jarrett, Karina, and Karin Reisinger. 2021. "Broderi som respons på förlust och sorg." *Täcklebo Broderiakademi* 2, no. 4: 26–29.

Johansson Jänkänpää, Magnus. 2014. "LKAB Presentation." Presentation at the Northern Lights Corridor Seminar in Muonio Olos, November 26, 2014, https://www.slideshare.net/KatriRantakokko/nlc3-lkab-presentation-by-magnus-johansson-jnknp-northern-lights-corridor-olos-finland-26112014 (accessed February 22, 2022).

Knobblock, Ina. 2021. "Att skriva från gränslandet: dekoloniala berättelser från Sábme." *Kulturella Perspektiv* 30: 1–7.

Knobblock, Ina. 2022. *Writing-Weaving Sámi Feminisms: Stories and Conversations*. Lund: Lund University.

Knobblock, Ina, and Rauna Kuokkanen. 2015. "Decolonizing Feminism in the North: A Conversation with Rauna Kuokkanen." *NORA – Nordic Journal of Feminist and Gender Research* 23, no. 4: 275–281. https://doi.org/10.1080/08038740.2015.1090480.

Kuokkanen, Rauna. 2008a. "From Research as Colonialism to Reclaiming Autonomy: Toward a Research Ethics Framework in Sápmi." In *Sáme- ja álgoálbmot-dutkama etihkka / Ethics in Sámi and Indigenous Research: Report from a Seminar in Kárášjohka, Norway*, 48–63. Kárášjohka: Sámi Instituhtta. http://rauna.files.wordpress.com/2007/10/2008-sami-research-ethics.pdf (accessed February 22, 2022).

Kuokkanen, Rauna. 2008b. *Reshaping the University: Responsiblity, Indigenous Epistemes, and the Logic of the Gift*. Vancouver and Toronto: UBC Press.

Laula, Elsa. 1904. *Inför lif eller död? Sanningsord I de lappska förhållandena*. Stockholm: Wilhelmssons Boktryckeri A.-B.

Ledman, Anna-Lill. 2021. *Att representera & representeras: Samisk kvinnor I svensk och samisk press 1966–2006*. Umeå: Umeå University.

Lilja, Petra, and Karin Reisinger. 2022. "sensing interdependency, experiencing embeddedness, extending the frame while zooming in." *Rogue Research*, http://dx.doi.org/10.14236/ewic/POM2021.10.

Lugones, María. 2010. "Toward a Decolonial Feminism." *Hypatia* 25, no. 4 (Fall): 742–759. https://www.jstor.org/stable/40928654 (accessed February 17, 2022).

Lundmark, Lennart. 2008. *Stulet land: Svensk makt på samisk mark*. Stockholm: Ordfront.

Öhman, May-Britt. 2010. "Being May-Britt Öhman: Or, Reflections on my own Colonized Mind Regarding Hydropower Constructions in Sápmi." In Pirjo Elovaara, Johanna Sefyrin, May-Britt Öhman, and Christina Björkman, eds., *Travelling Thoughtfulness – Feminist Technoscience Stories*, 269–292. Umeå: Umeå University.

Öhman, May-Britt. 2021a. "The Ski or the Wheel? Foregrounding Sámi Technological Innovation in the Arctic Region and Challenging its Invisibility in the History of Humanity." In Brendan Hokowhitu, Aileen Moreton-Robinson, Linda Tuhiwai-Smith, Chris Andersen, and Steve Larkin, eds., *Routledge Handbook of Critical Indigenous Studies*, 431–446. Abingdon and New York: Routledge.

Öhman, May-Britt. 2021b. "Gut la dån? Vem är du? Kukas sie olet? – Who are you? An Alternative Perspective on the History of the North." In Daniel Golling and Carlos Minguez Carrasco, eds., *Kiruna Forever*, 237–246. Stockholm: ArkDes.

Össbo, Åsa. 2014. *Nya vatten, dunkla speglingar. Industriell kolonialism genom svensk vattenkraftutbyggnad in renskötselområdet 1910–1968*. Umeå: Umeå University. http://umu.diva-portal.org/smash/get/diva2:697690/FULLTEXT01.pdf (accessed February 13, 2022).

Össbo, Åsa. 2021. "'A Constant Reminder of What We Had to Forfeit': Swedish Industrial Colonialism and Intergenerational Effects on Sámi Living Conditions in the Area of Upper Stuor Julevädno." *International Journal of Critical Indigenous Studies* 14, no. 1: 17–32.

Össbo, Åsa. 2022a. "Tillbaka till den koloniala framtiden." *Provins* 2: 20–23.

Össbo, Åsa. 2022b. "Hydropower Company Sites: A Study of Swedish Settler Colonialism." *Settler Colonial Studies*, February 10, 2022, https://doi.org/10.1080/2201473X.2022.2037293.

Össbo, Åsa, and Patrik Lantto. 2011. "Colonial Tutelage and Industrial Colonialism: Reindeer Husbandry and Early 20th-Century Hydroelectric Development in Sweden." *Scandinavian Journal of History* 36, no. 3: 324–348.

Persson, Curt. 2018. "Hjalmar Lundbohm: Demokrati och medbestämmande i Kiruna [Hjalmar Lundbohm: Democracy and Codetermination in Kiruna]." In Håkan A Bengtsson and Lars Ilshammar, eds., *Demokratins genombrott: Människor som formade 1900-talet*, 88–111. Lund: Historiska Media.

Rasmusson, Emma. 2017. "Fighting for Existence: Exposing, Questioning and Moving Beyond Colonial Practices within the Swedish Planning Framework for Mining Establishments." Master's Thesis, Örebro University.

Reinfors, Lis-Marie. 1989. *Kvinnoliv I kåkstadssamhället Malmberget 1890–1914* [*Women's Live in the Kåkstad Community of Malmberget 1890–1914*]. Stockholm: Stockholm University, Institutet för Folklivsforskning.

Reisinger, Karin. 2018. "Introduktion: En feministisk kartografi över ett växande hål [Introduction: A Feminist Cartography of a Growing Hole]." *PLAN* 6–7: 5–32.

Reisinger, Karin. 2022. "Struggles at the 'Peripheries': Situated knowledge production and Feminist Visions for Post-extractive Environments", *Cidades* 45. https://journals.openedition.org/cidades/6197 (accessed January 30, 2023).

Reisinger, Karin, and Karina Jarrett. 2021. "Karina Jarrett about the Embroidery Café." Video, 37:08 min. https://repository.akbild.ac.at/de/alle_inhalte/query;fq=%7B%22fulltext%22:%5B%22Reisinger%22%5D%7D;st=0;sz=50/25728 (accessed December 17, 2021).

Rendell, Jane. 2000. "Introduction: 'Gender, Space.'" In Jane Rendell, Barbara Penner, and Iain Borden, eds., *Gender Space Architecture: An Interdisciplinary Introduction*, 101–111. London: Routledge.

Rendell, Jane. 2016. "Giving an Account of Oneself: Architecturally." *Journal of Visual Culture* 15, no. 3: 334–348.

Rowe, Wendy E. 2014. "Positionality." In David Coghlan and Mary Brydon-Miller, eds., *The Sage Encyclopedia of Action Research*, 627–628. London: SAGE Publications.

Sehlin MacNeil, Kristina. 2017. *Extractive Violence on Indigenous Country: Sami and Aboriginal Views on Conflicts and Power Relations with Extractive Industries*. Umeå: Umeå University. http://www.diva-portal.org/smash/get/diva2:1068229/FULLTEXT02.pdf (accessed February 4, 2022).

Sehlin MacNeil, Kristina, and Niila Inga. 2019. "Extraktivt våld och urfolks koppling till mark [Extractive Violence and Indigenous Peoples' Connection to Land]." *Kulturella perspektiv – Svensk etnologisk tidskrift* 28, no. 1–2: 42–51.

Smith, Linda Tuhiwai. 2012. *Decolonizing Methodologies: Research and Indigenous Peoples*. London: Zed Books.

Sörlin, Sverker, ed. 2023. *Resource Extraction and Arctic Communities: The New Extractivist Paradigm*. Cambridge and New York: Cambridge University Press.

Stammler, Florian, and Aitalina Ivanova. 2016. "Confrontation, Coexistence or Co-ignorance? Negotiating Human-Resource Relations in two Russian Regions." *The Extractive Industries and Society* 3, no. 1: 60–72.

Stenberg, Karin. 1920. *Dat läh mijen situd! Det är vår vilja. En vädjan till den svenska nationen från samefolket* [*That is Our Will. An Appeal to the Swedish National from the Sami People*]. Örnsköldsvik: Ägrens boktryckeri.

Tlostanova, Madina, Suruchi Thapar-Björkert, and Ina Knobblock. 2019. "Do We Need Decolonial Feminism in Sweden?" *NORA – Nordic Journal of Feminist and Gender Research* 27, no. 4: 290–295. https://doi.org/10.1080/08038740.2019.1641552.

Truman, Sarah E. 2019. "Feminist New Materialisms." In P. A. Atkinson, S. Delamont, M. A. Hardy, & M. Williams, eds., *The SAGE Encyclopedia of Research Methods*, 13 pages. London: SAGE Publications.

Image Sources

1, 2 ArkDes Collections, photos by Björn Strömfeldt, 2021–2022.

3 ArkDes Collections, photo by Sune Sundahl, 1957.

4 Photo by Karin Reisinger, 2021.

5 Photo by Olesya Kleymenova / Wienwoche.

6 Photo by Karin Reisinger, 2021.

JOHANNA BLOKKER

Challenging Monuments

Heritage Conservation and the Difficult Legacies of Colonialism

Recent years have seen commemorative monuments become the focus of unusually heated public debate.[1] The question of whether statues of colonial rulers, slave owners and slave traders, or of Confederate soldiers and generals, should or should not be removed from the urban landscape has been widely discussed in the media, in politics, and in academia, not just in the United States but also internationally. The issue is not new, but with the murder of George Floyd by a white police officer in Minneapolis in May 2020 and the global wave of public protest it set in motion under the banner of the Black Lives Matter (BLM) movement, the question of monuments in our cities and our society has become a topic of urgent and almost universal interest.

In the clamor of public discussion over the past three years, however, and among all the statements and opinions of activists, experts, and opinion leaders that have been voiced and printed and broadcast, the perspective of those in society whose primary responsibility and daily business it is to deal with monuments—namely, conservationists and scholars of heritage—has rarely been canvassed or heard. Yet this perspective is highly relevant to the issues at the core of the current debate. For heritage conservation is not solely, as many might assume, a matter of "technical practices of conservation and processes of heritage management," that is, the preservation of the material substance of historic artifacts such as statues, although this too is an important concern. Rather, in the words of British heritage researcher Rodney Harrison, it is about "critical discussion of the nature of heritage and why we think particular objects, places and practices might be considered … [worthy] of conservation and protection."[2] Heritage scholars ask about the functions and effects of historic objects in society and the processes of remembering and forgetting, appropriating and rejecting, that they manifest and support.[3] Put another way: "Monuments are … values made visible."[4] It is of course values that are at the center of current debates about racism and discrimination in many countries around the world, as manifested in the international BLM movement, and it is precisely because monuments stand for values that they have become focal points in these debates.

In this contribution I will therefore introduce the special perspective of heritage conservation into the current discussion about the handling of public monuments dedicated to personalities of the colonial era and representatives of colonialism. I will outline some of the theoretical principles underlying conservation practice and, on this basis, critically examine some of the measures being proposed for dealing with statues and other artifacts. In doing so, I will refer primarily to examples from Germany, Great Britain, and the United States, drawing liberally on the research and insights of colleagues from these countries. It will come as little surprise that the consensus within the field is decidedly in favor of preserving commemorative monuments, and that heritage professionals in general reject the destruction or removal of these objects. Revealing this at the outset does not, however, spoil the effect of the chapter, for, as was suggested above, conservation is by no means about preserving for its own sake. On the contrary, the decision to preserve an object comes at the end of a careful process of thought and reflection, one that is worth examining in detail and that can help to advance the wider debate about monuments in a productive way.

Deliberate and Unintentional Monuments

In the following I will focus exclusively on so-called *gewollte Denkmale* or "deliberate monuments." The term was coined in 1903 by the Austrian art historian and early heritage theorist Alois Riegl and denotes

> a work of man erected for the specific purpose of keeping particular human deeds or destinies
> … alive and present in the consciousness of future generations. It may be a monument either
> of art or of writing, depending on whether the event to be eternalized is conveyed to the viewer solely through the expressive means of the fine arts or with the aid of inscription; most often
> both genres are combined in equal measure.[5]

In this definition, now a century old, it is easy to recognize the kinds of objects that are the main focus of the current debate: statues that represent and celebrate historical individuals, as well as obelisks, sculptures, and plaques that honor them, keep their memory alive, and embed their personalities and deeds in the structure of public space. Not addressed, on the other hand, will be so-called "unintentional monuments" (Riegl's *gewordene Denkmale*), the large category of objects that take on value gradually over time because of their artistic quality, their acquired historical associations, their age, or their increasing rarity. That said, it must be acknowledged that unintentional monuments, too, can manifest, reproduce, and perpetuate colonial structures. With reference to the city of Bristol, where the statue of slave trader Edward Colston was toppled by protesters in 2020 (fig. 1), historian Mirjam Brusius has noted that "many cities are now just realizing that their wealth"—and in fact much of their architectural and urban fabric—"is based, like Bristol's, on a system of exploitation."[6]

Both categories of monuments, the deliberate and the unintentional, are about "objects, places and practices that have some significance in the present which relates to the past," as Rodney Harrison explains.[7] This brings us into contact with a first fundamental point of heritage conservation theory: as a cultural phenomenon, heritage is always "present-centered"; that is, it involves objects or artifacts from the past that have meaning *in* and *for* the present. From this first insight, a second one immediately follows: the meaning or "value" of heritage is not inherent in the artifact, but is ascribed to it by viewers or users according to their own beliefs, needs, and aims.[8] Thus we can say with cultural anthropologist Regina Bendix that "cultural heritage is not a state of being, but a process of becoming."[9] The point is that heritage is not so much a thing as it is a practice performed by people—the practice of value-attribution and meaning-making.[10] Consequently, it is also a dynamic phenomenon, always changing with the shifting and evolving perspectives of people in the present.

It is clear that the members of any community or society do not always agree on what is important or valuable to them. For this reason, heritage theory describes valorization as a social

1   The statue of the slave trader Edward Colston (1636–1721) is dumped into Bristol Harbour by demonstrators on June 7, 2020.

process of negotiation: members must work toward a consensus on their common values and on what exactly—which objects, which artifacts—should represent these values in what way. Such negotiation processes may well involve friction and contention, and to this extent they must be understood as political processes. And just as in politics, not all participants in the discourse are equally well positioned: some are better able than others, thanks to their financial or social or cultural capital, to assert their own version of shared values and to dominate in the struggle for interpretive sovereignty over heritage. In other words, just like politics, heritage conservation too is about power relations. As Harrison puts it, "Heritage … is a dynamic process which involves competition over whose version of the past … will find official representation in the present."[11] Whose values a monument is meant to express, who exactly is using this medium and with what right, what intent, and what message, are thus questions at the heart of conservation research.

The great utility of heritage as an instrument of power is explained primarily by its legitimizing effect, by the perception of "the moral and legal rights which flow from [the] version of the past" it presents.[12] Indeed, heritage can not only express and reflect systems of values and relations of power, it can also reproduce them, solidify them, normalize and naturalize them, make them seem self-evident—sometimes so much so that they become invisible. This is what the writer Robert Musil was suggesting in his famous essay on "Monuments" of 1932: "The most striking thing about monuments is that one does not notice them," he wrote. "There is nothing in the world so invisible as monuments."[13] He explained the phenomenon as follows: "Everything that forms the walls of our lives, the backdrop, so to speak, of our consciousness, loses the ability to play a role in that consciousness."[14] The observation may seem banal, but it contains a deeper truth that is highly significant. This "backdrop of our consciousness," its contours and boundaries, shape and mold everything that takes place in our consciousness, our entire patterns of thought and behavior. And this is precisely the problem: the values attributed to heritage in turn become systemic and structural through heritage's own naturalized and naturalizing, legitimized and legitimizing effect.

When Monuments Become Visible

All of this can remain the case for decades, even centuries, until something occurs to challenge the prevailing consensus, to upset the established value system, to call into question the seemingly self-evident facts, and the monument becomes visible again—as appears to be occurring now. The immediate triggers for this development have been multiple: even before the murder of George Floyd in 2020, an attack by neo-Nazis on anti-racism demonstrators in Charlottesville, Virginia in 2017, and prior to that the massacre of nine attendees at a service in an African-American church in Charleston, North Carolina in 2015, brought monuments and symbols of the Confederacy to the center of public attention in these and other places. In Great Britain, by contrast, efforts by groups such as Bristol's "Countering Colston" to promote a broader discussion around the statue of the slave trader, and to generate public interest in developing a strategy for dealing with it, date back to the 1990s.[15] The efforts of activists in Berlin to persuade its Senate and City Council to change street names in the city's so-called African Quarter have a similarly long history.[16] The fact that all of these public monuments, previously "visible" only to certain groups in society, are now suddenly present in the consciousness and perception of all, is an indication that a major turning point has been reached.

Exactly why this point has arrived only now and not earlier is a question that will occupy scholars for years to come. What is clear is that monuments such as the Colston statue in Bristol, or the figure of Confederate General Robert E. Lee that was the focus of the violent clashes in Charlottesville, are now understood as symbols and manifestations of a value system that is no longer self-evident, and that this is the reason for their emergence as objects of contention. It is precisely this contentiousness that once again highlights the essential function of heritage in society, namely as a medium for the conduct of discourses on values, as places where people can come together—in many cases quite literally (fig. 2)—to participate in processes of negotiation. Seen in this light, such monuments should perhaps not be destroyed or removed without further ado, but should rather be kept standing and preserved. And this not because, as Musil writes, it is the surest method by which a *persona non grata* can be "plunged, as it were, with a memorial stone around its neck into the sea of oblivion"—an image that strongly if only coincidentally recalls the handling of the Colston statue by demonstrators in the summer of 2020.[17] On the contrary: these monuments should be kept standing because removing them would only make their invisibility complete and would thereby effectively foreclose any opportunity to revisit and re-negotiate their value once the "sea of oblivion" has ebbed away, as is happening now.

This cannot really be to the advantage of either side in the debate. Those opposed to removing colonialist statues for fear of "erasing" or "rewriting our history"[18] as well as "destroying

2   The equestrian monument of Confederate General Robert E. Lee in Richmond, Virginia becomes the focus of democratic processes of negotiation in June 2020.

our cultural heritage"[19] certainly do not want it. Their logic is faulty, of course: the past cannot be undone, nor can it be erased from memory using such simple means. History, on the other hand, can and should be rewritten. Indeed, it is always in motion and is constantly being revised and reinterpreted.[20] Mirjam Brusius makes this point succinctly in a statement on the Colston controversy: "Of course we want to rewrite history," she says. "That comes with the job, so to speak; you're always trying to close the gaps."[21] This also happens to be what most advocates of statue removal are demanding: the complication and completion of our image of the past, which is only partially and often falsely represented by public monuments as they still stand now. Far from wanting to destroy our cultural heritage, advocates of removal are thus pushing to create the conditions in which a heritage can emerge for the first time at these sites. For Confederate statues, at least, have never been "our cultural heritage," they have never been the outcome of a process of negotiation among members of society. Instead, they represent target-ed propaganda by interest groups. As various scholars have shown, "The purpose of their instal-lation was to intimidate the African American populations and … defy desegregation."[22] In fact there have been two historical moments at which the installation of Confederate monuments and other symbols reached particular heights: the first two decades of the twentieth century, when the so-called Jim Crow laws were enacted, and the 1950s and 1960s, when the civil rights movement was gaining momentum and celebrating some early victories.[23] In this sense, these statues, obelisks, plaques, and so on illustrate in a particularly striking way what Alois Riegl ob-served about deliberate and unintentional monuments: "In the case of deliberate monuments, the commemorative value is dictated to us by others (the former creators), while we define the value of unintentional monuments ourselves."[24]

It is precisely for this reason that I would urge the proponents of statue removal to reconsider their position: here is a chance to allow a true heritage in the modern sense to emerge, a heritage that can fulfill its indispensable social and political function and have a lasting impact. For if it is true that "it takes more than the removal of a statue to decenter whiteness,"[25] it is also true that "If you give the statues a shake, the structures will wobble."[26] It is precisely as handholds for such shaking that monuments are so useful—provided, of course, that they are still there.

This brings us to the third and most important point of heritage conservation theory that I would like to introduce into the discussion here. Among the essential values that heritage holds for society is included not only its artistic and historical value, but also its so-called "contestation value" (*Streitwert*). The term was coined in 2010 by Gabi Dolff-Bonekämper, professor of heritage conservation at the Technical University of Berlin, in a much-cited essay, and as a concept it has proved extremely fruitful.[27] It is also highly relevant to our topic and therefore merits closer examination. As Dolff-Bonekämper writes: "A contested monument—that is, a monument worth fighting over"—can be important, and this "not in spite of the fact that it attracts controversy, but precisely because it does so"; that is, because it sets in motion and drives forward dynamic processes of negotiation and engagement with the meaning of the past in the present:

> Contestation pervades all processes of value attribution … because every value can be contested … I see this kind of conflict as a culturally productive activity that advances both the cause of heritage and that of society.[28]

Furthermore, if we agree that the value and significance of cultural heritage is never definitively established, but changes constantly with time and with the perspective of the person ascribing significance to that heritage, then:

> It may be necessary to fight over a monument again and again. Certainties can be shaken up, new perspectives on the monument can lead to completely different conclusions and insights. *Provided that it is still there*. The open-endedness of the processes of interpretation thus makes the material substance of the monument all the more valuable, because it contains answers to questions that no one is asking yet.[29]

Applied to the question of how to deal with the contentious and contested monuments of colonialism today, this approach means in concrete terms the preservation of these objects intact, both with respect to their material condition and their context in urban space. For ultimately, what is "actually inherent to the heritage artifact" is solely "its form, its substance, and its location in space and time"—all of its other qualities arise and exist exclusively in the minds of viewers and users. It is for this reason, Dolff-Bonekämper concludes, that "we conservationists … have a critical relationship to the meaning of heritage, but an affirmative relationship to its material substance."[30]

Worth Fighting Over

This does not of course mean that monuments that glorify the idea of colonialism and reproduce structures of discrimination should simply be left as they are. Rather, they need to be placed in their historical context: their history needs to be completed and nuanced, this knowledge needs to be actively communicated, and the meaning of the colonial past for us in the present needs to be widely and publicly discussed. It is here that heritage conservation, as a field of historical and cultural study, can play an important role. Furthermore, as a design profession, it can contribute to the development of interpretation and presentation strategies that creatively question the "dictated" messages of "deliberate monuments" without damaging or destroying them, and without diminishing their power as witnesses to history or setting limits to the free play of interpretive processes in the present and future.

Contextualization and interpretation are, incidentally, also what most activist groups that focus their protest on colonialist statues and monuments are working for, alongside Countering Colston in Britain,[31] for example, or Decolonize Berlin in the German capital. The latter was named in 2019 as the coordinating body for the development of the "city-wide concept for memorializing and coming to terms with the history and consequences of colonialism in Berlin," in a law passed by the city's House of Representatives in August of that year.[32] In the group's 2021 annual report, the provision of "perspective-changing commentary on objects and sites having a connection to colonialism" was strongly recommended, but removals or substantial changes to these objects were not called for.[33] Similarly, the report for 2022 contained an appeal by literary scholar Dr. Ibou Diop to "identify and make visible the traces of colonialism in the life of Berlin" and to "preserve memories, to document and to question time and space."[34] When it comes to the appropriate way to handle public monuments, the positions of activists and heritage conservationists are thus often closely aligned.

For the elaboration of "profound, scholarship-based, coordinated, and balanced" commentaries on monuments of colonialism, however, as recommended by the heritage conservation authority in Bremen for the Bismarck statue in that city,[35] some participants in the discourse might lack the necessary endurance. After all, the processes of political negotiation that are required are often very slow, arduous, and wearisome—not least because many of the historical personalities now attracting critical attention reveal themselves on closer examination to be genuinely ambivalent figures: in addition to Bismarck, Colston, or Cecil Rhodes, also Thomas Jefferson, George Washington, Winston Churchill, and many others are now being shown to have held racist attitudes. Here, too, heritage conservationists are in demand, as "communication-organizing moderators"[36] with extensive experience both in making difficult decisions—one cannot preserve everything—and in dealing with complexity, contradiction, and uncomfortable historical truths. "It's possible to recognize people's contributions at the same time as recognizing their flaws," reminds Annette Gordon-Reed, professor of history at Harvard University.[37] In response to the question "Where does it stop?"[38] we need to find answers together, and to do so through open dialogue and on the basis of full knowledge of the historical circumstances.

Of course, the success of such processes of negotiation and rapprochement presupposes a level playing field in the struggle for interpretive sovereignty, as well as trust that all participants are acting in good faith. Unfortunately, this is not always the case: all too often, the balance of power remains skewed in favor of politically influential interest groups. In many instances, the forces that maintain the status quo have little to do with democracy or negotiation, but rather with the exercise of power by the establishment, which also uses the instruments of its power—among them the law—to assert its will. That is why, as a heritage scholar, I am appalled when heritage preservation laws, of all things, are used to prevent the public questioning of colonial monuments.[39] With Gabi Dolff-Bonekämper, I would argue that it is not and must not be the purpose of these laws—at least not in modern democracies—to secure the power position of particular groups in society. Rather, it is a matter of providing an orderly framework for constant

3   The equestrian monuments of Confederate Generals Robert E. Lee and Stonewall Jackson are removed under cover of darkness in Baltimore, Maryland on August 16, 2017.

reflection on, as well as further development and, where necessary, reinterpretation and adaptation of, the concept of heritage.[40]

To this extent, the attacks on colonialist monuments and the destructive interventions of some activist groups must be understood primarily as expressions of frustration at the failure of democratic processes, and not as examples of direct democracy in action. The violent toppling of the Colston statue after a decades-long and ultimately deadlocked dispute makes this particularly clear: even those who welcomed and cheered the action—among them the leadership of Countering Colston—would have much preferred that Bristol's elected representatives had taken on this task, and in doing so had explicitly committed themselves to the principle of decolonizing public space. In this way, the removal of the statue could have had the character of "legitimized popular anger"[41] and thus could have served as a genuine model for other cities. Instead, even state-supported decolonization measures are often still carried out more like technical procedures: one thinks of the unceremonious dismantling of the statue of slave trader Robert Milligan at London's Docklands in June 2020, or the unannounced, almost clandestine nighttime operations in which many public monuments in the United States, such as the statue of Generals Robert E. Lee and Stonewall Jackson in Baltimore in 2017 (fig. 3), have been brought down from their pedestals. While some of these removals are prepared for by clear statements on the part of political leaders—the eloquent speech by New Orleans Mayor Mitch Landrieu should be specifically noted here[42]—the general lack of official ceremony and attention sends the message that these measures are more about capitulation to circumstances than they are about fundamental change in public policy and principle. More courage and leadership of the kind shown by Landrieu is needed from policymakers; supporting and standing by them can be the role of a self-reflexive field of heritage conservation that is conscious of its political and social responsibilities.

No Blanket Rules

From the perspective of heritage conservation, historical contextualization and non-destructive, creative means of coming to terms with the past are thus the favored options for dealing with the difficult legacies of colonialism in the urban landscape. Ideally, this should also be done on-site in the original urban context; only in rare exceptions should statues or monuments be moved into sculpture parks or museums. Although such facilities offer ideal conditions for the communication and interpretation of culture and history, they ultimately represent closed spaces and are thus unsuited to the conduct of genuinely open and public discussion, as architectural historian and conservationist Daniela Spiegel rightly points out.[43] To this it should be added that the transfer into the museum removes the monument from its urban context once and for all, and thus necessitates even greater efforts to contextualize it. In the process, a part of the documentary value and the expressive power of the monument is unavoidably lost and can hardly be compensated by a panel bearing explanatory text. Indeed, it is public space as an integral whole that offers the greatest potential "to shake up the prevailing historical consciousness and provide food for thought for decolonization processes," as historian Bebero Lehmann argues in a further report published by Decolonize Berlin.[44] In cities shaped by colonialism and steeped in that legacy, public statues and monuments should function as landmarks in a broader urban topography of active remembrance.[45] Above all, it will be important to present colonialism not as a phenomenon of the museum—that is, as something that already belongs to the past—but as a present reality that can also be experienced in the spaces of everyday life.

"There are ways of remembering our history without glorifying those that were on the wrong side of it," writes Bristol native Tom Ravenscroft, editor of *Dezeen*.[46] Likewise, our responses to the question of the appropriate handling of colonialist monuments can and should be multiple and heterogeneous. Some can be transferred into museums, many more can be provided with "perspective-changing commentary," and still others—even the majority—can and perhaps should be turned into sites of artistic expression and interpretation.[47] A change in perspective was the explicit aim of the temporary installation *Discovering Columbus* created by the artist Tatzu Nishi in New York City in 2012 (fig. 4), for example, and many more works in this vein could be cited.[48]

4   The art installation *Discovering Columbus* by Tatzu Nishi on Columbus Circle in New York City in September 2012.

Toppling and destruction are of course themselves radically perspective-changing interventions, and there is an argument to be made that they, too, can be considered heritage practices and can contribute to the heritage value and meaning of a statue. As such, they can also become preservation-worthy—and indeed there have been several proposals for ways in which to make the act of toppling more permanent, for example in the artist Banksy's suggestion for a reworking of the Colston statue in Bristol (fig. 5).[49] Such a proposal—which would see the statue put back in place, with additional figures of protesters added—could also help to foster a broader understanding of heritage as something that is not threatened by the addition to it of layers of meaning and nuance, but is kept alive and vital by this activity. This seems like an important lesson, and not one that can easily be learned from an empty pedestal.

5   Banksy's proposal
for a new version of the
toppled statue of Edward
Colston in Bristol, 2020.

That said, a few of these objects clearly must be removed and made to disappear from view: specifically, those that do not inspire contestation, but rather engender conflict. With the latter term I intend to denote violence, both physical and psychological, which I see as the end of dialogue and therefore quite distinct from contestation. It will be recalled that the clashes that rocked Charlottesville in 2017, and that left one woman dead as well as dozens injured, were centered on an equestrian statue of General Lee, which was subsequently hidden from view with a tarp before being removed entirely from its site in 2021. The decision to do so was justifiable. Yet the example illustrates how conflict raises a different and more difficult set of questions with regard to heritage: How can a dialogue be started or restarted when the will to engage in contestation is absent, or has been abandoned? And conversely: How can processes of contestation be supported, such that they are never abandoned in favor of conflict? For capitulating to conflict and removing colonialist monuments, I argue, is ultimately counter-productive.

The example of Charlottesville also illustrates a final point of heritage conservation theory to be made here: there can be no blanket rules; rather, decisions must be made on a case-by-case basis. Above all, no approach should be considered definitive: the processes of negotiation must remain dynamic, the activity of interpretation incomplete. Only in this way can we guarantee that the heritage of the past will continue to function as a useful and constructive force for positive social change—in the knowledge that change will always be necessary, and improvement will always be possible.

1   An abridged, German-language version of this contribution was published under the title "Denkmalsturz und Denkmalschutz: Positionen der Denkmalpflege zum Umgang mit Denkmälern des Kolonialismus," see Blokker 2021.
2   Harrison 2010, 15.
3   Harrison 2010, 75.
4   Neiman 2019, 263.
5   Riegl 1996 [1903], 69.
6   Hondl and Brusius 2021.
7   Harrison 2010, 12.
8   Harrison 2010, 25.
9   Bendix 2007, 340.
10   Cf. Waterton and Smith 2009.
11   Harrison 2010, 8.
12   Harrison 2010, 8.
13   Musil 1936, 87.
14   Musil 1936, 89.
15   Cf. Countering Colston – Campaign to Decolonise Bristol, https://counteringcolston.wordpress.com/ (accessed June 19, 2023).
16   Cf. Förster et al. 2016.
17   Musil 1936, 93.
18   Cf. Graham 2017.
19   Cf. Burgard and Boucher 2018, 246.
20   Cf. Ravenscroft 2020.
21   Hondl and Brusius 2021.
22   Burgard and Boucher 2018, 246.
23   Cf. Gunther and Southern Poverty Law Center 2016, 11.

24   Riegl 1996 [1903], 72.

25   Burgard and Boucher 2018, 245.

26   Joanna Burch-Brown, member of the History Commission convened by Bristol's mayor in 2020, in a statement during the online book presentation of International Bar Association, ed., *Contested Histories: Principles, Processes, Best Practices* (London: IBA, 2021), February 11, 2021, https://www.ibanet.org/contested-histories (accessed June 19, 2023).

27   Dolff-Bonekämper 2010.

28   Dolff-Bonekämper 2010, 37.

29   Dolff-Bonekämper 2010, 39. Emphasis by the author.

30   Dolff-Bonekämper 2010, 39.

31   Cf. "What do we want?" [n.d.].

32   Cf. Koordinierungsstelle bei Decolonize Berlin e.V., https://decolonize-berlin.de/de/koordinierungsstelle/ (accessed June 19, 2023).

33   Koordinierungsstelle 2021, 52.

34   Diop 2023, 46, 47.

35   Scharfenberger 2020.

36   Dolff-Bonekämper 2010, 34.

37   Graham 2017.

38   Graham 2017.

39   Cf. Southern Poverty Law Center 2019.

40   Dolff-Bonekämper 2002.

41   Daniela Spiegel, "Volkszorn und Denkmalpflege: Überlegungen im Kontext der Black Lives Matter-Proteste im Sommer 2020." Lecture delivered in the online lecture series *Kulturerbe: Emotionen und Bedeutungen* (University of Heidelberg, June 14, 2021).

42   Cf. "Mitch Landrieu's Speech" 2017.

43   Cf. Daniela Spiegel's lecture "Volkszorn" (see note 41). See also Spiegel 2021.

44   Lehmann 2021, 35.

45   An impressive example is Barkley Brown and Kimball 1995.

46   Ravenscroft 2020.

47   See for example Rooney, Wingate, and Senie 2022.

48   Interestingly, many recent examples fall into the category of unauthorized or "guerilla" art, that is, art as public protest: they include the set of miniature plaster figures laid out in the configuration of prisoners on a slave ship, which was placed in front of the Edward Colston statue in Bristol by an anonymous artist on Anti-Slavery Day in October 2018; the figure of BLM protester Jen Reid produced by artist Quinn and set atop the empty plinth of the Colston statue after its toppling in July 2020; the spray-painted outline of the shadow cast by the monumental figure of Cecil Rhodes after its removal from the campus of Cape Town University in April 2019; and the laser-light images and texts projected onto the equestrian statue of General Lee in Richmond, VA on July 4, 2020. The latter "in its current state" was named one of "the 25 most influential works of American protest art since World War II" by *The New York Times Style Magazine*; see "The Most Influential" 2020. The projections were in turn inspired by artist Krzysztof Wodiczko's "Bunker Hill Monument Projection" in Boston in 1998, an installation described at the time as making it "hard for people … to view the monument the way they did before." See Temin 1998.

49   Ravenscroft 2020.

Bibliography

Barkley Brown, Elsa, and Gregg D. Kimball. 1995. "Mapping the Terrain of Black Richmond." In *Journal of Urban History* 21, no. 3 (March): 296–346.

Bendix, Regina. 2007. "Kulturelles Erbe zwischen Wirtschaft und Politik. Ein Ausblick." In Dorothee Hemme, Markus Tauschek, and Regina Bendix, eds., *Prädikat 'Heritage': Wertschöpfungen aus kulturellen Ressourcen*, 337–353. Berlin: LIT.

Blokker, Johanna. 2021. "Denkmalsturz und Denkmalschutz: Positionen der Denkmalpflege zum Umgang mit Denkmälern des Kolonialismus." *Aus Politik und Zeitgeschichte* 40–41 (October): 20–26.

Burgard, Karen, and Michael Boucher. 2018. "The Special Responsibility of Public Spaces to Dismantle White Supremacist Historical Narratives." In Angela Labrador and Neil Asher Silberman, eds., *The Oxford Handbook of Public History Theory and Practice*, 236–256. Oxford: Oxford University Press.

Diop, Ibou. 2023. "Ein Konzept zur Erinnerung der kolonialen Geschichte des Landes Berlin muss die Geschichte Berlins, Brandenburgs, Preußens sowie die des Wilhelminismus, des Faschismus und der zwei deutschen Staaten nach 1949 neu und anders lesen als bisher – und dadurch Zwischenräume sichtbar machen." In Koordinierungsstelle bei Decolonize Berlin e.V., ed., *Gesamtstädtisches Aufarbeitungskonzept der kolonialen Vergangenheit Berlins: Jahresbericht 2022*, 45–47. Berlin: Pinguin Druck.

Dolff-Bonekämper, Gabi. 2002. "Zur Streitseite der Denkmale." May 16, 2002, http://www.dolff-bonekaemper.de/denkmale-p.-1.html (accessed June 19, 2023).

Dolff-Bonekämper, Gabi. 2010. "Gegenwartswerte: Für eine Erneuerung von Alois Riegls Denkmalwerttheorie." In Hans-Rudolf Meier and Ingrid Scheurmann, eds., *DENKmalWERTE: Beiträge zur Theorie und Aktualität der Denkmalpflege*, 27–40. Munich: Deutscher Kunstverlag.

Förster, Susanne, et al. 2016. "Negotiating German Colonial Heritage in Berlin's Afrikanisches Viertel." *International Journal of Heritage Studies* 22: 515–529.

Graham, David. 2017. "Where Will the Removal of Confederate Monuments Stop?" *The Atlantic*, June 28, 2017, https://www.theatlantic.com/politics/archive/2017/06/where-will-the-removal-of-confederate-monuments-stop/532125/ (accessed June 19, 2023).

Gunther, Booth, and Southern Poverty Law Center, eds. 2016. *Whose Heritage? Public Symbols of the Confederacy*. Montgomery: SPLC.

Harrison, Rodney. 2010. *Understanding the Politics of Heritage*. Manchester: Manchester University Press.

Hondl, Katrin, and Mirjam Brusius. 2021. "Vielsagender Sturz einer Sklavenhändler-Statue: In Bristol beginnt der Prozess gegen Black-Lives-Matter-Demonstrant*innen." *SWR2 am Morgen*, February 8, 2021, https://www.academia.edu/49050628/Radio_Interview_Vielsagender_Sturz_einer_Sklavenhändler_Statue_In_Bristol_beginnt_der_Prozess_gegen_Black_Lives_Matter_Demonstrant_innen_ (accessed June 19, 2023).

Koordinierungsstelle bei Decolonize Berlin e.V., ed. 2021. *Gesamtstädtisches Aufarbeitungskonzept der kolonialen Vergangenheit Berlins: Jahresbericht 2021*. Berlin: Pinguin Druck.

Lehmann, Bebero. 2021. "Neue Erinnerungsorte im öffentlichen Raum." In Koordinierungsstelle bei Decolonize Berlin e.V., ed., *Gesamtstädtisches Aufarbeitungskonzept der kolonialen Vergangenheit Berlins: Zwischenbericht 2020*, 32–35. Berlin: Oktoberdruck.

"Mitch Landrieu's Speech on the Removal of Confederate Monuments in New Orleans." 2017. *New York Times*, May 23, 2017, https://www.nytimes.com/2017/05/23/opinion/mitch-landrieus-speech-transcript.html (accessed June 19, 2023).

Musil, Robert. 1936. "Denkmale." In *Nachlaß zu Lebzeiten*, 87–93. Zürich: Humanitas.

Neiman, Susan. 2019. *Learning from the Germans: Race and the Memory of Evil*. New York: Farrar, Strauss and Giroux.

Ravenscroft, Tom. 2020. "The Long-overdue Removal of Colston's Statue is Now Part of Bristol's History." *Dezeen*, June 10, 2020, https://www.dezeen.com/2020/06/10/the-long-overdue-removal-of-colstons-statue-is-now-part-of-bristols-history/ (accessed June 19, 2023).

Riegl, Alois. 1996. "The Modern Cult of Monuments: Its Essence and Its Development" (1903, translated by Karin Bruckner with Karen Williams). In Nicholas Stanley-Price, Mansfield Kirby Talley, and Alessandra Melucco Vaccaro, eds., *Historical and Philosophical Issues in the Conservation of Cultural Heritage*, 69–83. Los Angeles: Getty Conservation Institute.

Rooney, Sierra, Jennifer Wingate, and Harriet F. Senie, eds. 2022. *Teachable Monuments: Using Public Art to Spark Dialogue and Confront Controversies*. New York: Bloomsbury.

Scharfenberger, Lukas. 2020. "Erst sanieren, dann reden." *taz*, September 5, 2020, https://taz.de/Erst-sanieren-dann-reden/!5709420/ (accessed June 19, 2023).

Southern Poverty Law Center, ed. 2019. "A Closer Look: Laws in Seven States Protect Confederate Monuments." February 2, 2019, https://www.splcenter.org/20190201/whose-heritage-public-symbols-confederacy#state-laws (accessed June 19, 2023).

Spiegel, Daniela. 2021. "Volkszorn und Denkmalstürze: Überlegungen im Kontext der Black-Lives-Matter-Ereignisse im Jahr 2020." In Stephanie Herold and Gerhard Vinken, eds., *Denkmal:Emotion: Politisierung–Mobilisierung–Bindung*, 76–83. Holzminden: Mitzkat.

Temin, Christine. 1998. "Monument Message is Searing." *Boston Globe*, September 25, 1998.

"The 25 Most Influential Works of American Protest Art since World War II." 2020. *NYT Style Magazine*, October 15, 2020, https://www.nytimes.com/2020/10/15/t-magazine/most-influential-protest-art.html?action=click&module=Editors%20Picks&pgtype=Homepage (accessed June 19, 2023).

Waterton, Emma, and Laurajane Smith. 2009. "There is No Such Thing as Heritage." In Laurajane Smith and Emma Waterton, eds., *Taking Archaeology Out of Heritage*, 10–27. Cambridge: Cambridge Scholars Publishing.

"What Do We Want?" [n.d.] Countering Colston, https://counteringcolston.wordpress.com/what-do-we-want/ (accessed June 19, 2023).

Image Sources

1   Alamy Stock Photo / Ben Birchall.
2   picture alliance / Steve Helber.
3   picture alliance / Baltimore Sun / Denise Sanders.
4   Public Art Fund / Go Sugimoto.
5   Screenshot Instagram / @banksy, post from June 9, 2020, accessed July 1, 2023.

ANNA YEBOAH

(De)Colonial Berlin

Spatializations of German Colonialism

For me as a Black woman[1] in Germany, right-wing spaces unfold more quickly, more frequently, and sometimes more unexpectedly than for the white majority society. More precisely, depending on whom I encounter, these spaces can arise around me out of the blue. Leaving my house, my mere existence in public space is an irritation for many—and sometimes even a provocation for a society that has constructed whiteness as the standard and stubbornly clings to it.

I am often in Brandenburg, in an area called Oderbruch to be specific. In the summer, when the weather is nice, the supermarket parking lot in Neuhardenberg is sometimes filled with circular corrals of cars whose owners easily indicate their state of mind by large stickers on the hood or by certain combinations of numbers and letters on the license plate. I go shopping there, but never alone. I cross the parking lot by the quickest route to the entrance, always dead straight—and thus without a shopping cart. I don't go to the annual fishing festival. While the decolonization of the world formally came to an end in the last century, the racism underlying colonialism tenaciously persists in Germany.

Racism lives on not only in the thoughts and actions of individuals, but above all in the institutions that have established it socially. It is precisely these—schools, security agencies, and the like—that shape my existence and that of many other non-white people in Germany. Like many others who spoke out about their experiences of racist discrimination on Twitter as part of the #MeTwo campaign, I did not receive the recommendation for a *Gymnasium* (university-track secondary school) as a pupil. As a defendant, I would be punished significantly more harshly than white defendants for the same offenses, as studies prove. Bodies such as the police or the Federal Office for the Protection of the Constitution protect people like me less than others (as demonstrated once again by the extreme right-wing activities of the Hessian police that have recently come to light).[2] The journalist Anke Schwarzer speaks in this context of the "expression of a racist knowledge prevailing in society that is effective beyond individual attitudes."[3] Among other things, as will be shown in the following, this is also the case in architecture and urban planning, in monument and reconstruction projects such as the Potsdam Garnisonkirche (Garrison Church) and the Berlin Stadtschloss (City Palace), and not least in street names, which should not be underestimated as instruments of history policy and remembrance culture. The connections between the overt racism of Neuhardenberg parking-lot Nazis and educated trivializers of German colonialism in Berlin-Mitte are closer than the latter believe.

In Potsdam

In Potsdam, a building is currently being reconstructed that stands for the ghostly pair of militarism and imperialism like no other in Germany: the Garnisonkirche. Built between 1730 and 1735 after plans by architect Johann Philipp Gerlach, the church was badly damaged at the end of World War II and the ruins were finally demolished in 1968. In GDR times, the church was considered a "symbol of German militarism"[4] due to its popularity in nationalist, anti-democratic, and right-wing extremist circles. Here, in 1900, German soldiers sent to China during the Boxer Rebellion were sworn to a war of exploitation that cost the lives of numerous civilians. On March 21, 1933, the site became the infamous backdrop for the closing of ranks between Hitler and Hindenburg (fig. 1), and thus a symbol of the alliance between National Socialism and conservatism.[5] The reconstruction of the church was pushed in the 1980s by the historical revisionist initiative Traditionsgemeinschaft Potsdamer Glockenspiel e. V. and its then chairman Max Klaar, a right-wing extremist former Federal Army officer. Klaar not only had the glockenspiel of the Garnisonkirche rebuilt and officially presented to the city of Potsdam in a ceremony in 1991, but also collected six million euros for the complete reconstruction of the church—but please "not for one in which gays are married or conscientious objectors are counseled."[6] Klaar, who was classified as a right-wing extremist by the federal defense minister, ended his involvement in the reconstruction of the Garnisonkirche in 2015 because the aims of the Potsdam Garnisonkirche Foundation, founded in 2008 to use the site as an international reconciliation

1 On the "Day of Potsdam," March 21, 1933, on the occasion of the opening of the Reichstag, there is a handshake between Hindenburg and Hitler in front of the Garnisonkirche in the presence of the Reichswehr, the imperial army. Here, Hitler and the newly appointed Minister of Propaganda Goebbels staged the "reconciliation of the old with the young Germany" at a traditional site of Prussian history.

2   Paul Carl Leygebe, Tobacco College, 1709/10, oil on canvas, 130×166 cm, Neues Palais (New Palace) in Potsdam, showing the Tobacco College of King Frederick I in Prussia (1657–1713) in the Drap d'or Chamber of the Berlin Palace with Black Servants.

center, ran counter to his historical revisionist goals. Nevertheless, his decades-long efforts fell on fertile ground. Meanwhile, the reconstruction project has the support of a broad coalition in the churches, politics, business, and the public. The reconstruction of the tower of the Garnisonkirche is currently taking place and is scheduled for completion in 2024.

On August 9, 2018, Philipp Oswalt, Professor of Architectural Theory and Design at the University of Kassel, published an open letter addressed to the scientific advisory board of the Potsdam Garnisonkirche Foundation and, in particular, its chairman Paul Nolte,[7] in which he explains why the Garnisonkirche "for all its appreciation of Gerlach's architecture – [cannot] be primarily a place of pride for our society, but a place of shame and atonement."[8] Oswalt emphasizes the role of the Garnisonkirche not only in the Boxer Rebellion, but also in the genocide of the Herero and Nama in the early twentieth century in the colony of German Southwest Africa. In both cases, officers and soldiers of the Potsdam garrison were involved, but: "The role of the Garnisonkirche in blessing and paying homage to the German participants and the 'moral' support on the part of the church for these crimes have not yet been dealt with and require research. This has not yet been mentioned in the Foundation's historical accounts."[9]

In Berlin-Friedrichstadt and Groß-Friedrichsburg (in present-day Ghana)

When I cycle to and from work, I cross ~~Mohren~~straße ("Moor" Street, respectfully referred to as M-Straße) in Berlin-Mitte twice a day. The origin and naming of the street dates back to before 1700 and thus to the heyday of the first Electorate of Brandenburg colony in Africa—Groß-Friedrichsburg, a Prussian fort on the coast of what is now Ghana, of which I am a citizen in addition to being a German citizen. I saw the small cellars where a total of about 19,000 people[10] were imprisoned and tortured before being shipped to Central America. A dense black mass remained of them, covering the floor of the cellars like soft screed. I stood on a molasses of blood and human feces that had fossilized over the centuries.

3   The equestrian statue of the Great Elector Frederick William of Brandenburg by Andreas Schlüter was erected on the *Lange Brücke* (today's *Rathausbrücke*) in Berlin in 1703. Thus it stood prominently between the Berlin Stadtschloss, Cathedral and *Marstall* (in the background). It depicts the Great Elector holding a lowered scepter and four allegorical slave figures at the base, representing the defeated enemies Poland, Sweden, France, and the Ottoman Empire.

Among the European nobility during the seventeenth and eighteenth centuries, it was considered particularly chic to keep Black servants at court (fig. 2). The underage boys from Groß-Friedrichsburg who were enslaved and taken to the residence of the Prussian King Frederick I are said to have lived in this street of the newly developing Berlin-Friedrichstadt, which explains the name. The naming of the street thus not only stands for a degrading designation of Black people, but is also closely linked to the local history of enslavement and forced labor. The early triangular trade between Africa, Europe, and America was a profitable business for the Prussian rulers. The Brandenburg-African Company, founded in Groß-Friedrichsburg solely for overseas trade, was the first German joint stock company; at times it recorded profit margins of over 400 % and enabled the Hohenzollerns to redesign their Berlin residence, the Stadtschloss, with the most costly renovation work to date. The elaborate Baroque facade, which was reconstructed by 2020, was also created in the course of this work. Andreas Schlüter, who was entrusted with the extension as the palace architect, also designed the equestrian statue of Frederick William, the father of Frederick I, which stood opposite the palace until the middle of the Second World War (fig. 3). It shows the *Kurfürst* (Elector) on horseback with a lowered scepter. Below him, at the four corners of the pedestal, four chained slaves are writhing, allegorically representing the defeated enemies with whom the ruler fought wars: Poland and Sweden, France and the Ottoman Empire.

Particularly painful and humiliating for a daily passerby like me is the fact that in 1991 the name of the subway station was changed to M*****straße, although the station was originally called Kaiserhof from 1908 to 1950 and after World War II bore the name of communist politicians: Thälmannplatz from 1950, Otto-Grotewohl-Straße from 1986. May Ayim, Afro-German activist and author, wrote about this: "The renaming of the East Berlin subway station 'Thälmannstraße' to 'M*****straße' is a sure sign that even in the highest white ranks of the new republic, racist language and corresponding thinking are tolerated and handed down."[11] Ayim describes here a gloomy vision of the future that has unfortunately been confirmed time and again.

The "M-Straße," as it has been called in discrimination-sensitive linguistic usage for years, is one of many streets or places in Berlin and Germany that until recently bore an unacceptable, racist name or were dedicated to colonial perpetrators such as Adolf Lüderitz, Gustav Nachtigal, or Carl Peters.

In Berlin, these streets were preferentially located in the "African Quarter" in Wedding (Mitte district). The quarter is one of the oldest and largest neighborhoods in Germany, where the streets were named after people and events of German colonial history. At the same time, it was a *Flächendenkmal* (area monument) that celebrated German colonial rule through its names.[12]

In 2020, the Berlin Street Law regulations were specifically expanded to allow for "references to colonialism, insofar as the streets were named after pioneers and advocates of colonialism, slavery and racist-imperialist ideologies or after places, things, events, organizations, symbols, terms or similar related to this" to be a supplementary reason for renaming, besides positive references to regimes of injustice during National Socialism and the GDR or other anti-democratic contents.[13] In the aftermath of this change, the district assembly decided to rename the infamous M-Straße, igniting populist newspaper debates and right-wing agitation against the critical reappraisal of German colonial history. More than 1,100 legal objections, of which only thirty were eligible, were issued in local courts to prevent the implementation of the new name of Anton-Wilhelm-Amo-Straße. The same applies to the African Quarter where critical walking tours by civil society groups often get harassed and concerted legal actions try to delay the official renaming procedures—without success: since December 2, 2022 Manga-Bell-Platz and Cornelius-Fredericks-Straße commemorate anti-colonial resistance fighters and thus reverse the quarter's bitter claim into one that speaks of empowerment and liberation.

In Berlin-Treptow

With colonialism and nationalism, binary models of power and identity were established, discriminatorily dividing people into "belonging" and "foreign." The narrative of a culturally and ethnically homogeneous national collective remains intact—and over time took many forms that are still ubiquitous in the age of human rights. Historian Anja Laukötter describes in a text on the early history of "Völkerkunde" (a dated term for ethnology) that the museum institutionalized the encounter with the "other": "It trained a specific form of seeing based on the distinction between 'own' and 'foreign,' thus reiterating a colonial worldview based not only on difference but also on notions of superiority and inferiority."[14] An extreme version of this form of presentation can be found in the so-called "Völkerschauen" (human zoos) which appeared at about the same time as the "Völkerkundemuseen" (ethnological museums)—in which people from Africa and other parts of the world were presented like animals in a zoo, sometimes even alongside animals. An example of this is the German Colonial Exhibition, held in Berlin Treptower Park in 1896, which laid the foundation for the establishment of the German Colonial Museum that existed until 1915 and whose collection is now held in the Humboldt Forum.[15]

The director of the Africa and Oceania Department of the Royal Museum of Ethnology, Felix von Luschan, also sat on the board of the German Colonial Exhibition. In his time, he began to build a collection of skulls that would later be taken over by the Nazi eugenicist Eugen Fischer and thus became the basis of the pseudo-scientific National Socialist racial ideology. Currently, it is believed that there are about 8,000 skeletons, skulls, and other "human remains" in the Charité's (Berlin university hospital) repositories—a large part of it in the holdings of the Stiftung Preußischer Kulturbesitz (Prussian Cultural Heritage Foundation, SPK). In response to an inquiry by the politician Clara Herrmann (Green Party) in 2015, the SPK described the body parts as a "still indispensable part of the collections" that had a "high scientific knowledge value."[16] Felix von Luschan had also understood the captured humans presented at the colonial exhibition in Treptower Park as "rich material"[17] with great knowledge potential that needed to be measured and documented.

Von Luschan was by no means an isolated misguided individual with his attitude. Such objectifications of Black people can also be found in the first third of the nineteenth century, for example in Georg Wilhelm Friedrich Hegel's *Lectures on the Philosophy of History*. The German philosopher was of the opinion that "in the *Negroes* … nothing resembling the human … can be found."[18]

Today there is—rightly—a lot of movement and the postcolonial discourse made its way into the mainstream. In a recent interview in the cultural and social magazine *Dummy*, which bears the title *Dirty Kant und Flegel Hegel: Wie deutsche Philosophen den Rassismus salonfähig machten* (*Dirty Kant and Ruffian Hegel: How German Philosophers Made Racism Acceptable*), the German philosopher Rolf Elberfeld calls for rethinking the Enlightenment and dealing with its unpleasant facets in order to understand exactly at which points Hegel's or Kant's ways of thinking could lead to the devaluation of people.[19] What does it mean, not least against this background, when complete strangers run their fingers through my curls, as happens regularly on the bus or in bars? I get scared. I am not only frightened by the unexpected assault on my body, I am also frightened by this carefree gesture of superiority—by the familiar and unreflective curiosity that still stops at nothing and no one.

In Berlin-Mitte

The Humboldt Forum, containing the museums within the Berlin Stadtschloss, was opened digitally in 2020 and became accessible to the general public in 2021, with a new decorative facade on the outside, the non-European collections including those of former Prussian rulers on the inside, and a replica cross on the domed roof. Previously stored and displayed in remote Berlin-Dahlem, the SPK's non-European collections are among the most extensive and important ethnological collections in the world, although only a small percentage of the approximately 500,000 objects have ever been on public display. With the move to the reconstructed palace, the collection returns to its first presentation site in the center of Berlin. The SPK sees the Hohenzollern Chamber of Wonders as the historical starting point of the Humboldt Forum and postulates on its homepage that "the visions of the former Berlin Kunstkammer" will once again be felt "as a place for exploring the world."[20]

The completion and opening of the palace replica coincides with the hundredth anniversary of the end of German colonial rule. Around the same time, in 2018, a study entitled *The Restitution of African Cultural Heritage – Toward a New Relational Ethics*, commissioned by French President Emmanuel Macron and written by the French art historian Bénédicte Savoy, who teaches at the Technical University of Berlin, and Felwine Sarr, a Senegalese economist and professor at the Senegalese University Gaston Berger in Saint-Louis, was published in France.[21] Adopting a hitherto unknown radicalism, the report recommended that the French state permanently return African objects. A year earlier, in 2017, during a speech at the University of Ouagadougou, Burkina Faso, Macron had surprisingly promised that France would restitute African cultural heritage within the next five years.[22]

The French paradigm shift in dealing with cultural heritage located in Europe has caught the future operators of the Humboldt Forum off guard. Bénédicte Savoy was also a member of the Humboldt Forum's expert commission until she resigned in protest in June 2017. She accused the founders of the Humboldt Forum of "colonial amnesia"—and criticized Angela Merkel for the lack of support for the numerous initiatives of the African diaspora in Germany.[23] To this day, the SPK resists the transferability of the French report to German conditions, although some efforts have been made to keep up with the European partners. In 2018 the German art historian and professor emeritus at the Humboldt University in Berlin Horst Bredekamp, who together with SPK President Hermann Parzinger and Neil MacGregor held the founding directorship of the Humboldt Forum, announced in all seriousness in a radio interview on *Deutschlandfunk Kultur* that the German collections had been created in an "Enlightenment tradition" and there had been no colonial spirit in the museums of the German Empire. Meanwhile, the first twenty Benin Bronzes were returned by the end of 2022.[24]

Decolonization, now

Hardly any cultural-political topic has gained as much presence in recent years in Germany as the country's participation in European colonialism, a discussion of which had been suppressed for decades. More and more museums, cities and federal states are taking up the cause of decolonization. This is necessary, because the German Reich not only bequeathed direct responsibility for colonial-historical regimes of injustice, especially in Africa, to its legal successor, the Federal Republic of Germany. Like other European countries, it has itself developed over centuries into a racist colonial state, the legacy of which continues to be felt in perpetual exclusions and unequal treatment of people in domestic and foreign policy. The legacy of colonialism is omnipresent and can no longer be ignored. Under the euphemistic title "Colonial Heritage," the new federal government speaks for the first time in its coalition agreement of the need to "press ahead with coming to terms with colonial history."[25] However, the lack of an unambiguous classification of colonialism as a comprehensive and continuing system of injustice is a serious problem. Accordingly, the governing coalition lists only a self-determined selection of individual measures that cannot do justice to the overall social dimension of the task. It lacks a responsible, holistic approach.

Pressure on the Humboldt Forum has also increased noticeably in the wake of the Savoy and Sarr report, leading to new admissions by all institutions involved. Monika Grütters (Christian Democrats), Minister of State for Culture and Media, in collaboration with Michelle Müntefering

4   The reconstructed Berlin Stadtschloss in May 2020.

(Social Democrats), Minister of State for International Cultural Policy, wrote a guest article in the *FAZ* newspaper in December 2018 calling for "striking steps": "It is absolutely indisputable that looted human remains do not belong in European repositories, but in the hands of their descendants,"[26] the two write—and even put on paper the otherwise meticulously circumnavigated word "restitutions." Unfortunately, they have not matched words with deeds so far. In the 2019 budget law, a budget was quickly released for Müntefering's cultural department for the creation of an Agency for International Museum Cooperation, which is to promote exhibition cooperation and possible restitution processes.

The erection of the dome cross on the Berlin Stadtschloss, which was forcefully disputed and seriously questioned, was nevertheless completed (fig. 4). "Nervousness among political decision-makers" was "excessive because of the colonialism debate," said Bredekamp in an interview with *Herder Korrespondenz*.[27] Shortly thereafter, SPK President Hermann Parzinger spoke out, first with the idea of setting up an aid fund to support African museums, and a few days later with the idea of setting up a silence room for colonial injustice in the palace.[28] After all the failures of the last hundred years, the suggestion that the Stadtschloss should continue to be silent about colonial crimes seems downright cynical.

And yet the hope remains that silence will cease and action will begin. It is naive to believe that the reconstructed Hohenzollern Palace, of all places, was to be the stumbling block that set German decolonization in motion. This process of coming to terms with colonial racism has always been, and will continue to be, carried out by active citizenship, here and in the former colonies. The real confrontation awaits elsewhere anyway, namely the painstaking work of understanding, apologizing, and making amends. It will take longer than the reconstruction of a castle and require much greater political will. But above all, such a confrontation will not take place without bravery and civil courage. The Federal Republic of Germany will face up to its history if we force it to, and not only in the cultural sphere, but also and above all in education, domestic, and foreign policy.

The author would like to thank the decolonial and Black self-organizations, without whose work this text, as well as the positive developments described in it, would not have been possible.
The essay was first published in German in *ARCH+*, no. 235 (2019): "Rechte Räume – Bericht einer Europareise," 226–231, and has been updated for this volume.

1   "Black" is capitalized in the following to make clear that it is a political identity, a constructed pattern of attribution, and not a real characteristic attributable to the color of the skin.

2   See Jolls and Sunstein 2006. For a judge's perspective, see Bennett 2010.

3   Schwarzer 2018.

4   Cf. Grünzig 2017.

5   Cf. Trüby 2018.

6   Quoted from Weidner 2012.

7   Oswalt 2018.

8   Oswalt 2018.

9   Oswalt 2018.

10   Weindl 2001, 67.

11   Ayim 1993, 215.

12   Note from the *ARCH+* editors: Another glaring example is the streets around the Asian Museum in Dahlem, which opened in 1914. In their book on the history of Berlin museums, Hans Georg Hiller von Gaertringen and Katrin Hiller von Gaertringen (2014, 130) write: "In 1900, the colonial powers joined forces to put down the freedom efforts of the 'Boxer Rebellion' in China with military force. The dubious enterprise was commemorated in 1906 with the naming of three streets in Dahlem: The imperial gunboat 'Iltis' (Iltisstraße) under its commander Wilhelm Lans (Lansstraße) had successfully stormed Fort Taku (Takustraße) not far from Beijing in 1900. It was within this area, of all places, that the general director of the Prussian Art Collections, Wilhelm Bode, planned an 'Asian Museum' in 1907 – which was to pay tribute not least to Chinese culture."

13   Senatsverwaltung 2020, 2 (2) c).

14   Laukötter 2014, 238.

15   For its history, see Hiller von Gaertringen and Hiller von Gaertringen 2014, 151 ff.

16   Abgeordnetenhaus Berlin vom 7. Juli 2015, 17. Wahlperiode, Drucksache 17/16583.

17   Felix von Luschan: *Deutschland und seine Kolonien im Jahre 1896: Amtlicher Bericht über die erste Deutsche Kolonial-Ausstellung*, ed. by Graf v. Schweinitz et al., Berlin 1897, quoted from Heller and Peşmen 2018.

18   Hegel 1837, 90 (emphasis by the author).

19   Seufert 2018, 94.

20   Humboldt Forum 2019.

21   See Sarr and Savoy 2018, 54 ff.

22   Sarr and Savoy 2018, 1.

23   Sarr and Savoy 2018, 15.

24   Roelcke 2018.

25   Koalitionsvertrag 2021–2025 zwischen der Sozialdemokratischen Partei Deutschlands (SPD), Bündnis 90 / die Grünen und den Freien Demokraten (FDP), Berlin, December 7, 2021, https://www.spd.de/fileadmin/ Dokumente/Koalitionsvertrag/Koalitionsvertrag_2021-2025.pdf (accessed June 28, 2023).

26   Grütters and Müntefering 2018.

27   Cf. Wiegelmann 2019, 19.

28   "Koloniales Erbe" 2018; "Gedenkraum" 2019.

Bibliography

Ayim, May. 1993. "Das Jahr 1990: Heimat und Einheit aus afro-deutscher Perspektive." In Ika Hügel et al., eds., *Entfernte Verbindungen: Rassismus, Antisemitismus, Klassenunterdrückung*, 206–20. Berlin: Orlanda Frauenverlag.

Bennett, Mark W. 2010. "Unraveling the Gordian Knot of Implicit Bias in Jury Selection." *Harvard Law & Policy Review* 4, no. 1 (Winter): 149–71.

"Gedenkraum für koloniales Unrecht im Humboldt Forum gefordert." 2019. *WDR*, January 3, 2019, www1.wdr.de/kultur/kulturnachrichten/humboldt-forum-parzinger-gedenkraum-100.html (accessed February 25, 2019).

Grünzig, Matthias. 2017. *Für Deutschtum und Vaterland: Die Potsdamer Garnisonkirche im 20. Jahrhundert.* Berlin: Metropol.

Grütters, Monika, and Michelle Müntefering. 2018. "Eine Lücke in unserem Gedächtnis." *Frankfurter Allgemeine Zeitung*, December 15, 2018.

Hegel, Georg Wilhelm Friedrich. 1837. *Vorlesungen über die Philosophie der Geschichte.* Georg Friedrich Wilhelm Hegel's Werke, vol. 9. Berlin: Duncker & Humblot.

Heller, Lydia, and Azadê Peşmen. 2018. "Über die rassistischen Wurzeln von Wissenschaft." *Deutschlandfunk*, December 25, 2018, www.deutschlandfunk.de/rassendenken-teil-1-ueber-die-rassistischenwurzeln-von.740.de.html?dram:article_id=436585 (accessed February 25, 2019).

Hiller von Gaertringen, Hans Georg, and Katrin Hiller von Gaertringen. 2014. *Eine Geschichte der Berliner Museen in 227 Häusern.* Berlin: Deutscher Kunstverlag.

Humboldt Forum im Berliner Schloss. 2019. "Das Prinzip Kunstkammer". www.humboldtforum.com/de/inhalte/humboldt-forum (accessed February 29, 2019).

Jolls, Christine, and Cass R. Sunstein. 2006. "The Law of Implicit Bias." *California Law Review* 94, no. 4 (July): 969–96.

"Koloniales Erbe: Parzinger fordert Strukturfonds für afrikanische Museen." 2018. *Tagesspiegel*, December 30, 2018, www.tagesspiegel.de/kultur/koloniales-erbe-parzinger-fordert-strukturfonds-fuer-afrikanische-museen/23814546.html (accessed February 25, 2019).

Laukötter, Anja. 2014. "Das Völkerkundemuseum." In Jürgen Zimmerer, ed., *Kein Platz an der Sonne: Erinnerungsorte der deutschen Kolonialgeschichte*, 231–43. Bonn: Campus.

Oswalt, Philipp. 2018. "Offener Brief an Prof. Dr. Paul Nolte", August 9, 2018, www.baunetz.de/dl/2303029/Schreiben_Oswalt_Beirat_Garnisonkirche_180810.pdf (accessed August 9, 2018).

Roelcke, Eckhard. 2018. "Bredekamp widerspricht Savoys Empfehlungen: 'Ich lehne diese Argumentation der Gleichsetzerei ab'." *Deutschlandfunk Kultur*, November 26, 2018, www.deutschlandfunkkultur.de/bredekamp-widerspricht-savoys-empfehlungen-ich-lehne-diese.100.html (accessed January 29, 2019).

Sarr, Felwine, and Bénédicte Savoy. 2018. *The Restitution of African Heritage: Toward a New Relational Ethics.* November 2018, restitutionreport2018.com/sarr_savoy_en.pdf (accessed January 29, 2019).

Schwarzer, Anke. 2018. "Das verdrängte Verbrechen: Plädoyer für eine Dekolonialisierung der Bundesrepublik." *Blätter für deutsche und internationale Politik* 6: 85–92.

Senatsverwaltung für Umwelt, Verkehr und Klimaschutz. 2020. "Ausführungsvorschriften zu § 5 des Berliner Straßengesetzes (AV Benennung)". December 1, 2020, https://www.berlin.de/sen/uvk/_assets/verkehr/service/rechtsvorschriften/amtsblatt_av_gur5.pdf?ts=1683622437 (accessed June 19, 2023).

Seufert, Jonas. 2018. ""Wir müssen die Aufklärung noch einmal neu denken" / Dirty Kant und Flegel Hegel: Ein Gespräch über den Rassismus unserer großen Philosophen." *Dummy* 61 (December): 92–94.

Trüby, Stephan. 2018. "Wir haben das Haus am rechten Fleck." *Frankfurter Allgemeine Sonntagszeitung*, April 8, 2018.

Weidner, Anselm. 2012. "Kirchlicher Glanz für militärisches Gloria." *taz*, October 13, 2012, www.taz.de/!550903/ (accessed March 21, 2018).

Weindl, Andrea. 2001. *Die Kurbrandenburger im 'atlantischen System,' 1650–1720.* Arbeitspapiere zur Lateinamerikaforschung II-03, Cologne: Universität zu Köln. https://lateinamerika.phil-fak.uni-koeln.de/fileadmin/sites/aspla/bilder/arbeitspapiere/weindl.pdf (accessed February 25, 2019).

Wiegelmann, Lucas. 2019. "'Radikaler Laizismus erzeugt neue Probleme': Ein Gespräch mit dem Kunsthistoriker Horst Bredekamp." *Herder Korrespondenz* 1 (January): 17–20.

Image Sources

1   Photo by Georg Pahl © Bundesarchiv.

2   https://de.wikipedia.org/wiki/Datei:Paul_Carl_Leygebe_-_Tabakskollegium_of_Frederick_I_-_WGA12950.jpg.

3   Photo from 1938 © Bundesarchiv.

4   Photo by Dmicha, https://commons.wikimedia.org/wiki/File:DomSchlossRathaus.JPG; licensed under CC BY-SA 4.0: https://creativecommons.org/licenses/by-sa/4.0/deed.en.

REINHARD BERNBECK

Past and Present German Colonialism

From a Prisoner-of-War Camp of the First World War to the Refugees of the Year 2015

History, Memory, Politics

Collective memory in Germany has always been complex because of overlaps of a political and chronological nature. The Nazi period has acted like a wall against the historical constellations leading up to these twelve years of dictatorship,[1] especially the period of the German Empire and its colonialism between 1871 and 1918. I am concerned in this paper with a late episode of this period, which I contextualize with a preface. In doing so, I address German collective memory, from 1990 backwards, ending with the forgotten history of a Muslim prisoner-of-war camp in World War I.

As is well known, the two Germanies "re-united" thirty years ago. Between 1945 and 1990 when reunification took place, East and West Germany developed radically antagonistic understandings of the same national past.[2] Repercussions of these distinct collective memories reach into the present, into the politics of space and city planning in the middle of Berlin, an issue to which I turn at the end of this paper.

The East German past was officially an antifascist, heroic one. The ruling elite wanted to turn concentration camps into "positive heritage," as Lynn Meskell calls it,[3] by emphasizing solely the victims who had resisted the Nazis.[4] According to that narrative, the resisters were communists and socialists, not Jews, Roma and Sinti, homosexuals, or non-European minorities. The aesthetics of the memorial at the former Buchenwald concentration camp underscores these tendencies. The enforced official discourse produced an unfortunate backlash. Some East Germans started to be attracted by neo-Nazi ideas as a source of opposition to this single-party regime.

In sharp contrast, West German elites of the 1950s suppressed almost completely any discussion about the Nazi period and the Holocaust[5] until the Auschwitz trials in Frankfurt in the 1960s and the Eichmann trial in Jerusalem in 1961.[6] Other landmarks in the development of West German collective memory were the genuflection of then chancellor Willy Brandt at the memorial for the uprising in the Warsaw Ghetto and president Richard von Weizsäcker's 1985 speech commemorating Germany's victims of WWII.[7] Such events finally led to lifting the deadly silence about the Nazi past in West Germany and a fundamental change in the dominant discourse about Germany's horrendous past, accompanied by a sharp dispute between the post- and pre-war generations.[8] Under these conditions, reunification in 1990 was no easy task in the sphere of memory politics.[9]

The formation of the right-wing "Pegida" movement, mainly but not solely in former East Germany, the so-called "Patriotic Europeans against the Islamization of the Occident," as well as the racist right-wing nationalist party "Alternative für Deutschland," have to be seen in this context. Germany has reached a point where public discourse openly debates the advantages and dangers of past dictatorial rule. The Nazi period plays a prominent role in these reflections. The political right uses allusions to the Nazis to break taboos.[10]

Other right-wing populists follow a strategy of belittling rather than admiring the twelve years of Nazism. For example, the then chairman of the Alternative für Deutschland party, Alexander Gauland, has said in 2018 that "Hitler and the Nazis are just a speck of bird shit in over 1,000 years of successful German history."[11] These comments by the head of an extremist right-wing party have led to widespread reactions in both the former western and eastern Germany. However, to my knowledge, no one objected to the reference to "1,000 years of successful history." There is a convenient silence in the responses that includes forgetfulness about a ruthless colonialist past and connections between colonialism and the Nazis' wars of aggression.[12]

Public discourse was and still is so preoccupied with the role of the Holocaust, the SS, and Hitler that constellations of slightly earlier times, when Germany had colonialist aspirations, remain widely forgotten. Only in recent years, for example, has the genocide against the Herero and Nama in Namibia in the first years of the twentieth century become a prominent topic in politics because of disputes over reparations.[13] But Germany's colonialism also stretched into other directions. The empire was deeply involved in the late Ottoman Empire's Armenian genocide during the First World War. The German role in the latter atrocity remains deeply buried under various attempts to "come to terms" with the Holocaust, but politicians and intellectuals prefer to accuse Turkey of silencing this murderous episode rather than analyzing the details of Germany's involvement.[14]

Prisoner-of-War and Indoctrination Camp: Wünsdorf

This general memory constellation prevailed in July 2015, when a team of archaeologists from the Freie Universität Berlin started an excavation in the village of Wünsdorf, 40 kilometers south of Berlin. The site of the excavation had been a prisoner-of-war camp in World War I. This "Half Moon" camp, established in 1915, had been set up solely to house Muslim prisoners of war of Germany's enemies, the so-called Triple Entente of Tsarist Russia, Great Britain, and France.[15] The reasons for the establishment of this camp were complex. One was clearly racism: the British and French powers urged the German government not to incarcerate their white officers together with soldiers from the colonies—if the Germans did so, they would retaliate by doing the same to German PoWs.

The camp was also established as part of a much larger strategy dreamt up by an archaeologist who specialized in Western Asia, Max von Oppenheim. As a young adult with aspirations to enter the diplomatic service, Oppenheim had experienced racism himself. As a so-called half-Jew, he was not allowed to pursue a diplomatic career despite sufficient qualifications. This was the case even though his family, from the Oppenheim bank dynasty, was extremely well-connected in the political establishment. Oppenheim tried to further his diplomatic ambitions by working at the German Consulate in Cairo as an "attaché" from 1896 to 1909, but without any specific tasks. He learned to speak Arabic fluently, travelled widely, and sent reports to the Kaiser, who enjoyed reading them.[16] In 1899, claiming to be doing ethnographic research, Oppenheim travelled from Cairo to northern Syria and Mesopotamia. The trip was actually at the behest of the Deutsche Bank, which was the main source of finance for the *Baghdadbahn* (the Berlin–Baghdad railway).[17] Oppenheim was among the main advisers who were supposed to identify the best route for the railway.

This activity had long-term consequences. The route he proposed is largely that of the present-day railway, which is also the border between Syria and Turkey with its recently built wall, hundreds of kilometers long. The railway skirts Tell Halaf where Oppenheim himself conducted major excavations from 1911 to 1913. His findings there would eventually make him a well-known archaeological researcher.[18] In his triple role as consular attaché, spy, and archaeologist, Oppenheim took the initiative immediately after the start of World War I to suggest the establishment of the "Intelligence Bureau for the East," with a goal of subverting French and British colonial rule and fostering political instability among Germany's enemies in the First World War.[19] Together with General von Moltke and the Turkish General Enver, Oppenheim pushed for a politics of Muslim insurrection from Egypt to India in order to keep British military forces busy far away from the main WWI battlefields.

Among other activities, an expedition to Iran and Afghanistan was organized by Werner Otto von Hentig and Oskar von Niedermayer. In Iran, undercover agent Wilhelm Waßmuß was tasked with inciting guerilla warfare by Bakhtiyari and Qashqai nomads against British forces.[20] A larger contingent went on to Kabul to try to convince the Afghan Emir Habibullah to attack India (which at that time included present-day Pakistan) under a unit of Ottoman and German military officers. Habibullah remained undecided, and this whole mission failed. The contingent in Iraq consisted in part of Oppenheim's fellow archaeologists, for example, Conrad Preusser, Friedrich Wetzel, Oskar Reuther, and Walter Bachmann.[21]

Oppenheim's intelligence bureau was not content with initiatives aimed at armed uprisings in regions the British and Tsarist regimes tried to occupy. The unit also convinced the Ottoman Sultan Mehmet V to declare jihad or holy war against the Triple Entente.[22] The Sultan had the official right to declare jihad in a fatwa because of his claim to be not just a sultan but also the Muslim caliph, that is, the religious leader of all Sunni Muslims. This claim was based on the idea of "pan-Islamism," a movement that had become fashionable at the end of the nineteenth century as an oppositional force against the increasing grip of European colonial powers on populations across the Islamic world, from Algeria to the Indian subcontinent.[23]

During his time in Cairo, Oppenheim had befriended some major proponents of pan-Islamism at Al-Azhar University, Muhammad Abduh and Rashid Rida, and he tried to convince Egyptian and Ottoman politicians as well as academic orientalists in Germany that Germany was an ideal protector of an Istanbul-based caliphate. The mobilization of major contingents of Muslim soldiers by the Triple Entente certainly helped to fuel the Sultan's policies and Oppenheim's cause. Colonial soldiers fought a war the reasons for which must have remained entirely unintelligible to them, and hundreds of thousands died.[24]

In this situation, Oppenheim dreamt up yet another way to support Germany's war interests. He made a successful proposal to the foreign office to unite all Muslim prisoners of war in one camp and to build a mosque there.[25] He saw in this plan a great potential to promote pan-Islamism further, by bringing together Sunni and Shi'a as well as Deobandi Muslims from the Indian subcontinent. The main aim was not just an inversion of political allegiance, but much

1   Half Moon PoW camp in Wünsdorf with the mosque in the foreground and barracks at the back.

more: to fanaticize the prisoners so that they would commit acts of sabotage behind the military fronts of Germany's and the Ottoman Empire's enemies, or so that they could at least be inserted into the Ottoman army to fight against the Entente. As a perceptive commentator recently remarked, this was the "first state-organized terror camp" in the world.[26]

The camp was erected in the aforementioned village of Wünsdorf. The mosque, the oldest in Germany, was a calculated abuse of religious symbolism for military purposes (fig. 1). Architectural historian Martin Gussone has analyzed the mosque's stylistic elements, which combine Spanish-Islamic arches from the Alhambra, alternating colored bands in red and white that mimic the so-called tomb mosques from the Mamluk period in Cairo, an Ottoman-style minaret, and Mughal-style Indian arches in the area for ablutions in the courtyard.[27] Since the prisoners came from widely separated places such as Senegal, India, and even beyond there to the east, the architects concocted this curious mix of visual cues. Of particular importance is the effect of the main prayer hall, a ground plan that clearly alludes to the Dome of the Rock in Jerusalem. This octagonal structure is Islam's second most holy place, and the structural reference to it was surely intentionally chosen by the two people who advised on the design of the mosque: a Tunisian propagandist named Sahil al-Sharif and Max von Oppenheim himself.[28]

On the other hand, the mimbar inside the building where the imam gives the sermon looks, according to a sarcastic comment, very much like the interior fittings of a classicist German protestant church. The whole building fit well with the Orientalism of the time as well as with the European architectural eclecticism of neoclassical origin. However, if western Islamic architecture was attractive mainly to prisoners of war from French colonies, and the Egyptian or Indian elements to those from British colonies, there is nothing that would appeal directly to the Tatars from Tsarist Russia—mainly Crimea and the lower Volga region—who were held in particularly low regard by racist Germans.[29]

The mosque was not just a concealment in the form of a religious garb for politico-military goals. It was also a concealment in a much more direct way. When considering the relation between the original prototypes and the Wünsdorf mosque, the difference in building material is especially striking. On the one hand, sandstone, artistically elaborate tiles, and alabaster, on the other wooden boards. Oppenheim himself tried to sell his idea for the mosque to the war office that paid for it by claiming that it would be a cheap timber construction with adjacent possibilities for ablutions.[30] An internal document testifies that a more expensive version had been under consideration, but that the plan was to find a minimally elaborate design that would "satisfy as far as possible the senses and imagination of Muhamedan believers."[31]

In order to further this Islamization program, an imam was brought to Wünsdorf from the Ottoman Empire, and the German camp direction printed an official newspaper with the title *al Jihad* in several of the languages spoken in the camp. Preferential treatment of these prisoners had its own effects: one finds references to the fact that the material conditions of life in the camp were not as dismal as in PoW camps elsewhere. Journalists and photographers were invited to visit the Half Moon camp, in accordance with the goal of creating positive propaganda about Germany's good treatment of prisoners in general. This was an element of "privilege" to the camp: compared to many other PoW camps, this one needed to provide good services to pull the erstwhile enemy over to the German side.

The photographs of the camp, and particularly of the mosque, were turned into postcards. This mechanism deserves close analysis, and a dissertation currently underway by Ezel Güneş[32] will provide a systematic catalogue of these postcard images. Postcards functioned in certain respects like the Internet today. One needs to remember that in times of war families are often split up, resulting in a sharply increased desire to connect with those who are temporarily displaced to frontlines and in grave danger. Sending postcards was a way to maintain a connection. As a result, the camp must have been very well known both at home and on the war front, thanks to the hundreds if not thousands of postcards sent and received that are now in the archives of the Garnisonsmuseum Wünsdorf.

As an archaeologist, I see in the postcards a material record worth analyzing in several different dimensions. First, it is important to reconstruct the spots from where the photos used in the postcards were taken. In the case of views from above, the photographer was apparently located in one of the guard towers. In one photo, one can see the main gate and the tower above it, where a machine gun was installed (fig. 2). This insight became important for an explanation of some of the archaeological remains to which I return below.

A second dimension of the imagery is an unintended one. The views can help in the reconstruction of the camp's interior structure. For example, there must have been two types of standard barracks in which prisoners lived, as well as other kinds of buildings the purpose of which still eludes us. A few of them have a roof that suggests their function as kitchens. Some photos

2   Half Moon camp with barbed wire fences; the guard tower at the gate is visible at the back to the right.

show barbed wire within the camp. Apparently, prisoners were not free to move about in the camp. Oppenheim's proposal to separate the prisoners "according to religion, race and caste"[33] could be behind this fencing in of camp sections.

A third dimension of the images relates to the photographing of people. The images in which they occur can be divided into quotidian scenes and religious feasts. I discuss the quotidian ones below. Religious occasions include prayers and animal sacrifice. Some of the scenes of praying show a framing by German officers, a deliberate setting that seems odd for normal religious rituals.[34]

A Diachronic Material Assemblage: Archaeology at Wünsdorf

As clearly shown in the discussion above, Islam has a convoluted history in Berlin and its surroundings.[35] Our interest as archaeologists in this past was driven by the recognition that almost no material traces of this history remain apart from the Zehrensdorf cemetery,[36] the resting place for those Wünsdorf PoWs who perished in the nearby camp. The leading archaeologist of the State Office for Cultural Heritage Preservation in Brandenburg, Thomas Kersting, Susan Pollock, and the author therefore planned to explore whether remains of the mosque could be located in the area of the former PoW camp. Our plans for the excavations were to make a small series of soundings where we suspected the location of the mosque to be. Geophysical research carried out before our excavations had not delivered clear results.

However, in the weeks immediately before we began work, we learned that the state government planned to set up a camp for refugees on exactly the spot on which the former prisoner of war camp had stood! This was in 2015, when Chancellor Angela Merkel had temporarily opened the borders for refugees and there was a pressing need to find places for them to live. Given the new plans for Wünsdorf, we found ourselves working alongside private archaeological companies (ABD-Dressler and Archäologie Wiegmann)[37] in order to excavate the premises of the mosque and the former camp where potential archaeological remains from the First World War might be destroyed by the construction work for the new refugee camp.

Before we encountered any remains of the mosque, we had to clear thick layers of sterile sand to a depth of more than a meter below the present surface. After the removal of the mosque and barracks, major landscaping work must have been carried out. We were able to date this to the Nazi period when rows of tank garages were set up in this area. Only below the layer relating to that work did we discover a thin dark surface with impressions of footsteps (fig. 3).[38] The foundations of the mosque had been dug into that surface. The foundation trenches were filled with broken bricks, tiles and concrete from the mosque.[39] A few pieces of green and blue glass from the windows under the dome were also recovered, and we even found the remains of the chandelier in the main room.

Most noticeable were the many rusty twisted spans and bolts of the dome (fig. 4). They match exactly a technical drawing of the structure.[40] While we also recovered the lightning rod of the minaret, the exposure of a substantial walking surface of the former camp led to only one

3   Excavation team of the Freie Universität Berlin clearing a surface with the remains of the former mosque of the Half Moon camp.

4   Screws, bolts, and nails of the mosque's dome.

single personal item, a small rectangular mirror. Otherwise, the space in front of the mosque was completely empty. It is not easy to explain this situation: one would expect this to have been an area of much coming and going and of activity in general. One possibility is that this place was used for prayers and therefore was meant to be kept free of rubbish. More likely, the avoidance of the space in front of the mosque was due to the watchtower at the entry to the camp where guards with machine guns were positioned.

The archaeological excavations also reveal subsequent changes to the site that correspond to existing photographs and other information. For instance, after the war, Tatars stayed in the area, and the mosque is seen in a mid-1920s photo with trees that did not exist before—we found the traces of their roots. One enigma remains: we found no indication about why and how the mosque and the barracks were torn down. We only know that the destruction happened sometime around 1930[41] when the grounds were turned over in their entirety to the German military.

Soon after the Nazis came to power in 1933, an armored-vehicle school was built on the site with the above-mentioned garages for tanks. Remains of the massive foundations of these garages were the only material traces left from that time. Just north of the former Half Moon Camp, there are still the standing remains of two major bunker systems called Maybach I and II. The High Command of the Wehrmacht (Armed Forces) had been housed there during World War II. It was from there that the war of aggression against the Soviet Union was planned. This was the nerve center of the Wehrmacht in World War II.[42]

At the end of the war, the Soviet Army was able to take over the whole area without much damage, and its military infrastructure was directly transferred to the Soviet military. The premises were off-limits for East Germans because at least 35,000 Soviet soldiers, but at times more than double that number, were stationed there from 1945 to 1994. The relevance of this otherwise small, out-of-the-way place is clear when one knows that there was a direct train, once every week, from the small village of Wünsdorf to Moscow.[43]

In all the trenches that we excavated, traces from the Soviet occupation were obvious and showed up immediately below the surface. The material composition of these layers was strange, as we found canning jars next to the remains of tanks and ammunition. With the help of specialists, we were able to determine that the tank parts were fly-wheel elements of the treads from one of the most popular Soviet tanks called PT76 or BMP 1 (fig. 5). The pieces were partly galvanized but carelessly thrown away, like much other material of the Soviet military.[44]

The canning jars, on the other hand, fit with information that the Soviet occupation forces were mistrustful of East Germans. The area could not be accessed by local people. There were apparently Soviet plans to maintain independence from local food deliveries. Alcohol was generally forbidden.[45] However, we found not just remains of German beer bottles and a small advertisement that all date to the 1950s, but also local wine bottles. At least the officers had a very luxurious life in Wünsdorf. A movie theater, a huge swimming pool, and other facilities today slowly decay in the growing forest.

Jumping forward to the near present, it became clear that the longer we worked on the excavation, the more difficult it became to reach the site because of fences that prevented unrestricted access. One reason was that around the time we started the project, neo-Nazis carried out an arson attack on a neighboring building. Not because of our excavations in the "Mosque street" but because of the plans to construct a camp for over 1,000 asylum seekers on the spot. The planned presence of refugees led to angry responses amongst the neo-Nazi groups in Zossen, Wünsdorf, and surroundings.[46]

5   Sewage shaft, filled with parts of Soviet PMT tanks on the grounds of the Half Moon camp.

6 Containers for refugees on the grounds of the former Half Moon PoW camp (state of 2017).

What is more, among the politicians and administrators who chose the site for a camp, no one was apparently aware of the irony of putting refugees from the fallout of Islamist attacks on civilians in Syria and Afghanistan in a camp that was located exactly on the spot where one hundred years earlier the German Reich had established the first jihadist camp. Nor did they likely know that the so-called Islamic State is a movement driven by a pan-Islamist ideology that was the inspiration for Oppenheim's idea of the Intelligence Bureau for the East. Abu Bakr al-Baghdadi, the former head of the Islamic State who committed suicide in October 2019, saw himself as the contemporary caliph of all Muslims.

The refugee camp in Wünsdorf was indeed built. It consisted of identical, dark blue containers (fig. 6). The interior of these living units was divided by a long middle corridor with rooms arranged at regular intervals on both sides, similar in structure to Nazi forced labor camp barracks, the cages in Guantanamo, and other such "facilities."[47] As an architectural form, these barracks are a major framework for de-subjectivation. They suppress any individual use of space by forcing people to spend free time, *not working time*, in strongly standardized units. In the year 2019, the containers were removed again, as the number of refugees in Germany declined. Now, a barrack, several stories high, that once served to house soldiers is planned for enlargement once again by the installation of additional containers for 500 refugees.[48]

De-Subjectivation

Historical, archaeological, and present-day uses of the Wünsdorf camp ground turn the site into a landscape contaminated by the past, poisoned by a brutal heritage of two world wars and, in the case of the High Command of the Wehrmacht, a state-organized campaign of extinction. But this place is not just any piece of historically tainted ground. Paradoxically, the colonial prisoners of WWI were turned into subjects ready to give their lives for colonial overlords in a geographically and culturally inscrutable world. As soon as they had been captured by the German military, a different but equally non-understandable command of loyalty was imposed on them: to fight for their erstwhile enemies against their own former colonial masters. They received preferential treatment—to convince the PoWs to accept this radical change and to pursue a ruthless German jihadist instrumentalization, they were provided with relatively good living conditions. But at the same time, the PoWs were turned into anthropological objects.

The place also turned into a center of other colonialist-racist practices. During the war, the ethnographer Leo Frobenius opined that ethnographers would not have to travel to foreign countries any more: the "material" was just in front of their doors, on the outskirts of Berlin. People from so many different colonial origins gathered conveniently in one camp not far from the German capital were seen as a "laboratory" in which to pursue research. Artists came to make drawings of the prisoners, put together in a book by Frobenius with the title *The People's Circus of Our Enemies*,[49] very much reminiscent of the *Völkerschauen* at the turn of the century. The paradoxical nature of racist prejudice comes to the fore when one considers that Frobenius accused France and England of abusing colonial subjects, and at the same time he depicted the latter as subhuman.[50]

Physical anthropologists visited Wünsdorf and even stayed for weeks in the camp to take measurements of bodies, and especially the heads, of prisoners. The scholar Egon von Eickstädt, who worked under Felix von Luschan, noted that he painstakingly took skull measurements of sixty-eight Punjabi "Muhammedans," thirteen Garhwali, and seventy-six Sikhs, of whom he reported physical characteristics, published after the war in 1923 in the British journal *Man*. The goal was to statistically separate so-called "races," a kind of research that contributed to mass murder and the Holocaust only twenty years later.[51] Scholars of folklore forced the prisoners to dance and play German children's games, a humiliating way of "doing ethnography." Musicologists forced them to sing and play instruments.[52] Frobenius himself collected folk tales in Wünsdorf and published them, never mentioning where and under what circumstances he had documented them.[53]

Best known among these scientific and racist abuses of defenseless people are the more than 2,500 phonographic recordings made by linguists who used wax cylinders to register the sentences, poetry, and songs of the prisoners. Among the South Asian languages recorded in this way are Baluchi, Hindi, Bengali, Nepali, and Gurung.[54] Nowadays, they provide a means to study not just language, poetry, and oral history, but also the situation of the prisoners, as they sometimes made statements about their treatment in the war and in the camp.[55] For single individuals, it is sometimes even possible to trace their history relatively closely, as is the case for the Gurkha soldier Gangaram Gurung who was the painter of a number of colorful images that originally decorated a Hindu temple in one of the barracks. In one of the images, one can clearly recognize the Elephant god Ganesha with his animal, the rat.[56]

The phonographic archive includes—and in this it is exceptional—the voices of the subaltern, who speak to us even one hundred years later. However, it would be wrong to assume that the prisoners could talk freely. Often they were told which subject to speak about into a huge funnel that served as a device for recording. Still, the political dimension of some of the messages is clear.[57] Undertones in the pseudo-research reports resulting from those activities range from paternalism at best to dehumanizing racism. The privilege of becoming a jihadist was coupled with racist abuse in the process. The phonographic documentation has recently gained renewed interest because it was moved to a new building in the middle of Berlin, the so-called Humboldt Forum. I turn now from one hundred years of racism in the periphery of Berlin to the present colonialist condition at the center of the city.

Palaces and Museums as Colonialist Actants

Until the mid-twentieth century Berlin had a palace, the origins of which go back to the fifteenth century. However, only from the early eighteenth century onwards did the building with its Baroque additions become the seat of the Prussian kings, and from 1871 the residence of the German Kaiser. The palace stood on Berlin's main avenue, Unter den Linden, until 1950, when the structure, heavily bombarded and damaged during World War II, was dismantled by the socialist East German government (fig. 7). The East Germans constructed nearby the so-called *Staatsratsgebäude* and inserted into it a portal of the old palace. That was the portal from where Karl Liebknecht, the comrade of Rosa Luxemburg, had announced the founding of a socialist republic in November 1918. In the early 1970s, a new building was erected instead of the emperor's palace. This new "Palace of the Republic," as it was called, housed the East German parliament but also provided a space for public celebrations.[58]

The building had a short life: it was torn down in 2008. Politicians in the re-unified Germany and other interested parties claimed that the asbestos used in its construction could not be removed. Many East Germans did not believe that, but under the impression of this rhetoric,

Berlin, Imperial Castle (old part)   Berlin, Schloss (Alter Teil)   7

7   Berlin Schloss in ruins (old part). Postcard from c. 1951.

the German parliament decided to demolish the building and to reconstruct the palace in the state of the nineteenth century. In this way, a major symbol of an unsavory version of German socialism has been replaced with a structure that symbolizes the ruthlessly colonialist power of the pre-WWI *Kaiserreich*. Such an action could only happen in a country that has developed a highly effective mechanism to silence its colonial past.

The initiative for this curious architectural cleansing of Berlin's history came from a small number of business people, some of whom were or are of a decidedly anti-Semitic and anti-democratic persuasion.[59] They used their influence to instigate the 2002 Bundestag vote. Donations by multinational companies such as Siemens, BMW, and Thyssen allowed this group to claim international support and financial power. Resentment towards East Germany, and an urge to make a lasting victory statement over communism, were palpable motivations for this project. Instead of planning for the future needs of the city, the Bundestag decided to create an anachronistic building. Some call it an outright historical fake.

However, no German monarch can legitimately be made to live again in this concrete box with a veneer of historicizing decoration. What to do with such a retrogressive architectural colossus? A return to an imperialist past is never a simple "yes" or "no" question. Therefore, it was decided that one side of the fake palace should be modern, and the other three dummy facades. The rooms inside were also to remain largely plain although the Italian architect Frank Stella opted to reconstruct the historical dome on the western wing. One of the disputes concerns a 12m-high cross erected on top of the building. It was not part of the reconstruction plans, but when a mysterious donor coughed up the money for it, this symbol of a fundamental connection between Christianity and the state was also included.

What to do with this thing? Politicians and designers came up with the wonderful idea to move the collections of non-European origins from the ethnological museum in the southwest of Berlin as well as from other museums into the fake palace. The planning has its own winning logic and symbolism: re-erecting large-scale monarchist architecture by destroying the built environment of a regime that had just collapsed. It means elevating an architecture that is inextricably bound up with a Kaiser who was largely responsible for the start of World War I, and crowning it with Christianity's core symbol of domination. Apparently, the most celebratory heritage left behind by the Hohenzollern monarchy was colonialism. What was stolen from the colonies will now be on display in the abodes of the former thief-in-chief.[60]

And anything that is entangled with other former colonial empires can also be added to this collection. In order to justify this cultural imperialism with global reach, the palace has been re-named the Humboldt Forum after an intellectual whose research is supposedly beyond doubt, although recently criticism has emerged.[61]

The voice recordings of former prisoners-of-war from British and French colonies are also destined to move into this shell of a former palace. Collected for a "sound museum," the first step for their registration was a scientific objectification, a disregard for the personal origin of prisoners, for culture shock, and particularly for the trauma of a war fought in trenches with chemical weapons. A war fought for reasons entirely detached from any interest of the colonized soldiers themselves.[62]

Memory is always political. The official plans for the Humboldt Forum have naively assumed a coherent new "national history" of what is known as the "Berlin Republic", i.e. the reunified post-1989 Germany. However, sharp disputes over the design of this institution have led to counter-memories, most openly by organizations such as "Decolonize Berlin." On July 14, 2021, the Humboldt Forum opened its doors to the public. At the least, there are now efforts for restitution of a number of colonial objects, starting with the over 1,000 Benin bronzes that three German museums agreed to hand back to Nigeria in the summer of 2022.[63]

A Brief Summary

I started out this paper by discussing the complexities of the history of German collective memory. I tried to argue that the heavy weight of the Nazi past on collective memory has wiped out a differentiated analysis of the country's colonial past. Remembering produces amnesia in this as in many other cases. It is in such instances that archaeology takes on a role mentioned long ago by Sigmund Freud. For Freud, hidden individual memory can be brought back to the surface by way of a therapy, a purely verbal interaction. Archaeology has the same effect on collective consciousness, using practical and material means rather than discursive ones. Particularly in the realm of the archaeology of the twentieth century, a mostly dark and suppressed past re-enters the present. Its materiality creates a new configuration of collective memory.

I thank the editors of this volume for their invitation to contribute as well as for their patience with me. Susan Pollock and Ezel Güneş provided valuable critique and important information.

1   Fischer 1961.
2   Frei 1998.
3   Meskell 2002.
4   Münkler 2002; Ahbe 2007.
5   Ambros 2013; Heimannsberg and Schmidt 1992.
6   Arendt 1965; Yablonka 2012.
7   Bundespräsident 1985.
8   Jureit and Schneider 2010; Konitzer 2012.
9   Koselleck 1999; Funke 2000.
10   Kubitschek and Höcke 2014; Wildt 2017.
11   "Hitler und die Nazis sind nur ein Vogelschiss in über 1000 Jahren erfolgreicher deutscher Geschichte" (Wiederwald 2018).
12   Terkessidis 2019; see also Rothberg 2009.
13   Karch 2019.
14   Gottschlich 2015.
15   *The Halfmoon Files* 2007; Gordon 2011.
16   Gossman 2013.
17   Schöllgen 2003; Canis 2011, 48–64.
18   Cholidis and Martin 2011.
19   Oppenheim 2018.
20   Rogan 2016.
21   Andrae 1952, 238.
22   Lüdke 2005.
23   Aydın 2017.
24   For an overview, see McMeekin 2010.
25   Oppenheim 2018 [1914].
26   Maak 2015.

27 Gussone 2010.

28 Heine 1982.

29 Nagornaja 2010.

30 "Man sollte ihnen [den Kriegsgefangenen] eine kleine Moschee einrichten …, ferner eine Gelegenheit zur Verrichtung ihrer religiösen Waschungen" (Oppenheim 2018, 79).

31 Gussone 2016, 186.

32 Ezel Güneş, *Archäologie der Zossener Sonderlager für muslimische Kriegsgefangene im 1. Weltkrieg* (working title).

33 Oppenheim 2018, 85.

34 Kahleyss 2014, 86–87.

35 Yaldiz 2022.

36 Höpp 1997, 131–38.

37 See https://www.abd-dressler.de/.

38 See Dressler et al. 2017, 130–32; Kersting 2022, 330–34.

39 Bernbeck et al. 2016, 105–7.

40 Bernbeck et al. 2016, figs. 154 and 155.

41 Höpp 1996, 218.

42 Kaiser and Herrmann 2010.

43 Franke and Steinberg 2014.

44 Landesamt für Umwelt 2022.

45 Hoffmann and Stoof 2013, 164.

46 Fröhlich and Hampel 2015.

47 Bernbeck 2017, 260–72.

48 Lassiwe 2023.

49 Frobenius 1916.

50 Olusoga 2014, 259–60.

51 Preuß 2009.

52 Mahrenholz 2020.

53 Frobenius 1921.

54 Hilden 2022.

55 Berner, Hoffmann, and Lange 2011; Lange 2013.

56 Liebau 2018, 8, figure on the lower right.

57 Liebau 2018.

58 Schug 2007; Holfelder 2008, 53–66.

59 Häntzschel 2021.

60 See contributions in Sandkühler, Epple, and Zimmerer 2021.

61 Berlin postkolonial n.d.

62 Olusoga 2014.

63 Ethnologisches Museum 2022; see also Osadolor 2021.

Bibliography

Ahbe, Thomas. 2007. *Der DDR-Antifaschismus: Diskurse und Generationen – Kontexte und Identitäten: Ein Rückblick über 60 Jahre*. Texte zur politischen Bildung 39. Leipzig: Rosa Luxemburg-Stiftung Sachsen. http://www.thomas-ahbe.de/ddr-antifaschismus_%28download%29.pdf (accessed May 5, 2016).

Ambros, Peter. 2013. *Das wortreiche deutsche Schweigen*. Hamburg: Argument.

Andrae, Walter. 1952. *Babylon: Die versunkene Weltstadt und ihr Ausgräber Robert Koldewey*. Berlin: de Gruyter.

Arendt, Hannah. 1965. *Eichmann in Jerusalem: A Report on the Banality of Evil*. Rev. and enl. ed. New York: Viking Press.

Aydın, Cemil. 2017. *The Idea of the Muslim World: A Global Intellectual History*. Cambridge, MA: Harvard University Press.

Berlin postkolonial. n.d. "Störung der Totenruhe: Ein Interview mit Alexander von Humboldt." *No Humboldt 21!* https://www.no-humboldt21.de/information/humboldt/ (accessed June 8, 2022).

Bernbeck, Reinhard. 2017. *Materielle Spuren des nationalsozialistischen Terrors: Zu einer Archäologie der Zeitgeschichte*. Bielefeld: transcript.

Bernbeck, Reinhard, Torsten Dressler, Martin Gussone, Thomas Gersting, Susan Pollock, and Ulrich Wiegmann. 2016. "Wünsdorf: Archäologie der Moderne: Ausgrabungen im Gelände der Moschee und des 'Halbmondlagers' von 1915." *Brandenburgische Denkmalpflege* 2, no. 1: 99–113.

Berner, Margit, Anette Hoffmann, and Britta Lange, eds. 2011. *Sensible Sammlungen: Aus dem Anthropologischen Depot*. Hamburg: Philo Fine Arts.

Bundespräsident. 1985. *Gedenkveranstaltung im Plenarsaal des Deutschen Bundestages zum 40. Jahrestag des Endes des Zweiten Weltkrieges in Europa*. https://www.bundespraesident.de/SharedDocs/Reden/DE/Richard-von-Weizsaecker/Reden/1985/05/19850508_Rede.html (accessed June 5, 2023).

Canis, Konrad. 2011. *Der Weg in den Abgrund: Deutsche Außenpolitik 1902–1914*. Paderborn: Ferdinand Schöningh.

Cholidis, Nadia, and Lutz Martin, eds. 2011. *Die geretteten Götter aus dem Palast vom Tell Halaf*. Regensburg: Schnell & Steiner.

Dressler, Torsten, Manolo Escobedo, Martin Gussone, Thomas Kersting, Susan Pollock, Ulrich Wiegmann, and Reinhard Bernbeck. 2017. "Halbmond über Wünsdorf: Moschee im Kriegsgefangenenlager 1915." *Mitteilungen der Deutschen Gesellschaft für die Archäologie des Mittelalters und der Neuzeit* 30: 125–136.

Ethnologisches Museum. 2022. "Rückkehr der ersten zehn Benin-Objekte aus der Sammlung des Ethnologischen Museums der Staatlichen Museen zu Berlin." https://www.smb.museum/nachrichten/detail/rueckgabe-der-benin-bronzen-des-ethnologischen-museums-eigentum-an-nigeria-uebertragen/ (accessed May 31, 2023).

Fischer, Fritz. 1961. *Griff nach der Weltmacht: Die Kriegszielpolitik des kaiserlichen Deutschland 1914/1918*. Düsseldorf: Droste.

Franke, Andreas, and Detlev Steinberg. 2014. *Wünsdorf: Eine russische Stadt in der DDR – 20 Jahre nach dem Abzug der Sowjetarmee*. Halle: Mitteldeutscher Verlag.

Frei, Norbert. 1998. "Abschied von der Zeitgenossenschaft: Der Nationalsozialismus und seine Erforschung auf dem Weg in die Geschichte." *WerkstattGeschichte* 20: 69–83.

Frobenius, Leo. 1916. *Der Völkerzirkus unserer Feinde*. Berlin: Eckhart.

Frobenius, Leo. 1921. *Volksmärchen der Kabylen*, 3 vols. Jena: Eugen Diederichs.

Fröhlich, Alexander, and Torsten Hampel. 2015. "Brandanschlag in Zossen: Es flammt wieder auf." *Der Tagesspiegel*, May 17, 2015. https://www.tagesspiegel.de/themen/reportage/brandanschlag-in-zossen-es-flammt-wieder-auf/11787948.html (accessed May 31, 2023).

Funke, Hajo. 2000. "Andere Erinnerung: Zu Ästhetik und Kultur des Gedenkens." In Micha Brumlik, Hajo Funke, and Lars Rensmann, eds., *Umkämpftes Vergessen: Walser-Debatte, Holocaust-Mahnmal und neuere deutsche Gedächtnispolitik*, 168–173. Berlin: Das Arabische Buch.

Gordon, Avery F. 2011. "'I'm Already in a Sort of Tomb': A Reply to Philip Scheffner's *The Halfmoon Files*." *South Atlantic Quarterly* 110, no. 1: 121–154.

Gossman, Lionel. 2013. *The Passion of Max von Oppenheim: Archaeology and Intrigue in the Middle East from Wilhelm II to Hitler*. Open Book Publishers. http://www.openbookpublishers.com/product/163 (accessed May 31, 2023).

Gottschlich, Jürgen. 2015. *Beihilfe zum Völkermord: Deutschlands Rolle bei der Vernichtung der Armenier*. Berlin: Ch. Links.

Gussone, Martin. 2010. "Die Moschee im Wünsdorfer 'Halbmondlager' zwischen Gihād-Propaganda und Orientalismus." *Beiträge zur Islamischen Kunst und Archäologie* 2: 204–231.

Gussone, Martin. 2016. "Architectural Jihad: The "Halbmondlager" Mosque of Wünsdorf as an Instrument of Propaganda." In Erik-Jan Zürcher, ed., *Jihad and Islam in World War I: Studies on the Ottoman Jihad on the Centenary of Snouck Hurgronje's "Holy War Made in Germany"*, 179–222. Leiden: Leiden University Press.

Häntzschel, Jörg. 2021. "Rechte Spenden für das Berliner Stadtschloss: Wer hat's bezahlt?" *Süddeutsche Zeitung*, September 12, 2021. https://www.sueddeutsche.de/kultur/humboldt-forum-berliner-stadtschloss-afd-neue-rechte-rechte-spender-wer-hat-das-humboldt-forum-bezahlt-1.5483342 (accessed August 8, 2022).

The Halfmoon Files. A Ghost Story … 2007. Documentary film by Philip Scheffner, pong film GmbH. https://halfmoonfiles.de/de/4/film/synopsis (accessed May 31, 2023).

Heimannsberg, Barbara, and Christoph J. Schmidt, eds. 1992. *Das kollektive Schweigen: Nationalsozialistische Vergangenheit und gebrochene Identität in der Psychotherapie*. 2nd ext. ed. Köln: Edition Humanistische Psychologie.

Heine, Peter. 1982. "Sâlih Ash-Sharîf at-Tûnisî, a North African Nationalist in Berlin during the First World War." *Revue de l'Occident Musulman et de la Méditerranée* 33, no. 1: 89–95.

Hilden, Irene. 2022. *Absent Presences in the Colonial Archive: Dealing with the Berlin Sound Archive's Acoustic Legacies*. Leuven: Leuven University Press.

Hoffmann, Hans-Albert, and Siegfried Stoof. 2013. *Sowjetische Truppen in Deutschland und ihr Hauptquartier in Wünsdorf 1945–1994: Geschichte, Fakten, Hintergründe*. Berlin: Dr. Köster.

Holfelder, Moritz. 2008. *Palast der Republik: Aufstieg und Fall eines symbolischen Gebäudes*. Berlin: Ch. Links.

Höpp, Gerhard. 1996. "Die Wünsdorfer Moschee: Eine Episode islamischen Lebens in Deutschland, 1915–1930." *Welt des Islams* 36, no. 2: 204–218.

Höpp, Gerhard. 1997. *Muslime in der Mark: Als Kriegsgefangene und Internierte in Wünsdorf und Zossen*. Berlin: Das Arabische Buch.

Jureit, Ulrike, and Christian Schneider. 2010. *Gefühlte Opfer: Illusionen der Vergangenheitsbewältigung*. Stuttgart: Klett-Cotta.

Kahleyss, Margot. 2014. "Indische Kriegsgefangene im 1. Weltkrieg: Fotografien als Quellenmaterial." In Franziska Roy, Heike Liebau, and Ravi Ahuja, eds., *Soldat Ram Singh und der Kaiser: Indische Kriegsgefangene in deutschen Propagandalagern 1914–1918*, 233–260. Heidelberg: Draupadi.

Kaiser, Gerhard, and Bernd Herrmann. 2010. *Vom Sperrgebiet zur Waldstadt: Die Geschichte der geheimen Kommandozentralen in Wünsdorf und Umgebung*. 5th rev. ed. Berlin: Ch. Links.

Karch, Daniel. 2019. *Entgrenzte Gewalt in der kolonialen Peripherie: Die Kolonialkriege in "Deutsch-Südwestafrika" und die "Sioux Wars" in den nordamerikanischen Plains*. Stuttgart: Franz Steiner.

Kersting, Thomas. 2022. *Lagerland: Archäologie der Zwangslager des 20. Jahrhunderts in Brandenburg*. Berlin: BeBra Wissenschaft Verlag.

Konitzer, Werner. 2012. "Opferorientierung und Opferidentifizierung: Überlegungen zu einer begrifflichen Unterscheidung." In Margit Frölich, Ulrike Jureit, and Christian Schneider. eds., *Das Unbehagen an der Erinnerung: Wandlungsprozesse im Gedenken an den Holocaust*, 119–128. Frankfurt a.M.: Brandes & Apsel.

Koselleck, Reinhart. 1999. "Die Diskontinuität der Erinnerung." *Deutsche Zeitschrift für Philosophie* 47, no. 2: 213–222. https://www.degruyter.com/view/journals/dzph/47/2/article-p213.xml (accessed May 31, 2023).

Kubitschek, Götz, and Björn Höcke. 2014. "'Glücklich der Staat, der solche Bürger hat!': AfD-Landeschef Björn Höcke im Gespräch über die PEGIDA." *Sezession im Netz*. http://www.sezession.de/47597/gluecklich-der-staat-der-solche-buerger-hat-afd-landeschef-bjoern-hoecke-im-gespraech-ueber-die-pegida.html (accessed May 31, 2023).

Landesamt für Umwelt. 2022. *Land Brandenburg: Militärische Altlasten: Potsdam*. https://lfu.brandenburg.de/lfu/de/aufgaben/boden/altlasten/spezielle-altlastenthemen/militaerische-altlasten/# (accessed May 31, 2023).

Lange, Britta. 2013. "'Wenn der Krieg zu Ende ist, werden viele Erzählungen gedruckt werden': Südasiatische Positionen und europäische Forschungen im 'Halbmondlager.'" In Franziska Roy, Heike Liebau, and Ravi Ahuja, eds., *Soldat Ram Singh und der Kaiser: Indische Kriegsgefangene in deutschen Propagandalagern 1914–1918*, 165–210. Heidelberg: Draupadi.

Lassiwe, Benjamin. 2023. "Flüchtlinge in Brandenburg: Innenminister will 1500 Menschen in Containern unterbringen." *Der Tagesspiegel*, April 14, 2023. https://www.tagesspiegel.de/potsdam/brandenburg/fluchtlinge-in-brandenburg-innenminister-will-1500-menschen-in-containern-unterbringen-9659090.html (accessed June 3, 2023).

Liebau, Heike. 2018. "A Voice Recording, a Portrait Photo and Three Drawings: Tracing the Life of a Colonial Soldier." *Working Papers* 20. Berlin: Leibniz-Zentrum Moderner Orient. https://d-nb.info/1164997394/34 (accessed December 14, 2019).

Lüdke, Tilman. 2005. *Jihad Made in Germany: Ottoman and German Propaganda and Intelligence Operations in the First World War*. Münster: Lit Verlag.

Maak, Niklas. 2015. "Wünsdorf in Brandenburg bekommt größtes Flüchtlingslager." *Frankfurter Allgemeine Zeitung*, August 19, 2015. https://www.faz.net/aktuell/feuilleton/wuensdorf-in-brandenburg-bekommt-groesstes-fluechtlingslager-13750479.html (accessed October 8, 2022).

Mahrenholz, Jürgen-K. 2020. "Südasiatische Sprach- und Musikaufnahmen im Lautarchiv der Humboldt-Universität zu Berlin." *MIDA Archival Reflexicon*: 1–19. https://www.projekt-mida.de/reflexicon/suedasiatische-sprach-und-musikaufnahmen-im-lautarchiv-der-humboldt-universitaet-zu-berlin/ (accessed May 15, 2023).

McMeekin, Sean. 2010. *The Berlin-Baghdad Express: The Ottoman Empire and Germany's Bid for World Power*. Cambridge, MA: Belknap Press.

Meskell, Lynn. 2002. "Negative Heritage and Past Mastering in Archaeology." *Anthropological Quarterly* 75, no. 3: 557–574.

Münkler, Herfried. 2002. "Antifaschismus als Gründungsmythos der DDR: Abgrenzungsinstrument nach Westen und Herrschaftsmittel nach Innen." In Manfred Agethen, Eckhard Jesse, and Ehrhardt Neubert, eds., *Der missbrauchte Antifaschismus. DDR-Staatsdoktrin und Lebenslüge der deutschen Linken*, 79–99. Freiburg i.Br.: Herder.

Nagornaja, Oxana. 2010. "Des Kaisers Fünfte Kolonne? Kriegsgefangene aus dem Zarenreich im Kalkül deutscher Kolonisationskonzepte (1914 bis 1922)." *Vierteljahreshefte für Zeitgeschichte* 58, no. 2: 181–206.

Olusoga, David. 2014. *The World's War: Forgotten Soldiers of Empire*. London: Head of Zeus Ltd.

Oppenheim, Max von. 2018. *Denkschrift betreffend die Revolutionierung der islamischen Gebiete unserer Feinde*. Reprint from 1914. Berlin: Verlag Das Kulturelle Gedächtnis.

Osadolor, Osarhieme Benson. 2021. "The Benin Sculptures: Colonial Injustice and the Restitution Question." In Sandkühler et al. 2021, 207–23.

Preuß, Dirk. 2009. *"Anthropologe und Forschungsreisender": Biographie und Anthropologie Egon von Eickstedts*. Munich: Herbert Utz.

Rogan, Eugene. 2016. "Rival Jihads: Islam and the Great War in the Middle East, 1914–1918." *Journal of the British Academy* 4: 1–20. https://www.thebritishacademy.ac.uk/publications/rival-jihads-islam-and-great-war-middle-east-1914-1918 (accessed December 10, 2019).

Rothberg, Michael. 2009. *Multidirectional Memory: Remembering the Holocaust in the Age of Decolonization*. Stanford: Stanford University Press.

Sandkühler, Thomas, Angelika Epple, and Jürgen Zimmerer, eds. 2021. *Geschichtskultur durch Restitution? Ein Kunst-Historikerstreit*. Vienna: Böhlau.

Schöllgen, Gregor. 2016. "Instrument deutscher Weltmachtpolitik: Die Bagdadbahn im Zeitalter des Imperialismus." In Jürgen Franzke, ed., *Bagdadbahn und Hedjazbahn: Deutsche Eisenbahngeschichte im Vorderen Orient*, 108–111. Nuremberg: Tümmel.

Schug, Alexander, ed. 2007. *Palast der Republik: Politischer Diskurs und private Erinnerung*. Berlin: Berliner Wissenschaftsverlag.

Terkessidis, Mark. 2019. *Wessen Erinnerung zählt? Koloniale Vergangenheit und Rassismus heute*. Hamburg: Hoffmann und Campe.

Wiederwald, Rupert. 2018. "Gauland bezeichnet NS-Zeit als 'Vogelschiss in der Geschichte.'" *Deutsche Welle*. https://www.dw.com/de/gauland-bezeichnet-ns-zeit-als-vogelschiss-in-der-geschichte/a-44054219 (accessed August 17, 2022).

Wildt, Michael. 2017. *Volk, Volksgemeinschaft, AfD*. Hamburg: Hamburger Edition.

Yablonka, Hanna. 2012. "Die Bedeutung der Zeugenaussagen im Prozess gegen Adolf Eichmann." In Martin Sabrow and Norbert Frei, eds., *Die Geburt des Zeitzeugen nach 1945*, 176–198. Göttingen: Wallstein.

Yaldiz, Yunus. 2022. "Die Muslime Berlins und Brandenburgs: Diplomatische Beziehungen, islamische Bauten, Kriegsgefangene, Propaganda im Umfeld des Ersten Weltkriegs." In Matthias Asche and Thomas Brechenmacher, eds., *Hier geblieben? Brandenburg als Einwanderungsland vom Mittelalter bis heute*, 177–192. Potsdam: Universitätsverlag Potsdam.

Image Sources

1   Museum Europäischer Kulturen – Staatliche Museen zu Berlin.
2   Bildagentur für Kunst, Kultur und Geschichte.
3   Thomas Kersting.
4   Susan Pollock.
5   Georg Cyrus.
6   Jokeair Luftaufnahmen.
7   Attribution-ShareAlike 2.0 Generic (CC BY-SA 2.0; Author Sludge G) https://www.flickr.com/photos/sludgeulper/50002954247.

Biographies

Reinhard Bernbeck is Professor of Western Asian Archaeology at the Freie Universität Berlin and professor emeritus of Anthropology at Binghamton University. His interests include the prehistory of Iran, archaeological manifestations of social and material inequality, economic exploitation, and ideological dimensions of archaeological practice. He is the author of *Materielle Spuren des nationalsozialistischen Terrors* (2017), co-editor (with Gisela Eberhardt and Susan Pollock) of *Coming to Terms with the Future: Concepts of Resilience for the Study of Early Iranian Societies* (2023), (with Randall H. McGuire) of *Ideologies in Archaeology* (2011), and (with Ruth Van Dyke) of *Subjects and Narratives in Archaeology* (2015), among other works. He has carried out fieldwork in Iran, Iraq, Syria, Turkmenistan, and Germany.

Shraddha Bhatawadekar is a Lecturer and Research Associate at the Department of Art History, Chair for Transcultural Studies in Heinrich Heine University Düsseldorf, Germany. She completed her dissertation at the Brandenburg University of Technology Cottbus-Senftenberg, Germany in affiliation with the DFG Research Training Group 1913 "Cultural and Technological Significance of Historic Buildings." In her dissertation titled "A Place of Hybrid Encounters: Heritage Biography of a Railway Station. Story of Victoria Terminus, now Chhatrapati Shivaji Maharaj Terminus, Mumbai," she investigated how heritage and cultural significance of this World Heritage Site extend beyond the conventional approaches currently in use and emerge through the relationship between people, place, and objects. Dr. Bhatawadekar specializes in the field of heritage studies with a special interest in railway architecture, its representation and perception as well as its colonial and postcolonial intersections and transcultural dimensions.

Johanna Blokker holds the Chair in Architectural Conservation at the Brandenburg University of Technology Cottbus-Senftenberg. A native of Canada, she studied art and architectural history in Montréal and Toronto before joining the doctoral program at New York University's Institute of Fine Arts. Her dissertation research on the reconstruction of mediaeval churches after World War II brought her to Germany in the mid-2000s, where she went on to complete a large-scale investigation of Allied support for building projects aimed at fostering democracy in that country during the postwar occupation. In her subsequent research and teaching, Prof. Blokker continues to explore discourses of heritage as they relate to cultural and memory politics. Her most recent work addresses the role of heritage in democratic processes, including those active in the debate over monuments to colonialism and those affected by the conservative cultural critique of populist and right-wing groups.

Jorge Correia holds a degree and a PhD in Architecture by the Faculty of Architecture of the University of Porto, with the thesis "Implementation of the Portuguese City in North Africa." In 2020, he completed his habilitation at the University of Minho with the theme "Orientalism and Urban Space." He is Professor at the School of Architecture, Art and Design (EAAD) of the University of Minho, where he has chaired the Integrated Master in Architecture, headed the Pedagogical Council of EAAD, lectures and supervises theses on urban and architectural histories. Among other recent engagements, he was President of the European Architectural History Network (EAHN) and Director of the Landscapes, Heritage and Territory Laboratory (Lab2PT). His research focuses on intercultural aspects of the built environment and heritage, particularly urban and architectural narratives between early-modern colonial settlements and traditional Islamic urbanism.

Vera Egbers is an archaeologist specialized in ancient Western Asia with research interests in subjectivation processes, sensory archaeology, architecture, feminist approaches, and archaeology of modernity. After studying in Berlin, Istanbul, and Paris, she later held fellowships at the Department of Anthropology in Harvard as well as at the Research Center for Anatolian Studies of Koç University Istanbul. She received her PhD from the Institute of Near Eastern Archaeology at Freie Universität Berlin, published 2023 in Sidestone Press Leiden ("Thirdspace in Assyria and Urartu"). Vera Egbers participated in various field projects in Turkmenistan, Iraqi-Kurdistan, Turkey, and Germany. From 2020 to 2023 as Postdoc at the DFG Research Training Group 1913 "Cultural and Technological Significance of Historic Buildings" at Brandenburg University of Technology Cottbus-Senftenberg she worked on the meaning and impact of rural space in times of political and social change in twentieth-century (CE) Turkey. After traveling for one year with the Travel Grant of the German Archaeological Institute, she works now as Junior Professional Officer at the Living Heritage Entity of UNESCO.

Cornelia Escher teaches the history and theory of architecture at the Academy of Fine Arts Düsseldorf. Her research and publications focus on the architecture in the nineteenth and twentieth centuries, on architecture and its media, the global history of architecture, and architecture and sociology. She received her doctorate in 2014 from the ETH Zurich. Subsequently she was a postdoctoral fellow in the Leibniz Prize Research Group "Global Processes" at the University of Konstanz. Her publications include the book *Zukunft entwerfen* [Designing the Future] (gta Verlag 2017) as well as articles in *Arch+*, the *Journal of Urban History*, *Oase Journal*, and the *Journal of Architecture*. She has recently co-edited the books *Negotiating Ungers II: The Oberhausen Institute and the Materiality of the Social* (common books, 2022) and *Begegnung mit dem Materiellen* [Encounters with Materiality] (transcript, 2021). Recently, she curated exhibitions at the CIVA Brussels and at the FRAC Centre, Orleans.

Lisandra Franco de Mendonça is an architect, architectural historian, and researcher at the University of Minho, leading her own research project "Architecture of Decolonization," with specific expertise in Mozambique and its capital Maputo. She was an Alexander von Humboldt fellow at the DFG Research Training Group "Identity and Heritage" at TU Berlin, and obtained her double PhD degree in Architecture and Urbanism and History and Restoration of Architecture (Universities of Coimbra and Sapienza of Rome), with a study of twentieth-century architecture in Maputo. She was educated at the Universities of Porto (licentiate degree in Architecture) and Sapienza of Rome (MSc in Restoration of Monuments), and did her professional internship at Souto Moura Arquitectos Lda. in Porto. Her research field is the history of twentieth-century built production under dictatorial and colonial regimes in Europe and Africa. Within this field, she develops an interrogative view oriented towards the conservation of modern ensembles.

Zulfikar Hirji is Associate Professor in Anthropology at York University, Toronto (Canada). He received his DPhil in Social Anthropology from the University of Oxford (2002), MPhil in Islamic Studies from the University of Cambridge (1997), and BA (Joint Honours) in Religious Studies and Anthropology from McGill University (1989). His research focuses on knowledge production, representation and identity, and visual, material, and sensory cultures in a range of historical and contemporary contexts, particularly amongst Muslim communities around the Indian Ocean. He has conducted archival research and ethnographic fieldwork in East Africa, the Arabian Peninsula, South Asia, Europe, and North America. His publications include *Diversity and Pluralism in Muslim Contexts* (2010), *Between Empires: Sheikh Mbarak al-Hinawy 1896–1959* (2012), *Islam: An Illustrated Journey* (2018), *Approaches to the Qur'an in Sub-Saharan Africa* (2019), and "A Corpus of Illuminated Qur'ans from Coastal East Africa" in the *Journal of Islamic Manuscripts* (2023).

Christa Kamleithner is an architectural theorist and cultural historian, whose research focuses on the epistemological and cultural history of built spaces. After holding various academic positions in Austria and Germany, she is currently a postdoc researcher at the Centre for Cultural Inquiry (ZKF) at the University of Konstanz. Together with Susanne Hauser and Roland Meyer, she edited the anthology *Architekturwissen* (2011/2013), which assembles fundamental texts on the cultural history and theory of built space. In her PhD dissertation *Ströme und Zonen*, published in 2020 in the *Bauwelt Fundamente* series, she reconstructs the genealogy of the "functional city" as a media-based process of abstraction. In 2023, with Moritz Gleich, she published the co-edited volume *Medium unter Medien: Architektur und die Produktion moderner Raumverhältnisse*, which explores the intertwining of architecture and other media and their effects on knowledge, subjectivity, and the environment. Her current project is dedicated to the history of the "user."

Itohan Osayimwese is Associate Professor of the History of Art & Architecture and affiliate faculty in Africana Studies, Urban Studies, and the Center for Latin American and Caribbean Studies at Brown University. Her research engages with theories of modernity, postcolonialism, and globalization to analyze built and designed environments in nineteenth- and twentieth-century East and West Africa, the Caribbean, and Germany. Her book, *Colonialism and Modern Architecture in Germany* (Pittsburgh, 2017), received a 2016 Society of Architectural Historians/Mellon Foundation award. Her work has been published in the *Journal of Architecture*, *African Arts*, *Architectural Theory Review*, and *Traditional Dwellings and Settlements Review*. Her current book projects explore migration and the acquisition of property as the realization of freedom for Afro-Caribbean people, and translation as a critical source in the historiography of African architecture. She serves on the board of directors of the Society of Architectural Historians, the European Architectural History Network, and *Thresholds*.

Elizabeth Rankin, Professor Emeritus of the University of Auckland, was previously Professor of Art History and Dean of Arts at the University of the Witwatersrand, Johannesburg. There her research interest lay in the politics of art, particularly in sculpture, reflected in two important exhibitions and publications, *Images of Wood* (1989) and *Images of Metal* (1994). Her focus was often on the recovery of unrecorded histories of black artists, notably in two books co-authored with Philippa Hobbs: *Rorke's Drift: Empowering Prints* (2003) and *Listening to Distant Thunder: The*

Art of Peter Clarke (2011/2014) again with accompanying exhibitions. Her research in art, history, and politics continued in New Zealand, as in *Collateral: Printmaking as Social Commentary* (2011) and *Michael Shepherd: Reinventing History Painting* (2019). Alongside this she pursued a major project with Rolf Schneider on the historical frieze of the Voortrekker Monument, Pretoria, *From Memory to Marble* (2020).

Karin Reisinger is a researcher and lecturer at the Academy of Fine Arts Vienna (Institute for Education in the Arts) where she leads the two research projects "Two Ore Mountains: Feminist Ecologies of Spatial Practices" and "Stories of Post-extractive Feminist Futures," both funded by the Austrian Science Fund (https://www.mountains-of-ore.org). Her intersectional feminist research focuses on the mining towns Malmberget in Sábme / Sweden and Eisenerz in Austria and their situated knowledges. Her work with Malmberget started in 2016 during her post-doc fellowship at KTH Stockholm, School of Architecture, Critical Studies, and was pursued during a fellowship at the Architecture and Design Center Stockholm in 2019. Current publications include "Two Mining Areas: Spaces of Care amid Extraction" in *Architecture and Culture* 11, no. 3 (2024), "Ganz andere Erzählungen von zwei Orten des Erzabbaus: Feministische Materialgeschichten" in *Figurationen von Gender im zeitgenössischen Architekturdiskurs* (TU Berlin, forthcoming), and the co-edited volume *Material Practices: Positionality, Methodology and Ethics* (TU Munich, 2023). Karin Reisinger curated the exhibition *Fences Insects Embroideries (material communities)* as part of WIENWOCHE in Vienna in 2022.

Joaquim Rodrigues dos Santos is an architect, researcher, and visiting professor at the ARTIS Institute of Art History, School of Arts and Humanities of the University of Lisbon. He is developing a research project on the safeguarding of transcultural heritage in South Asia, after accomplishing a post-doctoral project on the preservation of architectural heritage with Portuguese influence in India. He holds a PhD in Architecture from the University of Alcalá, and a MArch in Architecture, Territory and Memory from the University of Coimbra, having investigated the creation of a cultural image of the "Portuguese castle" and the rehabilitation of medieval fortifications in Portugal. Coordinator of the research project "Oratorians in Ceylon: Survey of Oratorian churches with Portuguese influence in Sri Lanka," his research areas are the history of architecture (with a focus on buildings and cities in Portugal and its former colonies) and the preservation of built heritage.

Rolf Michael Schneider, Professor Emeritus of the Ludwig Maximilian University of Munich, has also taught in Berkeley, Cape Town (Honorary Professor), Cambridge (also Curator of the Museum of Classical Archaeology and Fellow of Downing College), Marburg, and Heidelberg. His main research interests concern the importance of non-Greeks and -Romans in classical art (*Bunte Barbaren: Orientalenstatuen aus farbigem Marmor*, 1986, and *Context Matters: Pliny's Phryges and the Basilica Paulli in Rome*, 2016); representing emotions (*Plädoyer für eine Geschichte des Lachens*, 2004/2008); and image, text, history (*Räume, Bauten, Bilder: Knotenpunkte der kaiserlichen Weltordnung Roms*, 2012). He is also the main editor of the series *Image and Context* (24 Volumes, 2008–2023, De Gruyter). Recently he wrote with Elizabeth Rankin the two-volume book *From Memory to Marble: The Historical Frieze of the Voortrekker Monument* (De Gruyter, 2020).

Beatriz Serrazina, holding a master in architecture from FAUL (Lisbon, 2016), is working on her PhD thesis "Building an Empire: Space, Connections and Architecture in Diamang, Angola" (CES/III-UC). Her research focuses on the role of private companies in the production of colonial space in Africa, with an interest in overlooked inter-imperial and international networks for a more complex and plural understanding of the spatialization of building grammars, practises, and forms. Current research interests span architectural and planning history, circulation of knowledge, and the possibilities and frontiers of (post)colonial heritage. She is a research fellow in the project "ArchWar: Dominance and Mass Violence through Housing and Architecture during Colonial Wars. The Portuguese Case" (DINÂMIA'CET-Iscte). Scientific contributions include the co-organization of the exhibition "Colonizing Africa: Reports on Colonial Public Works" (Lisbon, 2019) and several publications.

Özge Sezer received her bachelor's degree in architecture from Izmir Institute of Technology and her master's degree in architectural history from Istanbul Technical University. In 2019 she received her PhD with her dissertation "Idealization of the Land: Forming the New Rural Settlements in the Early Republican Period of Turkey" from TU Berlin. Her first monograph *Forming the Modern Turkish Village: Nation Building and Modernization in Rural Turkey during the Early Republic*, published by Transcript Verlag in 2022, was fully funded by Zeit Stiftung Ebelin und Gerd Bucerius. Özge Sezer worked as an architect in restoration and conservation projects of historic buildings and archeological sites in Turkey and as an adjunct lecturer in Art and Architectural History in Izmir and Berlin. From 2020 to 2023 she was a post-doctoral member and associated researcher in the DFG Research Training Group 1913 "Cultural and Technological Significance of Historic Buildings" at Brandenburg University of Technology Cottbus-Senftenberg.

Alexandra Skedzuhn-Safir is a senior lecturer and post-doctoral researcher at the Chair of Architectural Conservation at Brandenburg University of Technology Cottbus-Senftenberg. She trained as an art conservator in Florence at the Istituto per l'Arte e il Restauro for works in stone and ceramics. Later she focused on the conservation of architectural surfaces, working among other sites at the Neues Museum in Berlin and on Tibetan-Buddhist wall paintings in Ladakh/India. She obtained her BA for the conservation of architectural surfaces at the University of Applied Sciences in Hildesheim (HAWK) and her MA in World Heritage Studies at BTU in Cottbus. Her dissertation in conservation focused on the cultural significance of historic brothels in Florence. Her research interests are marginalization and conflicting values in the heritage discourse, as well as trans-disciplinary approaches to heritage protection. For her postdoctoral research project, she examines the significance of odours at heritage sites and their relevance for the conservation of architectural heritage.

Jens Wiedow graduated with a Masters in Architecture from the Nelson Mandela Metropolitan University in Gqeberha, South Africa before practicing in various offices in Cape Town, Berlin, and Windhoek. His academic career began in 2003 when he joined the Department of Architecture at the Namibian University of Science and Technology (NUST) as a lecturer in design and construction, with a specific research focus on the architectural history of Namibia. Jens Wiedow is a doctoral candidate at the Brandenburg University of Technology Cottbus-Senftenberg where he is writing a dissertation on State Housing in Namibia during the South African colonial period.

Anna Yeboah is an architect and curator. She studied architecture with a focus on cultural theory at the Technical University of Munich and UPC Barcelona. Her research and artistic practice deal with systems of power in architecture and urban planning. Her research on the topic has been shown at the 15th Venice Architecture Biennale and published in international professional media. Anna Yeboah was a lecturer at the Institute for History and Theory of Design at the Berlin University of the Arts. Since 2020, she has been responsible for the overall coordination of the five-year model project "Decolonial Remembrance Culture in the City" for the Initiative of Black People in Germany.

Ying Zhou is an architect and urban theorist teaching at the University of Hong Kong. Her research on the urban transformations of Shanghai, contextualizing contemporary developments in the institutional frameworks and historical legacies of the city, was published in the book *Urban Loopholes: Creative Alliances of Spatial Productions in Shanghai's City Center* in 2017. Her current research looks at how the burgeoning of art spaces manifests the shifts in the arts' ecologies of East Asian cities and their intersections with heritage conservation, gentrification, and the rhetorics of creative cities. Her writings appeared in *Critical Planning, Topos, Urban China, Art Journal, artplus,* and she has exhibited at the Rotterdam Biennale, Swiss Architecture Museum, and the Haus der Kunst, amongst others. She earned her BSE at Princeton, her MArch at Harvard, and her PhD at the ETH Zurich.